also by the editors at america's test kitchen

THE COOK'S ILLUSTRATED ALL-TIME BEST SERIES

COOK'S COUNTRY TITLES

FOR A FULL LISTING OF ALL OUR BOOKS

CooksIllustrated.com

AmericasTestKitchen.com

praise for other america's test kitchen titles

"The editors at America's Test Kitchen pack decades of baking experience into this impressive volume of 250 recipes. . .You'll find a wealth of keeper recipes within these pages."
LIBRARY JOURNAL (STARRED REVIEW) ON *THE PERFECT COOKIE*

"This book is a comprehensive, no-nonsense guide . . . a well-thought-out, clearly explained primer for every aspect of home baking."
THE WALL STREET JOURNAL ON *THE COOK'S ILLUSTRATED BAKING BOOK*

Selected as the Cookbook Award Winner of 2017 in the Baking Category
INTERNATIONAL ASSOCIATION OF CULINARY PROFESSIONALS (IACP) ON *BREAD ILLUSTRATED*

"With 1,000 photos and the expertise of the America's Test Kitchen editors, this title might be the definitive book on bread baking."
PUBLISHERS WEEKLY ON *BREAD ILLUSTRATED*

"Cooks with a powerful sweet tooth should scoop up this well-researched recipe book for healthier takes on classic sweet treats."
BOOKLIST ON *NATURALLY SWEET*

"The 21st-century *Fannie Farmer Cookbook* or *The Joy of Cooking*. If you had to have one cookbook and that's all you could have, this one would do it."
CBS SAN FRANCISCO ON *THE NEW FAMILY COOKBOOK*

"The sum total of exhaustive experimentation . . . anyone interested in gluten-free cookery simply shouldn't be without it."
NIGELLA LAWSON ON *THE HOW CAN IT BE GLUTEN-FREE COOKBOOK*

"A one-volume kitchen seminar, addressing in one smart chapter after another the sometimes surprising whys behind a cook's best practices. . .You get the myth, the theory, the science, and the proof, all rigorously interrogated as only America's Test Kitchen can do."
NPR ON *THE SCIENCE OF GOOD COOKING*

"Another winning cookbook from ATK. . . .The folks at America's Test Kitchen apply their rigorous experiments to determine the facts about these pans."
BOOKLIST ON *COOK IT IN CAST IRON*

Selected as one of Amazon's Best Books of 2015 in the Cookbooks and Food Writing Category
AMAZON ON *THE COMPLETE VEGETARIAN COOKBOOK*

"Some 2,500 photos walk readers through 600 painstakingly tested recipes, leaving little room for error."
ASSOCIATED PRESS ON *THE AMERICA'S TEST KITCHEN COOKING SCHOOL COOKBOOK*

"An exceptional resource for novice canners, though preserving veterans will find plenty here to love as well."
LIBRARY JOURNAL (STARRED REVIEW) ON *FOOLPROOF PRESERVING*

"A terrifically accessible and useful guide to grilling in all its forms that sets a new bar for its competitors."
PUBLISHERS WEEKLY (STARRED REVIEW) ON *MASTER OF THE GRILL*

"The go-to gift book for newlyweds, small families, or empty nesters."
ORLANDO SENTINEL ON *THE COMPLETE COOKING FOR TWO COOKBOOK*

"This encyclopedia of meat cookery would feel completely overwhelming if it weren't so meticulously organized and artfully designed. This is Cook's Illustrated at its finest."
THE KITCHN ON *THE COOK'S ILLUSTRATED MEAT BOOK*

"Further proof that practice makes perfect, if not transcendent. . .If an intermediate cook follows the directions exactly, the results will be better than takeout or Mom's."
THE NEW YORK TIMES ON *THE NEW BEST RECIPE*

"The perfect kitchen home companion. . . .The practical side of things is very much on display . . . cook-friendly and kitchen-oriented, illuminating the process of preparing food instead of mystifying it."
THE WALL STREET JOURNAL ON *THE COOK'S ILLUSTRATED COOKBOOK*

THE
perfect CAKE

YOUR ULTIMATE GUIDE TO CLASSIC, MODERN, AND WHIMSICAL CAKES

the editors at
America's Test Kitchen

Library of Congress Cataloging-in-Publication Data

Names: America's Test Kitchen (Firm)
Title: The perfect cake : your ultimate guide to classic, modern, and whimsical cakes / the editors at America's Test Kitchen.
Description: Boston, MA : America's Test Kitchen, 2018. | Includes bibliographical references and index.
Identifiers: LCCN 2017049045 | ISBN 9781945256264 (hardback)
Subjects: LCSH: Cake. | BISAC: COOKING / Courses & Dishes / Cakes. | COOKING / Methods / Baking. | COOKING / Courses & Dishes / Desserts. | LCGFT: Cookbooks.
Classification: LCC TX771 .P43 2018 | DDC 641.86/53--dc23
LC record available at https://lccn.loc.gov/2017049045

AMERICA'S TEST KITCHEN
21 Drydock Avenue, Suite 210E, Boston, MA 02210
Manufactured in the United States of America

10 9 8 7 6 5 4 3 2 1

Distributed by Penguin Random House
Publisher Services
Tel: 800.733.3000

Pictured on front cover **Blueberry Jam Cake (page 178)**

Pictured on back cover **Cornmeal Cake with Apricot-Bay Compote (page 187), Rainbow Cake (page 152), Chocolate-Raspberry Torte (page 194), Salted Caramel Cupcakes (page 70)**

Pictured opposite title page **Blackberry-Mascarpone Lemon Cake (page 164)**

Pictured opposite welcome page **Rainbow Cake (page 152)**

Chief Creative Officer **Jack Bishop**

Editorial Director, Books **Elizabeth Carduff**

Executive Editor **Julia Collin Davison**

Executive Food Editor **Suzannah McFerran**

Senior Editor **Stephanie Pixley**

Associate Editors **Kathryn Callahan, Leah Colins, Afton Cyrus, Nicole Konstantinakos, and Sacha Madadian**

Editorial Assistant **Alyssa Langer**

Design Director, Books **Carole Goodman**

Deputy Art Director **Jen Kanavos Hoffman**

Photography Director **Julie Bozzo Cote**

Photography Producer **Mary Ball**

Senior Staff Photographer **Daniel J. van Ackere**

Staff Photographers **Steve Klise and Kevin White**

Additional Photography **Keller + Keller and Carl Tremblay**

Food Styling **Catrine Kelty, Kendra McKnight, Marie Piraino, Elle Simone Scott, and Sally Staub**

Photoshoot Kitchen Team

Manager **Timothy McQuinn**

Associate Editor **Daniel Cellucci**

Assistant Test Cooks **Mady Nichas and Jessica Rudolph**

Production Director **Guy Rochford**

Senior Production Manager **Jessica Lindheimer Quirk**

Production Manager **Christine Spanger**

Imaging Manager **Lauren Robbins**

Production and Imaging Specialists **Heather Dube, Dennis Noble, and Jessica Voas**

Copy Editor **Elizabeth Wray Emery**

Proofreader **Jane Tunks Demel**

Indexer **Elizabeth Parson**

CONTENTS

WELCOME TO AMERICA'S TEST KITCHEN

This book has been tested, written, and edited by the folks at America's Test Kitchen. Located in Boston's Seaport District in the historic Innovation and Design Building, it features 15,000 square feet of kitchen space, including multiple photography and video studios. It is the home of *Cook's Illustrated* magazine and *Cook's Country* magazine and is the workday destination for more than 60 test cooks, editors, and cookware specialists. Our mission is to test recipes over and over again until we understand how and why they work and until we arrive at the best version.

We start the process of testing a recipe with a complete lack of preconceptions, which means that we accept no claim, no technique, and no recipe at face value. We simply assemble as many variations as possible, test a half-dozen of the most promising, and taste the results blind. We then construct our own recipe and continue to test it, varying ingredients, techniques, and cooking times until we reach a consensus. As we like to say in the test kitchen, "We make the mistakes so you don't have to." The result, we hope, is the best version of a particular recipe, but we realize that only you can be the final judge of our success (or failure). We use the same rigorous approach when we test equipment and taste ingredients.

All of this would not be possible without a belief that good cooking, much like good music, is based on a foundation of objective technique. Some people like spicy foods and others don't, but there is a right way to sauté, there is a best way to cook a pot roast, and there are measurable scientific principles involved in producing perfectly beaten, stable egg whites. Our ultimate goal is to investigate the fundamental principles of cooking to give you the techniques, tools, and ingredients you need to become a better cook. It is as simple as that.

To see what goes on behind the scenes at America's Test Kitchen, check out our social media channels for kitchen snapshots, exclusive content, video tips, and much more. You can watch us work (in our actual test kitchen) by tuning in to *America's Test Kitchen* or *Cook's Country from America's Test Kitchen* on public television or on our websites. Listen in to test kitchen experts on public radio (SplendidTable.org) to hear insights that illuminate the truth about real home cooking. Want to hone your cooking skills or finally learn how to bake—with an America's Test Kitchen test cook? Enroll in one of our online cooking classes. However you choose to visit us, we welcome you into our kitchen, where you can stand by our side as we test our way to the best recipes in America.

facebook.com/AmericasTestKitchen

twitter.com/TestKitchen

youtube.com/AmericasTestKitchen

instagram.com/TestKitchen

pinterest.com/TestKitchen

google.com/+AmericasTestKitchen

AmericasTestKitchen.com

CooksIllustrated.com

CooksCountry.com

OnlineCookingSchool.com

GETTING STARTED

Introduction

Feelings about cake can run deep and are often tied to regional recipes, family history, or simple flavor preferences. Maybe for you, the ultimate cake is the one you had on your birthday every year, perhaps a Fluffy Yellow Layer Cake with billows of chocolate frosting. Or maybe you like something audacious, like a three-layer rainbow sprinkle–filled Confetti Cake. Maybe your fondness isn't tied to celebrations at all: Few things are more comforting than an anytime treat of Sour Cream Coffee Cake. Or the pleasures of a Salted Caramel Cupcake—a delightful solo indulgence. And baking enthusiasts might love elegant projects like Raspberry Charlotte. Cake can be a single layer like Apple Upside-Down Cake topped with glistening fruit. Or it can be as statuesque as Rainbow Layer Cake that stands six colored layers tall.

Whichever kind of cake you prefer, you'll likely find it in this collection—America's Test Kitchen's first-ever cake cookbook—and also learn how to make the most perfect-looking and -tasting version of it. We've aggregated everything the test kitchen has discovered over 25 years of baking cakes into 10 chapters. You'll see standard favorites like a go-to Old-Fashioned Chocolate Layer Cake in our Classic Layer Cakes chapter, while in other chapters you can explore the vast world of cakes, from elegant ganache-slicked tortes to quirky treasured American cake recipes, sky-high stunners (there's a 24-layer crêpe cake!), the creamiest cheesecakes, whimsical ice cream cakes, and giftable cake pops. You can also bake your way through modern flavors with recipes like Tahini-Banana Snack Cake (that makes banana bread seem boring), Blackberry-Mascarpone Lemon Cake (with trendy bare sides), or Peanut Butter–Pretzel Cake (whose layers are made from pretzel "flour").

In addition, a handy appendix includes the building block recipes you'll turn to throughout the book. Combine these cake layers, frostings, and fillings according to our composed cake recipes or use your imagination to create your dream pairings of flavors and textures. You'll discover that cake isn't just vanilla or chocolate, buttercreams aren't made from only butter and sugar, and layers can be filled with not just frosting but with custards and jams too. Get creative while constructing cakes with our countless options.

The recipes here will grow the skills of novice bakers while also appealing to the most experienced of cake crafters. But no matter your skill level, there's no question that cake baking is an exacting art. Our foolproof recipes and clear instructions take away the intimidation factor. Among the recipes, we've included techniques for all aspects of cake baking, from how to eliminate air bubbles from heavy batters (swirl the batter in the pan with a small spatula) to slicing cake layers so your cake towers won't lean. Follow our tips for folding whipped egg whites into batters without deflating them (start by stirring in one-third of the whites) and mixing up a buttercream without it breaking (beat in softened butter for longer than you'd expect). You'll become just as comfortable piping professional-looking frosting on cakes as you are hand-mixing a snack cake on a weekday.

Another way we make cakes approachable is by teaching you the whys and hows in a comprehensive introduction. We clearly lay out key steps to cake baking and outline what you need to outfit your kitchen—both equipment and pantry items. Then we dig a little deeper, so you learn just what makes a cake's crumb fine and velvety versus open and rustic and whether you should use baking powder, baking soda, or both in a recipe. Once you understand the science, you'll be a more confident and successful baker.

We hope you'll bake your way through the never-fail recipes in this definitive guide and enjoy learning about how cake baking works along the way, so you can turn out perfect cakes every time.

Core Cake-Baking Techniques

This book covers cakes of all kinds, from single-layer fruit-filled cakes and individual-size desserts to those as many as 24 layers high (see our crêpe cake on page 168). But while different types of cakes require different techniques and methods to achieve the desired outcome, all cake recipes have six key steps in common: measuring, preparing the pan, mixing, transferring the batter to the pan, baking, and cooling. In the photos below, we use our Devil's Food Layer Cake (page 397) to illustrate each of those processes, as this recipe covers the most basic (but also most essential) techniques that apply to most cakes. In the pages that follow, we'll dive deeper into the process for a thorough explanation of why the proper execution of each step is important.

1 MEASURING

2 PREPARING THE PAN

3 MIXING

4 TRANSFERRING TO THE PAN

5 BAKING

6 COOLING

1 MEASURING

It might sound obvious, but measuring—the first step to creating perfect cakes—takes care: Baking is a science, and inexact measurements will yield inferior results. We provide weights for dry ingredients in our recipes and use a digital scale to weigh them; we strongly recommend you do too. But if you're dead set on measuring these ingredients by volume, there's a way to increase your accuracy: the dip and sweep method.

Dip the measuring cup into the flour, sugar, or other dry ingredient and sweep away the excess with a straight-edged object, such as the back of a butter knife.

For wet ingredients, we use a liquid measuring cup. For an accurate reading, set the cup on a level surface and bend down to read the bottom of the concave arc at the liquid's surface—known as the meniscus line—at eye level. And for sticky ingredients, we recommend using an adjustable measuring cup. If you don't own one, spray a dry measuring cup with vegetable oil spray before filling it; when emptied, the liquid should slide right out of the cup.

2 PREPARING THE PAN

If we're serving a cake right out of the pan, the pan usually needs only to be greased and floured. But if you want to remove the cake from the pan, you'll need to line it; otherwise the cake could stick and break into pieces as you attempt to remove it. Some exceptions: High-fat pound cakes, curved Bundt cakes, cheesecakes, and most important, chiffon and angel food cakes (these actually need to stick to the sides of the pan in order to maintain their delicate rise).

1 Place the cake pan on a sheet of parchment and trace around the bottom of pan. Cut out a parchment circle.

2 Evenly spray the bottom and sides of the pan with vegetable oil spray or rub with butter.

3 Fit parchment into the pan, grease the parchment, and then sprinkle with several tablespoons of flour. Shake and rotate the pan to coat it evenly and shake out the excess.

3 MIXING

Once your ingredients are measured, mixing can begin. Depending on the recipe and the type of cake you're making, batters can be mixed by hand, in a food processor, or by using a mixer (the most common method in this book). The most basic mixing method—which we use for the Devil's Food Layer Cake—is called creaming, and it's done in a stand mixer. With creaming, softened butter and sugar are beaten together until the mixture is pale and fluffy. Eggs are added next, sometimes followed by other liquid ingredients (here: sour cream and vanilla extract), and then the dry ingredients, which are sometimes added in alternating turns with additional liquid ingredients (here: a melted chocolate–cocoa mixture). Following this gradual series of events prevents overmixing, which can yield tough cakes. Creaming accomplishes two things: First, it makes the butter malleable, which allows other ingredients to blend in easily. Second, the tiny sugar crystals act like extra beaters, helping to incorporate air into the butter as it's creamed. These tiny air pockets expand during baking, giving the cake lift and forming its crumb. Occasionally scraping down the bowl with a spatula guarantees that all the ingredients are evenly incorporated.

any way you mix it
While creaming may be the most common mixing method, it's not the only one. Many of the recipes in this book use other methods, such as reverse creaming, whipping whites, ribboning, and the quick-bread method. Each serves a specific purpose and using the right technique ensures your cake will have the desired texture. See page 20 for more information on these other mixing methods and to discover how mixing technique can affect the texture of your cake.

4 TRANSFERRING TO PAN

While the hardest part of making a cake probably takes place in the mixing bowl, you still want to take care with the rest of the process—and that includes transferring the aerated batter to the pans. If making a layered cake, you'll want to divide the batter as evenly as possible between the pans to ensure that the layers will be the same height and will bake through in the same amount of time. Then, you typically want to smooth the top of the batter with a rubber spatula for a level result; this is particularly important with thick batters. Finally, if a batter isn't too delicate, tap it on the counter to further settle it or to release any air bubbles that could leave holes in the finished cake. Be sure to use a cake pan that's at least 2 inches tall and has a light interior. (For more information on cake pans, see page 8.)

5 ｜ BAKING

Once the batter is in the pan(s), the cake is ready to be baked, and although the process is usually straightforward, little details can make a big difference. Take care to adjust the oven racks as directed in the recipe and use an oven thermometer to guarantee your oven is at the proper temperature. Rotate the pan halfway through baking (and switch the position of the pans if baking more than one layer) to ensure even browning and baking.

when's the cake done?

The amount of time it will take for a cake to bake depends on many factors, such as the temperature of the oven and the depth of the batter. But don't rely on the recipe's time alone: The most foolproof way to test doneness is with the classic toothpick test. Most butter cakes are finished baking when a toothpick inserted in the center of the cake comes out clean. For moister, chocolate-based cakes like this Devil's Food Layer Cake, the toothpick should come out with a few crumbs attached to ensure the cake isn't dry.

6 ｜ COOLING

Some delicate cakes, like Angel Food Cake (page 354), need to cool completely in the pan before being turned out. Others, such as cheesecakes, need time to set up before being released from the springform pan. And some cakes, such as Jelly Roll Cake (page 226), need to be manipulated while warm and have to be removed from the pan immediately. But the majority of cakes need just a little cooling time in the pan—about 10 minutes—to set up, after which they should be removed from the pan so that the residual heat doesn't overbake them. Cool cakes on a wire cooling rack where air can circulate around them. After removing a cake from a pan, be sure to remove the parchment before reinverting the cake right side up on the cooling rack. If you're storing cooled cake layers at room temperature for a day before building your layer cake, wrap them well in plastic wrap. If you opt to freeze them, wrap them in plastic followed by a layer of aluminum foil. You can freeze layers for up to one month; defrost wrapped cakes at room temperature.

**Perfectly Baked
Chocolate Cake**

**Underbaked
Chocolate Cake**

Equipment and Tools

There are certain pieces of equipment that make cake baking easier (and more accurate). These are the basic tools you'll need and the specialty items you'll want.

PREPPING CAKES

digital scale

We weigh dry ingredients to ensure consistent results. We prefer digital scales for their readability and precision. Look for one that has a large weight range and that can be "zeroed." The **OXO Good Grips 11 lb. Food Scale with Pull Out Display** ($49.95) has clear buttons, and its display can be pulled out from the platform for easy viewing when weighing bulky items.

dry measuring cups

While we much prefer to weigh our dry ingredients for cake baking, we understand that many will measure by volume. (And you'll still want a set of measuring cups for many other purposes.) Look for heavy, well-constructed, evenly weighted stainless-steel models with easy-to-read measurement markings and long, straight handles. We use the very accurate **OXO Good Grips Stainless Steel Measuring Cups** ($19.99).

liquid measuring cups

We turn to the industry-standard durable, accurate **Pyrex Measuring Cups** (in multiple sizes) for measuring milk, buttermilk, water, and coffee. We also like to whisk our wet ingredients together in these cups when a recipe calls for adding them gradually to the mixer.

adjustable measuring cups

Sticky ingredients, such as peanut butter, molasses, and honey, can be difficult to measure and scrape out of liquid measuring cups. Enter: the adjustable-bottom liquid measuring cup. This style of measuring cup has a plunger-like bottom that you set to the correct measurement and then push up to extract the ingredient. Our favorite is the **KitchenArt Adjust-A-Cup Professional Series, 2-Cup** ($12.95).

measuring spoons

We prefer heavy, stainless steel measuring spoons with long, sturdy, well-designed handles. Choose deep bowls; leavener or extract is more likely to spill out of shallow bowls with the shake of an unsteady hand. The Cuisipro **Stainless Steel Measuring Spoons Set** ($11.95) is our recommended set.

chef's knife

When you think of cake baking, a sharp-bladed chef's knife might not be the first tool to come to mind. But this kitchen essential isn't just for savory cooking; lots of baking prep steps, such as chopping nuts and chocolate, require a good chef's knife. We think the best knife for this or any job is the inexpensive **Victorinox 8" Swiss Army Fibrox Pro Chef's Knife** ($39.95); it has been a test kitchen favorite for more than 20 years. We find that it maintains its edge long after its competitors have gone dull. Its textured grip feels secure for a wide range of hand sizes and is comfortable for a variety of different grips. You'll use it for everything.

rasp-style grater

We flavor many cakes and frostings with citrus zest, so you'll want a rasp-style grater. This essential tool can also be used for other sweet kitchen tasks such as grating fresh nutmeg or chocolate. Our top rasp-style grater is the **Microplane Premium Classic Zester/Grater** ($14.95); it came sharp, stayed sharp, and looked good as new after testing.

MIXING BATTERS

stand mixer

A stand mixer, with its hands-free operation, numerous attachments, and strong mixing arm, is a worthwhile investment if you plan on baking cakes regularly. Heft matters, as does a strong motor that doesn't give out when whipping for a long period of time. Our favorite stand mixer is the **KitchenAid Pro Line Series 7-Qt Bowl Lift Stand Mixer** ($549.95). Our best buy is the Kitchen Aid Classic Plus Series 4.5-Quart Tilt-Head Stand Mixer ($229.99).

food processor

A food processor is ideal for chopping nuts or grinding them to a fine flour with ease, but it can be used to make some cake batters as well. Look for a workbowl that has a capacity of at least 11 cups. With a powerful motor, responsive pulsing action, sharp blades, and a simple design, the **Cuisinart Custom 14 Food Processor** ($199.99) aced our tests.

whisk

Fat or skinny, tapered or short, with wires that twist at odd angles or sport a silicone coating, there seems to be a whisk for every facet of cooking. Could one all-purpose whisk tackle all of our cake needs? We tested 10 slim, tapered French-style models and skinny balloon whisks as they're best at getting into corners. What we found was that for an all-purpose whisk, we liked 10 moderately thin wires, and our favorite 10-wired whisk, with its grippy handle and lightweight frame for whipping, was the **OXO Good Grips 11" Balloon Whisk** ($9.99).

rubber spatulas

For scraping bowls, folding ingredients, mixing caramel, and smoothing batters you'll want the no-nonsense **Rubbermaid Professional 13½-Inch High-Heat Scraper** ($14.50) and the **Di Oro Living Seamless Silicone Spatula—Large** (10.97). The large head on the Rubbermaid spatula makes it easy to properly fold ingredients; the Di Oro Living spatula is a good multipurpose tool.

BAKING CAKES

parchment paper

Lining your cake pans with parchment paper is a simple way to make sure your cakes release effortlessly. We like **King Arthur Flour's Baking Parchment Paper** ($19.99 for 100 sheets), a commercial-inspired home product we're not sure how we lived without. After tearing, trimming, and flattening paper in our testing, we appreciated that this product combines precut sheets—which eliminate the need to trim and tear—with packaging that allows them to be stored flat.

oven thermometer

It's common for ovens to run hot or cold, which can lead to cakes that are either overbaked or underbaked. The easiest way to accurately gauge oven temperature is with a thermometer. The **CDN Pro Accurate Oven Thermometer** ($8.70) has a clear display and attaches to the oven rack securely. Note that it is manufactured in two factories, so your model may not look exactly like the picture.

cake strips

Cake strips, also known as magic strips, are engineered to correct uneven baking and doming by applying an insulating layer around the outside of a cake pan so the edges don't finish baking before the center of the cake is done. Some strips require a soaking in water before they can be wrapped around the pan, but not our winner, **Rose's Heavenly Cake Strip by Rose Levy Beranbaum** ($9.99). These are an optional accessory but provide extra insurance.

cooling rack

Properly cooling a cake is an essential step that shouldn't be overlooked. A good wire rack allows air to circulate all around the cake as it cools. The **Libertyware Half Size Sheet Pan Cooling Rack** ($15.99 for a set of two; $7.99 each) is our favorite.

Introduction

instant-read thermometer

When it comes to sweet tasks, thermometers aren't just for candy making. They're also incredibly helpful for judging the doneness of custard-based cakes such as Foolproof New York Cheesecake (page 360) and the temperature of ingredients or cake fillings such as Lemon Curd (page 407). Even caramel—a confection that must reach a specific temperature to achieve the proper consistency—can be found in some of our cakes (it is the sweet surprise in the center of our Salted Caramel Cupcakes on page 70). A digital instant-read thermometer—rather than a slow-registering stick candy thermometer—will provide you with an accurate reading almost immediately; this is especially important for items like Pastry Cream (page 407) that are prepared on the stovetop and can quickly overcook. Thermometers with long probes easily reach into deep pots. The **ThermoWorks Thermapen Mk4** ($99) has every bell and whistle.

CAKE PANS

round cake pan (8- and 9-inch)

While cake pans aren't used just for cakes—think deep-dish pizza and cinnamon rolls—in choosing the best round cake pans we rightfully had cake on the brain. This meant we had two requirements: sides that are at least two inches tall and a light color. Why? Tall sides reduce the risk of batter rising up over the edge of the pan, while a light finish produces evenly baked, taller, and more level cakes with a tender crust. (By contrast, a darker pan produces a darker cake. Dark-colored pans absorb heat more efficiently than light-colored ones, and while browning does improve flavor, darker pans also produced cakes that were distinctly domed.) We highly recommend the solidly built **Nordic Ware Naturals Nonstick Round Cake Pan** in 8- ($13.50) and 9-inch ($14.32) sizes.

8-inch square baking pan

Not surprisingly, pans with a light-colored interior ruled the day in the square pan category too. The **Williams-Sonoma Goldtouch Nonstick 8-Inch Square Cake Pan** ($21) yielded baked goods that stood a full 2 inches tall and sported straight (rather than flared) sides, making it easier to cut symmetrical pieces and split cakes two even layers.

13 by 9-inch baking pan

The rectangular sister to our favorite square pan is the **Williams-Sonoma Goldtouch Nonstick Rectangular Cake Pan, 9" x 13"** ($32.95), and it produced the most evenly cooked, professional-looking baked goods of all the baking pans we tested.

loaf pan

Cakes baked in a loaf pan should be golden, but the dark surfaces of many loaf pans brown pound cake a shade too much. Once again, the **Williams-Sonoma Goldtouch Nonstick Loaf Pan** ($21) yielded perfect browning. Note that loaf pan size really matters; all of our recipes were developed in this 8½ by 4½-inch pan. If your pan measures 9 by 5 inches, another common size, you'll need to check for doneness earlier than the recipe indicates; otherwise, the cake will bake up dry. It should also be noted that cakes baked in a 9 by 5-inch pan will be shorter and flatter than those baked in our winner.

muffin tin

We made 10 batches of muffins, 10 batches of cupcakes, and 10 batches of single-serve frittatas to determine the best muffin tin. Pan color proved to be the most important characteristic, as it affected not only the color but the shape of the baked goods. Because dark models conduct heat faster, the sides of cupcakes and muffins baked in these set quickly, leaving the rest of the batter to rise upward, which sometimes resulted in oddly conical or bulbous shapes. In addition to a light interior we liked a muffin tin with a large rim, which makes it easy to move around. Our favorite is the **OXO Good Grips Non-Stick Pro 12-Cup Muffin Pan** ($24.99).

bundt pan

The most important attribute of a Bundt pan is its ability to cleanly release a cake from its decorative ridges. But our winner had even more features we liked. The roomy **Nordic Ware Anniversary Bundt Pan** ($30.99) had large handles, making it easy to grip, maneuver, and flip. It also had the deepest, most well-defined ridges and produced the most eye-catching cakes. For more information on Bundt pans, see page 332.

The Perfect Cake

tube pan

It's essential to buy a tube pan with a removable bottom; otherwise, extracting the cake from the pan is nearly impossible. The **Chicago Metallic Professional Nonstick Angel Food Cake Pan with Feet** ($19.95) is a perfect specimen, yielding tall, evenly browned cakes. The removable bottom doesn't leak, and the feet on its rim elevate the cake while it cools (so we don't need to turn it upside down over a bottle).

springform pan

Bottom line: A completely leakproof springform pan doesn't exist. But there are design elements that make some much better than the rest. The **Williams-Sonoma Goldtouch Springform Pan, 9"** ($49.95) produced pristine cheesecakes with golden, evenly baked crusts. A ridge along the top was a great guide for leveling batters. Its wide, raised base easily caught leaking batter and provided support when cutting slices or removing cake.

baking sheet

Baking sheets aren't just for cookies. We bake thin layers and roulade cakes in this versatile pan. The **Vollrath Wear-Ever Heavy Duty Sheet Pan** (13 gauge) ($20.99) performs flawlessly.

ASSEMBLING AND DECORATING CAKES

serrated knife

There are many uses for serrated knives in the kitchen and one of them is to cut cake layers horizontally, so they must be longer than the diameter of a 9-inch cake layer. With the fewest, widest, and deepest serrations as well as a grippy handle, the **Mercer Culinary Millennia 10" Wide Bread Knife** ($22.10) is a standout.

cardboard rounds

Cardboard rounds—which you can buy online or in craft stores—are simple but immensely helpful: They're great for moving cake layers, building cakes, lifting and transporting cakes, and serving cakes.

cake stand

While you can frost and decorate cakes on any surface you like—such as a cutting board, platter, or cake pedestal—it's much easier to get smooth coatings on a rotating cake stand. The **Winco Revolving Cake Decorating Stand** ($29.98) is tall and provides excellent visibility and comfort. It rotates quickly and smoothly, and it has three shallow circles etched onto its surface for easy cake centering.

offset spatula

For frosting a cake, there's no better tool than an offset spatula. The long, narrow blade on the **OXO Good Grips Bent Icing Knife** ($9.99) is ideal for scooping and spreading frosting, and it bends like a stairstep where it meets the handle for better leverage. The 6.5-inch blade is sturdy but nimble and very comfortable in hand.

piping sets

Floppy cloth pastry bags can stain or cling to smells. Canvas bags tend to be too stiff. We prefer disposable plastic bags; they're easy to handle for neat cake decorating and effortless to clean. In addition, we consider six different tips essential to cover a range of decorating needs: #4 round, #12 round, #70 round, #103 petal, #2D large closed star, and #1M open star. You'll also want four couplers—plastic nozzles that adhere the tip to the bag. We like **Wilton** supplies.

cake carrier

There's nothing worse than trying to transport a cake you have painstakingly frosted for a special occasion, only to have all your hard work ruined by plastic wrap. We like to store and transport cakes in the **Progressive Collapsible Cupcake and Cake Carrier** ($29.95). It has comfortable handles and a sturdy locking system, as well as a collapsible design for easier storage. It can fit either 9-inch round or square layer cakes, or up to 24 cupcakes (with an included insert).

Flour, Butter, Sugar, Eggs, Milk: The Cake Building Blocks

Like all baking, cake making is a science. But it doesn't have to be intimidating, especially once you understand the workings of the five simple ingredients it typically relies on, all of which you probably stock regularly. These basic ingredients can be mixed and measured in countless ways to yield an incredible array of cakes. Here's how we put the Big Five to work.

FLOUR

Flour is arguably the most important ingredient for just about any cake; it gives baked goods structure, crumb, and texture, whether tough (bad), tender (good), or something in between (sometimes desired). While many of our cake recipes call for basic all-purpose flour, we also frequently use—unsurprisingly—cake flour. The main difference between types of flour is the amount of protein they contain. More protein leads to more gluten development, which translates to more structured cakes—or, depending on the proportion of other ingredients, tough, dense cakes. For that reason you won't see us using bread flour, which has the highest protein content of any white flour, in our cake recipes. (The one exception is our Ultimate Chocolate Cupcakes with Ganache Filling recipe; you can read about it on page 56.) Here are the flours we use in this book.

all-purpose flour

All-purpose flour has a moderate protein content (10 to 11.7 percent, depending on the brand) and is by far the most versatile variety for baking. We use it in cake recipes that require extra structure, such as chocolate cakes (chocolate contains tenderizers beyond the sugar, eggs, and butter already called for); cakes supporting a topping of fruit like Pineapple Upside-Down Cake (page 313); or cakes that also use a gluten-free flour like cornmeal, as in our Cornmeal Cake with Apricot-Bay Compote (page 187). We develop our recipes with easy-to-find Gold Medal Unbleached All-Purpose Flour (10.5 percent protein). Pillsbury All-Purpose Unbleached Flour (also 10.5 percent protein) offers comparable results. If you use an all-purpose flour with a higher protein content (such as King Arthur Unbleached All-Purpose Flour, with 11.7 percent protein) in our recipes that call for all-purpose flour, the cakes may be a bit drier and denser.

cake flour

Cake flour has a low protein content (6 to 8 percent) and delivers delicate, fine-crumbed cakes. You'll find it used widely throughout the book for layer cakes, Pound Cake (page 322), and light cakes such as Angel Food Cake (page 354). You can approximate cake flour by mixing cornstarch with all-purpose flour. For each cup of cake flour, use 7/8 cup of all-purpose flour mixed with 2 tablespoons cornstarch. Most cake flour is bleached, which affects the starches in the flour and enables it to absorb greater amounts of liquid and fat.

whole-wheat flour

Whole-wheat flour gives baked goods a distinctive flavor and texture because it's made from the entire wheat berry, unlike white flours, which are ground solely from the grain's endosperm. Because whole-wheat flour has a high protein content (about 13 percent), it behaves differently than white flour and can result in dense baked goods. For that reason, we usually combine whole-wheat flour with all-purpose flour in recipes like Chocolate-Beet Cupcakes (page 72) for the best balance of nutty flavor and good texture. We use King Arthur Premium Whole Wheat Flour in the test kitchen.

nut flours

Grinding nuts to a fine flour can add a beautiful aroma and delicate flavor to cakes; we use ground hazelnuts in the crêpe layers of our Hazelnut-Chocolate Crêpe Cake (page 168) and ground almonds in our take on the classic Italian Almond Cake (page 184). A small amount can fortify the structure of an almost-flourless cake, like our Chocolate-Raspberry Torte (page 194), while a larger amount can provide the bulk of it, as in Chocolate-Hazelnut Cake (page 193). As nuts are not a grain and contain no gluten, we typically combine them with all-purpose flour in baked goods. You can purchase preground nut flours but they're expensive and prone to rancidity, so we like to grind our own; we provide instruction in the recipes for doing so.

cornmeal

While you might not think of cornmeal as a flour, it functions like one in some cake recipes. However, because it doesn't contain gluten it won't provide cakes with much structure. What it does provide: nutty, sweet flavor and a pleasant texture. Because the texture of cornmeal varies, it's important to use the variety that a recipe calls for. Coarse stone-ground cornmeal, for example, doesn't soften and can make cakes gritty.

storing flour

It's best to store all-purpose and cake flour in the pantry, away from light and heat. Whole-wheat and nut flours contain more fat and quickly turn rancid at room temperature, so they should be stored in the freezer. Make sure to bring flour kept in the freezer to room temperature before using. To quickly accomplish this, spread the flour in a thin layer on a baking sheet and let it sit for about 30 minutes.

BUTTER

Most of the recipes in this book use butter—rather than oil or shortening—for its satisfyingly rich flavor. But fat in cakes isn't just for flavor; the amount of fat in a recipe helps determine the texture of the cake's crumb as well. Typically, the more fat you add, the more tender your cake will be—and sometimes, the more crumbly: Fat coats the flour proteins, inhibiting their ability to form a strong gluten network.

use unsalted butter

Our recipes call for unsalted butter. That's because the amount of salt in salted butter varies from brand to brand. This is problematic for a couple of reasons: First, it makes it impossible to know how much salt to call for in a recipe. Second, salted butter contains more water than unsalted does, and the excess water can affect gluten development.

plain, premium, and cultured butter

We use regular unsalted butter in all the cakes in this book. We usually don't think high-fat butters are worth their higher price tag; **Land O'Lakes Unsalted Sweet Butter** has received top ratings in our taste tests for its clean dairy flavor. Regular supermarket butter contains about 82 percent fat or less. (The rest is mostly water, with some milk solids too.) Premium butters, many of which are imported from Europe, have a slightly higher fat level—up to 86 percent. But in baking tests, we've had trouble telling the difference. Our favorite premium butter, Plugrá European-Style Unsalted Butter, is better saved for spreading on toast or for making croissants. Similarly, we leave cultured butter on the supermarket shelves when baking. Culturing, or fermenting, cream before churning it into butter builds tangy, complex flavors—which are lost when baked into cakes.

Though it may be tenderizing, vegetable shortening is a poor choice for cakes: It's simply flavorless, and where it could be used, butter is a better option. However, vegetable oil can sometimes be a welcome addition to cakes. It provides tenderizing fat without water and remains fluid at colder temperatures, which can yield a softer crumb in the cooled cake. Vegetable oil can also be used in conjunction with butter. In our Fluffy Yellow Layer Cake (page 32)—which, by definition, needs to be buttery—we combine melted butter with a small amount of vegetable oil; the oil ensures tenderness and gives our cake a moistness that's so often missing from homemade yellow cakes.

And sometimes, oil's neutral flavor is key: In our Chocolate Sheet Cake with Milk Chocolate Frosting (page 108), using vegetable oil lets the chocolate flavor shine (unlike butter, which can mute it).

Cakes made with oil are often of the rustic variety, as oil can't be creamed and aerated the way butter can. And, of course, an abundance of oil can make cakes—you guessed it—oily. So oil has its place, but you can't simply substitute it for butter in any application. Below are two samples of Lemon Bundt Cake (page 335), one made with creamed butter, as the recipe calls for, and the other made with oil. The cake made with oil (right), has less rise, is dense, and has a coarser crumb and a pale exterior. The cake made with butter (left) is lofty, with a finer, softer crumb and a deep golden exterior.

Made with Butter   **Made with Oil**

storing butter

Butter can pick up off-flavors and turn rancid when kept in the refrigerator for longer than a month, as its fatty acids oxidize. For longer storage (up to 4 months), move it to the freezer. And because butter quickly picks up odors and flavors, we like to slip the sticks into a zipper-lock bag, whether it's stored in the refrigerator or in the freezer.

butter temperature

The temperature of butter affects the texture of finished cakes. We soften butter for creaming so it's malleable enough to be whipped but firm enough to retain air, which provides structure and leavening for cakes like Red Velvet Layer Cake (page 42). If the butter is too soft, it can't hold air bubbles and the cake will be flat and dense. With reverse creaming, softened butter coats the flour particles for an ultratender texture, as in our Classic White Layer Cake (page 35). Some recipes such as Genoise Sponge Cake (page 40) get enough lift and a fluffy crumb from the whipped eggs in the recipe; in these instances we use melted butter, which is more easily incorporated. And when we desire a rustic crumb, as with our Applesauce Snack Cake (page 298), we simply stir in the butter for a mess-free affair using the quick-bread method. Here are our techniques for achieving the right butter temperature for a recipe.

Softened Butter (65 to 67 degrees)

- *Method:* Let refrigerated butter sit at room temperature for about 30 minutes; cut the butter into pieces for faster softening. (Or, if you are in a hurry, you can place the cold butter in a zipper-lock bag and pound it with a rolling pin to the desired temperature and consistency.)
- *How to Test It:* The stick will easily bend without breaking and will give slightly when pressed.

Melted and Cooled Butter (85 to 90 degrees)

- *Method:* Melt butter in a small saucepan or microwave-safe bowl; let cool for about 5 minutes.
- *How to Test It:* The butter should be fluid and slightly warm.

SUGAR

As a sweet treat, cakes require sugar. But in addition to providing the requisite sweetness, sugar affects the moisture level, crumb, structure, and browning of cakes. Sweeteners come in many forms, from conventional white sugar to sticky-sweet honey or molasses. These are the sweeteners we use in this book.

granulated sugar

White granulated sugar, made from either sugarcane or sugar beets, is the type of sugar used most often in our cake recipes. It has a clean flavor and an evenly ground, loose texture that incorporates well with butter during creaming; it aerates the butter (by allowing it to retain small air bubbles) and dissolves easily into batters.

confectioners' sugar

Also called powdered sugar, confectioners' sugar is the most finely ground sugar. It's commonly used for dusting finished cakes, but it's also used for sweetening glazes, icings, and frostings because its fine texture can go undetected in raw applications and because it thickens and stabilizes these mixtures. You can approximate confectioners' sugar with this substitution: For 1 cup of confectioners' sugar, process 1 cup granulated sugar with 1 tablespoon cornstarch in a blender (not a food processor) until fine, 30 to 40 seconds.

brown sugar

Brown sugar is granulated sugar that has been combined with molasses, giving it a deep caramel flavor. If important, an ingredient list will indicate "light" or "dark" brown sugar; if either can be used, we simply call for "brown sugar." Store brown sugar in an airtight container to prevent it from drying out. (We pop in a Sugar Bears Inc. Brown Sugar Bear ($3.25), a clay bear that keeps the sugar soft.) If brown sugar does become hard, place it in a bowl with a slice of sandwich bread, cover, and microwave for 10 to 20 seconds to revive it.

To approximate 1 cup of light brown sugar, pulse 1 cup of granulated sugar with 1 tablespoon of mild molasses in a food processor until blended. Use 2 tablespoons molasses for dark brown sugar. Brown sugar is so moist and clumpy that it must be packed into a measuring cup to get an accurate reading. To do this, use your fingers or the bottom of a smaller cup to tap and press the sugar into the cup.

molasses

Molasses is a dark, thick syrup that's the by-product of sugarcane refining. It comes in three types: light or mild, dark or robust, and blackstrap. We prefer either light or dark molasses in baking and generally avoid using bitter blackstrap molasses. Store molasses in the pantry, not in the fridge, where it turns into a thick sludge.

honey

Made by bees from flower nectar, honey's mechanically filtered and strained to remove wax and debris. Color can indicate depth of flavor: Lighter shades will be more mellow, while darker shades tend to be richer or even slightly bitter. Honey crystallizes in the refrigerator; store it in the pantry.

If your honey is crystallized, put the opened jar in a saucepan filled with 1 inch of water, and heat the honey until it reaches 160 degrees. (Make sure the container is heatproof.)

maple syrup

This syrup is made by boiling down sap from maple trees. It has a high moisture level, so you should refrigerate it not only to retain flavor but also to prevent microorganisms from growing. It will keep for six months to a year. For long-term storage, maple syrup can be stored in the freezer. If it crystallizes, a zap in the microwave will restore it.

EGGS

Eggs are a baking essential. Their yolks and whites have different properties and functions, but together they can bind, thicken, emulsify, and leaven. Theoretically, eggs come in three grades (AA, A, and B), six sizes (from peewee to jumbo), and a rainbow of colors. But the only grade you'll find in a standard supermarket is grade A, the only colors brown and white, and the only sizes jumbo, extra-large, large, and medium. After extensive tasting, we could not discern any flavor differences among egg sizes or these two colors. For consistency's sake, however, the size of the eggs is important. Thus, in all of our recipes, we use large eggs.

storing eggs

Properly stored eggs will last up to three months, but both the yolks and the whites will become looser and they'll begin to lose their structure-lending properties. To be sure your eggs are fresh, check the sell-by date on the carton. By law, the sell-by date must be no more than 30 days after the packing date. To ensure freshness, store eggs in the back of the refrigerator (the coldest area), not in the door (the warmest area), and keep them in the carton; it holds in moisture and protects the eggs from odors. Separated egg whites can be frozen, but in our tests we found that their rising properties were compromised, so it's best not to use them in cakes.

egg substitutes

Egg substitutes are made with egg whites (some brands contain up to 99 percent whites) along with a mixture of vegetable gums, dairy products, vitamins and other nutrients, water, and coloring agents. While we don't like any of these products in savory egg-based recipes such as omelets, egg substitutes fared much better in baking tests: We couldn't distinguish between cakes, cookies, and brownies made with real eggs and those made with substitutes. You can use egg substitutes in cake recipes calling for whole eggs only, replacing each egg with ¼ cup of substitute.

liquid egg whites

If you're tossing egg yolks when making recipes that call for egg whites only, you might think liquid whites are a better option. But we've found that in baked goods most liquid egg whites come up short—literally. The pasteurization process they undergo compromises the whites' structure; as a result, they can't achieve the same volume as fresh whites when whipped. While we'd rather use conventional whites from whole eggs, we have found Eggology 100% Egg Whites to be satisfactory.

egg temperature

For good measure, many of our cake recipes call for room-temperature eggs, but for most recipes the differences between a cake made with cold eggs and one made with room-temperature eggs are fairly minimal: When we made our Fluffy Yellow Layer Cake (page 32) with cold eggs rather than room-temperature eggs, the cake took 5 extra minutes to bake and the crumb was slightly less fine and even. That said, the cold-egg cake was acceptable.

However, letting eggs come to room temperature is critical in more finicky cakes, such as Angel Food Cake (page 354), Chiffon Cake (page 356), and Pound Cake (page 322), which rely on air incorporated into the beaten eggs as a primary means of leavening. In these cases, we found that cold eggs didn't whip nearly as well as room-temperature eggs and the cakes didn't rise properly and were too dense.

WHIPPING EGG WHITES

Perfectly whipped egg whites begin with a scrupulously clean bowl, as fat will inhibit egg whites from whipping properly. Bowls made from porous plastic retain an oily film even when washed carefully and should not be used for whipping. Glass and ceramic should be avoided as well; their slippery surfaces make it harder for whites to billow up. The two best choices are stainless steel and copper. First wash the bowl in soapy, hot-as-you-can-stand-it water, rinse with more hot water, and dry with paper towels. (A dish towel may have traces of oil within its fibers.) Make sure the bowl is cool when you use it. Be careful not to puncture the yolk as you separate the eggs.

Egg whites whipped to stiff peaks leaven heavenly Angel Food Cake (page 354), lighten Fluffy Yellow Layer Cake (page 32) and give a delicate structure to Apricot-Almond Meringue Cake (page 155). They also provide Seven-Minute Frosting (page 402) with a confection-like flavor and the ability to stand in swoops, so it's important to whip them right. If whipped shy of stiff peaks, their structure will be too weak in these applications; but if overwhipped, the same will be true. Sometimes less structure, a tender texture, and a little less lift is desired, as with the cake base for our Summer Berry Trifle (page 160). When that's the case, we whip our whites to delicate soft peaks.

Soft Peaks

Stiff Peaks

Overwhipped

To quickly warm whole eggs, place them in a bowl and cover them with hot—but not boiling—tap water for 5 minutes. Since it's easier to separate eggs when they're cold, you can separate eggs first and allow them to warm up while the remaining ingredients are assembled. If necessary, the whites or yolks can be placed in a bowl nestled within another bowl filled with warm water to speed up the process.

MILK

Liquid thins out batters and contributes to a cakey crumb as the liquid generates steam in the oven. But it's also responsible for gluten development; when it interacts with flour, it allows the proteins in wheat to crosslink into strands of gluten. Therefore, knowing which milk to use and when and how to add it is key for the best-textured cakes. We most often use whole milk in our cake recipes; the fat in whole milk tenderizes the crumb and can weaken gluten just enough for a cake that has structure (after all, milk is still mostly water) but isn't tough and chewy.

acidic dairy

Buttermilk can add a tangy flavor to baked goods, but its inclusion is often more about texture: As an acidic ingredient, buttermilk tenderizes. Also, when an acidic ingredient is used, baking soda (or a combination of baking soda and powder) is typically the leavener of choice; the two interact for extra fluffiness. If a recipe calls for just a cup or so of buttermilk, however, you may not want to buy an entire quart, so we tested a couple of substitutes—shelf-stable powdered buttermilk or soured milk (a tablespoon of vinegar to a cup of milk)—in cakes. Cakes made with powdered buttermilk were more mellow-tasting, whereas cakes made with liquid buttermilk had a detectable, rich tang. However, cake made with powdered buttermilk had the fluffiest, most even texture, making it an able stand-in. The soured-milk cakes were flat-tasting and overly moist, but the differences were small enough that we think soured milk can be used in a pinch.

Yogurt and sour cream, both acidic, produce similar results to buttermilk but sour cream can make for an even more tender cake, as it's higher in fat than low-fat buttermilk and thus has two tenderizing properties.

WHAT ABOUT WATER?

Water is our liquid of choice only in high-fat chocolate cakes. (It would make other cakes tough and lean-tasting.) We often boil water to bloom the cocoa powder in a chocolate recipe. And sometimes we substitute coffee for the water in chocolate cakes; the coffee points up the flavor of the chocolate.

The Cake Cabinet: Staples and Miscellany

CHEMICAL LEAVENERS

A majority of cakes include some kind of chemical leavener to help them rise during baking. Baking soda is an alkali and therefore must be used in conjunction with an acidic ingredient—such as buttermilk, sour cream, molasses, or brown sugar—in order to produce carbon dioxide. The leavening action happens right after mixing, so you should bake right away. In addition to leavening, baking soda also promotes browning. Baking powder is a mixture of baking soda, a dry acid, and double-dried cornstarch. The cornstarch absorbs moisture and prevents the premature production of gas. Baking powder works twice—when it first comes in contact with a liquid, and again in response to heat. Once a container is opened, it will lose its effectiveness after six months. Our favorite baking powder is **Argo Double Acting Baking Powder**.

two leaveners are (sometimes) better than one

Using both baking powder and soda in a recipe rather than just baking powder can give you better control over rise and over the alkalinity of the batter. If a batter with powder is highly acidic, we'll add soda as well for extra support so that the powder isn't neutralized and deactivated. The soda will make the batter more alkaline. Alkaline batters brown more (amino acids thrive in an alkaline environment and react with sugar to create browning) and have a weaker gluten structure so they bake up with a more tender, porous crumb. So while baking powder alone is sufficient for leavening, in the presence of acid, the addition of soda can lighten a cake's crumb when desired and create better browning, which means more flavor.

VANILLA EXTRACT

Vanilla is the most commonly used flavoring in cakes. It's sold in pure and imitation varieties. Which should you buy? If you want to buy just one bottle of extract for all kitchen tasks, our top choice is a real extract—real vanilla has around 250 flavor compounds compared to imitation vanilla's one, giving it a complexity tasters appreciated when we tried it in cooked applications and in cold and creamy desserts. Our favorite pure vanilla is **McCormick Pure Vanilla Extract**. But if you use vanilla only for baking, we have to admit there's not much of a difference between a well-made synthetic vanilla and the real thing (the flavor and aroma compounds in pure vanilla begin to bake off at higher temperatures, so the subtleties are lost). Our top-rated imitation vanilla, **CF Sauer Co. Gold Medal Imitation Vanilla Extract**, has a well-balanced and full vanilla flavor—and a budget-friendly price to boot.

VANILLA BEANS

For cake accompaniments in which you're really going to taste the vanilla—such as Pastry Cream (page 407) or the elegant topping on our Lavender Tea Cakes with Vanilla Bean Glaze (page 99)—we've found that beans impart deeper flavor than extract. We tested five vanilla beans, three mail-order and two from the supermarket. Although all samples were acceptable—including cheaper Spice Islands ($8.49 for two)—we recommend splurging on **McCormick Madagascar Vanilla Beans** ($15.99 for two) for their plump, seed-filled pods and complex caramel-like flavor.

1 To remove the seeds from vanilla bean pods, first use a paring knife to cut the bean in half lengthwise.

2 Scrape the seeds out of the bean with the blade of the knife.

ALMOND EXTRACT

After vanilla extract, our most common cake flavoring is almond extract. To find out if brand matters, we tasted four nationally distributed supermarket extracts (three pure and one imitation) in whipped cream and in our recipe for Almond Pound Cake (page 323). Pure almond extract is made from three primary ingredients: alcohol, water, and bitter almond oil. The last is extracted from almonds or (more frequently) their kin, drupes, the botanical term for stone fruits such as peaches and apricots. Imitation almond extract also starts with water and alcohol, but it gets its flavor from synthetic benzaldehyde, created in a lab. To even greater degree than in our vanilla tests, our tasters couldn't tell the imitation almond extract from the pure stuff. And, in fact, the brand we ranked last (recommended with reservations) was the only one that derives some of its almond flavor from actual almonds. We found it too mild. Our favorite is **Nielsen-Massey Pure Almond Extract**. It was more assertive than others we tested without being harsh.

NUTS

We love the richness and texture nuts contribute to cakes. We grind them into flour for cakes throughout this book (for more information on nut flours, see page 10), and also use them for decoration.

storing nuts

All nuts are high in oil and will become rancid rather quickly. We store nuts in the freezer in zipper-lock bags. Frozen nuts will keep for months, and there's no need to defrost before toasting or chopping. Do defrost before grinding.

nut varieties

Nut nomenclature can be confusing. Recipes may call for raw, roasted, blanched, slivered, or sliced nuts. If there is no descriptor in the ingredient list, raw is assumed. Roasted nuts have already been toasted but we rarely use these, as we like to control the degree of toasting ourselves. However, they're a good choice for peanuts because we like the flavor of salted peanuts, which are nearly always roasted. We often use blanched nuts for grinding because the sweet nuts are stripped of their skins, which can add too much nuttiness or even bitterness to nut flours. If almonds aren't whole, they're often slivered or sliced. Slivered almonds are blanched and easier than whole nuts to break down, so we use them for grinding. Sliced almonds are just that: Almonds that are sliced very thin lengthwise. They most often still have the skin so they're a great choice for decorating.

skinning hazelnuts

The skins from hazelnuts can impart a bitter flavor and undesirable texture.

To remove the skins, simply rub the hot toasted nuts inside a clean dish towel.

PEANUT BUTTER

Peanut butter makes it into whimsical cakes like the sweet-salty Peanut Butter Pretzel Cake (page 166) and our Peanut Butter and Jam Cake (page 244). It comes salted and unsalted; in creamy, chunky, and even extra-chunky varieties; and conventional and natural. Natural peanut butter refers either to butters made simply from ground peanuts without added partially hydrogenated fats or emulsifiers (these butters exhibit natural oil separation and require stirring) or to those

---

CANDIED WALNUTS OR PECANS

Looking for an easy way to decorate an elegant frosted cake? Try using candied walnuts or pecans to adorn the tops or sides. (For more information on decorating cakes, see page 26.)

Makes about 1 cup

1 cup walnut or pecan halves, toasted
¼ cup sugar
¼ cup water
½ teaspoon salt

Line baking sheet with parchment paper. Bring all ingredients to boil in medium saucepan over medium heat. Cook, stirring constantly, until water evaporates and sugar mixture coats nuts and looks glossy, about 5 minutes. Transfer walnuts to prepared sheet and spread in even layer. Let cool completely, about 10 minutes.

---

made with only ground peanuts and palm oil (these do not require stirring). We avoid no-stir varieties as they make for oily frostings and fillings. And we like the flavor boost provided by salt. Our favorite creamy peanut butter is **Skippy Peanut Butter**.

BAKING SPICES

The addition of spices is a great way to round out the flavor of a cake or to give it a bolder profile. We recommend following a few tips: Label them with the purchase date; store them in a cool, dry place; and use within 12 months. Buy whole spices when you can and grind them in a coffee grinder devoted solely to this purpose; the flavors of preground spices fade fast. We use the following spices in our cake baking.

cinnamon

Cinnamon is Americans' favorite baking spice; while basic versions abound, you can also choose from among bottles labeled "Vietnamese" or even "Saigon." These specialty cinnamons also command a higher price—up to about $4.00 per ounce, compared with as little as $0.90 per ounce for those with generic labeling. Does origin really matter? We found that cinnamons are indeed markedly different from each other. The Vietnamese cinnamons, for example, all fell on the spicier end of the spectrum, while the Indonesian cinnamons were mild. If you like a big, spicy flavor, we recommend springing for **Penzeys Vietnamese Cinnamon Ground**. At $4.09 per ounce, it was the most expensive product in our lineup, but it also had the highest percentage of volatile oils, which carry the flavor of cinnamon. We particularly love this cinnamon in streusel-packed Sour Cream Coffee Cake (page 292), but if you prefer a milder spice, stick with less expensive cinnamons that make no claim to origin. Our favorite basic cinnamon is **Morton & Bassett Spices Ground Cinnamon**.

nutmeg

Nutmeg is a hard, brown seed from a tropical tree that, when ground, offers a heady, potent aroma and flavor. We compared fresh with preground and found that in recipes in which nutmeg is the sole spice—such as our Eggnog Bundt Cake on page 271—grinding it yourself is important (we like to use a rasp-style grater for this task). But in foods with lots of spices, preground nutmeg is fine.

cardamom

Fragrant cardamom comes in pods—either black or the more common green—and each holds many tiny seeds. Most of the highly aromatic flavors live in the seeds, which we grind ourselves for recipes like Ginger-Cardamom Applesauce Snack Cake (page 298) rather than buy it preground.

ground ginger

Ground ginger comes from the dried fresh root, but you can't substitute one for the other: fresh has a floral flavor, while dry is spicier. They also function differently in baking (fresh is moister). Our favorite is **Spice Islands Ground Ginger**.

black pepper

While we generally associate this spice with savory applications, it makes an intriguing addition to spiced cakes like our Bold and Spicy Gingerbread Bundt Cake (page 348). The flavor of preground doesn't compare with fresh ground. The test kitchen's favorite peppercorns are mail-order: **Kalustyan's Indian Tellicherry Black Peppercorns**. Our favorite supermarket option is from Morton & Bassett.

lavender

Lavender is actually a relative of mint, and the dried buds give sweets a pleasant floral quality. The key to using lavender successfully is restraint; we use a light hand in our Lavender Tea Cakes with Vanilla Bean Glaze (page 99).

saffron

Sometimes referred to as "red gold," saffron is the world's most expensive spice. It's made from the delicate dried stigmas of *Crocus sativus* flowers; it takes about 200 hours to pick enough stigmas to produce just 1 pound of saffron! Luckily, a little goes a long way toward contributing its distinct gold color, notes of honey and grass, and a slight hint of bitterness to foods and baked goods like our Saffron-Orange Bundt Cake (page 342). The major producers are Iran and Spain;

supermarket saffron is usually Spanish. Look for bottles that contain dark red threads—saffron is graded, and the richly hued, high-grade threads from the top of the stigma yield more flavor. Our favorite is **Morton & Bassett**.

spicing up spices

Depending on the amount used, spices can taste a bit dusty right out of the jar. For our cake recipes, we sometimes like to cook spices briefly in melted butter or whisk them into just-melted butter; this technique, known as blooming, removes any raw flavor. It also releases their essential oils from a solid state into solution form, where they interact, producing a more complex flavor. But be careful: This technique requires a close eye to avoid burning them.

Blooming spices in hot butter releases their flavor.

COCONUT

Packaged coconut products all start as raw coconut meat that's then boiled, grated, and dried. Dried coconut comes in large flakes, shreds, or desiccated. There are two types of shredded coconut—sweetened and unsweetened. The dehydrated shreds are either immediately packaged and sold as unsweetened coconut or soaked in a liquid sugar solution and dried again to make sweetened coconut. We use the moister sweetened shredded coconut for the recipes in this book. Flaked coconut is too large to incorporate into batters, but it makes a good decoration.

DRIED FRUIT

The process of drying fruit concentrates flavor and sugar. We use a variety of dried fruits in our cakes, such as earthy-tasting raisins (regular and golden raisins can be used interchangeably), tart dried cranberries (they're infused with sweetened cranberry juice in the process of being dried), dried cherries (usually the tart variety for the biggest cherry punch), dried figs (we often choose Calimyrna figs; this caramel-y fruit is the California version of the Turkish Smyrna fig), dried apricots (for more information on dried apricots, see page 269), and dates (buy whole dates and pit them yourself). Sometimes we simply mix dried fruits into the batter; other times we cook them into a puree or plump them in the microwave with water or liquor to rehydrate them a bit.

Introduction

All About Chocolate

All chocolate begins as cacao beans found in large pods that grow on cacao trees. These beans are fermented, dried, and roasted and then the inner meat (or nib) of the bean is removed from the shell and ground into a paste called chocolate liquor, which consists of cocoa solids and cocoa butter. Chocolate liquor is then further processed and mixed with sugar and flavorings to make the various types of chocolate. White chocolate is made from just the cocoa butter and doesn't contain any cocoa solids. Milk, semisweet, and bittersweet chocolate go through a refining process known as conching, where the liquor and the other ingredients are smeared against rollers until smooth.

TYPES OF CHOCOLATE

The type and brand of chocolate you use can make a big difference. Here's what you need to know.

cocoa powder

Cocoa powder is chocolate liquor that has been processed to remove all but 10 to 24 percent of the cocoa butter. Cocoa powder comes in natural and Dutched versions. Dutching, which was invented in the 19th century by a Dutch chemist and chocolatier, raises the powder's pH, which neutralizes its acids and astringent notes and rounds out its flavor. (It also darkens the color.) We often bloom cocoa powder in a hot liquid such as water or coffee. This dissolves the remaining cocoa butter and disperses water-soluble flavor compounds for a deeper, stronger flavor. Our favorites? All-purpose: **Hershey's Natural Cocoa Unsweetened.** Dutched: **Droste Cocoa.**

unsweetened chocolate

Unsweetened chocolate is the traditional choice for recipes in which a bold hit of chocolate flavor is paramount; however, we don't use it too often because the high proportion of cocoa solids can interfere with a delicate texture. If a recipe calls for unsweetened chocolate but you don't have any on hand, you can replace 1 ounce of unsweetened chocolate with 3 tablespoons of cocoa powder and 1 tablespoon of butter or oil. This substitution is best for small quantities, as it ignores the important differences between butter, oil, and cocoa butter. Our favorite? **Hershey's Unsweetened Baking Bar.**

semisweet and bittersweet chocolate

Semisweet and bittersweet chocolates, both called dark chocolate, must contain at least 35 percent chocolate liquor, although most contain more than 55 percent and some go as high as 99 percent. (Chocolates containing 70 percent or more cacao usually require recipe adjustments to get good results.)

For substitutions, we found that you can replace 1 ounce of semisweet or bittersweet chocolate with ⅔ ounce of unsweetened chocolate and 2 teaspoons of granulated sugar—but because the unsweetened chocolate has not been conched it will not provide the same smooth, creamy texture. We prefer **Ghirardelli 60% Cacao Bittersweet Chocolate Premium Baking Bar.**

milk chocolate

Milk chocolate must contain at least 10 percent chocolate liquor and 12 percent milk solids. The result is a smooth but mellow flavor (milk chocolate is usually more than 50 percent sugar), so we use it only in very specific applications such as our Milk Chocolate Cheesecake (page 369), where a more bitter chocolate flavor would clash with the tangy cream cheese, or in the frosting for our Chocolate Sheet Cake with Milk Chocolate Frosting (page 108), which has a rich, milky flavor that counterbalances the rich, deep chocolate of the cake. Our favorite is **Dove Silky Smooth Milk Chocolate.**

white chocolate

White chocolate is technically not chocolate since it contains no cocoa solids. Authentic white chocolate contains at least 20 percent cocoa butter, which provides its meltingly smooth texture. Many brands rely on palm oil in place of some or all of the cocoa butter and can't be labeled "chocolate." If the product is called "white chips" or "white confection," it's made with little or no cocoa butter. That said, since both styles derive their flavor from milk and sugar, not the fat, we find this distinction makes little difference in recipes. Our favorite? **Guittard Choc-Au-Lait White Chips**.

chocolate chips

While chocolate chips contain less cocoa butter than bar chocolate, they have stabilizers and emulsifiers that help them hold their shape when baked and are also a better choice in applications that need that extra stability, such as Creamy Vegan Chocolate Frosting (page 405) and the coating for Party Cake Pops (page 80). Our favorites? Dark chocolate: **Ghirardelli 60% Cacao Bittersweet Chocolate Chips**. Milk chocolate: **Hershey's Milk Chocolate Chips**.

storing chocolate

Wrap open bars of chocolate tightly in plastic wrap and store them in a cool pantry. Avoid the refrigerator or freezer, as cocoa butter easily absorbs off-flavors from other foods and temperature changes can alter its crystal structure so it behaves differently in recipes. Stored properly, unsweetened and dark chocolate will last about 2 years. The milk solids in white and milk chocolate give them a shorter shelf life of about 6 months.

WAKING UP CHOCOLATE FLAVOR

Sometimes we call for espresso powder in cakes even when coffee flavor isn't the goal. Why? Just a pinch pumps up chocolate flavor considerably, making it more intense and complex without imparting a noticeable coffee presence. Our favorite instant espresso powder for brewing a demitasse or baking brownies is Cafe D'Vita Imported Premium Instant Espresso, which contributes dark, deep, fruity, roast-y notes to baked goods.

CHOPPING CHOCOLATE

There are two ways to chop a large block of chocolate into pieces.

Hold a chef's knife at a 45-degree angle to one of the corners and bear down evenly. After cutting about an inch from the corner, repeat with the other corners.

Alternatively, you can use a sharp two-tined meat fork to break the chocolate into smaller pieces.

MELTING CHOCOLATE

Chocolate can burn easily, so it's best to use a gentle approach for melting. The two best methods for melting chocolate are using an improvised double boiler or microwaving it at 50 percent power. Do not let the slightest amount of water get in melted chocolate or it will seize and turn grainy: The liquid forms a syrup with the sugar in the chocolate to which the cocoa particles will cling, creating clumps.

On the Stovetop

Chop the chocolate (so it melts evenly) and place it in a heatproof bowl set over a saucepan of barely simmering water. (Be sure the bowl is not touching the water or the chocolate could scorch.) Stir occasionally.

In the Microwave

Microwave the chopped chocolate at 50 percent power. (The time will depend on the amount.) Stir the chocolate and continue microwaving until melted, stirring occasionally.

Mixing, an In-Depth Look

Most cakes share the same five basic ingredients (see page 10); it's the way those ingredients are combined that makes all the difference in the style and crumb of the final product. Here we'll take a closer look at the major cake mixing methods.

CREAMING

If you know just one mixing method by name, it's likely the creaming method (for more information, see page 4). Creaming is a fundamental technique that helps cakes rise: The tiny pockets of air created during the process get filled by the leavener in the recipe. As with this Lemon Bundt Cake (page 335) below, it creates a fluffy crumb and a cake with good height.

The result?
- Fluffy, somewhat open crumb
- Tall rise

Good for
- Bundt cakes
- Everyday cakes
- Some layer cakes

CREAMING VERSUS REVERSE CREAMING
One technique isn't better than the other, but each results in a unique texture and shape. A creamed cake will have a higher rise with a domed top. A cake made with reverse creaming will have a flat top and a finer crumb—perfect for stacking and frosting.

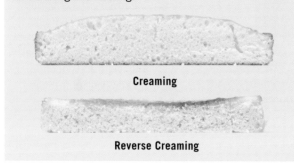

Creaming

Reverse Creaming

REVERSE CREAMING

While creaming butter and sugar is probably the most common first mixing step in the world of baking, we don't use this method all that much for layer cakes. When we want a tender but sturdy cake with an ultrafine, downy crumb, we turn to reverse creaming. This process starts with combining all of the dry ingredients, after which softened butter is incorporated followed by any liquid ingredients. During reverse creaming, the butter coats the flour particles, therefore minimizing gluten development for a tender, fine crumb. Just as important, since the butter isn't beaten with sugar, less air is incorporated, which translates to less rise and a sturdier cake perfect for the Classic White Layer Cake (page 35) below that needs to be stacked and frosted.

The result?
- Ultratender but sturdy structure; resists crumbling
- Fine, velvety crumb
- Even rise

Good for
- Layer cakes
- Coffee cakes with heavy toppings
- Filled cupcakes

WHIPPED WHITES

Whipped egg whites are often thought of as another form of leavening, and this is basically true: Many cakes, like the following Angel Food Cake (page 354), gain impressive height (and lightness) from whipped whites. But it's not the egg itself that grows the cake, it's air. As egg whites are whipped, their proteins loosen and stretch, capturing and trapping air inside a fluffy foam that gives cakes lift. The whipped whites are then gently added to a batter made from flour and liquids; sometimes, melted fat is added.

The result?
- Light texture
- Airy, springy crumb

Good for
- Angel food cakes
- Jelly roll cakes
- Some pound-style cakes

adding sugar to whipped whites

Often sugar is added to egg whites partway through the whipping process. The sugar dissolves in the water from the whites to form a viscous liquid that helps stabilize the structure. If the sugar is added too early, it interferes with the egg proteins' ability to unfold for a weaker network that supports only small air bubbles. If added too late, it draws water from the foam and causes its structure to weaken. Gradually add sugar according to the visual of the recipe; usually, for ideal volume and stability, you'll want to add the sugar after the whites have started to get foamy but well before they form peaks.

incorporating whipped whites

After carefully whipping your egg whites to just the right point, you don't want them to deflate upon being incorporated into the batter. Most often we take the following precaution: Combine (essentially deflating) a third of the whipped whites with the batter to lighten it and then carefully fold in the remaining whites with a rubber spatula; lightening the batter ensures the whites won't collapse under its weight.

RIBBONING

When you think of whipping eggs, you probably think of just the whites. But whipping whole eggs with sugar until they double in volume is another mixing method that can act as leavener for a cake that's incredibly light—though not as whisper-light as one leavened with egg whites alone—yet still rich in flavor. We use this method for the pictured sponge cake for our Refined Strawberry Shortcake (page 204). The term "ribboning" refers to the ribbon-like strands that form between the whisk and batter when the eggs and sugar are whipped.

The result?
- Light and fluffy but substantial texture
- Rich flavor

Good for
- Genoise cakes
- Sponge cakes that require the structure to stand up to a filling
- Chocolate cakes that need help with lift

heating it up

Sometimes the eggs and sugar are heated together before whipping. This ensures that all of the sugar dissolves, which makes for a more viscous mixture. And the more viscous a liquid, the slower the water escapes. This leads to a more stable foam and, in turn, a loftier, sturdier cake.

THE QUICK-BREAD METHOD

This method is the easiest of all the mixing methods: First, the dry ingredients (flour, baking powder and/or baking soda, and salt) are whisked together in one bowl. Next, the wet ingredients (milk or buttermilk, melted butter or oil, sugar, and eggs) are whisked in another bowl or a liquid measuring cup. Finally, the wet ingredients are stirred into to the dry ingredients until just combined to avoid overmixing; despite the fact that melted butter (or oil), eggs, and sugar have a great tenderizing effect, overmixing will yield tough results. This technique doesn't introduce extra air into the batter and the result is a cake with a rustic crumb. This mixing method virtually eliminates doming and makes for a sturdy cake that can support a topping like the one on this Apple Upside-Down Cake (page 314).

The result?
- Coarse crumb
- Sturdy structure

Good for
- Upside-down cakes
- Snack cakes

Making a Masterpiece

In the previous pages, you've learned just about everything you need to know in terms of the science of cake baking; here we move on to the art. We know we can make a great-tasting cake, and with just a bit more effort it's easy enough to make a beautiful one. Here are our tips for slicing, filling, and frosting cakes with panache.

WORKING WITH BUTTERCREAM

We love our basic Vanilla Frosting (page 398): Softened butter and confectioners' sugar are beaten together and a little cream is added. It's simple and sweet and works on most cakes. But there's a world beyond this American frosting to explore. This tutorial for Vanilla Buttercream (page 403) will give you the confidence to try your hand at a classic buttercream, which is made with melted sugar and egg yolks for an ultrasilky texture. (For more information on frosting varieties, see page 24.)

1 Whip the Egg Yolks Using a stand mixer fitted with the whisk attachment, whip the egg yolks on medium speed until they're slightly thickened and pale yellow, 4 to 6 minutes. You must whip the yolks until they're thick and pale before you pour the sugar mixture into the mixing bowl or else it won't come together properly.

2 Cook the Sugar and Corn Syrup Bring the sugar and corn syrup to a boil in a small saucepan over medium heat, stirring occasionally to dissolve the sugar, about 3 minutes. You want to heat the sugar syrup at the same time the yolks are whipping so the hot syrup will be ready once the yolks are done. The corn syrup gives the buttercream a fluid but stable consistency.

3 Slowly Add the Hot Syrup With the mixer on low speed, pour the hot sugar syrup into the whipped egg yolks. Pouring the hot syrup into the egg yolks gently raises their temperature to a safe level. If you dump the syrup into the bowl all at once you can scramble the eggs. Aim to pour the syrup into the bowl so that it avoids both the whisk and the sides (where it can seize).

4 Whip the Mixture Until Cool Increase the mixer speed to medium-high and whip the mixture until it's light and fluffy and the bowl is no longer warm, 5 to 10 minutes. Whipping aerates the yolk mixture and makes it easier to add the butter in the next step.

5 Beat in the Softened Butter Reduce the mixer speed to medium-low and add the vanilla and salt. Gradually add the softened butter until it's completely incorporated. Cold butter will clump up and you will have to overbeat the frosting to smooth it back out.

6 Whip the Frosting Until Silky Increase the mixer speed to medium-high and whip the buttercream until it's smooth and silky. If the finished frosting looks curdled, the butter was probably too cold. Wrap a hot wet towel around the bowl and whip until smooth.

FROSTING A LAYER CAKE

You may think a bakery-quality frosted cake isn't possible at home and so you settle for a more homemade, rustic appearance. But the truth is that a polished frosting is easy if you have the right tools and use the right technique. We provide steps for frosting a two-layer cake but the technique is transferable to a cake with more layers.

1 Remove the Dome Cool, flat layers are paramount to a good cake. Not only does this make for a sleeker appearance, it guarantees that the cake maintains its structural integrity. We engineer our layer cake recipes to emerge from the oven nice and level, but if your layers do dome, use a serrated knife to gently slice back and forth with a sawing motion to remove the domed portion from each cake layer. Brush the crumbs off the cake since they can mar the frosting.

2 Keep the Platter Clean Cover the edges of the cake stand or platter with 4 strips of parchment paper. The strips ensure that extra frosting doesn't end up on the platter. Once the cake is frosted, you can slide out and discard the parchment for a neat presentation.

3 Frost the First Layer For elaborate cakes, you may want to anchor your cake in place. Start by dolloping a small amount of frosting in the center of the cake stand and then place a cake layer on top. Dollop the correct portion of frosting in the center of the cake layer (see page 24). Using an offset spatula, spread the frosting evenly from the center to the edge of the cake. (Depending on the nature of the filling, the recipe may instruct you to leave a border unfrosted.)

4 Place the Second Layer Place the second layer on top, making sure it's aligned with the first layer. As you place the top layer, don't push down on it or you risk squeezing the frosting out the sides of the cake, but do press gently to make sure it adheres. Careful placement of the top layer allows you to frost the cake properly with smooth sides.

5 Frost the Top, Then the Sides If frosting a three-layer cake, continue with another layer of frosting and cake. If frosting a two-layer cake, finish by spreading more frosting evenly over the top layer, pushing it over the edge of the cake. Gather several tablespoons of frosting with the tip of an offset spatula and gently smear it onto the sides of the cake. Repeat until the sides are covered with frosting. If you spread a large amount of frosting on the sides, you risk getting crumbs in the frosting or causing the layers to shift. Clean off the spatula as needed.

6 Smooth It Out Gently run the edge of the spatula around the sides of the cake to smooth out bumps and tidy areas where the frosting on the top and sides merge. You can run the edge of the spatula over the top of the cake to give it a smooth look too. Remove the strips of parchment before serving.

KNOW YOUR FROSTING

We like to have fun pairing different cake layers with the frostings and buttercreams in this book. (See "Appendix: Essential Cake Components" on page 392 for recipe options.) And with many variation recipes, the frosting flavor choices are ample. Frostings and buttercreams are different in their ingredients, the way they're mixed, and their final texture, all of which could be considerations when you're determining what frosting you'd like to pair with your cake. Here we distinguish between the frostings and buttercreams in this book as well as how to best put them to use for neatly filled and evenly frosted cakes that look and taste their best.

cool layers

Letting cake layers cool completely is more than a formality. A cake layer that is even slightly warm is too delicate to move without breaking, making stacking uncooled layers a precarious situation. And if you want a picture-perfect layer cake with fluffy frosting, it's equally essential that the cake be fully cooled before applying the frosting; nearly all frostings contain butter, which means that if the frosting comes in contact with a cake that's warmer than room temperature, it will melt and reveal spotty patches of cake—and lose its volume. Depending on the temperature of your kitchen, it can take up to 2 hours to fully cool cake layers, so be patient!

Frosted When Cool   Frosted When Warm

smoothing the frosting

We provide decorating tips and tricks throughout these pages, but here's a simple trick to employ for perfectly slick sides on modest two-layer cakes. Instead of pulling out the large offset spatula—which is one of our absolute favorite cake decorating tools but which is flexible—we sometimes pull out our trusty all-purpose bench scraper. With the cake firmly anchored on a rotating cake stand, spread a generous amount of frosting onto the sides of the cake and then slowly spin the cake while gently pressing the bottom edge of the bench scraper against the cake sides. After a few spins, the cake will look perfect.

frosting amounts

We have unique sky-high cakes in chapter four of this book (page 130) with their own set of rules, but for simple, mix-and-match cake layers and frostings consisting of two or three layers, it's helpful to know how to divide a batch of frosting among the layers. The last thing you want is to overfill the layers and find yourself left without enough frosting to cover the top and sides. Our frosting yields leave a generous amount after filling so you can decorate as you like.

	Filling	Top and sides
Two-layer cake	1½ cups	3½ cups
Three-layer cake	1 cup	4 cups

frosting varieties

American Buttercream (A) is basically regular old frosting—a timeless fluffy combination of butter and sugar. Confectioners' sugar is the best choice because it thickens the frosting, eliminating the need for eggs, and—owing to its superfine texture—provides stability without the grit. We add a little heavy cream for an ultracreamy consistency you can't get from butter and sugar alone. This is typically the sweetest frosting option. Our Vanilla Frosting (page 398) is an American Buttercream.

Swiss Meringue Buttercream (B) is less sweet than most frostings, and it's also one of the easiest buttercreams to make. It starts with a cooked egg-white meringue, to which you gradually add softened butter—and lots of it—until the mixture becomes light and fluffy. Its ultrasatiny texture makes it an elegant and decadent option. Our Chocolate Buttercream (page 399) is a Swiss meringue buttercream.

French Buttercream (C) is also a moderately sweet, butter-packed frosting. It's richer than Swiss meringue buttercream because its egg base is egg yolks rather than whites. Pouring a hot sugar syrup over the yolks ensures they are cooked to a safe temperature. Then, as with a Swiss meringue buttercream, a generous amount of softened butter is whipped in. Our luxurious Vanilla Buttercream (page 403) is a French meringue buttercream.

German Buttercream (D) starts out like American buttercream—butter is beaten until light and fluffy—but then an egg-based pastry cream (that has already been cooked and cooled) is added. The custard contributes a super-creamy texture for a soft, light buttercream that, while rich, isn't overwhelming. We fill layers of our Chocolate-Espresso Dacquoise (page 206) with a German buttercream.

Seven-Minute Frosting (E) is the frosting for you if you like marshmallows or meringues. This frosting is playful, simple, and sweet; and since it doesn't contain butter, it isn't very rich. Although the egg white base requires cooking, the frosting is easy to prepare, taking just 7 minutes to whip up (hence the name). The sticky frosting looks particularly nice in swirls and billows.

Ganache (F) is simply a decadent, truffle-like mixture of melted chocolate and cream. Depending on the amount of cream used, ganache can be a pourable glaze, a fudgy filling, or a whipped frosting (like our Chocolate Ganache Frosting on page 400), making it a versatile option.

Whipped Cream (G) is all that's needed for rustic cakes or those that are particularly rich. When whipped cream is being used in place of frosting, we prefer to make it in the food processor. Whereas whipping cream in a stand mixer produces light, billowy peaks, the sharp, fast-moving blades of a food processor can't add as much air. The result is whipped cream with a denser, creamier consistency that's ideal for spreading over a cake; it can also be piped on to make a decorative edge. And because the smaller air bubbles created by the food processor are more stable than the bigger bubbles created by a stand mixer, we've found that processed cream keeps its thick, dense texture for two full weeks.

DECORATING CAKES

Once you know how to make a smooth-frosted layer cake, you have a canvas for showcasing more elaborate decorations, from toppings that you can adhere to swirls and swoops of piped frosting. Here are some of our favorite ways to dress up our cakes.

texture with a spoon

One of the simplest ways to decorate a cake is to give the frosting some texture. Using the back of a soupspoon, press into the frosting and then twirl as you lift it away for artful swoops. You can also make wavy lines or a striped pattern by dragging a cake comb (or fork) around the cake's sides, or by adorning the top with a wave from the serrations of a knife.

coating the sides

Coating the sides with small adornments—sprinkles, toasted coconut, chocolate shavings, crushed candies, cookies, or nuts—is an easy way to add visual appeal. (It also hides any messy frosting jobs.) You can take a small amount of the ingredient in your hand and press it against the sides. If you built your cake on a cake round and it's light enough pick it up with one hand, you can press on the toppings with your free hand for the most even coating.

bottom border

This simple trick is one of the most elegant treatments, but it also camouflages any imperfections at the base of the cake. Press whole toasted or candied nuts (page 16), one at a time, around the bottom edge of the cake. You can also chop toasted or candied nuts and press them a third of the way up from the bottom of the cake. Instead of nuts, you can also use fruit, sprinkles, candies, or even crushed cookies.

mark each slice

Try marking each future slice with a small garnish. When you slice the cake, you'll cut between the garnishes so that each slice has a garnish in the center. The garnish can hint at the flavors inside the cake (such as fruit or nuts) or simply be decorative. And of course you can always place a small pile of garnish in the center of the cake or all along the edge, as well.

cover the top

Garnishing the top of a cake makes it look tall and impressive, but you want to choose a topping that won't weigh down the cake. We particularly like chocolate shavings.

NAKED CAKES

One of the biggest trends in cake making is the naked cake—layer cakes with sheer coatings or completely bare sides. At once elegant and rustic, these cakes showcase the juxtaposition of layer and filling to beautiful effect. If you're filling a cake and leaving the sides unfrosted, as we do for our Pomegranate Walnut Cake (page 188), you'll want to be a bit more graceful in your filling of the cakes, as it will show through the sides. Another option is to scrape frosting along the sides of the cake—just enough to give the cake a thin veil but not so much that you can't see the stacked layers. We use this technique in our Blackberry-Mascarpone Lemon Cake (page 164).

WHEN TO USE A CRUMB COAT

A crumb coat is a thin veil of frosting that's used to cover the sides of the cake before the real frosting job to prevent it from picking up crumbs. A crumb coat can be used at your discretion, but we only find it necessary on really tall cakes, like our Rainbow Cake (page 152). For directions on how to make a crumb coat, see page 153.

LOVELY LAYERS

Sometimes our cakes reach even greater heights than those featured in the preceding pages. In fact, we have a whole chapter devoted to sky-high cakes (see page 130). If we're making a four-layer cake, it usually means we're slicing standard layers in half. The task seems daunting, but if you follow these instructions, you'll achieve thin, even layers without stress.

1 Measure the height of the cake. Using a paring knife, mark the midpoint at several places around the sides of the cake.

2 Using the marks as a guide, score the entire circumference of the cake with a long serrated knife.

3 Following the scored lines, run the knife around the cake several times, cutting inward. Once the knife is inside the cake, use a back-and-forth motion.

4 Once the knife cuts through the cake, separate the layers and gently insert your fingers between them. Lift the top layer and place it on the counter.

HOW TO USE A PASTRY BAG

For special occasions, you may want to go all out and pipe more elaborate decorations on your cake. But before you get decorating, you'll want to be adept with a piping bag. Here are the steps to filling and using one. (For information on buying a pastry bag, see page 9.)

1 Fit the Tip Inside the Bag Holding the pastry bag in one hand, fold the top down about halfway. Insert the selected tip into the point of the bag and press it securely in place. Ideally, about ½ inch of the tip should be peeking through the hole in the bag. Be careful: If the hole is too big, the force of the frosting will dislodge the tip, and you'll have a mess.

2 Fill the Bag Scrape the frosting into the bag until the bag is half full. Don't overfill the bag or frosting will pop out of the top.

3 Squeeze Out the Air Pull up the sides of the bag, push down the frosting, and twist tightly. Push down on the bag to squeeze air out and move the frosting into the tip. The twisted top serves two functions: It helps keep the frosting away from your hands, and it also gives you a place to exert pressure that will start the flow of frosting through and out of the tip. Make sure to squeeze out air bubbles in the frosting; if you don't, the frosting will come out of the tip in spurts.

4 Practice First Grab the base of the bag, twist, and squeeze to pipe out frosting. Practice briefly on a sheet of parchment paper before decorating the cake. Steady pressure with both hands will keep the frosting flowing. Practicing on parchment will give you a chance to remove air bubbles that often form in the flow of frosting.

PROFESSIONAL PIPING

You can use your imagination when applying piping to your cakes. But these are our four favorite classic decorations for inspiration. If you want to switch tips on the bag, owning a coupler (see page 9) is worthwhile.

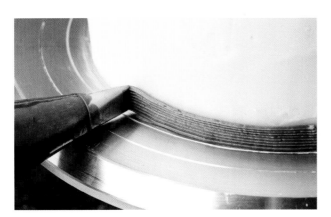

1 Dot Patterns Use a round tip and hold the bag perpendicular to the surface of the cake. Pipe out a small amount of frosting and then stop piping and pull bag straight away from the cake to ensure neat dots that hold their shape.

2 Rosettes Use a closed star tip and hold the bag perpendicular to the surface of the cake. Slowly pipe out the frosting while directing the tip in a tight, circular motion, then top piping and pull bag straight away from the cake. You can top rosettes with a garnish if desired.

3 Striped Border Use a basket weave tip and hold the pastry bag perpendicular to the surface of the cake. Slowly pipe out the frosting in a horizontal band along the bottom and/or top edge of the cake. Piping along the bottom can seal the space between the cake and the platter.

4 Shell Border To make a ruffled border, use a star (or leaf) tip and hold the bag at an angle to the surface of the cake. Pipe out a small amount of frosting, then lightly draw the tip forward while reducing the flow of icing to make a tail; pipe the next ruffle on the tail of the previous ruffle.

1

CLASSIC LAYER CAKES

fluffy yellow layer cake

serves 10 to 12

2½ cups (10 ounces) cake flour

1¼ teaspoons baking powder

¼ teaspoon baking soda

¾ teaspoon salt

1¾ cups (12¼ ounces) sugar

1 cup buttermilk, room temperature

10 tablespoons unsalted butter, melted and cooled

3 large eggs, separated, plus 3 large yolks, room temperature

3 tablespoons vegetable oil

2 teaspoons vanilla extract

Pinch cream of tartar

5 cups Chocolate Frosting (page 399)

why this recipe works When we think of birthday cake, the first thing that comes to mind is yellow cake covered in billowy chocolate frosting. But many recipes turn out dry, heavy, or cottony rounds rather than rich, buttery, tender cake. Our first step toward an ultralight texture was to skip the traditional creaming method (for more information on creaming, see page 4) and adopt a chiffon cake technique—using whipped egg whites to get high volume and a light texture. This gave us a fluffy cake that was still sturdy enough to support a substantial frosting. A combination of butter and vegetable oil gave our cake layers a buttery-rich flavor while ensuring they remained incredibly moist. Substituting buttermilk for milk produced a downy, fine crumb.

1 Adjust oven rack to middle position and heat oven to 350 degrees. Grease two 9-inch round cake pans, line with parchment paper, grease parchment, and flour pans. Whisk flour, baking powder, baking soda, salt, and 1½ cups sugar together in bowl. Whisk buttermilk, melted butter, egg yolks, oil, and vanilla together in second bowl.

2 Using stand mixer fitted with whisk attachment, whip egg whites and cream of tartar on medium-low speed until foamy, about 1 minute. Increase speed to medium-high and whip whites to soft billowy mounds, about 1 minute. Gradually add remaining ¼ cup sugar and whip until glossy, stiff peaks form, 2 to 3 minutes; transfer to third bowl.

3 Add flour mixture to now-empty mixer bowl and mix on low speed, gradually adding buttermilk mixture and mixing until almost incorporated (a few streaks of dry flour will remain), about 15 seconds. Scrape down bowl, then mix on medium-low speed until smooth and fully incorporated, 10 to 15 seconds.

4 Using rubber spatula, stir one-third of whites into batter. Gently fold remaining whites into batter until no white streaks remain. Divide batter evenly between prepared pans and smooth tops with rubber spatula. Gently tap pans on counter to settle batter. Bake until toothpick inserted in center comes out clean, 20 to 22 minutes, switching and rotating pans halfway through baking. Let cakes cool in pans on wire rack for 10 minutes. Remove cakes from pans, discarding parchment, and let cool completely on rack, about 2 hours. (Cake layers can be stored at room temperature for up to 24 hours or frozen for up to 1 month; defrost at room temperature.)

5 Line edges of cake platter with 4 strips of parchment paper to keep platter clean. Place 1 cake layer on platter. Spread 1½ cups frosting evenly over top, right to edge of cake. Top with second cake layer, press lightly to adhere, then spread remaining frosting evenly over top and sides of cake. Carefully remove parchment strips before serving.

classic white layer cake

serves 10 to 12

1 cup whole milk, room temperature

6 large egg whites, room temperature

1 teaspoon vanilla extract

2¼ cups (9 ounces) cake flour

1¾ cups (12¼ ounces) sugar

4 teaspoons baking powder

1 teaspoon salt

12 tablespoons unsalted butter,
cut into 12 pieces and softened

5 cups Vanilla Frosting (page 398)

why this recipe works A white layer cake is an elegant choice for special occasions. White cake is simply a butter cake made with whipped egg whites instead of whole eggs (using the latter would make it a—you guessed it—yellow cake). Using whites only is intended to give the cake a soft, fine crumb. Unfortunately, most white cakes emerge from the oven dry, cottony, and riddled with small holes. Tackling the texture problem first, we mixed the cake using the reverse creaming method—adding the butter to the dry ingredients so that it coated the flour particles for an ultratender crumb. (For more information on cake mixing methods, see page 20.) As for the large air pockets and holes, we suspected that the stiffly beaten whites were the culprit. So instead of folding whipped whites into the batter, we simply mixed the whites with the milk before beating them into the flour-butter mixture. This cake was fine-grained, free of holes, and delightfully tall and light. And with no special mixing techniques required, this foolproof method couldn't be easier.

1 Adjust oven rack to middle position and heat oven to 350 degrees. Grease two 9-inch round cake pans, line with parchment paper, grease parchment, and flour pans. Whisk milk, egg whites, and vanilla together in bowl.

2 Using stand mixer fitted with paddle, mix flour, sugar, baking powder, and salt on low speed until combined. Add butter, 1 piece at a time, and mix until only pea-size pieces remain, about 1 minute. Add all but ½ cup milk mixture, increase speed to medium-high, and beat until light and fluffy, about 1 minute. Reduce speed to medium-low, add remaining ½ cup milk mixture, and beat until incorporated, about 30 seconds (batter may look curdled). Give batter final stir by hand.

3 Divide batter evenly between prepared pans and smooth tops with rubber spatula. Gently tap pans on counter to settle batter. Bake until toothpick inserted in center comes out with few crumbs attached, 23 to 25 minutes, switching and rotating pans halfway through baking. Let cakes cool in pans on wire rack for 10 minutes. Remove cakes from pans, discarding parchment, and let cool completely on rack, about 2 hours. (Cake layers can be stored at room temperature for up to 24 hours or frozen for up to 1 month; defrost at room temperature.)

4 Line edges of cake platter with 4 strips of parchment paper to keep platter clean. Place 1 cake layer on platter. Spread 1½ cups frosting evenly over top, right to edge of cake. Top with second cake layer, press lightly to adhere, then spread remaining frosting evenly over top and sides of cake. Carefully remove parchment strips before serving.

old-fashioned chocolate layer cake

serves 10 to 12

4 ounces unsweetened chocolate, chopped coarse

½ cup hot water

¼ cup (¾ ounce) Dutch-processed cocoa powder

1¾ cups (12¼ ounces) sugar

1¾ cups (8¾ ounces) all-purpose flour

1½ teaspoons baking soda

1 teaspoon salt

1 cup buttermilk

2 teaspoons vanilla extract

4 large eggs plus 2 large yolks, room temperature

12 tablespoons unsalted butter, cut into 12 pieces and softened

5 cups Chocolate Frosting (page 399)

why this recipe works Over the years, chocolate cakes have become denser, richer, and squatter. We wanted a more traditional chocolate layer cake with a tender, airy, open crumb. To start, we turned to a popular old-fashioned method called ribboning, a technique in which eggs are whipped with sugar until they double in volume before the butter, dry ingredients, and milk are added. This process of aerating the eggs gave our cake height and structure, but also made it remarkably tender. To achieve a moist cake with rich chocolate flavor, we once again looked to historical sources, which suggested using buttermilk instead of the milk and making a "pudding" with a mixture of chocolate, water, and sugar. The results were just what we were looking for: a moist, tender chocolate cake that's sure to have people clamoring for seconds. Do not substitute natural cocoa powder for the Dutch-processed cocoa powder. We recommend using milk chocolate for the Chocolate Frosting (page 399).

1 Adjust oven rack to middle position and heat oven to 350 degrees. Grease two 9-inch round cake pans, line with parchment paper, grease parchment, and flour pans.

2 Combine chocolate, hot water, and cocoa in medium heatproof bowl set over saucepan filled with 1 inch barely simmering water, making sure that water does not touch bottom of bowl and stirring with heat-resistant rubber spatula until chocolate is melted, about 2 minutes. Add ½ cup sugar to chocolate mixture and stir until thick and glossy, 1 to 2 minutes. Remove bowl from heat; set aside to cool.

3 Whisk flour, baking soda, and salt together in medium bowl. Combine buttermilk and vanilla in second bowl. Using stand mixer fitted with whisk attachment, whip eggs and yolks on medium-low speed until combined, about 10 seconds. Add remaining 1¼ cups sugar, increase speed to high, and whip until light and fluffy, 2 to 3 minutes. Fit stand mixer with paddle. Add cooled chocolate mixture to egg mixture and mix on medium speed until thoroughly combined, 30 to 45 seconds, scraping down bowl as needed. Add butter, 1 piece at a time, mixing for about 10 seconds after each addition. Add flour mixture in 3 additions, alternating with buttermilk mixture in 2 additions, mixing until incorporated after each addition (about 15 seconds) and scraping down bowl as needed. Reduce speed to medium-low and mix until batter is thoroughly combined, about 15 seconds. Give batter final stir by hand.

4 Divide batter evenly between prepared pans and smooth tops with rubber spatula. Bake until toothpick inserted in center comes out with few moist crumbs attached, 25 to 30 minutes, switching and rotating pans halfway through baking. Let cakes cool in pans on wire rack for 10 minutes. Remove cakes from pans, discarding parchment, and let cool completely on rack, about 2 hours. (Cake layers can be stored at room temperature for up to 24 hours or frozen for up to 1 month; defrost at room temperature.)

5 Line edges of cake platter with 4 strips of parchment paper to keep platter clean. Place 1 cake layer on platter. Spread 1½ cups frosting evenly over top, right to edge of cake. Top with second cake layer, press lightly to adhere, then spread remaining frosting evenly over top and sides of cake. Carefully remove parchment strips before serving.

devil's food layer cake

serves 10 to 12

½ cup (1½ ounces) Dutch-processed cocoa powder, plus extra for pan

1½ cups (7½ ounces) all-purpose flour

1 teaspoon baking soda

½ teaspoon baking powder

¼ teaspoon salt

1¼ cups boiling water

4 ounces unsweetened chocolate, chopped

1 teaspoon instant espresso powder or instant coffee powder

10 tablespoons unsalted butter, cut into 10 pieces and softened

1½ cups packed (10½ ounces) light brown sugar

3 large eggs, room temperature

½ cup sour cream, room temperature

1 teaspoon vanilla extract

5 cups Seven-Minute Frosting (page 402)

why this recipe works The name of this cake refers to its color, which is a very dark—almost black. Unfortunately, the flavor often fails to match the rich hue. For an intensely chocolate devil's food cake, we used a combination of unsweetened chocolate and Dutch-processed cocoa powder (which is less acidic than natural cocoa and enhances browning). Mixing the chocolate and cocoa with hot water, rather than the milk found in recipes, ensured a strong presence. Brown sugar and some espresso powder further underscored the deep chocolate notes. The chocolaty impact of this dark-as-night cake was clear as day. Sweet, marshmallowy seven-minute frosting tempers the cakes' darkness. For an accurate measurement of boiling water, bring a full kettle of water to a boil and then measure out the desired amount. Do not substitute natural cocoa powder for the Dutch-processed cocoa powder.

1 Adjust oven rack to middle position and heat oven to 350 degrees. Grease two 9-inch round cake pans, then dust with cocoa powder and line bottoms with parchment paper.

2 Whisk flour, baking soda, baking powder, and salt together in bowl. Whisk boiling water, chocolate, cocoa, and espresso powder in second bowl until smooth.

3 Using stand mixer fitted with paddle, beat butter and sugar on medium-high speed until pale and fluffy, about 3 minutes. Add eggs, one at a time, and beat until combined, about 30 seconds. Beat in sour cream and vanilla until incorporated. Reduce speed to low and add flour mixture in 3 additions, alternating with chocolate mixture in 2 additions, scraping down bowl as needed. Give batter final stir by hand.

4 Divide batter evenly between prepared pans and smooth tops with rubber spatula. Gently tap pans on counter to settle batter. Bake until toothpick inserted in center comes out with few crumbs attached, 18 to 22 minutes, switching and rotating pans halfway through baking. Let cakes cool in pans on wire rack for 10 minutes. Remove cakes from pans, discarding parchment, and let cool completely on rack, about 2 hours. (Cake layers can be stored at room temperature for up to 24 hours or frozen for up to 1 month; defrost at room temperature.)

5 Line edges of cake platter with 4 strips of parchment paper to keep platter clean. Place 1 cake layer on platter. Spread 1½ cups frosting evenly over top, right to edge of cake. Top with second cake layer, press lightly to adhere, then spread remaining frosting evenly over top and sides of cake. Carefully remove parchment strips before serving.

genoise sponge cake

serves 10 to 12

4 tablespoons unsalted butter, melted and cooled slightly

1 teaspoon vanilla extract

½ teaspoon grated lemon zest

1¼ cups (5 ounces) cake flour

¼ teaspoon salt

5 large eggs

¾ cup (5¼ ounces) granulated sugar

⅔ cup raspberry jam

Confectioners' sugar

why this recipe works Genoise-style sponge cakes are a study in contrasts. They are light but have good structure (making them ideal for layering with fruit or cream fillings); they're elegant even when unadorned; and unlike other egg-aerated cakes with a light, delicate texture (such as chiffon and angel food), they contain both whole eggs and melted butter for rich flavor. But genoise isn't without problems. Recipes call for whipping the eggs and sugar until the mixture has more than tripled in volume and then gently folding in the dry ingredients, followed by the melted butter. This seems straightforward enough, but since the batter contains no chemical leaveners the cake can be dense, flat, and rubbery if the eggs aren't perfectly aerated. To ensure the ideal texture, we followed a number of key steps. First, fully dissolving the sugar in the eggs by heating the mixture over simmering water made for a more viscous mixture that's extremely capable of holding air. Next, transferring the egg mixture to a wide, shallow bowl made folding more efficient, which also helped the batter retain air. Finally, lightening the melted butter by combining it with some of the egg foam before folding it in made it easier to combine.

1 Adjust oven rack to middle position and heat oven to 350 degrees. Spray two 9-inch round cake pans with baking spray with flour, line with parchment paper, and spray parchment with baking spray with flour. Combine melted butter, vanilla, and lemon zest in bowl. Whisk flour and salt together in second bowl.

2 Combine eggs and sugar in bowl of stand mixer; place bowl over medium saucepan filled with 2 inches simmering water, making sure that water does not touch bottom of bowl. Whisking constantly, heat until sugar is dissolved and mixture registers 115 to 120 degrees, about 3 minutes.

3 Transfer bowl to stand mixer fitted with whisk attachment. Whip on high speed until eggs are pale yellow and have tripled in volume, about 5 minutes. (Egg foam will form ribbon that sits on top of mixture for 5 seconds when dribbled from whisk.) Measure out ¾ cup egg foam, whisk into butter mixture until well combined, and set aside.

4 Transfer remaining egg foam to large, wide bowl and sift one-third of flour mixture over egg foam in even layer. Using rubber spatula, gently fold batter 6 to 8 times until small streaks of flour remain. Repeat folding 6 to 8 times with half of remaining flour mixture. Sift remaining flour mixture over batter and gently fold 10 to 12 times until flour is completely incorporated.

5 Pour butter mixture over batter in even layer. Gently fold until just incorporated, taking care not to deflate batter. Divide batter evenly between prepared pans. Bake until centers of cakes are set and bounce back when gently pressed and toothpick inserted in center comes out clean, 13 to 16 minutes. Remove cakes from pans, discarding parchment, and let cool completely on wire rack, about 2 hours.

6 Place 1 cake layer on platter. Spread jam evenly over top. Top with second cake layer, press lightly to adhere. Dust with confectioners' sugar before serving.

red velvet layer cake

serves 10 to 12

2¼ cups (11¼ ounces) all-purpose flour

1½ teaspoons baking soda

Pinch salt

1 cup buttermilk

2 large eggs

1 tablespoon distilled white vinegar

1 teaspoon vanilla extract

2 tablespoons natural unsweetened
cocoa powder

2 tablespoons (1 ounce) red food coloring

12 tablespoons unsalted butter,
cut into 12 pieces and softened

1½ cups (10½ ounces) sugar

5 cups Cream Cheese Frosting (page 401)

why this recipe works Although it's perhaps best known for its shocking bright color, red velvet layer cake is more than just a novelty: Its tender, light, and moist texture is also a hallmark of the cake. For the ideal red velvet cake, we discovered that two ingredients were essential: buttermilk and vinegar. This combination of liquids reacted with the baking soda in our recipe to create a fine, tender crumb. We also found that the type of cocoa powder we used was important. Unlike Dutch-processed cocoa, natural cocoa powder is acidic; so in addition to providing a light chocolate flavor to the cake, natural cocoa further enhanced the cake's light and airy texture. (In fact, the ruddy color of the original red velvet cake didn't come from dye but from the reaction of the natural cocoa and the buttermilk and vinegar.) Do not substitute Dutch-processed cocoa powder for the natural cocoa powder.

1 Adjust oven rack to middle position and heat oven to 350 degrees. Grease two 9-inch round cake pans, line with parchment paper, grease parchment, and flour pans. Whisk flour, baking soda, and salt together in bowl. Whisk buttermilk, eggs, vinegar, and vanilla together in second bowl. Mix cocoa and red food coloring in third bowl until smooth paste forms.

2 Using stand mixer fitted with paddle, beat butter and sugar on medium-high speed until pale and fluffy, about 3 minutes. Reduce speed to low and add flour mixture in 3 additions, alternating with buttermilk mixture in 2 additions, scraping down bowl as needed. Beat in cocoa mixture until batter is uniform. Give batter final stir by hand.

3 Divide batter evenly between prepared pans and smooth tops with rubber spatula. Gently tap pans on counter to settle batter. Bake until toothpick inserted in center comes out clean, about 25 minutes, switching and rotating pans halfway through baking. Let cakes cool in pans on wire rack for 10 minutes. Remove cakes from pans, discarding parchment, and let cool completely on rack, about 2 hours. (Cake layers can be stored at room temperature for up to 24 hours or frozen for up to 1 month; defrost at room temperature.)

4 Line edges of cake platter with 4 strips of parchment paper to keep platter clean. Place 1 cake layer on platter. Spread 1½ cups frosting evenly over top, right to edge of cake. Top with second cake layer, press lightly to adhere, then spread remaining frosting evenly over top and sides of cake. Carefully remove parchment strips before serving.

carrot-honey layer cake

serves 10 to 12

1¾ cups (8¾ ounces) all-purpose flour

2 teaspoons baking powder

1 teaspoon baking soda

2 teaspoons ground cinnamon

1 teaspoon ground nutmeg

½ teaspoon ground cloves

½ teaspoon salt

¾ cup vegetable oil

3 large eggs

⅓ cup plus ¼ cup honey

1 tablespoon vanilla extract

2⅔ cups shredded carrots (4 carrots)

5 cups Honey Cream Cheese Frosting
(page 402)

why this recipe works We love our recipe for sky-high Carrot Layer Cake (page 132), but we also wanted a more modest two-layer version of this crowd-pleasing classic. For a unique spin on traditional carrot cake, we sweetened this one with honey; its floral nuances added an intriguing layer of complexity and paired well with the sweet carrots and warm spices. We further bolstered the cake's flavor by increasing the amounts of cinnamon, nutmeg, and cloves. To keep our recipe streamlined, we found that we could forgo the stand mixer and simply stir everything together by hand, making this layer cake recipe as easy as our carrot cupcakes and sheet cake. Cream cheese frosting sweetened with honey brought out the honey in the cake. Shred the carrots on the large holes of a box grater or in a food processor fitted with the shredding disk.

1 Adjust oven rack to middle position and heat oven to 350 degrees. Grease two 9-inch round cake pans, line with parchment paper, grease parchment, and flour pans.

2 Whisk flour, baking powder, baking soda, cinnamon, nutmeg, cloves, and salt together in bowl. Whisk oil, eggs, honey, and vanilla in large bowl until smooth. Stir in carrots. Add flour mixture and fold with rubber spatula until mixture is just combined.

3 Divide batter evenly between prepared pans and smooth tops with rubber spatula. Bake until cakes are set and center is just firm to touch, 16 to 20 minutes, switching and rotating pans halfway through baking. Let cakes cool in pans on wire rack for 10 minutes. Remove cakes from pans, discarding parchment, and let cool completely on rack, about 1 hour. (Cake layers can be stored at room temperature for up to 3 days.)

4 Line edges of cake platter with 4 strips of parchment paper to keep platter clean. Place 1 cake layer on platter. Spread 1½ cups frosting evenly over top, right to edge of cake. Top with second cake layer, press lightly to adhere, then spread remaining frosting evenly over top and sides of cake. Carefully remove parchment strips before serving.

maple layer cake

serves 10 to 12

2½ cups (10 ounces) cake flour

2 teaspoons baking powder

½ teaspoon salt

¾ cup plus 2 tablespoons vegetable oil

1¼ cups maple syrup

3 large eggs

4 teaspoons vanilla extract

5 cups Maple Cream Cheese Frosting
(page 402)

why this recipe works Simple yellow cake is a universal favorite; here we take this classic recipe up a notch by introducing the subtle yet welcoming flavor and aroma of maple syrup. While our Fluffy Yellow Layer Cake (page 32) relies on a delicate balance of ingredients to ensure a moist cake, here maple syrup gave us an advantage: This liquid sweetener is hygroscopic (meaning it attracts moisture), which virtually guarantees a moist crumb. Although many yellow cakes rely on butter as the fat, a simple test revealed that oil worked much better; it produced a cake that was not only tender and rich but also sturdy enough to support thick layers of frosting. As an added bonus, using oil meant that we didn't have to break out the stand mixer and could simply stir everything together by hand. Most frostings detracted from the delicate maple flavor of our cake. For the taste of maple-on-maple, we filled and frosted the cake layers with a maple cream cheese frosting.

1 Adjust oven rack to middle position and heat oven to 325 degrees. Grease two 9-inch round cake pans, line with parchment paper, grease parchment, and flour pans.

2 Whisk flour, baking powder, and salt together in bowl. Whisk oil, maple syrup, eggs, and vanilla in large bowl until smooth. Whisk in flour mixture until smooth. Divide batter evenly between prepared pans. Bake until cakes are set and center is just firm to touch, 22 to 25 minutes, switching and rotating pans halfway through baking. Let cakes cool in pans on wire rack for 10 minutes. Remove cakes from pans, discarding parchment, and let cool completely on rack, about 1 hour. (Cake layers can be stored at room temperature for up to 3 days.)

3 Line edges of cake platter with 4 strips of parchment paper to keep platter clean. Place 1 cake layer on platter. Spread 1½ cups frosting evenly over top, right to edge of cake. Top with second cake layer, press lightly to adhere, then spread remaining frosting evenly over top and sides of cake. Carefully remove parchment strips before serving.

vegan yellow layer cake

serves 10 to 12

1¾ cups unsweetened oat milk, room temperature

½ cup coconut oil, melted and cooled

1½ tablespoons vanilla extract

5 tablespoons aquafaba

1 teaspoon cream of tartar

4 cups (16 ounces) cake flour

1¾ cups (12¼ ounces) organic sugar

1 tablespoon baking powder

1 teaspoon salt

4 cups Creamy Vegan Chocolate Frosting (page 405)

Measuring Aquafaba

To measure out the amount of aquafaba called for in a recipe, start by shaking the unopened can of chickpeas well. Drain the chickpeas through a fine-mesh strainer over a bowl and reserve the beans for another use. Whisk the aquafaba liquid and then measure. While it may not be visible, the starches in the chickpea liquid settle in the can; in order to take advantage of them, you'll want to make sure they're evenly distributed throughout the liquid.

---

why this recipe works Our vegan yellow layer cake stands tall for any celebration. But nailing the recipe was a big challenge. After all, none of the ingredients that give yellow cake structure or lightness are vegan. And with yellow cake, off-flavors have nowhere to hide. Replacing the eggs would be no small feat. Eggs provide cakes with lift and structure, and most of the common substitutes we tried left us with heavy cakes. Then, after lots of testing, we landed on aquafaba; the liquid found in canned chickpeas, whipped to stiff peaks like egg whites and folded into the batter, acted as the perfect stand-in, trapping tiny air bubbles for a classic fluffy crumb. To enhance fluffiness more, we baked the cake in a hot oven—400 degrees—to boost oven spring (the rise that baked goods experience when they first hit the oven). And a lengthy baking time of 25 to 30 minutes helped dry out the layers so there was no pastiness. Using oat milk further promoted browning thanks to its sugar content. Most conventional white sugar is filtered through animal bone char; if you're not a strict vegan, feel free to use it in place of the organic sugar.

1 Adjust oven rack to middle position and heat oven to 400 degrees. Grease two 9-inch round cake pans, line with parchment paper, and grease parchment.

2 Whisk oat milk, melted oil, and vanilla together in bowl. Using stand mixer fitted with whisk attachment, whip aquafaba and cream of tartar on high speed until stiff foam that clings to whisk forms, 3 to 9 minutes; transfer to clean bowl.

3 Add flour, sugar, baking powder, and salt to now-empty mixer bowl and mix on low speed until well combined, about 1 minute. Gradually add milk mixture and continue to mix until just incorporated, about 15 seconds. Scrape down bowl and whisk attachment, then continue to whip on medium-low speed until smooth and fully incorporated, 10 to 15 seconds.

4 Using rubber spatula, stir one-third of whipped aquafaba into batter to lighten, then gently fold in remaining aquafaba until no white streaks remain. Divide batter evenly between prepared pans. Bake until cakes are set and spring back when pressed lightly, 25 to 30 minutes, switching and rotating pans halfway through baking. Let cakes cool in pans on wire rack for 10 minutes. Remove cakes from pans, discarding parchment, and let cool completely on rack, about 2 hours.

5 Line edges of cake platter with 4 strips of parchment paper to keep platter clean. Place 1 cake layer on platter. Spread 1½ cups frosting evenly over top, right to edge of cake. Top with second cake layer, press lightly to adhere, then spread remaining frosting evenly over top and sides of cake. Carefully remove parchment strips before serving.

gluten-free chocolate layer cake

serves 10 to 12

1 cup vegetable oil

6 ounces bittersweet chocolate, chopped

2 ounces (⅔ cup) unsweetened cocoa powder

7 ounces (1¼ cups) gluten-free all-purpose flour blend

1½ teaspoons baking powder

1 teaspoon baking soda

1 teaspoon xanthan gum (see page 77)

1 teaspoon salt

4 large eggs

2 teaspoons vanilla extract

10½ ounces (1½ cups) sugar

1 cup whole milk

5 cups Chocolate Buttercream (page 399)

Gluten-Free Flour Blends
Each store-bought gluten-free flour blend relies on a mix of different ingredients, yielding cakes and other baked goods with varying textures, colors, and flavors. Some work well, while others carry off-flavors or less-than-satisfactory textures. We've had good luck with and recommend **King Arthur Gluten-Free All-Purpose Flour** and **Betty Crocker All-Purpose Gluten Free Rice Flour Blend**, which both turned out tender cakes. Bob's Red Mill Gluten Free All-Purpose Baking Flour also works, but it will add a noticeable bean flavor in most instances.

why this recipe works Everyone loves (and deserves!) a rich chocolate cake, but too often the gluten-free translation is less than appealing; our initial survey of recipes turned out dense, brick-like cakes. We wanted a recipe for truly great gluten-free cake. A combination of cocoa powder and bittersweet chocolate provided the best chocolate flavor, but the bar chocolate weighed down our cake. When we tried a cake made with all cocoa powder, however, the results were dismal. Instead, we kept the chocolate and cocoa combination and swapped out the traditional butter for oil, which lightened our cake. A combination of ingredients—baking powder, baking soda, and xanthan gum—was necessary for leavening these rich layers. The soda helped keep the cake tender, while the powder gave it lift; xanthan gum contributed the structure typically provided by gluten. It's essential to weigh the flour. Seven ounces of King Arthur Gluten-Free All-Purpose Flour is equal to 1¼ cups, while 7 ounces of Betty Crocker All-Purpose Gluten-Free Flour Blend is equal to 1¼ cups plus 2 tablespoons. Volumes of other blends will vary, so we strongly recommend measuring by weight. Once it's frosted, serve the cake within a few hours.

1 Adjust oven rack to lower-middle position and heat oven to 350 degrees. Grease two 9-inch round cake pans, line bottoms with parchment paper, and grease parchment.

2 Microwave oil, chocolate, and cocoa in bowl at 50 percent power, stirring occasionally, until melted, about 2 minutes. Whisk mixture until smooth, then set aside to cool slightly. Whisk flour blend, baking powder, baking soda, xanthan gum, and salt together in second bowl.

3 Whisk eggs and vanilla together in large bowl. Whisk in sugar until well combined. Whisk in cooled chocolate mixture and milk until combined. Whisk in flour blend mixture until batter is thoroughly combined and smooth. Divide batter evenly between prepared pans and smooth tops with rubber spatula. Bake until toothpick inserted in center comes out clean, 30 to 32 minutes, switching and rotating pans halfway through baking.

4 Let cakes cool in pans on wire rack for 10 minutes. Run thin knife around edge of cake pans. Remove cakes from pans, discarding parchment, and let cool completely on rack, about 1½ hours. (Cake layers can stored at room temperature for up to 24 hours.)

5 Line edges of cake platter with 4 strips of parchment paper to keep platter clean. Place 1 cake layer on platter. Spread 1½ cups frosting evenly over top, right to edge of cake. Top with second cake layer, press lightly to adhere, then spread remaining frosting evenly over top and sides of cake. Carefully remove parchment strips before serving.

CUPCAKES, CAKE POPS, MUG CAKES & MORE

yellow cupcakes

makes 12 cupcakes

1½ cups (7½ ounces) all-purpose flour

1 cup (7 ounces) sugar

1½ teaspoons baking powder

½ teaspoon salt

8 tablespoons unsalted butter,
cut into 8 pieces and softened

½ cup sour cream

1 large egg plus 2 large yolks

1½ teaspoons vanilla extract

3 cups Vanilla Buttercream (page 403)

why this recipe works The cake part of a yellow cupcake sometimes seems like an afterthought—nothing more than a vehicle for mounds of frosting. We wanted a rich and tender yellow cupcake that would be delicious on its own merit, one that didn't need to hide under a blanket of frosting; in short, we wanted a crowd-pleasing cupcake that would satisfy the kids as well as the parents at any birthday party. We started with a simple ingredient list: all-purpose flour (cake flour produced too fine a crumb), a combination of a whole egg and two yolks (fewer whites meant richer flavor), sugar, butter, and sour cream (for tangy richness). As for mixing technique, we tried the classic creaming method as well as reverse creaming, but the difference in texture between the two was minimal. Instead, we decided to try a slightly unconventional approach: simply throwing everything into the mixer together. Surprisingly, the easiest method gave us the best cupcakes of the bunch. Why? One possible answer is that egg yolks contain emulsifiers, and with three in this recipe, there was enough to hold the fat and liquid together even when mixed in such a haphazard fashion. The cupcakes that emerged from the oven were buttery, tender, and lightly golden.

1 Adjust oven rack to middle position and heat oven to 350 degrees. Line 12-cup muffin tin with paper or foil liners.

2 Using stand mixer fitted with paddle, mix flour, sugar, baking powder, and salt on low speed until combined. Increase speed to medium, add butter, sour cream, egg and yolks, and vanilla and beat until smooth and satiny, about 30 seconds. Scrape down bowl with rubber spatula and stir by hand until smooth and no flour pockets remain.

3 Divide batter evenly among prepared muffin cups. Bake until tops are light golden and toothpick inserted in center comes out clean, 20 to 24 minutes, rotating muffin tin halfway through baking.

4 Let cupcakes cool in muffin tin on wire rack for 15 minutes. Remove cupcakes from muffin tin and let cool completely on rack, about 30 minutes. (Unfrosted cupcakes can be stored at room temperature for up to 24 hours.) Spread or pipe frosting evenly on cupcakes. Serve.

ultimate chocolate cupcakes with ganache filling

makes 12 cupcakes

filling

2 ounces bittersweet chocolate, chopped fine

¼ cup heavy cream

1 tablespoon confectioners' sugar

cupcakes

3 ounces bittersweet chocolate, chopped fine

⅓ cup (1 ounce) Dutch-processed cocoa powder

¾ cup brewed coffee, hot

¾ cup (4⅛ ounces) bread flour

¾ cup (5¼ ounces) granulated sugar

½ teaspoon salt

½ teaspoon baking soda

6 tablespoons vegetable oil

2 large eggs

2 teaspoons distilled white vinegar

1 teaspoon vanilla extract

3 cups Chocolate Buttercream (page 399)

why this recipe works When it comes to chocolate, a cupcake catch-22 befalls bakery and homemade confections alike: If the cupcakes are packed with enough chocolate to be worthy of their name, their structure usually suffers and they fall apart into a crumbly mess. Conversely, if the cakes strike just the right balance between moisture and tenderness to avoid crumbling, the chocolate flavor is barely discernible. Figuring that a cupcake is just a cake in miniature, we started by making cupcakes using a tried-and-tested cake recipe. But while tasters liked their chocolate flavor, their crumbly texture made them impossible to eat without a fork. We were loath to compromise the chocolate's intensity, so instead we tried fortifying the structure of the cupcakes, substituting higher-protein bread flour for the all-purpose flour. Specifically engineered for gluten development, bread flour turned out a cupcake that was markedly less crumbly yet not tough. But we still needed to reduce the amount of bar chocolate a bit. To compensate, we mixed the chocolate and cocoa with hot coffee to intensify their flavor and replaced the butter with neutral-flavored vegetable oil, which allowed the chocolate flavor to dominate. For a final bit of decadence, we spooned ganache onto the cupcakes before baking, giving them a truffle-like center. Use high-quality bittersweet chocolate for this recipe. Though we highly recommend the ganache filling, you can omit it for a more traditional cupcake.

1 *For the filling* Microwave chocolate, cream, and sugar in bowl until mixture is warm to touch, about 30 seconds. Whisk until smooth, then transfer bowl to refrigerator and let sit until filling is just chilled, no longer than 30 minutes.

2 *For the cupcakes* Adjust oven rack to middle position and heat oven to 350 degrees. Line 12-cup muffin tin with paper or foil liners. Place chocolate and cocoa in heatproof bowl. Pour hot coffee over mixture and let sit, covered, for 5 minutes. Whisk chocolate mixture gently until smooth, then transfer to refrigerator and let cool completely, about 20 minutes.

3 Whisk flour, sugar, salt, and baking soda together in bowl. Whisk oil, eggs, vinegar, and vanilla into cooled chocolate mixture until smooth. Add flour mixture and whisk until smooth.

4 Divide batter evenly among prepared muffin cups. Place 1 slightly rounded teaspoon filling on top of each portion of batter. Bake until set and just firm to touch, 17 to 19 minutes, rotating muffin tin halfway through baking. Let cupcakes cool in muffin tin on wire rack until cool enough to handle, about 10 minutes. Remove cupcakes from muffin tin and let cool completely on rack, about 1 hour. (Unfrosted cupcakes can be stored at room temperature for up to 24 hours.) Spread or pipe frosting evenly on cupcakes. Serve.

carrot cupcakes

makes 12 cupcakes

8 tablespoons unsalted butter, melted and cooled

¾ cup (5¼ ounces) granulated sugar

¼ cup packed (1¾ ounces) dark brown sugar

2 large eggs

1¼ cups (6¼ ounces) all-purpose flour

3 carrots, peeled and grated

¾ teaspoon baking powder

½ teaspoon baking soda

½ teaspoon salt

½ teaspoon ground cinnamon

¼ teaspoon ground nutmeg

⅛ teaspoon ground cloves

3 cups Cream Cheese Frosting (page 401)

½ cup walnuts, toasted and chopped (optional)

why this recipe works The very quality that makes carrot cake so appealing— the moist, dense texture provided by the carrots and oil—makes it an unlikely candidate for reimagining as cupcakes, which tend toward lightness. But carrot cake is ever-popular, and a miniature version would make an ideal bake sale treat or birthday party favorite, so we were determined to make it work. First, a healthy amount of baking soda and baking powder provided the upward push that the little cakes needed to reach a proper height. As for sweetener, many carrot cake recipes call for a good deal of brown sugar, but we found it turned our cupcakes' crumb into a gooey mess. Blending one part brown sugar with three parts white sugar solved the problem. Most carrot cake recipes use vegetable oil for its neutral flavor and to ensure a moist texture, but we wondered if butter might work better here. Swapping in melted butter for the oil gave us good results; the water in the butter evaporated quickly in the oven to provide a fluffy crumb, yielding cupcakes that were significantly more cakey. Grate the carrots on the small holes of a box grater. Be careful not to overmix the batter or the cupcakes will be dense and tough.

1 Adjust oven rack to middle position and heat oven to 350 degrees. Line 12-cup muffin tin with paper or foil liners.

2 Whisk melted butter, granulated sugar, brown sugar, and eggs in large bowl until combined. Using rubber spatula, gently fold in flour, carrots, baking powder, baking soda, salt, cinnamon, nutmeg, and cloves until mixture just comes together (do not overmix).

3 Divide batter evenly among prepared muffin cups. Bake until toothpick inserted in center comes out clean, 15 to 18 minutes, rotating muffin tin halfway through baking. Let cupcakes cool in muffin tin on wire rack for 5 minutes. Remove cupcakes from muffin tin and let cool completely on rack, about 1 hour. (Unfrosted cupcakes can be stored at room temperature for up to 3 days.) Spread or pipe frosting evenly on cupcakes. Sprinkle with walnuts, if using. Serve. (Frosted cupcakes can be refrigerated for up to 5 days.)

chocolate cream cupcakes

makes 12 cupcakes

cupcakes

1 cup (5 ounces) all-purpose flour

½ teaspoon baking soda

¼ teaspoon salt

½ cup boiling water

⅓ cup (1 ounce) unsweetened cocoa powder

⅓ cup (2 ounces) semisweet chocolate chips

1 tablespoon instant espresso powder

¾ cup (5¼ ounces) sugar

½ cup sour cream

½ cup vegetable oil

2 large eggs

1 teaspoon vanilla extract

filling

¾ teaspoon unflavored gelatin

3 tablespoons water

4 tablespoons unsalted butter, softened

1 teaspoon vanilla extract

Pinch salt

1¼ cups marshmallow crème

glaze

½ cup (3 ounces) semisweet chocolate chips

3 tablespoons unsalted butter

why this recipe works Hostess CupCakes conjure memories of envied lunchbox meals and beloved after-school snacks. But America's most iconic cupcake could stand some improvement—starting with the plasticky packaged flavor of the filling. Our goal was simple: We wanted a substantial filling with rich, creamy flavor that wouldn't dribble out. First, we tried simply plopping a marshmallow into the batter, but this created craters in our cupcakes. Combining marshmallow crème with a small amount of gelatin gave us a perfectly creamy filling that stayed put. Injecting the filling into the cupcakes caused them to crumble and tear, so we cut inverted cones from the tops of the cupcakes instead. We prefer a stiffer marshmallow crème in this filling; do not use marshmallow sauce. For an accurate measurement of boiling water, bring a full kettle of water to a boil and then measure out the desired amount.

1 *For the cupcakes* Adjust oven rack to middle position and heat oven to 325 degrees. Grease and flour 12-cup muffin tin.

2 Whisk flour, baking soda, and salt together in bowl. Whisk boiling water, cocoa, chocolate chips, and espresso powder in large bowl until smooth. Whisk sugar, sour cream, oil, eggs, and vanilla into cocoa mixture until combined. Whisk in flour mixture until just incorporated. Divide batter evenly among prepared muffin cups. Bake until toothpick inserted in center comes out with few crumbs attached, 18 to 22 minutes, rotating muffin tin halfway through baking. Let cupcakes cool in muffin tin on wire rack for 10 minutes. Remove cupcakes from muffin tin and let cool completely on rack, about 1 hour.

3 *For the filling* Sprinkle gelatin over water in bowl and let sit until gelatin softens, about 5 minutes. Microwave until mixture is bubbling around edges and gelatin dissolves, about 30 seconds. Whisk in butter, vanilla, and salt until combined. Let mixture cool until just warm to touch, about 5 minutes, then whisk in marshmallow crème until smooth. Refrigerate filling until set, about 30 minutes. Transfer ⅓ cup filling to pastry bag fitted with small plain tip; set aside remaining mixture for filling cupcakes.

4 *For the glaze* Microwave chocolate chips and butter in small bowl at 50 percent power, stirring occasionally, until melted and smooth, 1 to 2 minutes. Let glaze cool completely, about 10 minutes.

5 Insert tip of paring knife at 45-degree angle ¼ inch from edge of each cupcake and cut cone from top of cupcake. Slice off bottom ½ inch from each cone and discard. Place 1 tablespoon filling inside each cupcake and place tops on filling, pressing to adhere. Frost each cupcake with 2 teaspoons cooled glaze and let sit for 10 minutes. Using pastry bag, pipe curlicues across tops of glazed cupcakes. Serve. (Cupcakes can be stored at room temperature for up to 2 days.)

red velvet cupcakes

makes 12 cupcakes

1⅛ cups (5⅔ ounces) all-purpose flour

¾ teaspoon baking soda

Pinch salt

½ cup buttermilk, room temperature

1 large egg

1½ teaspoons distilled white vinegar

1 teaspoon vanilla extract

1 tablespoon natural unsweetened cocoa powder

1 tablespoon (½ ounce) red food coloring

6 tablespoons unsalted butter, softened

¾ cup (5¼ ounces) sugar

3 cups Cream Cheese Frosting (page 401)

why this recipe works The darling of boutique cupcake shops, red velvet cupcakes are a perennial favorite—perhaps even more beloved than the traditional layered cake. But many bakery versions get by on good looks alone; we wanted a cupcake that not only looked the part, but that tasted great and sported a light, tender crumb too. We figured we had a good starting place with our recipe for Red Velvet Layer Cake (page 42), but sometimes full-scale cake recipes don't translate to the muffin tin. Fortunately, that wasn't the case here and the transition to cupcakes was an easy one. Halving the recipe resulted in perfectly scaled treats that rose high and formed nice flat tops—perfect for sporting billows of frosting. With this foolproof recipe for fluffy, moist, lightly chocolaty red velvet cupcakes, we'll never overpay for a display-case cupcake again. Do not substitute Dutch-processed cocoa powder for the natural cocoa powder.

1 Adjust oven rack to middle position and heat oven to 350 degrees. Line 12-cup muffin tin with paper or foil liners.

2 Whisk flour, baking soda, and salt together in bowl. Whisk buttermilk, egg, vinegar, and vanilla together in second bowl. Mix cocoa and food coloring into smooth paste in small bowl.

3 Using stand mixer fitted with paddle, beat butter and sugar on medium-high speed until pale and fluffy, about 3 minutes. Reduce speed to low and add flour mixture in 3 additions, alternating with buttermilk mixture in 2 additions, scraping down bowl as needed. Beat in cocoa mixture until batter is uniform. Give batter final stir by hand.

4 Divide batter evenly among prepared muffin cups. Bake until toothpick inserted in center comes out with few crumbs attached, 15 to 20 minutes, rotating muffin tin halfway through baking.

5 Let cupcakes cool in muffin tin on wire rack for 10 minutes. Remove cupcakes from muffin tin and let cool completely on rack, about 1 hour. (Unfrosted cupcakes can be stored at room temperature for up to 24 hours.) Spread or pipe frosting evenly on cupcakes. Serve.

boston cream cupcakes

makes 12 cupcakes

pastry cream

1⅓ cups heavy cream

3 large egg yolks

⅓ cup (2⅓ ounces) sugar

Pinch salt

1 tablespoon plus 1 teaspoon cornstarch

2 tablespoons unsalted butter,
cut into 2 pieces and chilled

1½ teaspoons vanilla extract

cupcakes

1¾ cups (8¾ ounces) all-purpose flour

1 cup (7 ounces) sugar

1½ teaspoons baking powder

¾ teaspoon salt

12 tablespoons unsalted butter,
cut into 12 pieces and softened

3 large eggs

¾ cup milk

1½ teaspoons vanilla extract

glaze

¾ cup heavy cream

¼ cup light corn syrup

8 ounces bittersweet chocolate, chopped

½ teaspoon vanilla extract

why this recipe works The cool and creamy vanilla pastry cream, tender cake, and shiny chocolate glaze of Boston cream pie are a trio of flavors that make any dessert special. To successfully translate Boston cream pie into petite form (our large-scale cake is on page 232), we knew we'd need a uniquely sturdy—but still very tender—cake and a rich, creamy custard that would be thick and substantial enough to stay put. Using the reverse creaming method to combine the ingredients gave us a moist cake with a fine crumb; this cake had the structure it needed to withstand filling and handling. Heavy cream, egg yolks, and cornstarch created the perfect consistency for the custard without making it taste stodgy. To assemble the components, we carved out a cone from the top of each cake to make a crater for the filling. We cut off and discarded all but the top disk of the cake cone, spooned the custard into the middle of the cupcake, and replaced the top disk. The glaze concealed the incision for a flawless finish.

1 *For the pastry cream* Heat cream in medium saucepan over medium heat until simmering, stirring occasionally. Meanwhile, whisk egg yolks, sugar, and salt in bowl until smooth. Add cornstarch and whisk until mixture is pale yellow and thick, about 15 seconds. Remove cream from heat and slowly whisk into yolk mixture.

2 Return mixture to saucepan and cook over medium heat, whisking constantly, until thick and glossy, 1 to 2 minutes. Off heat, whisk in butter and vanilla until incorporated. Transfer pastry cream to small bowl, press plastic wrap directly on surface, and refrigerate until set, at least 2 hours or up to 2 days.

3 *For the cupcakes* Adjust oven rack to middle position and heat oven to 350 degrees. Spray 12-cup muffin tin with vegetable oil spray, flour generously, and tap pan to remove excess flour.

4 Using stand mixer fitted with paddle, mix flour, baking powder, salt, and sugar on low speed until combined. Add butter, 1 piece at a time, and mix until mixture resembles coarse sand, about 1 minute. Add eggs, one at a time, and mix until combined. Add milk and vanilla, increase speed to medium, and beat until light and fluffy and no lumps remain, about 3 minutes.

5 Divide batter evenly among prepared muffin cups. Bake until toothpick inserted in center comes out clean, 18 to 20 minutes, rotating muffin tin halfway through baking. Let cupcakes cool in muffin tin on wire rack for 5 minutes. Remove cupcakes from muffin tin and let cool completely on rack, about 1 hour. (Cupcakes can be refrigerated for up to 2 days; bring to room temperature before continuing with recipe.)

6 *For the glaze* Cook cream, corn syrup, chocolate, and vanilla in small saucepan over medium heat, stirring constantly, until smooth. Set glaze aside to cool and thicken for 30 minutes.

7 Insert tip of paring knife at 45-degree angle ¼ inch from edge of each cupcake and cut cone from top of cupcake. Slice off and discard all but top ¼ inch from each cone, leaving small disk of cake. Place 2 tablespoons pastry cream inside each cupcake and place tops on filling, pressing to adhere. Place cupcakes on wire rack set over parchment paper; spoon glaze evenly over cupcakes, allowing it to drip down sides. Refrigerate until glaze is just set, about 10 minutes, before serving. (Cupcakes can be refrigerated for up to 2 days; bring to room temperature before serving.)

Filling Boston Cream Cupcakes

1 Insert tip of paring knife at 45-degree angle about ¼ inch from edge of cupcake and cut cone from top of cupcake.

2 Slice off all but top ¼ inch from each cone, leaving small disk of cake. Place 2 tablespoons pastry cream inside each cupcake and place tops on filling.

Cupcakes, Cake Pops, Mug Cakes, and More

pumpkin cupcakes

makes 12 cupcakes

1 cup (5 ounces) all-purpose flour

1 teaspoon ground cinnamon

1 teaspoon baking powder

½ teaspoon baking soda

½ teaspoon salt

⅛ teaspoon ground allspice

⅛ teaspoon ground ginger

¾ cup canned unsweetened pumpkin puree

7 tablespoons (3 ounces) sugar

½ cup vegetable oil

2 large eggs

3 cups Cream Cheese Frosting (page 401)

why this recipe works Most pumpkin-flavored desserts share the same flaws: They're overly sweet and so heavily spiced that the pumpkin flavor is completely hidden. For just-sweet-enough cupcakes with undeniable pumpkin flavor, we began by avoiding the cans of overly sweet preseasoned pumpkin pie filling. Using unsweetened pumpkin puree allowed us to control the sweetness level and the spices that went into our cake. Cinnamon, allspice, nutmeg, cloves, and ginger are go-to seasonings for anything pumpkin-flavored, but we wanted to keep the flavor profile simple and streamlined. We found that 1 teaspoon of cinnamon provided plenty of warmth, while small amounts of allspice and ginger added the right background notes. With the pumpkin and spice flavorings nailed down, we turned our attention to the texture of our cupcakes. The ideal pumpkin cupcakes should be moist, but not damp and heavy. Determining the right quantities of oil and egg was key: Too much of either would weigh the cupcakes down, but with too little the cakes would be dry and crumbly. A combination of two eggs and ½ cup of vegetable oil yielded cupcakes that were tender, fine-crumbed, and perfectly moist. To help open the crumb and tenderize the cake, we used 1 teaspoon of baking powder and ½ teaspoon of baking soda.

1 Adjust oven rack to middle position and heat oven to 350 degrees. Line 12-cup muffin tin with paper or foil liners.

2 Whisk flour, cinnamon, baking powder, baking soda, salt, allspice, and ginger together in large bowl. Whisk pumpkin, sugar, oil, and eggs together in second bowl until smooth. Using rubber spatula, stir pumpkin puree mixture into flour mixture until combined.

3 Divide batter evenly among prepared muffin cups. Bake until toothpick inserted in center comes out with few crumbs attached, 15 to 20 minutes, rotating muffin tin halfway through baking.

4 Let cupcakes cool in muffin tin on wire rack for 10 minutes. Remove cupcakes from muffin tin and let cool completely on rack, about 1 hour. (Unfrosted cupcakes can be stored at room temperature for up to 3 days.) Spread or pipe frosting evenly on cupcakes. Serve.

Pumpkin Puree

To be sure we were opening the best canned pumpkin puree for our Pumpkin Cupcakes, we selected three widely available purees and tasted them plain, baked into pumpkin cake, and whipped into pumpkin chiffon pie. We were flummoxed by the variety of textures and colors. One yellow puree was a pulpy paste and reminiscent of baby food; it made a too-thick pie filling and an overly dense cake. Another product was fibrous when sampled plain and therefore created a gritty pie filling. Both of these products contained 33 percent more fiber than our top-ranking puree, **Libby's 100% Pure Pumpkin**, which had a silky consistency and subtle sweetness. Fortunately, it's also the easiest to find.

strawberry cupcakes

makes 12 cupcakes

1⅛ cups (4½ ounces) cake flour

2 teaspoons baking powder

½ teaspoon salt

10 ounces (2 cups) frozen whole
strawberries

6 tablespoons whole milk

2 large eggs

2 teaspoons vanilla extract

6 tablespoons unsalted butter, softened

7 tablespoons (3 ounces) sugar

3 cups Honey Cream Cheese Frosting
(page 402)

why this recipe works As with our Strawberry Dream Cake (page 220), we were amazed to discover how many recipes for strawberry cupcakes rely on a packet of strawberry-flavored Jell-O for the flavor base. We resolved to use real berries in our cupcakes for a naturally flavored strawberry treat. We put together a quick cake base by creaming butter and sugar (using a moderate amount of sugar so the sweetness of the strawberries could shine), adding a couple of eggs, and stirring in cake flour. For the strawberry component, we started by adding chopped frozen strawberries (which are of reliable quality year-round) to the cake batter, but they disrupted the fine crumb of the cake and left behind mushy pockets. For our next round of testing, we pressed the liquid out of the strawberries and added just the juice to the batter. This time our cakes had good flavor, but the texture was still mushy. Reducing the liquid on the stovetop—to a mere ¼ cup—was the solution: This concentrated the strawberry flavor beautifully and eliminated the excess moisture. Instead of discarding the strawberry solids left behind from straining the berries, we added them to our frosting for another dose of strawberry flavor.

1 Adjust oven rack to middle position and heat oven to 350 degrees. Line 12-cup muffin tin with paper or foil liners. Whisk flour, baking powder, and salt together in bowl. Microwave strawberries in covered bowl until softened and very juicy, about 4 minutes.

2 Transfer strawberries to fine-mesh strainer set over small saucepan and press firmly with rubber spatula to extract as much liquid as possible; set aside solids for frosting. Boil strained strawberry juice over medium-high heat, stirring occasionally, until syrupy and measures ¼ cup, about 8 minutes. Transfer juice to bowl and let cool for 5 minutes. Whisk in milk until combined, followed by eggs and vanilla.

3 Using stand mixer fitted with paddle, beat butter and sugar on medium-high speed until pale and fluffy, about 3 minutes. Slowly add juice mixture and beat until well combined, about 1 minute, scraping down bowl as needed (mixture will look soupy). Reduce speed to low, add flour mixture, and mix until combined, about 1 minute. Give batter final stir by hand.

4 Divide batter evenly among prepared muffin cups. Bake until toothpick inserted in center comes out with few crumbs attached, 15 to 20 minutes, rotating muffin tin halfway through baking.

5 Let cupcakes cool in muffin tin on wire rack for 10 minutes. Remove cupcakes from muffin tin and let cool completely on rack, about 1 hour. (Unfrosted cupcakes can be stored at room temperature for up to 3 days.) Stir reserved strawberry solids into frosting until combined. Spread or pipe frosting evenly on cupcakes. Serve.

salted caramel cupcakes

makes 12 cupcakes

cupcakes

1¾ cups (8¾ ounces) all-purpose flour

1 cup (7 ounces) granulated sugar

1½ teaspoons baking powder

¾ teaspoon salt

12 tablespoons unsalted butter, cut into 12 pieces and softened

3 large eggs

¾ cup milk

1½ teaspoons vanilla extract

salted caramel sauce

⅔ cup (4⅔ ounces) granulated sugar

2 tablespoons light corn syrup

2 tablespoons water

½ cup heavy cream

4 tablespoons unsalted butter, cut into 4 pieces

½ teaspoon vanilla extract

½ teaspoon salt

frosting

20 tablespoons (2½ sticks) unsalted butter, cut into 10 pieces and softened

2 tablespoons heavy cream

2 teaspoons vanilla extract

⅛ teaspoon salt

2½ cups (10 ounces) confectioners' sugar

Flake sea salt

why this recipe works The pairing of savory salt and sweet caramel is a hard one to resist. We wanted to create a cupcake that highlighted this combo, one that would be dressed up enough for any celebration. For caramel flavor in every bite, we started by giving our cupcakes a core of salted caramel sauce. We cooked the sauce until it was dark (but not burnt) for added complexity. And to ensure the sauce didn't ooze out of the cupcakes at first bite, we added extra butter to help it set up. Since we were already putting in the effort to prepare a delicious homemade caramel sauce for the cupcakes, we decided to add it to our frosting as well for a double hit of caramel flavor. We started with an easy vanilla frosting as our base and then simply whipped in ¼ cup of the caramel sauce. We like to pipe the frosting into swirls before drizzling it with more caramel sauce and sprinkling it with sea salt for an eye-catching topping. When taking the temperature of the caramel in steps 3 and 4, remove the pot from the heat and tilt the pan to one side. Use your thermometer to stir the caramel back and forth to equalize hot and cool spots, which will help ensure an accurate reading.

1 *For the cupcakes* Adjust oven rack to middle position and heat oven to 350 degrees. Line 12-cup muffin tin with paper or foil liners. Using stand mixer fitted with paddle, mix flour, sugar, baking powder, and salt on low speed until combined. Add butter, 1 piece at a time, and mix until mixture resembles coarse sand, about 1 minute. Add eggs, one at a time, and mix until combined. Add milk and vanilla, increase speed to medium, and mix until light, fluffy, and no lumps remain, about 3 minutes.

2 Divide batter evenly among prepared muffin cups. Bake until toothpick inserted in center comes out clean, 18 to 20 minutes, rotating muffin tin halfway through baking. Let cupcakes cool in muffin tin on wire rack for 10 minutes. Remove cupcakes from muffin tin and let cool completely on rack, about 1 hour. (Cupcakes can be refrigerated for up to 2 days; bring to room temperature before continuing with recipe.)

3 *For the salted caramel sauce* Combine sugar, corn syrup, and water in small saucepan. Bring to boil over medium-high heat and cook, without stirring, until mixture is light amber colored, 4 to 6 minutes. Reduce heat to low and continue to cook, swirling saucepan occasionally, until mixture is medium amber and registers 355 to 360 degrees, about 1 minute longer.

4 Off heat, carefully stir in cream, butter, vanilla, and salt (mixture will bubble and steam). Return saucepan to medium heat and cook, stirring frequently, until smooth and caramel reaches 240 to 245 degrees, 2 to 4 minutes. Remove from heat and allow bubbles to subside. Carefully measure ¼ cup caramel into heatproof liquid measuring

cup and set aside for frosting. Transfer remaining caramel to heatproof bowl and let both cool until just warm to touch, 15 to 20 minutes.

5 While caramel is cooling, use paring knife to cut out cone-shaped wedge from top of each cupcake, about 1-inch from cupcake edge and 1-inch-deep into center of cupcake. Discard cones. Fill each cupcake with 2 teaspoons warm caramel sauce; set aside remaining caramel for frosting.

6 *For the frosting* Using stand mixer fitted with paddle, beat butter, cream, vanilla, and salt on medium-high speed until smooth, about 1 minutes. Reduce speed to medium-low, slowly add sugar, and beat until incorporated and smooth, about 4 minutes. Increase speed to medium-high and beat until frosting is light and fluffy, about 5 minutes. Stop mixer and add ¼ cup caramel to bowl. Beat on medium-high speed until fully incorporated, about 2 minutes.

7 Spread or pipe frosting evenly on cupcakes, drizzle with remaining caramel sauce (rewarming sauce as needed to keep fluid), and sprinkle with sea salt. Serve. (Cupcakes can be stored at room temperature for up to 4 hours before serving.)

Cupcakes, Cake Pops, Mug Cakes, and More

chocolate-beet cupcakes

makes 12 cupcakes

12 ounces beets, trimmed, peeled, and quartered

2 ounces 70 percent dark chocolate, chopped

½ cup (1½ ounces) Dutch-processed cocoa powder

⅓ cup vegetable oil

¾ cup (5¼ ounces) sugar

2 large eggs

3 tablespoons milk

1 teaspoon vanilla extract

½ teaspoon baking soda

½ teaspoon salt

¾ cup (4⅛ ounces) whole-wheat flour

3 cups Cream Cheese Frosting (page 401)

why this recipe works In the Victorian era, beets were sometimes added to cakes for a natural boost of moisture and sweetness. Intrigued by this bit of culinary history, we decided to try our hand at adding this vibrantly hued root vegetable to our own cupcakes. We wanted something similar to a red velvet cupcake minus the dye and plus intense chocolate flavor and a delicate earthiness. Whole-wheat flour—rather than all-purpose or cake flour, which we use in most of our cupcake recipes—underscored the beets' earthy flavor. An optional topping of homemade beet sprinkles gave these cupcakes festive flair. Do not substitute natural cocoa powder for the Dutch-processed cocoa powder. We prefer the flavor of 70 percent dark chocolate; we tested with higher percentages and found the cupcakes too bitter. These cupcakes are best served the day they're made.

1 Adjust oven rack to lower-middle position and heat oven to 350 degrees. Line 12-cup muffin tin with paper or foil liners.

2 Working in batches, use food processor fitted with shredding disk to process beets until shredded. Transfer to bowl and microwave, covered, until beets are tender and have released their juices, about 4 minutes, stirring halfway through microwaving. Fit now-empty processor with chopping blade and transfer cooked beets to processor. Microwave chocolate in second bowl at 50 percent power, stirring occasionally, until melted, about 2 minutes. Whisk in cocoa and oil until smooth and transfer chocolate mixture to food processor with beets; let cool slightly.

3 Process beets and chocolate mixture until smooth, about 45 seconds, scraping down sides of bowl as needed. Add sugar, eggs, milk, vanilla, baking soda, and salt and process until sugar is mostly dissolved and mixture is emulsified, about 15 seconds. Add flour and pulse until just incorporated, about 5 pulses; do not overmix.

4 Divide batter evenly among prepared muffin cups. Bake until toothpick inserted in center comes out clean, 20 to 22 minutes, rotating muffin tin halfway through baking. Let cupcakes cool in muffin tin on wire rack for 15 minutes. Remove cupcakes from muffin tin and let cool completely on rack, about 1 hour. Spread or pipe frosting evenly on cupcakes. Serve.

beet "sprinkles"
makes about ¼ cup
Top Beet-Chocolate Cupcakes with these veggie sprinkles.

4 ounces beets, trimmed, peeled, and cut into 1-inch pieces

Adjust oven rack to middle position and heat oven to 200 degrees. Process beets in food processor until finely ground, about 20 seconds, scraping down sides of bowl as needed. Place in triple layer of cheesecloth; wring out as much liquid as possible. Spread into even layer on rimmed baking sheet lined with parchment paper. Bake, stirring occasionally, until dry and crisp, 45 to 55 minutes. Let cool completely before serving. (Beet sprinkles can be stored at room temperature for up to 2 days.)

Cupcakes, Cake Pops, Mug Cakes, and More

vegan dark chocolate cupcakes

makes 12 cupcakes

1⅓ cups (6⅔ ounces) all-purpose flour

1 cup (7 ounces) organic sugar

¾ teaspoon baking powder

¼ teaspoon baking soda

½ teaspoon salt

1 cup water

½ cup (1½ ounces) Dutch-processed cocoa powder

1 ounce bittersweet chocolate, chopped

¼ cup coconut oil

¾ teaspoon vanilla extract

¼ cup aquafaba (see page 48)

1 teaspoon cream of tartar

2 cups Creamy Vegan Chocolate Frosting (page 405)

Vegan Chocolate

Many chocolates aren't vegan. Even bittersweet or dark chocolates can contain milk fat. Also, chocolate contains sugar that may or may not be vegan. We used dairy-free chocolates when developing our Vegan Dark Chocolate Cupcakes and Creamy Vegan Chocolate Frosting (page 405). We cannot guarantee that these chocolates use vegan sugar, however, so if you're a strict vegan, you may choose to purchase only chocolates that are labeled "vegan." We used Lindt Excellence 70%, which does not contain milk fat, for these cupcakes. And chocolate chips are critical for our vegan frosting. Ghirardelli Semi-Sweet Chocolate Baking Chips do not contain milk fat, and we used them for our testing.

---

why this recipe works Dark chocolate cupcakes, vegan or not, need to be rich and tender and with deep chocolate flavor. To make dairy- and egg-free chocolate cupcakes that fit this description, we took a cue from the success of our Vegan Yellow Layer Cake (page 48) and folded whipped aquafaba, stabilized with cream of tartar, into our cupcake batter. Like whipped egg whites, this mixture helped us achieve a light, fluffy crumb. Next we focused on creating complex chocolate flavor, which was easily achieved with bittersweet chocolate. But when we added enough to satisfy our chocolate craving, the cupcakes developed a chalky texture. To fortify the dark chocolate flavor without overloading our cupcakes with cocoa butter, we added a generous ½ cup of cocoa powder to the mix, which kept our cupcakes tender. Many conventional granulated sugars are processed with animal bone char but will work in this recipe; use organic sugar if you're a strict vegan. Not all brands of bittersweet chocolate are vegan, so check ingredient lists carefully. Do not substitute natural cocoa powder for the Dutch-processed cocoa powder. These cupcakes are best served the day they're made.

1 Adjust oven rack to middle position and heat oven to 400 degrees. Line 12-cup muffin tin with paper or foil liners. Whisk flour, sugar, baking powder, baking soda, and salt together in large bowl.

2 Microwave water, cocoa, chocolate, oil, and vanilla in second bowl at 50 percent power, whisking occasionally, until melted and smooth, about 2 minutes; set aside to cool slightly.

3 Meanwhile, using stand mixer fitted with whisk attachment, whip aquafaba and cream of tartar on high speed until stiff foam that clings to whisk forms, 3 to 9 minutes. Using rubber spatula, stir chocolate mixture into flour mixture until batter is thoroughly combined and smooth (batter will be thick). Stir one-third of whipped aquafaba into batter to lighten, then gently fold in remaining aquafaba until no white streaks remain.

4 Divide batter evenly among prepared muffin cups. Bake until tops are set and spring back when pressed lightly, 16 to 20 minutes, rotating muffin tin halfway through baking. Let cupcakes cool in muffin tin on wire rack for 10 minutes. Remove cupcakes from muffin tin and let cool completely on rack, about 1 hour. Spread frosting evenly on cupcakes. Serve.

gluten-free confetti cupcakes

makes 12 cupcakes

cupcakes

4 ounces white chocolate, chopped coarse

6 tablespoons vegetable oil

6½ ounces (⅔ cup plus ½ cup) gluten-free all-purpose flour blend

1 teaspoon baking powder

⅛ teaspoon baking soda

½ teaspoon xanthan gum

½ teaspoon salt

2 large eggs

2 teaspoons vanilla extract

3½ ounces (½ cup) sugar

⅓ cup sour cream

¼ cup rainbow sprinkles

frosting

3 cups Vanilla Frosting (page 398)

3 tablespoons rainbow sprinkles

Xanthan Gum

Because there's less protein in gluten-free flours than in wheat flours, gluten-free flours aren't capable of forming the strong network required to stretch and surround starch granules. In our testing, we found that gluten-free flours require some help from a binder, and we use xanthan gum in our cake recipes. Xanthan gum strengthens protein networks in baked goods and makes them more elastic so they can act as the glue that gives gluten-free baked goods the proper shape. You should store xanthan gum in the refrigerator or in the freezer. Do not omit xanthan gum in recipes that call for it.

---

why this recipe works Confetti (or rainbow) cupcakes are festive and especially popular with children, so we wanted to develop an easy-to-make gluten-free version that would deliver on flavor and looks alike. First we needed a foolproof recipe for light, fluffy yellow cake. Following the lead of our regular Yellow Cupcakes (page 55), we turned to a super-easy mixing method: We simply combined everything in the same bowl. The problem with our gluten-free version? Gluten-free flour doesn't absorb fat as readily as wheat flour does, so the cakes were greasy. Reducing the amount of fat and also swapping in oil for the butter fixed the greasiness, but we missed the rich flavor butter contributed. The addition of sour cream and white chocolate added flavor and kept the cupcakes rich and moist, but not slick. To speckle the cupcakes with confetti, we simply mixed rainbow sprinkles into the batter. As the cupcakes baked, the sprinkles dissolved, forming colorful spots suspended in every bite. Mixing more sprinkles into the frosting completed the festive look and added a pleasantly crunchy texture on top. Six and a half ounces of King Arthur Gluten-Free All-Purpose Flour is equal to ⅔ plus ½ cup flour, while 6½ ounces of Betty Crocker All-Purpose Gluten-Free Flour Blend is equal to 1⅓ cups. Volumes of other blends will vary, so we strongly recommend measuring by weight.

1 *For the cupcakes* Adjust oven rack to middle position and heat oven to 325 degrees. Line 12-cup muffin tin with paper or foil liners. Microwave chocolate and oil in bowl at 50 percent power, stirring often, until chocolate is melted, about 2 minutes; whisk until smooth and let cool slightly. Whisk flour blend, baking powder, baking soda, xanthan gum, and salt together in second bowl.

2 Whisk eggs and vanilla together in large bowl. Whisk in sugar until well combined. Whisk in cooled chocolate mixture and sour cream until combined. Whisk in flour blend mixture until batter is thoroughly combined and smooth. Gently whisk in sprinkles until thoroughly incorporated.

3 Divide batter evenly among prepared muffin cups. Bake until tops are set and toothpick inserted in center comes out clean, 19 to 22 minutes, rotating muffin tin halfway through baking. Let cupcakes cool in muffin tin on wire rack for 10 minutes. Remove cupcakes from muffin tin and let cool completely on rack, about 1 hour. (Unfrosted cupcakes can be stored at room temperature for up to 24 hours.)

4 *For the frosting* Stir sprinkles into frosting. Spread or pipe frosting evenly on cupcakes. Serve.

ALL ABOUT CUPCAKES

Most things are better when you don't have to share, including (or especially!) dessert. That's one of the many reasons cupcakes are so appealing (their dainty package and high hats of frosting don't hurt either). Here are some ways to make these individual desserts extra special.

DECORATING CUPCAKES

There are countless ways to decorate a cupcake. We simply spread cupcakes with frosting for an easy and classically elegant look. For a fancier display, we pipe frosting with a pastry bag fitted with a large star tip to create intricate swirls. These techniques are illustrated below.

Flat Top with Coated Sides

1 Place 2 to 3 tablespoons of frosting on each cupcake, forming a thick layer. Using a small offset spatula, spread to create a flat top.

2 Using the spatula, smooth the frosting so its flush with the edges of the cupcake. Reflatten the top as necessary.

3 Place a topping such as chopped nuts on a plate. Holding the cupcake at its base, gently roll the outer edges of the frosting in the topping.

Piped and Topped

1 Place the frosting in a pastry bag fitted with a ½-inch plain or star tip. Starting at the outside edge and working inward, pipe the frosting into a spiral.

2 Sprinkle lightly with a topping, if desired.

MAKING CUPCAKES SPARKLE

When you want to add your own special touch to freshly frosted cupcakes, you can draw designs (see our recipe for Icing for Writing on page 113), but there's another way to give your cupcakes flair. Try this easy method for creating fun sprinkle shapes.

Press a simply shaped cookie cutter into smooth frosting on a cupcake. Using the cookie cutter outline as a guide, fill the shape with sprinkles, colored sugar, or another confection of a contrasting color. Carefully remove the cookie cutter, leaving behind a festive decoration.

PORTIONING BATTER

Spring-loaded ice cream scoops aren't our favorite for ice cream, but we found a better use for them: portioning cupcake batter. Our foolproof way for filling muffin tins is to portion ⅓ cup of the batter into each cup and then circle back and evenly add the remaining batter with a spoon. A #12 ice scoop (which holds ⅓ cup batter) makes it easy to portion batter without making a mess around the edges of the pan. Spray the scoop with vegetable oil spray so the batter slides off.

BAKING OUTSIDE THE TIN

If you don't own a muffin tin, we found that foil liners are sturdy enough to hold our cupcake batters. Simply arrange the liners on a rimmed baking sheet and then fill them with batter. Note that cupcakes baked in a muffin tin brown on both the bottom and sides. If the cupcakes are baked without a muffin tin, only the bottoms (and not the sides) will brown.

CUPCAKES TO GO

Toting a single cupcake for a take-along snack sounds like a good idea—until you're faced with squished cake and frosting. To safely transport a cupcake, lay the lid of a clean pint-size deli container upside down and place your cupcake on it. Invert the container, slip it over the cupcake and down onto the lid, and seal it shut, thus creating a safe shell around the cupcake.

MUFFIN PAN MYTH

It's commonly taught that if you're making a half batch of cupcakes or muffins and thus don't fill all the cups in the pan with batter, you should fill the empty cups with water. Proponents of this practice contend that filling empty cups with water serves two functions: It prevents the pan from warping and acts as a "heat sink" to ensure that cupcakes next to empty cups heat evenly (avoiding stunted growth or spotty browning). We tested this theory by baking one muffin tin completely filled with batter, one tin in which only half of the 12 cups were filled with batter and the remaining six with water, and one tin in which six of the cups were filled with batter and the other six left empty. The results? All the muffins had the same height, texture, and color and none of the tins warped. This actually makes sense: In a full 12-cup muffin tin, all but the two center cupcakes are directly exposed to the oven's heat on at least one side to no ill effect. Furthermore, if your muffin tin warps, that's a sign that you need to find a better quality pan. (For our favorite muffin tin, see page 8.)

TOP-NOTCH TOOL

An offset spatula is a must-have tool for creating smooth frosting coatings for layer cakes. But don't dismiss its little sister—a small offset spatula is much better than a butter knife for neatly topping cupcakes with frosting.

We tested five offset spatula models and, to our surprise, found significant differences. Thin blades wobbled and wooden handles absorbed odors. Our top choice, the **Wilton 9-inch Angled Spatula** ($4.79), has a sturdy, round-tipped blade and an easy-to-grip polypropylene handle that offers great control. Sleek, sturdy, and comfortable, this blade was just about flawless.

Tool of the Trade

Cupcakes, Cake Pops, Mug Cakes, and More

party cake pops

makes about 36 cake pops

1½ cups (7½ ounces) all-purpose flour

1 cup (7 ounces) granulated sugar

1½ teaspoons baking powder

½ teaspoon salt

8 tablespoons unsalted butter, softened

½ cup sour cream

1 large egg plus 2 large yolks,
room temperature

1½ teaspoons vanilla extract

¼ cup milk

2 tablespoons confectioners' sugar

2½ cups (15 ounces) white chocolate chips
or semisweet chocolate chips

Lollipop sticks

Multicolored nonpareil sprinkles

why this recipe works There's no denying the novel appeal of cake pops; after all, everyone loves food on a stick, and if it's dessert, even better. Most recipes call for starting with cake made from a store-bought mix, breaking it into crumbs, combining it with canned frosting, and forming the mixture into balls. We knew we could do better. Making a simple homemade yellow cake was easy enough and far superior to anything from a box; baking it in an 8-inch square pan gave us just enough cake for about three dozen pops. While traditional frosting worked as a binder, tasters found the pops overwhelmingly sweet. Moistening the crumbs with milk worked just as well, and a couple of tablespoons of confectioners' sugar provided just enough sweetness. Briefly freezing the cookie dough–like cake balls made them firm enough to stay put on their sticks, and also helped set the coating of melted chocolate chips (chips worked better than bar chocolate because their stabilizers created a smooth, snappy coating). We like to use a 2-cup liquid measuring cup to melt the chocolate; its tall, narrow sides allow for easier coating of the cake balls. You'll need a floral foam block (available at craft stores and online) to stand the cake pops upright as the coating sets. If you're unable to find one, stand the dipped cake pops upside down on a parchment paper–lined baking sheet (note that this will give the tops a flat appearance). To make different colors for the coating, add drops of food coloring to the melted white chocolate chips.

1 Adjust oven rack to middle position and heat oven to 350 degrees. Grease 8-inch square baking pan, line with parchment paper, grease parchment, and flour pan.

2 Whisk flour, granulated sugar, baking powder, and salt together in bowl of stand mixer. Fit stand mixer with paddle; add butter, sour cream, egg and yolks, and vanilla; and beat on medium speed until smooth and satiny, about 30 seconds. Scrape down bowl with rubber spatula and stir by hand until smooth and no flour pockets remain.

3 Scrape batter into prepared pan and smooth top with rubber spatula. Gently tap pan on counter to release air bubbles. Bake until light golden and toothpick inserted in center comes out clean, 25 to 30 minutes, rotating pan halfway through baking. Let cake cool in pan on wire rack for 10 minutes. Remove cake from pan, discarding parchment, and let cool completely on rack, about 2 hours. (Cake can be wrapped in plastic wrap and stored at room temperature for up to 24 hours.)

4 In clean, dry bowl of stand mixer fitted with paddle, break cake into rough 1-inch pieces. Add milk and confectioners' sugar and beat on medium-low speed until broken into fine, evenly moistened crumbs and cohesive dough begins to form, about 1 minute, scraping down bowl as needed.

5 Line baking sheet with parchment paper. Working with 1 packed tablespoon cake mixture at a time, roll into balls and place in single layer on prepared sheet. Cover with plastic wrap and freeze until firm but still pliable, 45 minutes to 1 hour.

6 Microwave 2 cups chocolate chips in 2-cup liquid measuring cup at 50 percent power, stirring occasionally, until melted, 1 to 2 minutes. Working with 1 cake ball at a time, insert lollipop stick into cake ball, stopping at center. Dip entire cake ball into melted chocolate and turn until completely coated (tipping measuring cup to the side as needed). Lift up from chocolate (do not turn upright) and gently shake side to side to allow excess coating to drip off evenly. Turn cake pop upright, gently twist back and forth to even out coating, and insert stick into foam block. Sprinkle with nonpareils. Stir and rewarm chocolate in microwave as needed to stay fluid; add remaining ½ cup chocolate chips and melt when chocolate level becomes too low to dip easily. (If cake balls become too soft, refreeze until firm.)

7 Let cake pops sit at room temperature until coating is set, about 30 minutes. Serve. (Cake pops can be kept at room temperature for up to 4 hours or refrigerated for up to 3 days; bring to room temperature before serving.)

Cupcakes, Cake Pops, Mug Cakes, and More

cookies and cream cake pops

makes about 36 cake pops

¾ cup (5¼ ounces) sugar

10 tablespoons (3⅛ ounces)
all-purpose flour

¼ teaspoon baking soda

¼ teaspoon salt

½ cup plus 2 tablespoons whole milk

4 ounces bittersweet chocolate,
chopped fine

6 tablespoons (1⅛ ounces)
Dutch-processed cocoa powder

⅓ cup vegetable oil

2 large eggs

½ teaspoon vanilla extract

6 Oreo cookies

2½ cups (15 ounces) white chocolate chips

Lollipop sticks

why this recipe works The flavor variations for cake pops are truly endless. After sampling a few different flavor profiles, we zeroed in on cookies and cream as a whimsical favorite of young and old. We quickly settled on a fudgy cake base; next, we tried incorporating crushed cookies but found they were absorbed into the cake and lost their distinct crunch. Instead, we dipped our coated pops into a bowl of cookie pieces, creating a delightfully crunchy cookie-coated exterior. A striking white chocolate coating won out as a nod to the "cream" element of the recipe. Enjoyed by kids and kids-at-heart alike, these cake pops are a sweet, giftable treat. We like to use a 2-cup liquid measuring cup to melt the chocolate; its tall, narrow sides allow for easier coating of the cake balls. Do not substitute natural cocoa powder for the Dutch-processed cocoa powder. You'll need a floral foam block (available at craft stores and online) to stand the cake pops upright as the coating sets. If you're unable to find one, stand the dipped cake pops upside down on a parchment paper–lined baking sheet (note that this will give the tops a flat appearance).

1 Adjust oven rack to middle position and heat oven to 325 degrees. Grease 8-inch square baking pan, line with parchment paper, grease parchment, and flour pan.

2 Whisk sugar, flour, baking soda, and salt together in medium bowl; set aside. Combine ½ cup milk, chocolate, and cocoa in medium saucepan. Place saucepan over low heat and cook, whisking frequently, until chocolate is melted and mixture is smooth. Remove from heat and let cool slightly, about 5 minutes. Whisk oil, eggs, and vanilla into chocolate mixture (mixture may initially look curdled) until smooth and homogeneous. Add sugar mixture and whisk until combined, making sure to scrape corners of saucepan.

3 Scrape batter into prepared pan and smooth top with rubber spatula. Gently tap pan on counter to release air bubbles. Bake until toothpick inserted in center comes out clean, 30 to 35 minutes, rotating pan halfway through baking. Let cake cool in pan on wire rack for 10 minutes. Remove cake from pan, discarding parchment, and let cool completely on wire rack, about 2 hours. (Cake can be wrapped in plastic wrap and stored at room temperature for up to 24 hours.)

4 In bowl of stand mixer fitted with paddle, break cake into rough 1-inch pieces. Add remaining 2 tablespoons milk and beat on medium-low speed until broken into fine, evenly moistened crumbs and cohesive dough begins to form, about 1 minute, scraping down bowl as needed.

5 Line baking sheet with parchment paper. Working with 1 packed tablespoon cake mixture at a time, roll into balls and place in single layer on prepared sheet. Cover with plastic wrap and freeze until firm but still pliable, 45 minutes to 1 hour.

6 Place cookies in zipper-lock bag and crush with rolling pin until broken into small pieces; transfer to small bowl. Microwave 2 cups chocolate chips in 2-cup liquid measuring cup at 50 percent power, stirring occasionally, until melted, 1 to 2 minutes. Working with 1 cake ball at a time, insert lollipop stick into cake ball, stopping at center. Dip entire cake ball into melted chocolate and turn until completely coated. Lift up from chocolate (do not turn upright) and gently shake side to side

to allow excess coating to drip off evenly. Turn cake pop upright and gently twist back and forth to even out coating. Dip into crushed cookies, pressing gently to adhere. Turn cake pop upright and insert stick into foam block. Stir and rewarm chocolate in microwave as needed to stay fluid; add remaining ½ cup chocolate chips and melt when chocolate level becomes too low to dip easily. (If cake balls become too soft, refreeze until firm.)

7 Let cake pops stand at room temperature until coating is set, about 30 minutes. Serve. (Assembled cake pops can be kept at room temperature for up to 4 hours or refrigerated for up to 3 days; bring to room temperature before serving.)

ALL ABOUT MAKING CAKE POPS

The cake pop–making process may seem counterintuitive: You bake a cake just to mash it up. But the result is a fun party centerpiece or favor featuring a pop with a truffle-like center and snappy coating. When it comes to decorating the pops, use your imagination. You can use white or semisweet chocolate chips for the coating; if you choose white chocolate chips, you can dye the melted chocolate. And then sprinkle them with the decorations: sanding sugar, crushed nuts, candies or cookies, or sprinkles. For the neatest party-ready cake pops, you'll want a floral foam block. This allows the pops to stand upright while the coating sets without becoming flat on top as they would if you set them on a parchment paper–lined baking sheet. Below, we break down the steps to this crafty project.

FORMING CAKE POPS

1 Bake the Cake Bake the cake and remove it from pan, letting the cake cool completely on a wire rack.

2 Break Up the Cake Break the cooled cake into rough 1-inch pieces and add them to the bowl of a stand mixer.

3 Make a Dough Add the milk and confectioners' sugar to the bowl with the cake and beat on medium-low speed until the cake is broken into fine, evenly moistened crumbs and a cohesive dough begins to form, about 1 minute, scraping down the bowl as needed.

4 Roll Them Working with 1 packed tablespoon cake mixture at a time, roll into balls and place in a single layer on a parchment paper–lined baking sheet.

5 Freeze Them Cover the baking sheet with plastic wrap and freeze the cake balls until they're firm but still pliable, 45 minutes to 1 hour.

6 Stick Them Working with 1 cake ball at a time, insert a lollipop stick into the cake ball, stopping at the center.

1 Dip Them Dip the entire cake ball into the melted chocolate and turn it until it's completely coated (tipping the measuring cup to the side as needed as the chocolate level gets low).

2 Lift Them Lift the pop up from the chocolate without turning it upright and gently shake it from side to side to allow excess coating to drip off evenly.

3 Stand Them Up Turn the cake pop upright, gently twisting it back and forth to even out the coating, and insert the stick into the foam block.

4 Sprinkle Them Before the coating starts to set, sprinkle the pop with your decoration.

5 Keep It Warm As you're coating the pops, stir and rewarm the chocolate in the microwave as needed to keep it fluid; add more chocolate chips and melt when the chocolate level becomes too low to dip easily. Meanwhile, if the cake balls become too soft to manipulate, refreeze them until they're firm.

6 Let Them Rest Let the cake pops sit at room temperature until the coating is set, about 30 minutes, before serving.

Cupcakes, Cake Pops, Mug Cakes, and More

molten chocolate microwave mug cake

makes 2 mug cakes

4 tablespoons unsalted butter

1 ounce bittersweet chocolate, chopped, plus 1 ounce broken into 4 equal pieces

¼ cup (1¾ ounces) sugar

2 large eggs

2 tablespoons unsweetened cocoa powder

1 teaspoon vanilla extract

¼ teaspoon salt

¼ cup (1¼ ounces) all-purpose flour

½ teaspoon baking powder

why this recipe works Molten chocolate cake is a restaurant classic that has long held a spot on many a dessert menu. We have a recipe of our own (see page 96)—the kind you bake in individual ramekins and then carefully turn out on a plate. These little cakes are refined, but since the craving for decadent, fudgy cake and warm chocolate filling can strike at any moment, we needed a way to satisfy it regularly—and fast. Enter: the microwave. We'd heard a lot about mug cakes, and the promise of homemade molten chocolate cake in about 10 minutes from start to finish was alluring. But while the recipes we tried did indeed deliver on the time front, the hype was unwarranted: These cakes were rubbery, heavy, chalky, and bland. Even worse, they often exploded over the brim. To keep our cakes from overflowing, we had to supplement bittersweet chocolate with cocoa powder; because cocoa powder has less fat it produces less steam, thus decreasing the chance of an overflow. (The cocoa powder also provided a flavor boost, of course.) For a light, tender crumb, we found we needed to microwave the cakes gently at 50 percent power. Stirring the batter halfway through ensured even cooking. Finally, we created the requisite gooey, molten center by simply dropping a couple of pieces of bittersweet chocolate into each cake. We developed this recipe in a full-size, 1200-watt microwave. If you're using a compact microwave with 800 watts or fewer, increase the cooking time to 90 seconds for each interval. For either size microwave, reset to 50 percent power at each stage of cooking. Use a mug that holds at least 12 ounces, or the batter will overflow.

1 Microwave butter and chopped chocolate in large bowl at 50 percent power, stirring often, until melted, about 1 minute. Whisk sugar, eggs, cocoa, vanilla, and salt into chocolate mixture until smooth. In separate bowl, combine flour and baking powder. Whisk flour mixture into chocolate mixture until combined. Divide batter evenly between 2 (12-ounce) coffee mugs.

2 Place mugs on opposite sides of microwave turntable. Microwave at 50 percent power for 45 seconds. Stir batter and microwave at 50 percent power for 45 seconds (batter will rise to just below rim of mug).

3 Press 2 chocolate pieces into center of each cake until chocolate is flush with top of cake. Microwave at 50 percent power for 30 seconds to 1 minute (chocolate pieces should be melted and cake should be slightly wet around edges of mug and somewhat drier toward center). Let cakes sit for 2 minutes before serving.

variation
molten mocha microwave mug cake
Add 1 tablespoon instant espresso powder along with
sugar to chocolate mixture in step 1.

Cooking Microwave Cake

Stopping the microwave
and giving the batter a stir
after 45 seconds doesn't
disturb the cake as it cooks;
it ensures that the cake
cooks through evenly.

s'mores molten microwave mug cake

makes 2 mug cakes

4 tablespoons unsalted butter

1 ounce bittersweet chocolate, chopped

¼ cup (1¾ ounces) sugar

2 large eggs

2 tablespoons unsweetened cocoa powder

1 teaspoon vanilla extract

⅛ teaspoon salt

¼ cup (1¼ ounces) all-purpose flour

½ teaspoon baking powder

6 marshmallows

2 whole graham crackers, crushed into crumbs, plus 1 whole graham cracker, broken into quarters

why this recipe works S'mores may be a favorite summertime treat, but we crave their flavors all year long. For a fast indoor creation, we turned to the microwave and grabbed a coffee mug. To incorporate the classic s'more flavors into a chocolate microwave mug cake, we first tried making a graham cracker crust on the bottom of each mug, but it dissolved into the warm cake batter. Topping the cake with graham cracker sections didn't work well either—the crackers grew soggy and were an awkward fit for the mugs. Instead, we crushed the graham crackers into crumbs and sprinkled them into an even layer for an attractive topping. Marshmallows were also a must, and they grew pleasantly puffy in the microwave when placed atop the layer of cracker crumbs. For added decadence, we also pushed one into the center of each cake for a molten core. Served with extra graham crackers as a fun garnish, our s'mores mug cakes were complete—no campfire required. We developed this recipe in a full-size, 1200-watt microwave. If you're using a compact microwave with 800 watts or fewer, increase the cooking time to 90 seconds for each interval. For either size microwave, reset to 50 percent power at each stage of cooking. Use a mug that holds at least 12 ounces, or the batter will overflow.

1 Microwave butter and chocolate in large bowl at 50 percent power, stirring often, until melted, about 1 minute. Whisk sugar, eggs, cocoa, vanilla, and salt into chocolate mixture until smooth. In separate bowl, combine flour and baking powder. Whisk flour mixture into chocolate mixture until combined. Divide batter evenly between 2 (12-ounce) coffee mugs.

2 Place mugs on opposite sides of microwave turntable. Microwave at 50 percent power for 45 seconds. Stir batter and microwave at 50 percent power for 45 seconds (batter will rise to just below rim of mug).

3 Press 1 marshmallow into center of each cake until marshmallow is flush with top of cake. Sprinkle top of each cake with 2 tablespoons graham cracker crumbs and top with remaining marshmallows, pressing to adhere to top of cake. Microwave at 50 percent power for 30 seconds to 1 minute (marshmallows should be softened and puffed). Let cakes sit for 2 minutes. Sprinkle with remaining graham cracker crumbs and garnish with graham cracker quarters. Serve.

Cupcakes, Cake Pops, Mug Cakes, and More

blackberry-walnut buckles

serves 8

½ cup walnuts, chopped coarse

4 tablespoons unsalted butter, softened

¾ cup (5¼ ounces) sugar

¼ teaspoon salt

2 large eggs

⅓ cup heavy cream

1 teaspoon vanilla extract

¾ cup (3¾ ounces) all-purpose flour

½ teaspoon baking powder

15 ounces (3 cups) blackberries

why this recipe works A buckle is a simple cake filled with fresh seasonal fruit and topped with a crunchy, buttery streusel. We wanted to up the elegance of this humble dessert by reimagining the buckle in miniature form, creating individual desserts that would be ideal for entertaining. While the base for buckles is typically just a yellow butter cake, we took a sophisticated turn by replacing some of the flour in our batter with ground nuts. The nuts provided richness and a substantial flavor boost, and we found that different nuts paired well with specific fruits; we particularly liked blackberry with walnut, cherry with almond, and raspberry with pistachio. Since we already had the food processor out for grinding the nuts, we decided to streamline our recipe and make the rest of the batter right in the processor, reserving the berries to fold in at the end. Rather than weigh down our buckles with a heavy streusel topping, we simply topped each batter-filled ramekin with a sprinkling of nuts. Coating the ramekins with vegetable oil spray prevents the buckles from sticking. Do not substitute frozen berries here. Serve warm with vanilla ice cream or Whipped Cream (page 405).

1 Adjust oven rack to middle position and heat oven to 375 degrees. Lightly spray eight 6-ounce ramekins with vegetable oil spray; set aside. Toast ¼ cup walnuts in dry 8-inch skillet over medium heat until lightly browned and fragrant, 3 to 4 minutes; let cool completely.

2 Process toasted walnuts, butter, sugar, and salt in food processor until finely ground, 10 to 15 seconds. With processor running, add eggs, cream, and vanilla and continue to process until smooth, about 5 seconds. Add flour and baking powder and pulse until just incorporated, about 5 pulses.

3 Transfer batter to large bowl. Using rubber spatula, gently fold in blackberries. Divide batter evenly among prepared ramekins and sprinkle top of each buckle with remaining ¼ cup walnuts.

4 Bake buckles on rimmed baking sheet until golden and cake begins to pull away from sides of ramekins, 25 to 35 minutes. Let cool completely on wire rack, about 45 minutes. Serve.

to make ahead Unbaked buckles can be wrapped in plastic wrap, then in aluminum foil, and refrigerated for up to 3 days or frozen for up to 1 month. If frozen, let buckles sit at room temperature for 30 minutes before baking. Baked buckles can also be wrapped tightly in plastic and stored at room temperature for up to 24 hours.

variations

cherry-almond buckles

You can substitute fresh pitted sweet cherries or canned sweet cherries in syrup for the frozen cherries; make sure they have been rinsed and patted dry.

Substitute sliced or slivered almonds for walnuts; almond extract for vanilla extract; and 3 cups frozen sweet cherries, thawed, drained, and patted dry, for blackberries.

raspberry-pistachio buckles

Don't use frozen raspberries in this recipe; they're too mushy.

Substitute pistachios for walnuts and raspberries for blackberries.

lemon pudding cakes

serves 6

1 cup whole milk

½ cup heavy cream

3 tablespoons grated lemon zest plus ½ cup juice (3 lemons)

1 cup (7 ounces) sugar

¼ cup (1¼ ounces) all-purpose flour

½ teaspoon baking powder

⅛ teaspoon salt

2 large eggs, separated, plus 2 large whites

½ teaspoon vanilla extract

why this recipe works The appeal of lemon pudding cake—aside from its vibrant citrus flavor—lies in the magic of a single batter producing two texturally distinct layers. But all too often, it emerges from the oven as an underbaked cake sitting atop a grainy pudding. We wanted tender cake, rich and creamy pudding, and lots of lemon flavor in one individual-size dessert. Whipping the egg whites to stiff peaks produced a too-tall, tough cake layer, while barely whipping the whites resulted in a squat, rubbery cake; the midpoint, soft peaks, produced a tender cake with moderate lift. Baking the cakes in a water bath prevented the pudding from curdling while still allowing the cake to cook through. With the most challenging piece of the puzzle—the texture—solved, we turned to the lemon flavor. Lemon zest, in addition to plenty of juice, was essential for balanced flavor, but the pieces of zest marred the pudding's silky texture. Instead, we infused the milk and cream with subtle lemon flavor by steeping the zest in the liquid. To take the temperature of the pudding layer, touch the probe tip of a thermometer to the bottom of the ramekin and pull it up ¼ inch. We like this dessert served at room temperature, but it can also be served chilled (the texture will be firmer). Serve with Blueberry Compote (recipe follows), if desired, or simply dust with confectioners' sugar.

1 Adjust oven rack to middle position and heat oven to 325 degrees. Bring milk and cream to simmer in medium saucepan over medium-high heat. Off heat, whisk in lemon zest, cover saucepan, and let stand for 15 minutes. Meanwhile, fold dish towel in half and place in bottom of large roasting pan. Place six 6-ounce ramekins on top of towel; set aside pan.

2 Strain milk mixture through fine-mesh strainer into bowl, pressing on lemon zest to extract liquid; discard lemon zest. Whisk ¾ cup sugar, flour, baking powder, and salt together in second bowl. Add egg yolks, vanilla, lemon juice, and milk mixture and whisk until combined. (Batter will have consistency of milk.)

3 Using stand mixer fitted with whisk attachment, whip egg whites on medium-low speed until foamy, about 1 minute. Increase speed to medium-high and whip whites to soft, billowy mounds, about 1 minute. Gradually add remaining ¼ cup sugar and whip until glossy, soft peaks form, 1 to 2 minutes.

4 Whisk one-quarter of whites into batter to lighten. Using rubber spatula, gently fold in remaining whites until no clumps or streaks remain. Divide batter evenly among ramekins (ramekins should be nearly full). Pour enough cold water into roasting pan to come one-third of way up sides of ramekins. Bake until cake is set and pale golden brown and pudding layer registers 172 to 175 degrees at center, 50 to 55 minutes. Remove pan from oven and let ramekins stand in water bath for 10 minutes. Transfer ramekins to wire rack and let cool completely. Serve.

blueberry compote
makes about 1 cup
To use fresh blueberries, crush one-third of them against the side of the saucepan with a wooden spoon after adding them to the butter and then proceed as directed.

1 tablespoon unsalted butter
10 ounces (2 cups) frozen blueberries
2 tablespoons sugar, plus extra for seasoning
Pinch salt
½ teaspoon lemon juice

Melt butter in small saucepan over medium heat. Add blueberries, sugar, and salt; bring to boil. Reduce to simmer and stir occasionally until thickened and about one-quarter of juice remains, 8 to 10 minutes. Remove pan from heat and stir in lemon juice. Season with extra sugar to taste.

Cupcakes, Cake Pops, Mug Cakes, and More

sticky toffee pudding

serves 8

cakes

8 ounces pitted dates, cut crosswise into ¼-inch-thick slices (1⅓ cups)

¾ cup warm water (110 degrees)

½ teaspoon baking soda

1¼ cups (6¼ ounces) all-purpose flour

½ teaspoon baking powder

½ teaspoon salt

¾ cup packed (5¼ ounces) brown sugar

2 large eggs

4 tablespoons unsalted butter, melted

1½ tablespoons vanilla extract

sauce

4 tablespoons unsalted butter

1 cup packed (7 ounces) brown sugar

¼ teaspoon salt

1 cup heavy cream

1 tablespoon rum

¼ teaspoon lemon juice

why this recipe works Sticky toffee pudding is a British dessert that's sticky in a good way: It features a moist date-studded cake soaked in toffee sauce. To bring this dessert stateside, we knew we'd first have to find a substitute for treacle, a sweetener similar to molasses that's traditionally used in these cakes. We also wanted to perfect the texture of the cake and showcase the rich, fruity flavor of the dates. These "puddings" are supposed to be sticky, not mushy, so we needed a fairly sturdy cake that would hold up to the sauce. Cakes made using the creaming method disintegrated once soaked in sauce. Happily, the easier quick-bread technique (dry and wet ingredients are mixed separately and then combined) produced the desired dense-yet-springy crumb. Substituting molasses for treacle overwhelmed the caramel flavor of the dates; brown sugar was a better option, but the dates still needed a flavor boost. Typically, sliced dates are soaked in baking soda–laced water to soften their skins. Replacing the water that was already in our batter recipe with the date soaking liquid improved the flavor significantly, and pulverizing half the dates in the food processor before mixing them in guaranteed that every bite was laced with date flavor. Baking the cakes in a water bath ensured they remained moist. Be sure to form a tight seal with the foil before baking the cakes.

1 *For the cakes* Adjust oven rack to middle position and heat oven to 350 degrees. Grease and flour eight 6-ounce ramekins. Fold dish towel in half and place in bottom of large roasting pan. Place prepared ramekins on top of towel; set aside pan. Bring kettle of water to boil.

2 Combine half of dates, warm water, and baking soda in 2-cup liquid measuring cup (dates should be submerged beneath water); soak dates for 5 minutes. Meanwhile, whisk flour, baking powder, and salt together in large bowl.

3 Process sugar and remaining dates in food processor until no large chunks remain and mixture has texture of damp, coarse sand, about 45 seconds, scraping down sides of bowl as needed. Drain soaked dates and add soaking liquid to processor. Add eggs, melted butter, and vanilla and process until smooth, about 15 seconds. Transfer sugar mixture to bowl with flour mixture and sprinkle soaked dates on top. Using rubber spatula or wooden spoon, gently fold sugar mixture into flour mixture until just combined and date pieces are evenly dispersed.

4 Divide batter evenly among prepared ramekins (ramekins should be two-thirds full). Quickly pour enough boiling water into roasting pan to come ¼ inch up sides of ramekins. Cover pan tightly with aluminum foil, crimping edges to seal. Bake until cakes are puffed and surfaces are spongy, firm, and moist to touch, about 40 minutes. Immediately transfer ramekins from water bath to wire rack and let cool for 10 minutes.

5 *For the sauce* While cakes cool, melt butter in medium saucepan over medium-high heat. Whisk in sugar and salt until smooth. Continue to cook, stirring occasionally, until sugar is dissolved and slightly darkened, 3 to 4 minutes. Stir in ⅓ cup cream until smooth, about 30 seconds. Slowly pour in rum and remaining ⅔ cup cream, whisking constantly until smooth. Reduce heat to low; simmer until frothy, about 3 minutes. Remove from heat and stir in lemon juice.

6 Using toothpick, poke 25 holes in top of each cake and spoon 1 tablespoon toffee sauce over each cake. Let cakes sit until sauce is absorbed, about 5 minutes. Invert each ramekin onto plate or shallow bowl; lift off ramekin. Divide remaining toffee sauce evenly among cakes and serve immediately.

Soaking Sticky Toffee Pudding

1 Using toothpick, poke 25 holes in top of each cake.

2 Spoon 1 tablespoon toffee sauce over each cake and let sit until sauce is absorbed, about 5 minutes.

Cupcakes, Cake Pops, Mug Cakes, and More

fallen chocolate cakes

serves 8

Unsweetened cocoa powder, for dusting

8 ounces semisweet chocolate, chopped coarse

8 tablespoons unsalted butter, cut into 8 pieces

4 large eggs plus 1 large yolk, room temperature

½ cup (3½ ounces) granulated sugar

1 teaspoon vanilla extract

¼ teaspoon salt

2 tablespoons all-purpose flour

Confectioners' sugar

why this recipe works Fallen chocolate cake, or molten chocolate cake, is an undercooked-in-the-center mound of intense, buttery chocolate cake. We wanted to turn this restaurant-menu standard into a practical recipe for home cooks. Beating the egg whites and yolks separately and then folding them together as some recipes instruct resulted in a cottony cake; we found that beating the eggs with sugar to a foam and then folding them into melted chocolate delivered cakes with the rich, moist texture we wanted. A mere 2 tablespoons of flour did an able job of holding the soufflé-like cakes together—any more and the cakes were dry, with no fluid center. Finally, we wanted to ensure that these decadent desserts would arrive at the table hot and still molten; happily, we found that we could prepare the batter ahead of time, refrigerating the filled ramekins until ready to use and then placing them in the oven to bake during dinner. You can substitute bittersweet chocolate for the semisweet; the flavor will be slightly more intense. Serve the cakes with Whipped Cream (page 405) or ice cream, if desired.

1 Adjust oven rack to middle position and heat oven to 400 degrees. Grease eight 6-ounce ramekins and dust with cocoa. Arrange ramekins on rimmed baking sheet. Microwave chocolate in large bowl at 50 percent power for 2 minutes. Stir chocolate, add butter, and microwave at 50 percent power for 2 minutes longer, stopping to stir after 1 minute. If chocolate is not yet entirely melted, microwave for an additional 30 seconds; set aside.

2 Using stand mixer fitted with whisk attachment, whip eggs, yolk, granulated sugar, vanilla, and salt on high speed until eggs are pale yellow and have nearly tripled in volume. (Egg foam will form ribbon that sits on top of mixture for 5 seconds when dribbled from whisk.) Scrape egg mixture over chocolate mixture, then sprinkle flour on top. Using rubber spatula, gently fold egg mixture and flour into chocolate until mixture is uniformly colored.

3 Divide batter evenly among prepared ramekins. (Unbaked cakes can be refrigerated for up to 8 hours. Return to room temperature for 30 minutes before baking.) Bake until cakes have puffed about ½ inch above rims of ramekins, have thin crust on top, and jiggle slightly at center when ramekins are shaken very gently, 12 to 13 minutes. Run thin knife around edges of ramekins to loosen cakes. Invert each ramekin onto plate and let sit until cakes release themselves from ramekins, about 1 minute. Lift off ramekins, dust with confectioners' sugar, and serve.

variation

orange fallen chocolate cakes

Fold 2 tablespoons orange liqueur and 1 tablespoon grated orange zest into chocolate with egg mixture and flour in step 2.

lavender tea cakes with vanilla bean glaze

makes 12 tea cakes

cakes

⅔ cup (4⅔ ounces) granulated sugar, plus 2 tablespoons for pan

6 tablespoons unsalted butter, cut into 6 pieces and softened, plus 2 tablespoons melted, for pan

1 cup (5 ounces) all-purpose flour

½ teaspoon salt

½ teaspoon baking powder

¼ teaspoon baking soda

¼ cup buttermilk, room temperature

1½ teaspoons dried lavender, coarsely ground

1 teaspoon vanilla extract

2 large eggs, room temperature

glaze

1 vanilla bean

1¾ cups (7 ounces) confectioners' sugar

2–4 tablespoons milk

why this recipe works With tender, buttery interiors and fine, crisp exteriors, these lavender-infused tea cakes are a sophisticated treat. Our starting point was a simple butter cake, and we found that increasing the butter and replacing the milk with buttermilk gave us rich yet delicate cakes. For petite cakes that didn't dome, we baked them in a muffin tin and carefully adjusted the leaveners and batter amounts. To keep the cakes from sticking and to ensure an attractive, crackly exterior, we brushed the pan with butter and sugar. After baking, we inverted the cakes so that their flat bottoms became the tops. We then bathed each cake in a bright-white glaze made from vanilla bean, confectioners' sugar, and milk. For a darling touch, decorate the cakes with candied violets. To coarsely grind dried lavender, pound the dried flowers in a mortar and pestle or pulse several times in a spice grinder.

1 *For the cakes* Adjust oven rack to lower-middle position and heat oven to 325 degrees. Whisk 2 tablespoons sugar and melted butter together in bowl. Brush 12-cup muffin tin with butter-sugar mixture.

2 Whisk flour, salt, baking powder, and baking soda together in bowl. Whisk buttermilk, lavender, and vanilla together in small bowl. Using stand mixer fitted with paddle, beat butter and remaining ⅔ cup sugar on medium-high speed until pale and fluffy, about 3 minutes. Add eggs, one at a time, and beat until combined. Reduce speed to low and add flour mixture in 3 additions, alternating with buttermilk mixture in 2 additions, scraping down bowl as needed. Increase speed to medium-high and beat until completely smooth, about 30 seconds. Give batter final stir by hand.

3 Divide batter evenly among prepared muffin cups and smooth tops. Bake until golden brown and toothpick inserted in center comes out clean, about 15 minutes, rotating muffin tin halfway through baking.

4 Let cakes cool in muffin tin on wire rack for 10 minutes. Invert muffin tin over wire rack and gently tap pan several times to help cakes release. Let cakes cool completely on rack, bottom side up, about 30 minutes. (Unglazed cakes can be stored at room temperature for up to 24 hours.)

5 *For the glaze* Cut vanilla bean in half lengthwise. Using tip of paring knife, scrape out seeds. Whisk vanilla seeds, sugar, and 2 tablespoons milk together in bowl until smooth. Gradually add remaining 2 tablespoons milk as needed, teaspoon by teaspoon, until glaze is thick but pourable. Spoon glaze over top of each cooled cake, letting some drip down sides. Let glaze set for 10 minutes before serving.

Cupcakes, Cake Pops, Mug Cakes, and More

petit fours

makes 60 petit fours

filling

7½ ounces (1½ cups) raspberries

¾ cup (5¼ ounces) sugar

2 teaspoons lemon juice

1 ounce bittersweet chocolate, chopped

cake

1½ cups (10½ ounces) sugar

8 ounces almond paste,
cut into 1-inch pieces

7 large eggs

1 teaspoon vanilla extract

½ teaspoon baking powder

½ teaspoon salt

8 tablespoons unsalted butter, melted and
cooled slightly

2 cups (8 ounces) cake flour

topping

2 cups (12 ounces) white chocolate chips

¼ cup (1½ ounces) bittersweet
chocolate chips

why this recipe works Petit fours are small confections typically presented at the end of a classic French meal. We wanted an easy-to-make recipe for these bite-size, decorative cakes that would make a statement at any party. We started by baking three thin layers of almond sponge cake, one at a time, in a 13 by 9-inch baking pan. Once the quick-cooking cakes cooled, we stacked them together, spreading a luscious raspberry-chocolate jam between the layers. Rather than bathing the cake pieces in sugary glaze (which tasters thought was outmoded), we simply spread a layer of melted white chocolate over the cake, drizzled dark chocolate in lines over the white, and ran the tines of a fork through the chocolates to create an elegant weblike pattern.

1 *For the filling* In large saucepan, bring raspberries, sugar, and lemon juice to boil over medium-high heat, stirring often. Boil until raspberries have broken down and released their juices, about 5 minutes.

2 Whisk in chocolate until completely melted, about 1 minute. Continue to boil mixture, stirring and adjusting heat as needed, until jam has thickened and measures 1 cup, 10 to 15 minutes. Remove pot from heat. Transfer jam to bowl and let cool completely, about 1 hour.

3 *For the cake* Adjust oven rack to middle position and heat oven to 350 degrees. Grease 13 by 9-inch baking pan, line with parchment paper, and grease parchment.

4 Process sugar and almond paste in food processor until mixture resembles coarse sand, 20 to 30 seconds. Add eggs, vanilla, baking powder, and salt and process until pale yellow and frothy, about 2 minutes. With processor running, slowly add melted butter in steady stream until incorporated, about 10 seconds. Add flour and pulse to combine, 4 or 5 pulses.

5 Transfer 1⅔ cups batter to prepared pan and spread in even layer with offset spatula; set remaining batter aside. Bake until top is set and edges are just starting to brown, 8 to 10 minutes. Let cake cool in pan on wire rack for 5 minutes. Remove cake from pan, discarding parchment, and let cake cool completely on rack. Let pan cool slightly, about 10 minutes. Line now-empty and cooled pan with clean parchment paper, and grease parchment. Transfer 1⅔ cups batter to prepared pan and repeat baking cake and cooling pan. Repeat baking and cooling with remaining 1⅔ cups batter.

6 Transfer one cooled cake layer, bottom side up, to cutting board. Spread ½ cup filling evenly over top, right to edge of cake. Top with second cake layer, bottom side up, and spread remaining ½ cup jam evenly over top. Top with third cake layer, bottom side up.

7 *For the topping* Microwave white chocolate chips and bittersweet chocolate chips in separate bowls at 50 percent power, stirring occasionally, until melted, 2 to 4 minutes. Using small offset spatula, spread white chocolate evenly over top of cake, right to edges of cake. While white chocolate is still warm, use small spoon to drizzle dark chocolate crosswise in thin parallel lines over white chocolate. Gently run tines of fork lengthwise across top of cake to create delicate, webbed pattern. Let cool until chocolate has set, 1 to 2 hours.

8 Dip serrated knife in very hot water and wipe dry before each cut. Trim away edges. Slice cake lengthwise into 5 equal strips (about 1½ inches wide), and then crosswise into 12 equal strips (about 1 inch wide). Serve. (Petit fours can be refrigerated for up to 24 hours.)

Topping Petit Fours

1 Spread white chocolate evenly over cake. Working quickly, use small spoon to drizzle melted dark chocolate crosswise in thin parallel lines.

2 Gently run tines of fork lengthwise across top of cake to create webbed pattern.

Cupcakes, Cake Pops, Mug Cakes, and More

CROWD-PLEASING SHEET CAKES

yellow sheet cake

serves 12 to 15

2½ cups (10 ounces) cake flour

1¾ cups (12¼ ounces) sugar ✓

1¼ teaspoons baking powder ✓

¼ teaspoon baking soda ✓

¾ teaspoon salt

1 cup buttermilk, room temperature ✓

3 large eggs, separated, plus 3 large yolks, room temperature

10 tablespoons unsalted butter, melted and cooled

3 tablespoons vegetable oil

2 teaspoons vanilla extract

Pinch cream of tartar

3 cups Vanilla Frosting (page 398)

why this recipe works Ideal for everything from birthday parties to potlucks and cookouts, sheet cake is easy to make and doesn't require many ingredients. Classic yellow sheet cake is a must-have in any baker's repertoire, and we wanted a perfect version. Our Fluffy Yellow Layer Cake (page 32) is so delicious—and foolproof—that we saw no reason not to use it as our starting point. Happily, it worked great—and better yet, we didn't even need to rescale the recipe; the amount of batter fit nicely into one 13 by 9-inch baking pan, yielding a sheet cake with just the right height. It's perfectly fine to serve this and all sheet cakes straight from the pan, but for special occasions, taking the baked and cooled cake out of the pan is as easy as flipping it onto a rack, peeling off the parchment, and inverting it onto a platter. If you want to take the cake out of the pan, grease the pan, line with parchment paper, grease the parchment, and then flour the pan.

1 Adjust oven rack to middle position and heat oven to 325 degrees. Grease and flour 13 by 9-inch baking pan. Whisk flour, 1½ cups sugar, baking powder, baking soda, and salt together in bowl. Whisk buttermilk, egg yolks, melted butter, oil, and vanilla together in second bowl.

2 Using stand mixer fitted with whisk attachment, whip egg whites and cream of tartar on medium-low speed until foamy, about 1 minute. Increase speed to medium-high and whip whites to soft billowy mounds, about 1 minute. Gradually add remaining ¼ cup sugar and whip until glossy, stiff peaks form, 2 to 3 minutes; transfer to third bowl.

3 Add flour mixture to now-empty mixer bowl and mix on low speed, gradually adding buttermilk mixture and mixing until almost incorporated (a few streaks of dry flour will remain), about 15 seconds. Scrape down bowl, then mix on medium-low speed until smooth and fully incorporated, 10 to 15 seconds.

4 Using rubber spatula, stir one-third of whites into batter. Gently fold remaining whites into batter until no white streaks remain. Transfer batter to prepared pan and smooth top with rubber spatula. Gently tap pan on counter to settle batter. Bake until toothpick inserted in center comes out clean, 28 to 32 minutes, rotating pan halfway through baking.

5 Let cake cool completely in pan on wire rack, about 2 hours. Spread frosting evenly over top of cake. Serve.

white sheet cake

serves 12 to 15

1 cup whole milk, room temperature

6 large egg whites, room temperature

1 teaspoon vanilla extract

2¼ cups (9 ounces) cake flour

1¾ cups (12¼ ounces) sugar

4 teaspoons baking powder

1 teaspoon salt

12 tablespoons unsalted butter, cut into 12 pieces and softened

3 cups Malted Milk Chocolate Buttercream (page 400)

why this recipe works Though simple, this crowd-serving white cake is just as appropriate at a child's party as it is at a wedding shower or other elegant celebration. As with our Yellow Sheet Cake (page 105), this white sheet cake is born from an already perfected layer cake recipe (in this case, the Classic White Layer Cake on page 35); we simply added all the batter to one pan and adjusted the baking time accordingly. The moist, fine crumb and hint of vanilla are the perfect base for just about any frosting you'd like to pair the cake with; we go with an interesting choice, an ultracreamy malted milk chocolate buttercream, which doesn't overpower the delicate cake like a heavier chocolate frosting might. If you want to take the cake out of the pan, grease the pan, line with parchment paper, grease the parchment, and then flour the pan.

1 Adjust oven rack to middle position and heat oven to 350 degrees. Grease and flour 13 by 9-inch baking pan. Whisk milk, egg whites, and vanilla together in bowl.

2 Using stand mixer fitted with paddle, mix flour, sugar, baking powder, and salt on low speed until combined. Add butter, 1 piece at a time, and mix until only pea-size pieces remain, about 1 minute. Add half of milk mixture, increase speed to medium-high, and beat until light and fluffy, about 1 minute. Reduce speed to medium-low, add remaining milk mixture, and beat until incorporated, about 30 seconds (batter may look curdled). Give batter final stir by hand.

3 Transfer batter to prepared pan and smooth top with rubber spatula. Gently tap pan on counter to settle batter. Bake until toothpick inserted in center comes out with few crumbs attached, 25 to 30 minutes, rotating pan halfway through baking.

4 Let cake cool completely in pan on wire rack, about 2 hours. Spread frosting evenly over top of cake. Serve.

chocolate sheet cake with milk chocolate frosting

serves 12 to 15

cake

1½ cups (10½ ounces) sugar

1¼ cups (6¼ ounces) all-purpose flour

½ teaspoon baking soda

½ teaspoon salt

1 cup whole milk

8 ounces bittersweet chocolate, chopped fine

¾ cup (2¼ ounces) Dutch-processed cocoa powder

⅔ cup vegetable oil

4 large eggs

1 teaspoon vanilla extract

frosting

1 pound milk chocolate, chopped

⅔ cup heavy cream

16 tablespoons unsalted butter, cut into 16 pieces and softened

why this recipe works When the results are good, chocolate sheet cake yields great reward for relatively minimal effort. But most chocolate sheet cakes we've made disappoint: They're dry and crumbly, have barely a whisper of chocolate flavor, or are so dense that they veer into brownie territory. For a cake that boasted deep chocolate flavor and color, we used a combination of Dutch-processed cocoa and melted bittersweet chocolate; the cocoa offered pure, assertive chocolate flavor while the bittersweet chocolate contributed complexity as well as the right amount of fat and sugar. We knew we wanted a milk chocolate ganache frosting to offset the intense flavor of the cake, but we needed to get the texture just right: Loose, drippy frostings made the cake too messy to eat out of hand, while stiff, fudgy ones weighed down the crumb. To make our ganache thicker, richer, and creamier than the norm, we added plenty of softened butter to the warm chocolate-cream mixture. Once assembled, we refrigerated the frosting to cool it quickly so that it would spread nicely, and then gave it a quick whisk to smooth it out and lighten its texture. The best part: This cake comes together with everyday staples and basic equipment— no mixers or food processors needed. Do not substitute natural cocoa powder for the Dutch-processed cocoa powder. If you want to take the cake out of the pan, grease the pan, line with parchment paper, grease the parchment, and then flour the pan.

1 *For the cake* Adjust oven rack to middle position and heat oven to 325 degrees. Lightly spray 13 by 9-inch baking pan with vegetable oil spray. Whisk sugar, flour, baking soda, and salt together in bowl; set aside.

2 Combine milk, chocolate, and cocoa in large saucepan. Place saucepan over low heat and cook, whisking frequently, until chocolate is melted and mixture is smooth. Remove from heat and let cool slightly, about 5 minutes. Whisk oil, eggs, and vanilla into chocolate mixture (mixture may initially look curdled) until smooth and homogeneous. Add sugar mixture and whisk until combined, making sure to scrape corners of saucepan.

3 Transfer batter to prepared pan. Bake until firm in center when lightly pressed and toothpick inserted in center comes out with few crumbs attached, 30 to 35 minutes, rotating pan halfway through baking. Let cake cool completely in pan on wire rack, 1 to 2 hours.

4 *For the frosting* While cake is baking, combine chocolate and cream in large heatproof bowl set over saucepan filled with 1 inch barely simmering water, making sure that water does not touch bottom of bowl. Whisk mixture occasionally until chocolate is uniformly smooth and glossy, 10 to 15 minutes. Remove bowl from saucepan. Add butter, whisking once or twice to break up pieces. Let mixture stand for 5 minutes to finish melting butter, then whisk until completely smooth. Refrigerate frosting, without stirring, until cooled and thickened, 30 minutes to 1 hour.

5 Once cool, whisk frosting until smooth. (Whisked frosting will lighten in color slightly and should hold its shape on whisk.) Spread frosting evenly over top of cake. Serve. (Leftover cake can be refrigerated for up to 2 days.)

simple carrot sheet cake

serves 12 to 15

2½ cups (12½ ounces) all-purpose flour

1¼ teaspoons ground cinnamon

1¼ teaspoons baking powder

1 teaspoon baking soda

½ teaspoon salt

½ teaspoon ground nutmeg

⅛ teaspoon ground cloves

4 large eggs

1½ cups (10½ ounces) granulated sugar

½ cup packed (3½ ounces) light brown sugar

1½ cups vegetable oil

1 pound carrots, peeled and grated

3 cups Cream Cheese Frosting (page 401)

why this recipe works Carrot cake was once heralded as a more healthful dessert option, with carrots (a vegetable!) providing natural sweetness. Sure, carrots add sweetness, but they also add a lot of moisture that can result in a dense, wet slice. And the oil the recipes include? It can make the cake dense and, well, oily. We wanted a moist (not soggy), rich cake that was rich, featuring a tender crumb, balanced spice, and the light sweetness of carrot. Cake flour proved too delicate to support the grated carrots, so we started with all-purpose. Some carrot cakes use a heavy hand with the spices but we took a more conservative approach, using modest amounts of cinnamon, nutmeg, and cloves. Finally, we tackled the most problematic elements: the carrots and oil. We found that 1 pound of grated carrots provided plenty of flavor and a pleasantly moist texture, while 1½ cups of vegetable oil added just enough richness without making the cake greasy. With the ingredients and quantities settled, the cake came together quickly: We mixed the dry ingredients separately from the wet ingredients before slowly whisking them together and then stirring in the carrots. If you want to take the cake out of the pan, grease the pan, line with parchment paper, grease the parchment, and then flour the pan.

1 Adjust oven rack to middle position and heat oven to 350 degrees. Grease and flour 13 by 9-inch baking pan. Whisk flour, cinnamon, baking powder, baking soda, salt, nutmeg, and cloves together in bowl.

2 Whisk eggs, granulated sugar, and brown sugar in large bowl until sugars are mostly dissolved and mixture is frothy. Continue to whisk while slowly drizzling in oil until thoroughly combined and emulsified. Whisk in flour mixture until just incorporated. Stir in carrots. Give batter final stir by hand.

3 Transfer batter to prepared pan and smooth top with rubber spatula. Gently tap pan on counter to settle batter. Bake until toothpick inserted in center comes out clean, 35 to 40 minutes, rotating pan halfway through baking.

4 Let cake cool completely in pan on wire rack, about 2 hours. Spread frosting evenly over top of cake. Serve.

ALL ABOUT SHEET CAKES

Not every occasion calls for a two- or three-decker affair. The reasons to love sheet cake are many: They're generally easy to make and transport, they serve a crowd, and they feature the perfect ratio of cake to frosting. Here are some pointers for making sheet cakes extra special.

DETERMINING DONENESS

The toothpick test is the gold standard for determining the doneness of most cakes, and sheet cakes are no different. However, with sheet cakes it's important to also use any other cues given in the recipe; because of the cake's large surface area, it may take a few tests to determine doneness. Use the baking times as a guide and refer to visual cues to determine doneness. A toothpick inserted in the center of the cake should come out with a few crumbs attached (unless otherwise stated in the recipe), and the cake should spring back when pressed lightly.

Underdone Cake

Perfectly Baked Cake

REMOVING A SHEET CAKE FROM THE PAN

Sheet cakes are all about ease, so most of the time we simply frost them and then serve them right from the pan. But some situations call for a more elegant presentation, in which case you may want to turn out the cake. Because of its large surface area, removing a sheet cake from the pan isn't as easy as removing a round cake layer. Below are our tricks. (Make sure to line the bottom of the pan with parchment in addition to greasing and flouring it if you choose to remove the cake from the pan.)

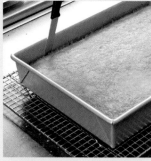
1 Run a paring knife around the edge of the cooled cake to loosen it. (Be careful not to scratch the bottom of the baking pan.)

2 Gently flip the cake out of the pan onto a wire rack.

3 Peel the parchment paper off the bottom of the cake and invert a large platter over the cake.

4 Holding both the rack and the platter firmly, gently flip the cake right side up onto the platter.

WRITING ON A CAKE

Writing a festive message on a sheet cake is easy because there's a lot of space to work with. Here are a few tricks. First, skip the writing glazes and gels at the supermarket. We tested those that are sold in small tubes and those sold in aerosol cans, but we found both were awkward to use and neither tasted very good. (In addition, the glazes often didn't set up well.) Instead, make your own simple icing for writing (recipe follows).

To write out your message, first make sure the top of the cake is level and evenly frosted. Use a very small pastry bag fitted with a round tip, which allows for sure control. Before writing on the cake, practice on a piece of parchment paper (roughly the same size as the cake) to get yourself accustomed to the icing, the size and style of your letters, and the overall spacing of your message. You can use your free hand to steady your writing hand for a smooth, even script.

FROSTING FOR SHEET CAKES

We've paired these sheet cakes with frostings, often classic, always complementary. But there's room to play. While some of our recipes like German Chocolate Sheet Cake (page 119) or Strawberry Poke Cake (page 128) are unique and call for their own frosting or icing recipes, others like Yellow Sheet Cake (page 105) or Pumpkin Sheet Cake (page 123) are blank canvases for the frosting of your choice if you'd prefer something else. (The same applies for the layer cakes in chapter 1 and more basic cupcakes in chapter 2.) And if you're the kind of person who eats cake for the frosting, the ratio of frosting to cake for a sheet cake makes it perfect for showing off your favorite frostings and icings. Take a look at our collection of frostings and buttercreams on pages 398–405.

icing for writing
makes about ⅔ cup
This recipe makes plenty of icing for both practice and the actual cake. If you find the icing stiff and difficult to pipe, return it to the bowl and add additional water, a little at a time, to loosen. If the icing is too thin and runny, return it to the bowl and add more confectioners' sugar, a little at a time, to stiffen.

1½ cups (6 ounces) confectioners' sugar
2 tablespoons unsalted butter, melted and cooled
Water, as needed
Food coloring (optional)

1 Mix sugar, melted butter, and 1 tablespoon water in small bowl with rubber spatula to make smooth paste. Add more water, 1 teaspoon at a time, until icing is very smooth and creamy (similar to room-temperature peanut butter).

2 Stir in drops of food coloring, if using, one drop at a time, until you achieve desired color. (Icing can be stored in piping bag at room temperature for up to 3 hours. For longer storage, refrigerate icing in covered container for up to 3 days.)

variation
chocolate icing for writing
Whisk 2 tablespoons unsweetened cocoa powder into sugar before adding butter. Add 2 tablespoons water with butter, then continue to add water as needed to adjust icing's consistency.

lemon buttermilk sheet cake

serves 12 to 15

cake

2½ cups (10 ounces) cake flour

1 teaspoon baking powder

½ teaspoon baking soda

½ teaspoon salt

¾ cup buttermilk, room temperature

3 tablespoons grated lemon zest plus ¼ cup juice (3 lemons)

1 teaspoon vanilla extract

1¾ cups (12¼ ounces) granulated sugar

12 tablespoons unsalted butter, cut into 12 pieces and softened

3 large eggs plus 1 large yolk, room temperature

glaze

3 cups (12 ounces) confectioners' sugar

3 tablespoons lemon juice

2 tablespoons buttermilk

why this recipe works A sweet-tart lemon sheet cake holds a lot of promise as a bright and lovely dessert. But because we wanted to serve this cake without a rich frosting, it would need to look perfect. That's a difficult feat for a sheet cake; with its large diameter, it can be difficult to achieve even browning and a perfectly flat top. Replacing some of the baking powder in our recipe with baking soda reduced doming, as did lowering the baking temperature. As for flavor, we wanted a bright, but not puckering, lemon presence. We added grated zest in addition to the lemon juice for round lemon flavor. Combining the fragrant zest with sugar worked even better; creaming this lemon sugar with the butter enhanced the zest's flavorful oil. Using buttermilk for the liquid in our batter added another layer of tangy richness. A simple glaze of confectioners' sugar, lemon juice, and more buttermilk was the perfect complement to our cake, and a sprinkle of reserved lemon sugar added crunch, shine, and a final flourish of lemon flavor.

1 *For the cake* Adjust oven rack to middle position and heat oven to 325 degrees. Grease and flour 13 by 9-inch baking pan. Whisk flour, baking powder, baking soda, and salt together in bowl. Combine buttermilk, lemon juice, and vanilla in 2-cup liquid measuring cup.

2 Using stand mixer fitted with paddle, beat sugar and lemon zest on medium speed until moist and fragrant, about 1 minute. Transfer ¼ cup sugar mixture to small bowl, cover, and set aside. Add butter to remaining sugar mixture and beat until pale and fluffy, about 2 minutes. Add eggs and yolk, one at a time, and beat until combined. Reduce speed to low and add flour mixture in 3 additions, alternating with buttermilk mixture in 2 additions, and mix until smooth, about 30 seconds.

3 Transfer batter to prepared pan and smooth top with rubber spatula. Bake until cake is golden brown and toothpick inserted in center comes out clean, 25 to 35 minutes, rotating pan halfway through baking. Let cake cool in pan on wire rack for 10 minutes.

4 *For the glaze* Whisk confectioners' sugar, lemon juice, and buttermilk in bowl until smooth. Gently spread glaze over warm cake and sprinkle evenly with reserved lemon sugar mixture. Let cool completely, at least 2 hours, before serving.

spice cake

serves 12 to 15

1 tablespoon ground cinnamon

¾ teaspoon ground cardamom

½ teaspoon ground allspice

½ teaspoon ground cloves

¼ teaspoon ground nutmeg

16 tablespoons unsalted butter,
cut into 16 pieces and softened

2¼ cups (11¼ ounces) all-purpose flour

½ teaspoon baking powder

½ teaspoon baking soda

½ teaspoon salt

2 large eggs plus 3 large yolks,
room temperature

1 teaspoon vanilla extract

1¾ cups (12¼ ounces) sugar

2 tablespoons molasses

1 tablespoon grated fresh ginger

1 cup buttermilk, room temperature

3 cups Cream Cheese Frosting (page 401)

¾ cup walnuts, toasted and chopped
(optional)

why this recipe works What's the problem with spice cakes? Well, the spice. Many versions suffer from spice overload, which results in a gritty, dusty cake. Others are so lacking in spice flavor, it's as if a lone cinnamon stick has merely been waved in their general direction. We wanted an old-fashioned, moist, and substantial spice cake with a warm, bold—but not overpowering— spice presence. All-purpose flour, rather than more tender cake flour, added the volume and heft we were looking for. And to build that spice flavor? Simply adding more spices didn't lead to increased spiciness; the spices smelled stronger than they tasted. Blooming a moderate amount of spices in butter was the way to go: This intensified their aromas and heightened their impact throughout. We'd been using the classic mixture of cinnamon, cloves, carda- mom, allspice, and nutmeg, but found that a tablespoon of grated fresh ginger and a couple tablespoons of molasses were welcome additions, giving the cake extra zing. And reserving a little of the spice mixture to add to the cream cheese frosting united the frosting and the cake. If you want to take the cake out of the pan, grease the pan, line with parchment paper, grease the parchment, and then flour the pan.

1 Adjust oven rack to middle position and heat oven to 350 degrees. Grease and flour 13 by 9-inch baking pan. Combine cinnamon, cardamom, allspice, cloves, and nutmeg in small bowl; set aside ½ teaspoon spice mixture for frosting.

2 Melt 4 tablespoons butter in 8-inch skillet over medium heat. Cook, swirling pan constantly, until butter is light brown and has faint nutty aroma, 2 to 4 minutes. Add spice mixture and continue to cook, stirring constantly, for 15 seconds. Remove from heat and let cool completely, about 30 minutes.

3 Whisk flour, baking powder, baking soda, and salt together in bowl. Gently whisk eggs and yolks and vanilla in small bowl until combined. Using stand mixer fitted with paddle, beat remaining 12 tablespoons butter, sugar, and molasses on medium-high speed until fluffy, about 3 minutes, scraping down bowl as needed. Reduce speed to medium, add ginger, cooled butter-spice mixture, and half of egg mixture, and mix until incorporated, about 15 seconds. Repeat with remain- ing egg mixture and scrape down bowl. Reduce speed to low and add flour mixture in 3 additions, alternating with buttermilk in 2 additions, scraping down bowl as needed. Increase speed to medium and continue to mix until batter is thoroughly combined, about 15 seconds. Give batter final stir by hand.

4 Transfer batter to prepared pan and smooth top with rubber spatula. Run tip of metal spatula through batter in zigzag motion to edges of pan, then gently tap pan on counter to release air bubbles. Bake until toothpick inserted in center comes out clean, 32 to 37 minutes, rotating pan halfway through baking. Let cake cool completely in pan on wire rack, about 2 hours.

5 Stir reserved spice mixture into frosting. Spread frosting evenly over top of cake. Sprinkle with walnuts, if using, and serve. (Cake can be refrigerated for up to 2 days; bring to room temperature before serving.)

Removing Trapped Air Bubbles

Our spice cake has a particularly thick batter that can easily trap air bubbles. These air bubbles can lead to a finished cake with unsightly holes. Here's how to get rid of them.

Run tip of metal spatula through batter in zigzag motion, pulling it to edges of pan.

Crowd-Pleasing Sheet Cakes

german chocolate sheet cake

serves 12 to 15

topping

4 large egg yolks

1 (12-ounce) can evaporated milk

1 cup (7 ounces) granulated sugar

¼ cup packed (1¾ ounces) light brown sugar

6 tablespoons unsalted butter, cut into 6 pieces

⅛ teaspoon salt

2 teaspoons vanilla extract

2⅓ cups (7 ounces) sweetened shredded coconut

1½ cups pecans, toasted and chopped fine

cake

4 ounces semisweet or bittersweet chocolate, chopped fine

¼ cup (¾ ounce) Dutch-processed cocoa powder

½ cup boiling water

2 cups (10 ounces) all-purpose flour

¾ teaspoon baking soda

12 tablespoons unsalted butter, softened

1 cup (7 ounces) granulated sugar

⅔ cup packed (4⅔ ounces) light brown sugar

¾ teaspoon salt

4 large eggs

1 teaspoon vanilla extract

¾ cup sour cream

why this recipe works Our German Chocolate Cake (page 222) puts on an impressive show with its towering layers of cake and sweet coconut filling, but splitting the cake layers and assembling the cake is a fair amount of work. To enjoy the irresistible combination of chocolate, coconut, and pecans with less fuss, we developed a simplified sheet cake version—which is essentially a large chocolate cake topped with a thick layer of the coconut-pecan filling. When you frost the cake, the frosting should be cool or cold (or room temperature, at the very warmest). For efficiency, make the topping first and then use the refrigeration time to prepare, bake, and cool the cake. The toasted pecans are stirred into the topping just before the cake is frosted so they retain a little crunch. If you want to take the cake out of the pan, grease the pan, line with parchment paper, grease the parchment, and then flour the pan. For an accurate measurement of boiling water, bring a full kettle of water to a boil and then measure out the desired amount.

1 *For the topping* Whisk egg yolks in medium saucepan, then gradually whisk in evaporated milk. Whisk in granulated sugar, brown sugar, butter, and salt and cook over medium-high heat, whisking constantly, until mixture is boiling, frothy, and slightly thickened, about 6 minutes. Transfer mixture to bowl, whisk in vanilla, then stir in coconut. Let cool until just warm, then refrigerate until completely cool, at least 2 hours or up to 3 days. (Pecans are added later.)

2 *For the cake* Adjust oven rack to lower-middle position and heat oven to 350 degrees. Grease and flour 13 by 9-inch baking pan. Combine chocolate and cocoa in bowl, add boiling water, cover, and let sit for 5 minutes. Whisk chocolate mixture until smooth; let cool completely. Whisk flour and baking soda together in second bowl.

3 Using stand mixer fitted with paddle, beat butter, granulated sugar, brown sugar, and salt on medium-high speed until fluffy, about 3 minutes. Reduce speed to medium, add eggs, one at a time, and beat until combined. Add vanilla, increase speed to medium-high, and beat until light and fluffy, about 45 seconds. Reduce speed to low, add chocolate mixture, then increase speed to medium and beat until combined, about 30 seconds, scraping down bowl once (batter may look curdled). Reduce speed to low and add flour mixture in 3 additions, alternating with sour cream in 2 additions, scraping down bowl as needed. Give batter final stir by hand (batter will be thick).

4 Transfer batter to prepared pan and smooth top with rubber spatula. Gently tap pan on counter to release air bubbles. Bake until toothpick inserted in center comes out clean, 30 to 35 minutes, rotating pan halfway through baking. Let cake cool completely in pan on wire rack, about 2 hours. Stir pecans into topping. Spread frosting evenly over top of cake. Serve. (Refrigerate cake if not serving immediately for up to 3 days; bring to room temperature before serving.)

tres leches cake

serves 12 to 15

milk mixture

1 (14-ounce) can sweetened condensed milk

1 (12-ounce) can evaporated milk

1 cup heavy cream

1 teaspoon vanilla extract

cake

2 cups (10 ounces) all-purpose flour

2 teaspoons baking powder

1 teaspoon salt

½ teaspoon ground cinnamon

8 tablespoons unsalted butter

1 cup whole milk

4 large eggs, room temperature

2 cups (14 ounces) sugar

2 teaspoons vanilla extract

topping

1 cup heavy cream

3 tablespoons corn syrup

1 teaspoon vanilla extract

why this recipe works Tres leches cake is a light, sweet sponge cake soaked with a mixture of "three milks" (heavy cream, evaporated milk, and sweetened condensed milk). And making a great one requires a careful balancing act: The cake should be moist, but not mushy, and the clean dairy flavor of the milks should be clear and sweet, but not sickeningly so. For the ideal tres leches cake that hit all the right notes, we first needed a sponge cake that would be sturdy enough to hold up to the milk mixture. This was easily solved by using whipped whole eggs instead of the usual egg whites. Although some recipes use equal amounts of evaporated milk, sweetened condensed milk, and cream for the soak, we found that cutting back on the cream produced a thicker mixture that didn't oversaturate the cake. For a more complex sweetness, we cooked down the condensed milk in the microwave until it was thickened and straw-colored before mixing it with the other milks. This one simple step gave each dairy-soaked bite a hint of caramel flavor. The cake is best frosted with its fluffy whipped topping just before serving.

1 *For the milk mixture* Pour condensed milk into large bowl. Microwave, covered, at 10 percent power, stirring every 3 to 5 minutes until milk is slightly darkened and thickened, 9 to 15 minutes. Slowly whisk in evaporated milk, cream, and vanilla until incorporated. Let mixture cool completely.

2 *For the cake* Adjust oven rack to middle position and heat oven to 325 degrees. Grease and flour 13 by 9-inch baking pan. Whisk flour, baking powder, salt, and cinnamon together in bowl. Heat butter and milk in small saucepan over low heat until butter is melted; remove from heat and set aside.

3 Using stand mixer fitted with whisk attachment, whip eggs on medium speed until foamy, about 30 seconds. Slowly add sugar and continue to whip until fully incorporated, 5 to 10 seconds. Increase speed to medium-high and whip until mixture is thick and glossy, 5 to 7 minutes. Reduce speed to low, add butter-milk mixture and vanilla, and mix until combined, about 15 seconds. Add flour mixture in 3 additions, mixing on medium speed after each addition and scraping down bowl as needed, until flour is fully incorporated, about 30 seconds. Transfer batter to prepared pan. Bake until toothpick inserted in center comes out clean, 30 to 35 minutes, rotating pan halfway through baking. Let cake cool in pan on wire rack for 10 minutes.

4 Using skewer, poke holes at ½-inch intervals in top of cake. Slowly pour milk mixture over cake. Let sit at room temperature for 15 minutes, then refrigerate, uncovered, for at least 3 hours or up to 24 hours.

5 *For the topping* Thirty minutes before serving, remove cake from refrigerator. Using stand mixer fitted with whisk attachment, whip cream, corn syrup, and vanilla on medium-low speed until foamy, about 1 minute. Increase speed to high and whip until soft peaks form, 1 to 3 minutes. Spread topping evenly over top of cake. Serve.

Oven Method for Dulce de Leche
Instead of cooking sweetened condensed milk to the pudding-like texture of classic dulce de leche for this recipe, we microwaved the milk until it was only slightly thickened and honey-colored. This allowed for a fluid texture that was readily absorbed into the cake. But if you don't have a microwave, simply pour the sweetened condensed milk into a 9-inch pie plate, cover the plate with foil, and set it in a roasting pan. Carefully add enough boiling water to the roasting pan to reach halfway up the side of the pie plate and bake in a 425-degree oven. In just 35 to 40 minutes, the milk mixture will be the right texture for our Tres Leches Cake (and after about 1 hour and 20 minutes, you'll have a dark, thick dulce de leche that's perfect for pouring over ice cream).

Crowd-Pleasing Sheet Cakes

pumpkin sheet cake

serves 12 to 15

2 cups (10 ounces) all-purpose flour

2 teaspoons ground cinnamon

2 teaspoons baking powder

1 teaspoon baking soda

1 teaspoon salt

¼ teaspoon ground allspice

¼ teaspoon ground ginger

1⅔ cups (11⅔ ounces) sugar

4 large eggs

1 cup vegetable oil

1 (15-ounce) can unsweetened pumpkin puree

3 cups Cream Cheese Frosting (page 401)

why this recipe works We figured that developing a recipe for pumpkin sheet cake would be an easy affair; after all, it's essentially a variation on spice cake and shouldn't require any fancy mixing techniques. But we quickly learned that for a pumpkin sheet cake, the common quick-bread mixing method—combining wet and dry ingredients separately and then simply mixing them together—wouldn't do: Cakes made this way were damp, leaden, and sunken in the middle. For a cake with such a large surface area, we'd need to build more structure. Fortunately, this was an easy fix: Four whole eggs helped us get there. To add fluffy volume, we changed up the mixing method by beating the eggs, sugar, and oil together vigorously to aerate the batter. Incorporating the pumpkin and dry ingredients on low speed was key; adding them carefully prevented the egg mixture from deflating. If you want to take the cake out of the pan, grease the pan, line with parchment paper, grease the parchment, and then flour the pan.

1 Adjust oven rack to middle position and heat oven to 350 degrees. Grease and flour 13 by 9-inch baking pan.

2 Whisk flour, cinnamon, baking powder, baking soda, salt, allspice, and ginger together in bowl. Using stand mixer fitted with paddle, beat sugar, eggs, and oil on medium-high speed until thick and fluffy, about 5 minutes. Reduce speed to low, add pumpkin, and mix until incorporated. Slowly add flour mixture and mix until only a few small lumps of flour remain, about 1 minute.

3 Transfer batter to prepared pan. Bake until toothpick inserted in center comes out clean, 30 to 35 minutes, rotating pan halfway through baking. Let cake cool completely in pan on wire rack, about 2 hours. Spread frosting evenly over top of cake. Serve.

texas sheet cake

serves 12 to 15

cake

2 cups (10 ounces) all-purpose flour

2 cups (14 ounces) granulated sugar

½ teaspoon baking soda

½ teaspoon salt

2 large eggs plus 2 large yolks

¼ cup sour cream

2 teaspoons vanilla extract

8 ounces semisweet chocolate, chopped

¾ cup vegetable oil

¾ cup water

½ cup (1½ ounces) Dutch-processed cocoa powder

4 tablespoons unsalted butter

icing

8 tablespoons unsalted butter

½ cup heavy cream

½ cup (1½ ounces) Dutch-processed cocoa powder

1 tablespoon light corn syrup

3 cups (12 ounces) confectioners' sugar

1 tablespoon vanilla extract

1 cup pecans, toasted and chopped

why this recipe works Texas sheet cake, the official cake of the Lone Star State, is a sheet pan–size, pecan-topped chocolate cake with three distinct layers of chocolaty goodness. A diverse range of textures is created when the sweet chocolate icing is poured over a cake that's still hot from the oven. Once the cake has cooled, you're left with a layer of icing on top, a fudgy middle layer where the icing and hot cake have melded, and a bottom layer of moist chocolate cake. For the cake, we relied on a combination of butter and vegetable oil for fat, which produced a dense, brownie-like texture. We wanted the cake's fudgy chocolate flavor to match its fudgy texture, so we used both cocoa powder and melted semisweet chocolate for a cake that was ultrachocolaty yet still moist and dense. The icing was the final element, and getting its texture right was key to this cake's success—replacing milk with heavy cream gave it more body, while adding corn syrup produced a lustrous finish. The traditional frosting method ensured a cake with the signature fudge-like layer between the icing and cake: We poured the warm icing over the cake straight out of the oven, smoothed it with a spatula, and let it soak into the hot cake.

1 *For the cake* Adjust oven rack to middle position and heat oven to 350 degrees. Grease 18 by 13-inch rimmed baking sheet. Whisk flour, sugar, baking soda, and salt together in large bowl. Whisk eggs and yolks, sour cream, and vanilla in second bowl until smooth.

2 Heat chocolate, oil, water, cocoa, and butter in large saucepan over medium heat, stirring occasionally, until smooth, 3 to 5 minutes. Whisk chocolate mixture into flour mixture until incorporated. Whisk egg mixture into batter, then transfer batter to prepared sheet. Bake until toothpick inserted in center comes out clean, 18 to 20 minutes, rotating sheet halfway through baking. Transfer sheet to wire rack.

3 *For the icing* About 5 minutes before cake is done baking, heat butter, cream, cocoa, and corn syrup in large saucepan over medium heat, stirring occasionally, until smooth. Off heat, whisk in sugar and vanilla. Spread warm icing evenly over hot cake and sprinkle with pecans. Let cake cool completely in pan on wire rack, about 1 hour, then refrigerate until icing is set, about 1 hour longer. Serve.

buttermilk-caramel cake

serves 12 to 15

cake

2¾ cups (11 ounces) cake flour

2 teaspoons baking powder

¾ teaspoon salt

16 tablespoons unsalted butter,
cut into 16 pieces and softened

1¾ cups (12¼ ounces) granulated sugar

4 large eggs, room temperature

1 tablespoon vanilla extract

1½ cups buttermilk, room temperature

icing

8 tablespoons unsalted butter

1 cup packed (7 ounces) dark brown sugar

¼ cup whole milk

2 cups (8 ounces) confectioners' sugar

1 teaspoon vanilla extract

why this recipe works Caramel cake is a true Southern specialty. The thick, toffee-flavored caramel icing forms a crystalline crust on top—a perfect complement to the rich, buttery yellow cake beneath. First, we needed to perfect the cake. Using cake flour instead of all-purpose flour gave us a tender, fine-crumbed cake that was a nice foil for the thick icing so our cake combination wasn't too heavy. But the pairing was too sweet. Cutting back on sugar made the cake too dry; we had better luck replacing the milk in the cake with tangy buttermilk, which offset the frosting's sweetness. For best results, spread the frosting over the cake while the frosting is still warm; if the frosting stiffens, reheat it until softened. Allow the frosting to firm up before slicing and serving the cake. If you want to take the cake out of the pan, grease the pan, line with parchment paper, grease the parchment, and then flour the pan.

1 *For the cake* Adjust oven rack to middle position and heat oven to 350 degrees. Grease and flour 13 by 9-inch baking pan. Whisk flour, baking powder, and salt together in bowl.

2 Using stand mixer fitted with paddle, beat butter and sugar on medium speed until pale and fluffy, about 3 minutes. Add eggs, one at a time, and beat until combined. Beat in vanilla. Reduce speed to low and add flour mixture in 3 additions, alternating with buttermilk in 2 additions. Give batter final stir by hand.

3 Transfer batter to prepared pan and smooth top with rubber spatula. Gently tap pan on counter to settle batter. Bake until toothpick inserted in center comes out with few moist crumbs attached, 25 to 30 minutes, rotating pan halfway through baking. Let cake cool completely in pan on wire rack, about 2 hours

4 *For the icing* Bring butter and brown sugar to boil in medium saucepan over medium heat, stirring constantly, until sugar is dissolved and mixture is foamy, 3 to 5 minutes. Whisk in milk, return mixture to brief boil, then remove from heat. Stir in confectioners' sugar and vanilla with a wooden spoon and beat frosting until smooth, 2 to 3 minutes. Spread warm frosting evenly over cake and let set, about 25 minutes, before serving.

strawberry poke cake

serves 12 to 15

cake

2¼ cups (11¼ ounces) all-purpose flour

4 teaspoons baking powder

1 teaspoon salt

1 cup whole milk

6 large egg whites

2 teaspoons vanilla extract

12 tablespoons unsalted butter,
cut into 12 pieces and softened

1¾ cups (12¼ ounces) sugar

syrup and topping

1¼ pounds (4 cups) frozen strawberries

½ cup water

6 tablespoons (2⅔ ounces) sugar

2 tablespoons orange juice

2 tablespoons strawberry-flavored gelatin

2 cups heavy cream, chilled

why this recipe works Strawberry poke cake was invented in 1969 as a way to increase Jell-O sales, and it quickly became popular thanks to its festive look and easy assembly. True to its name, this cake is poked full of holes, which are then filled with a gelatin mixture. We encountered two problems: dull strawberry flavor and soggy box-mix cake. First, we opted to make our own cake; lackluster box-mix cakes are simply too tender and turn to mush when saturated. To improve the strawberry flavor of the gelatin, we combined it with the juice from cooked strawberries. Making a homemade "jam" from the berry solids and spreading the mixture over the cake gave it an extra layer of flavor. The top of the cake will look slightly overbaked—this prevents the cake from becoming too soggy after the gelatin is poured on top.

1 *For the cake* Adjust oven rack to middle position and heat oven to 350 degrees. Grease and flour 13 by 9-inch baking pan. Whisk flour, baking powder, and salt together in bowl. Whisk milk, egg whites, and vanilla in 4-cup liquid measuring cup.

2 Using stand mixer fitted with paddle, beat butter and sugar on medium-high speed until pale and fluffy, about 2 minutes, scraping down bowl as needed. Reduce speed to low and add flour mixture in 3 additions, alternating with milk mixture in 2 additions, beating after each addition until combined, about 30 seconds each time, scraping down bowl as needed. Give batter final stir by hand. Transfer batter to prepared pan. Bake until toothpick inserted in center comes out clean, about 35 minutes, rotating pan halfway through baking. Let cake cool completely in pan on wire rack, about 2 hours. (Cake can be covered tightly with plastic wrap and stored at room temperature for up to 2 days.)

3 *For the syrup and topping* Cook 3 cups strawberries, water, 2 tablespoons sugar, and orange juice in medium saucepan over medium-low heat, covered, until strawberries are softened, about 10 minutes. Strain liquid into bowl, reserving solids, then whisk gelatin into liquid. Let cool completely, about 20 minutes.

4 Meanwhile, poke 50 deep holes all over top of cake with skewer. Pour cooled liquid evenly over top of cake. Cover with plastic wrap and refrigerate until gelatin is set, at least 3 hours or up to 2 days.

5 Pulse reserved strained strawberries, 2 tablespoons sugar, and remaining 1 cup strawberries in food processor until mixture resembles strawberry jam, about 15 pulses. Spread mixture evenly over cake. Using stand mixer fitted with whisk attachment, whip cream with remaining 2 tablespoons sugar on medium-low speed until foamy, about 1 minute. Increase speed to high and whip until soft peaks form, 1 to 3 minutes. Spread cream over strawberry mixture. Serve. (Frosted cake can be refrigerated for up to 2 days.)

4
SKY-HIGH CAKES

carrot layer cake

serves 12 to 16

cake

1¾ cups (8¾ ounces) all-purpose flour

2 teaspoons baking powder

1 teaspoon baking soda

1½ teaspoons ground cinnamon

¾ teaspoon ground nutmeg

½ teaspoon salt

¼ teaspoon ground cloves

1¼ cups packed (8¾ ounces) light brown sugar

¾ cup vegetable oil

3 large eggs

1 teaspoon vanilla extract

2⅔ cups shredded carrots (4 carrots)

⅔ cup dried currants

frosting and nuts

16 tablespoons unsalted butter, softened

3 cups (12 ounces) confectioners' sugar

⅓ cup (1 ounce) buttermilk powder

2 teaspoons vanilla extract

¼ teaspoon salt

12 ounces cream cheese, cut into 12 equal pieces and chilled

2 cups pecans, toasted and chopped coarse

why this recipe works We love carrot cake in all its many forms. And while our recipes for Carrot-Honey Layer Cake (page 45), Carrot Cupcakes (page 58), and Simple Carrot Sheet Cake (page 110) are easy enough to make at just about any time, we thought it would be nice to also have a carrot cake showpiece. We wanted a sleek, stacked, dressed-up version of carrot cake with thin layers of light cake and a sturdy, tangy cream cheese frosting. We baked our cake in a rimmed baking sheet, sliced it into four pieces, and stacked them. This thin cake baked in about 15 minutes, but that wasn't enough time for the carrots to soften; adding a little baking soda to the batter solved this problem by helping the carrots break down. We tried incorporating sour cream into our standard Cream Cheese Frosting (page 401) for extra tang, but this made a frosting that was too soft for this towering creation. Replacing the sour cream with buttermilk powder worked much better; it provided the desired tang and also thickened the frosting to just the right consistency. Shred the carrots on the large holes of a box grater or in a food processor fitted with the shredding disk. To ensure the proper consistency for the frosting, use cold cream cheese. If your baked cake is of an uneven thickness, adjust the orientation of the layers as they are stacked to produce a level cake. Assembling this cake on a cardboard cake rectangle trimmed to an 8 by 6-inch rectangle makes it easy to pick it up and press the pecans onto the sides.

1 *For the cake* Adjust oven rack to middle position and heat oven to 350 degrees. Grease 18 by 13-inch rimmed baking sheet, line with parchment paper, and grease parchment.

2 Whisk flour, baking powder, baking soda, cinnamon, nutmeg, salt, and cloves together in large bowl. Whisk sugar, oil, eggs, and vanilla in second large bowl until mixture is smooth. Stir in carrots and currants. Add flour mixture and fold with rubber spatula until mixture is just combined.

3 Transfer batter to prepared sheet and smooth top with offset spatula. Bake until center is firm to touch, 15 to 18 minutes, rotating sheet halfway through baking. Let cake cool in pan on wire rack for 5 minutes. Invert cake onto rack (do not remove parchment), then reinvert onto second rack. Let cake cool completely, about 30 minutes.

4 *For the frosting and nuts* Using stand mixer fitted with paddle, beat butter, sugar, buttermilk powder, vanilla, and salt on low speed until smooth, about 2 minutes, scraping down bowl as needed. Increase speed to medium-low, add cream cheese, 1 piece at a time, and mix until smooth, about 2 minutes.

5 Transfer cooled cake to cutting board, parchment side down. Using sharp chef's knife, cut cake and parchment in half crosswise, then lengthwise, making 4 equal rectangles, about 8 by 6 inches each.

6 Place 1 cake layer, parchment side up, on 8 by 6-inch cardboard rectangle and carefully remove parchment. Spread ⅔ cup frosting evenly over top, right to edge of cake. Repeat with 2 more cake layers, pressing lightly to adhere and spreading ⅔ cup frosting evenly over each layer. Top with remaining cake layer and spread 1 cup frosting evenly over top. Spread remaining frosting evenly over sides of cake. (It's fine if some crumbs show through frosting on sides, but if you go back to smooth top of cake, be sure that spatula is free of crumbs.)

7 Hold cake with your hand and gently press pecans onto sides with your other hand. Refrigerate for at least 1 hour. Transfer cake to platter and serve. (Cake can be refrigerated for up to 24 hours; bring to room temperature before serving.)

Buttermilk Powder

For a cream cheese frosting that's stiff enough to hold several layers of cake in place, we used tangy buttermilk powder—along with the confectioners' sugar—to add body. Powdered buttermilk is made from the byproduct of butter making; it's simply old-fashioned buttermilk without the water. In addition to its use here, we recommend it as a substitute for buttermilk in baking recipes; the powder can be added to the recipe along with the dry ingredients, and the correct amount of water is added to the wet ingredients. What's more? Buttermilk powder is inexpensive and has a long shelf life.

Making Carrot Layer Cake

1 Smooth batter in baking sheet to create thin, level cake.

2 Slice cooled sheet cake into 4 equal rectangles.

3 Spread frosting over rectangular layer placed on cardboard; repeat with remaining layers.

4 Press chopped pecans onto sides of cake to hide any imperfections and add crunch.

black forest cake

serves 10 to 12

cherries

2 cups jarred sour cherries in light syrup, drained with 1 cup syrup reserved

½ cup (3½ ounces) sugar

½ cup kirsch or other cherry-flavored liqueur

cake

3 (8-inch) Devil's Food Cake Layers (page 397)

whipped cream

¼ cup (1¾ ounces) sugar

1 tablespoon cornstarch

3 cups heavy cream, chilled

1½ teaspoons vanilla extract

Shaved semisweet chocolate

why this recipe works In Germany, Black Forest cake is an architectural masterpiece that sandwiches layers of chocolate cake with marinated cherries and thick drifts of sweetened whipped cream. Finished with a garnish of chocolate shavings and additional cherries, it is quite the showpiece. To streamline this impressive dessert, we started by examining each component separately. The cake was easy: The deep, dark color and flavor of our Devil's Food Cake Layers provided the perfect base on which to layer the other elements. For the frosting, we knew that anything richer than a whipped cream would be overwhelming, but we also knew simple whipped cream didn't have enough structure to hold up under the weight of this towering cake. Simmering some of the cream with cornstarch (raw cornstarch was chalky) and then whipping it with the rest of the cream created a whipped cream with voluminous body, strength, and staying power. Jarred sour cherries (Morello are some of the best), halved for the filling and left whole for the topping, tasted great straight from the jar but were even better when galvanized by a generous amount of kirsch. The cake's trademark garnish of chocolate shavings and whole cherries gave the cake a stunning crown. If you can't find jarred sour cherries, you can substitute high-quality canned cherries. Be sure to whip the cream only until soft peaks start to form. We use an 8-ounce block of semisweet Callebaut chocolate for the shavings.

1 *For the cherries* Reserve 8 prettiest cherries for garnish in small bowl. Slice remaining cherries in half and place in second bowl. Bring reserved cherry syrup and sugar to simmer in medium saucepan over medium heat and cook until syrup is thickened and measures about ½ cup, 8 to 10 minutes. Off heat, stir in kirsch. Toss 1 tablespoon syrup with cherries reserved for garnish. Toss 3 tablespoons more syrup with halved cherries.

2 *For the cake* Poke top of cake layers thoroughly with wooden skewer and brush with remaining syrup.

3 *For the whipped cream* Whisk sugar and cornstarch together in small saucepan and slowly whisk in ½ cup cream. Bring mixture to simmer over medium heat, whisking constantly, until mixture thickens, 2 to 3 minutes. Let mixture cool completely, about 30 minutes.

4 Using stand mixer fitted with whisk attachment, whip remaining 2½ cups cream and vanilla on low speed until frothy, about 30 seconds. Increase speed to medium and continue to whip until mixture begins to thicken, about 30 seconds. Slowly add cooled sugar mixture and continue to whip until soft peaks form, about 1 minute.

5 Line edges of cake platter with 4 strips of parchment paper to keep platter clean. Place 1 cake layer on platter. Spread ½ cup whipped cream over top, right to edge of cake, then cover with half of sliced cherries. Repeat with 1 more cake layer, ½ cup more whipped cream, and remaining sliced cherries. Top with remaining cake layer, pressing lightly to adhere. Spread remaining whipped cream evenly over top and sides of cake.

6 Refrigerate cake so it absorbs soaking syrup, at least 2 hours or up to 24 hours. Before serving, let cake sit at room temperature for 30 minutes to 1 hour, then gently press shaved chocolate into sides of cake. Evenly space 8 small piles shaved chocolate around top of cake and top each with cherry. Carefully remove parchment strips before serving.

Cherries for Baking

Tart sour cherries are a defining ingredient of Black Forest cake—their bracing acidity balances the richness of the cake and whipped cream. Fresh sour cherries are available only for a few weeks during the summer, and regionally at that. But sweet cherries just aren't a suitable substitute for sour. That left us with frozen, canned, and jarred sour cherries. So which kind of sour cherries should you use in desserts? The water that canned cherries are packed in muted their flavor, while the texture of frozen cherries was too soft. We found that only jarred cherries (ideally Morello, an especially flavorful variety) were a good replacement for fresh. They're bright, fruity, and have a firm-textured chew right out of the jar.

Working with Shaved Chocolate

1 Using vegetable peeler, scrape shavings from 8-ounce block of semisweet chocolate. Using spatula, transfer to plate and store in cool, dry place.

2 Gently press chocolate shavings into sides of cake, reserving about ½ cup shavings for top of cake.

3 Working with 1 tablespoon shavings at a time, evenly space 8 piles of shavings around top perimeter of cake.

chocolate turtle cake

serves 10 to 12

icing

½ cup heavy cream

6 ounces bittersweet chocolate, chopped

2 tablespoons light corn syrup

caramel

2 cups pecans, toasted

1 pound soft caramels

½ cup heavy cream

⅛ teaspoon salt

3 (8-inch) Chocolate Cake Layers
(page 395)

Making the Caramel Topping

1 Combine candies, cream, and salt in saucepan. Whisk over medium-low heat until smooth.

2 Using offset spatula, spread caramel over top of iced cake, letting it drip down sides.

why this recipe works Pecan turtles are immensely satisfying because they pack multiple flavors and textures into every bite: Crunchy, buttery pecans are held together with chewy, sweet, slightly salty caramel, and the whole thing is coated with rich chocolate. We wanted to translate this beloved confection into an impressive, multilayered cake. Chocolate was the obvious choice for our cake layers, and fortunately we already had the ideal chocolate layer cake in our repertoire. Rather than going to the trouble of making a from-scratch caramel filling, we opted to melt caramel candies (a whopping 57 candies gave us the 1 pound we needed) on the stovetop with some cream and a pinch of salt. We stirred chopped toasted pecans into some of the caramel to create a filling with true turtle character. After sandwiching three cake layers with the caramel-nut mixture, we covered the cake with a simple but rich chocolate icing before pouring extra caramel over the top and decorating the cake with whole pecans for an elegant finish. It is important to let the cake rest in the refrigerator before serving; it will be sturdier and much easier to slice.

1 *For the icing* Combine cream, chocolate, and corn syrup in medium saucepan and cook over medium-low heat, whisking constantly, until smooth. Transfer mixture to bowl and refrigerate until thickened but still spreadable, about 2 hours, stirring occasionally. (Mixture can be refrigerated for up to 12 hours. Let sit at room temperature until softened and spreadable, about 1 hour.)

2 *For the caramel* Finely chop 1½ cups pecans. Combine caramels, cream, and salt in clean, dry saucepan and cook over medium-low heat, whisking constantly, until smooth. Set aside ¾ cup caramel mixture for topping. Stir chopped pecans into remaining caramel mixture.

3 Line edges of cake platter with 4 strips of parchment paper to keep platter clean. Place 1 cake layer on platter. Spread half of caramel-pecan mixture evenly over top, leaving ½-inch border around edge of cake. Repeat with 1 more cake layer and remaining caramel-pecan mixture. Top with remaining cake layer, pressing lightly to adhere. Spread icing evenly over top and sides of cake and refrigerate until set, about 30 minutes. Spread reserved caramel mixture over top of cake, allowing caramel to drip over sides. Garnish with remaining ½ cup pecans. Carefully remove parchment strips before serving.

smith island cake

serves 10 to 12

The Perfect Cake

frosting

10 ounces bittersweet chocolate, chopped

1 cup heavy cream

1 cup (7 ounces) sugar

¼ teaspoon salt

1 teaspoon vanilla extract

8 tablespoons unsalted butter, softened

cake

2½ cups (10 ounces) cake flour

1¼ teaspoons baking powder

¼ teaspoon baking soda

¾ teaspoon salt

1¾ cups (12¼ ounces) sugar

1 cup buttermilk, room temperature

10 tablespoons unsalted butter, melted and cooled

3 large eggs, separated, plus 3 large yolks, room temperature

3 tablespoons vegetable oil

2 teaspoons vanilla extract

Pinch cream of tartar

why this recipe works Smith Island, Maryland, may be a small place, but it boasts a cake with a reputation so grand, it recently became the official state dessert. Multiple thin layers of buttery yellow cake are sleekly separated with a shiny, rich, fudgy frosting. With all the impressively thin layers that make up this tall cake, we assumed we'd need impossibly precise knife skills. Luckily, we found a work-around: We simply made the batter for our Yellow Cake Layers (page 394) and baked them in eight portions, spreading a thin layer of the batter in two cake pans at a time and baking the layers in four intervals for about 10 minutes each. Many recipes for the sleek ganache-like frosting include milk, but we used heavy cream to give the frosting more body for supporting the cake's many layers. Using an offset spatula helped to apply the icing in a sleek, even layer. You may have extra batter after baking all of the cake layers. Be sure to let the cake pans cool completely before filling with more batter.

1 *For the frosting* Place chocolate in large bowl. Heat cream, sugar, and salt in saucepan over medium-low heat, stirring occasionally, until sugar dissolves and mixture begins to simmer. Pour hot cream mixture over chocolate and whisk until smooth. Whisk in vanilla and butter until glossy. Cover and refrigerate until icing is firm but still spreadable, about 1 hour.

2 *For the cake* Adjust oven rack to middle position and heat oven to 350 degrees. Generously grease two 9-inch round cake pans, line with parchment paper, grease parchment, and flour pans. Whisk flour, baking powder, baking soda, salt, and 1½ cups sugar together in bowl. Whisk buttermilk, melted butter, egg yolks, oil, and vanilla together in second bowl.

3 Using stand mixer fitted with whisk attachment, whip egg whites and cream of tartar on medium-low speed until foamy, about 1 minute. Increase speed to medium-high and whip whites to soft billowy mounds, about 1 minute. Gradually add remaining ¼ cup sugar and whip until glossy, stiff peaks form, 2 to 3 minutes; transfer to third bowl.

4 Add flour mixture to now-empty mixer bowl and mix on low speed, gradually adding buttermilk mixture and mixing until almost incorporated (a few streaks of dry flour will remain), about 15 seconds. Scrape down bowl, then mix on medium-low speed until smooth and fully incorporated, 10 to 15 seconds.

5 Using rubber spatula, stir one-third of whites into batter. Gently fold remaining whites into batter until no white streaks remain. Spread about ⅔ cup batter in even layer in each prepared pan. Bake until edges are golden brown and cake springs back when touched, 10 to 14 minutes. Let cakes cool in pan on wire rack for 5 minutes. Run thin knife around edge of pans, remove cakes from pan, discarding parchment, and let cool completely on rack. Let pans cool completely, reline pans with parchment, grease parchment, and flour pans. Repeat process 3 times for a total of 8 layers.

6 Line edges of cake platter with 4 strips of parchment to keep platter clean. Place 1 cake layer on platter. Spread ¼ cup frosting evenly over top, right to edge of cake. (If frosting is too stiff, let stand at room temperature 5 minutes, then stir to soften.) Repeat with 6 more cake layers, spreading ¼ cup frosting evenly over each layer. Top with remaining cake layer and spread remaining frosting evenly over top and sides of cake. To smooth frosting, run edge of offset spatula around cake sides and over top. Carefully remove parchment strips before serving.

strawberry cream cake

serves 10 to 12

cake

1 cup (7 ounces) sugar

1¼ cups (5 ounces) cake flour

1½ teaspoons baking powder

¼ teaspoon salt

5 large eggs (2 whole, 3 separated), room temperature

6 tablespoons unsalted butter, melted and cooled

2 tablespoons water

2 teaspoons vanilla extract

Pinch cream of tartar

filling

2 pounds strawberries, hulled (6 cups)

4–6 tablespoons sugar

2 tablespoons kirsch

Pinch salt

whipped cream

8 ounces cream cheese, softened

½ cup (3½ ounces) sugar

1 teaspoon vanilla extract

⅛ teaspoon salt

2 cups heavy cream, chilled

why this recipe works It's hard to believe that the well-loved combination of cake, cream, and strawberries could be anything other than perfection, but soggy cake, squishy cream, or bland, underripe berries can easily ruin this heavenly trio. We wanted a sturdy multilayer cake with a firm filling and unmistakable strawberry flavor fit for a starring role—a berry-filled showpiece that could serve a formal occasion. We quickly realized that layers of tender butter cake couldn't support a substantial strawberry filling, so we developed a chiffon-style cake that combined the rich flavor of a butter cake with the light-yet-sturdy texture of a sponge cake. For a bright, prominent fruit filling, we made a berry "mash" with half of the berries and then reduced the macerated juice in a saucepan (with a little kirsch) to help concentrate and round out the flavor. The remaining element—the whipped cream—presented one final challenge: When the cake was assembled, the cream squished out the sides and the layers fell apart. To correct this problem, we reduced the number of layers from four to three and fortified the whipped-cream filling with cream cheese for a filling that stayed put. Sliced berries were the perfect finishing touch for this spectacular summertime cake. If your berries aren't very sweet, use the higher amount of sugar in the filling.

1 *For the cake* Adjust oven rack to lower-middle position and heat oven to 325 degrees. Grease 9-inch round cake pan or 9-inch springform pan, line with parchment paper, grease parchment, and flour pan. Reserve 3 tablespoons sugar in small bowl. Whisk flour, baking powder, salt, and remaining sugar together in bowl. Whisk in 2 eggs and 3 yolks, melted butter, water, and vanilla until smooth.

2 Using stand mixer fitted with whisk attachment, whip egg whites and cream of tartar on medium-low speed until foamy, about 1 minute. Increase speed to medium-high and whip whites to soft billowy mounds, about 1 minute. Gradually add reserved 3 tablespoons sugar and whip until glossy, soft peaks form, 1 to 2 minutes. Using rubber spatula, stir one-third of whites into batter. Gently fold remaining whites into batter until no white streaks remain.

3 Transfer batter to prepared pan and smooth top with rubber spatula. Bake until toothpick inserted in center comes out clean, 30 to 40 minutes. Let cake cool in pan on wire rack for 10 minutes. Remove cake from pan, discarding parchment, and let cool completely on rack, about 2 hours.

4 *For the filling* Halve 24 of best-looking berries and reserve. Quarter remaining berries, toss with sugar in bowl, and let sit for 1 hour, stirring occasionally. Drain berries in fine-mesh strainer set over bowl and reserve juice (you should have about ½ cup). Pulse macerated berries in food processor until coarsely chopped, about 5 pulses (you should have about 1½ cups). Simmer kirsch and reserved juice in small saucepan over medium-high heat until syrupy and reduced to about 3 tablespoons, 3 to 5 minutes. Add reduced syrup and salt to macerated berries and toss to combine. Set aside.

5 *For the whipped cream* When cake has cooled, fit stand mixer with whisk attachment and whip cream cheese, sugar, vanilla, and salt on medium-high speed until light and fluffy, 1 to 2 minutes, scraping down bowl as needed. Reduce speed to low and add cream in slow, steady stream; when almost fully combined, increase speed to medium-high and whip until stiff peaks form, 2 to 2½ minutes, scraping down bowl as needed (you should have about 4½ cups).

6 Using long serrated knife, cut 2 horizontal lines around sides of cake; then, following scored lines, cut cake into 3 even layers.

7 Place bottom cake layer on platter. Arrange 20 strawberry halves, cut sides down and stem ends facing out, in ring around perimeter of cake layer. Pour half of pureed berry mixture (about ¾ cup) in center, then spread evenly to cover cake. Gently spread one-third of whipped cream (about 1½ cups) evenly over berry layer, leaving ½-inch border around edge. Top with middle cake layer, pressing lightly to adhere (whipped cream layer should become flush with cake edge). Repeat with 20 strawberry halves, remaining berry mixture, and half of remaining whipped cream. Top with remaining cake layer, pressing lightly to adhere. Spread remaining whipped cream evenly over top and decorate with remaining strawberry halves. Serve. (Cake can be refrigerated for up to 4 hours.)

Assembling Strawberry Cream Cake

1 Using serrated knife and sawing motion, cut cake into three layers, rotating cake as you go. Place sliced berries evenly around edges.

2 Cover center of cake completely with half of pureed strawberries.

3 Spread one-third of the whipped cream over berries, leaving ½-inch border. Repeat layering.

4 Press final layer into place, spread with the remaining cream, and decorate with remaining berries.

rainbow cake

serves 20 to 24

2 cups whole milk, room temperature

12 large egg whites, room temperature

2 teaspoons vanilla extract

4½ cups (18 ounces) cake flour

3½ cups (24½ ounces) sugar

2 tablespoons plus 2 teaspoon
baking powder

2 teaspoons salt

24 tablespoons (3 sticks) unsalted butter,
cut into 24 pieces and softened

Gel food dye (red, orange, yellow, green,
blue, and purple)

10 cups Vanilla Frosting (page 398)

why this recipe works If it's possible that just looking at a cake can make you happy, this is the cake to do it. The array of vibrant colors will liven the mood at any celebration and is sure to appeal to guests of all ages. We started with our classic white layer cake recipe as the base. It's rich and tender and has the structure to stand tall in six layers; plus, it was the obvious choice for easy dyeing. We separated the batter into six portions and stirred in food dye right before baking. Baking our colorful layers in two batches of three cakes each ensured they were evenly cooked. We had the best luck using Betty Crocker Food Gel Colors. The amount of food dye required and the resulting color will differ from brand to brand. We strongly recommend using food gel coloring over liquid food dye for best results. Be sure to let the cake pans cool completely before repeating with more batter. Align layers evenly to ensure this tall cake stands straight. To make 10 cups of frosting, prepare the 5-cup recipe for Vanilla Frosting twice. (Do not try doubling the recipe; it won't fit in the mixer.) You may have leftover frosting after decorating.

1 Adjust oven racks to upper-middle and lower-middle positions and heat oven to 350 degrees. Grease three 9-inch round cake pans, line with parchment paper, grease parchment, and flour pans.

2 Whisk 1 cup milk, 6 egg whites, and 1 teaspoon vanilla together in 2-cup liquid measuring cup. Using stand mixer fitted with paddle, mix 2¼ cups (9 ounces) flour, 1¾ cups (12¼ ounces) sugar, 4 teaspoons baking powder, and 1 teaspoon salt on low speed until combined. Add 12 tablespoons butter, 1 piece at a time, and mix until only pea-size pieces remain, about 1 minute. Add half of milk mixture, increase speed to medium-high, and beat until light and fluffy, about 1 minute. Reduce speed to medium-low, add remaining milk mixture, and beat until incorporated, about 30 seconds (batter may look slightly curdled). Give batter final stir by hand.

3 Divide batter evenly among three bowls. Add ½ teaspoon red gel food dye to one bowl, ¼ teaspoon yellow to second bowl, and ¼ tea-spoon orange to third bowl. Stir each to combine. Transfer each colored batter to separate prepared pans. Smooth tops with rubber spatula and gently tap pans on counter to release air bubbles. Place 2 pans on upper rack and one pan on lower rack. Bake until toothpick inserted in center comes out clean, 18 to 22 minutes, switching and rotating pans halfway through baking. Let cakes cool in pans on wire rack for 10 minutes. Remove cakes from pans, discarding parchment, and let cool completely on rack, about 2 hours.

4 Repeat steps 1 through 3 with remaining ingredients, using ½ teaspoon blue, ½ teaspoon green, and ½ teaspoon purple gel food dye in each bowl of batter. (Cakes can be stored at room temperature for up to 24 hours or frozen for up to 1 month; defrost cakes at room temperature.)

5 Line edges of cake platter with 4 strips of parchment to keep platter clean and place small dab of frosting in center of platter to anchor cake. Place purple cake layer on platter. Spread ¾ cup frosting evenly over top, right to edge of cake. Top with blue cake layer, pressing lightly to adhere, and repeat process with green, yellow, orange, and red layers, pressing lightly to adhere and spreading ¾ cup frosting evenly over each layer. Place ¾ cup frosting in center of top of cake and spread to outer edges, letting any excess hang over edges; smooth top. Spread half of remaining frosting along sides of cake with short side-by-side strokes until entire side is covered with thin coat of frosting. Refrigerate cake until frosting is set, about 15 minutes.

6 Spread remaining frosting evenly over top and sides of cake. Carefully remove parchment strips before serving.

Applying the Crumb Coat

1 Place ¾ cup frosting in center of top of cake and spread to outer edges, letting any excess hang over edges; smooth top.

2 Spread half of remaining frosting along sides of cake with short side-by-side strokes. Continue until entire side is covered with thin coat of frosting.

3 Refrigerate cake until frosting is set, about 15 minutes. Spread remaining frosting evenly over top and sides.

apricot-almond meringue cake

serves 10 to 12

meringue

1⅛ cups (7¾ ounces) granulated sugar

1 tablespoon cornstarch

6 large egg whites

¾ teaspoon almond extract

¼ teaspoon salt

1⅓ cups sliced almonds, lightly toasted

filling

2 pounds apricots, halved, pitted, and cut into ½-inch wedges

½ cup apricot jam

2 teaspoons lemon juice

whipped cream

1½ cups heavy cream, chilled

1½ tablespoons confectioners' sugar

¾ teaspoon vanilla extract

Confectioners' sugar

why this recipe works Fluffy butter cakes are always delicious, but there are plenty of other layers you can stack for a stunning dessert. In search of a unique but elegant layered cake featuring a variety of textures, we decided to fill crisp meringue layers with soft, sweet fruit and whipped cream. We chose apricots for the fruit, and added toasted, sliced almonds and almond extract to our meringue for a complementary flavor pairing. We started by making the billowy meringue, which we spread into disks on parchment paper–lined baking sheets and then baked in a low 225-degree oven for nearly 2 hours. Turning off the heat and letting our meringues cool in the still-warm oven for at least 1 hour ensured that they were crisp throughout. For a substantial fruit filling, we cut the apricots into wedges and tossed them with jam and a little bit of lemon juice. As the meringue layers absorbed the flavor of the apricots and jam, they also softened slightly, creating a pleasing contrast of crunchy and creamy textures.

1 *For the meringue* Adjust oven racks to upper-middle and lower-middle positions and heat oven to 225 degrees. Using 8-inch round cake pan as guide, trace two 8-inch circles on each of 2 sheets of parchment paper; flip parchment sheets over and use to line 2 rimmed baking sheets.

2 Combine sugar and cornstarch in bowl. Using stand mixer fitted with whisk attachment, whip egg whites, almond extract, and salt on medium-low speed until foamy, about 1 minute. Increase speed to medium-high and whip whites to soft, billowy mounds, about 1 minute. Gradually add sugar mixture and whip until glossy, stiff peaks form, 2 to 3 minutes.

3 Divide meringue evenly among 4 circles on prepared sheets and gently spread into even layers. Sprinkle each round with ⅓ cup almonds. Bake for 1¾ hours, switching and rotating sheets halfway through baking. Turn off oven and let meringues cool in oven for 1 hour. Remove from oven and let cool completely, about 15 minutes.

4 *For the filling* Toss apricots, jam, and lemon juice together in bowl.

5 *For the whipped cream* Using stand mixer fitted with whisk attachment, whip cream, sugar, and vanilla on medium-low speed until foamy, about 1 minute. Increase speed to high and whip until stiff peaks form, 1 to 3 minutes.

6 Place 1 meringue round on platter. Spread 1 cup whipped cream over top and scatter generous 1 cup apricot filling in even layer over top. Repeat with remaining meringue rounds, whipped cream, and apricot filling, finishing with final meringue layer. Dust with confectioners' sugar. Serve immediately.

strawberry stack cake

serves 10 to 12

filling

2½ pounds strawberries, hulled and halved (8 cups)

½ cup (3½ ounces) granulated sugar

2 tablespoons lemon juice

Pinch salt

cake

5 cups (25 ounces) all-purpose flour

1 teaspoon baking powder

1 teaspoon baking soda

½ teaspoon salt

¼ cup buttermilk

2 teaspoons vanilla extract

8 tablespoons unsalted butter, softened

4 ounces cream cheese, softened

2½ cups (17½ ounces) granulated sugar

2 large eggs

2 tablespoons confectioners' sugar

why this recipe works Appalachian stack cakes were born of necessity. During tough times, resourceful Appalachian cooks unable to spare eggs and butter for conventional cake baked up thin, crisp, spiced rounds, filled them with various fruit mixtures, and left them to "ripen." After a couple of days, the filling moistened the sturdy layers, yielding a soft, fruity cake with robust flavor. We thought this unique cake was worth eating whether times were hard or not. So our version is enriched with some eggs and butter but still turns out a dough that bakes into hearty, cookie-like layers. Using cream cheese in the dough added a gentle tang and helped the layers hold up to a moist filling. Forming the dough rounds in a cake pan instead of rolling them out individually made for much easier prep. While a stewed apple filling was common, we decided to use strawberries for a bright update. We found that cooking the strawberries to a jam-like consistency helped keep the cake moist without it becoming a soggy mess. You can substitute frozen berries for the fresh. Be sure to let the baking sheet cool completely before repeating with more layers.

1 *For the filling* Bring strawberries, sugar, lemon juice, and salt to simmer in large saucepan over medium heat. Mash strawberries with potato masher and cook until thick and jam-like, about 30 minutes (mixture should measure 2¾ cups). Transfer to shallow dish and refrigerate until cool, about 30 minutes. (Filling can be frozen for up to 1 month.)

2 *For the cake* Adjust oven racks to upper-middle and lower-middle positions and heat oven to 350 degrees. Whisk flour, baking powder, baking soda, and salt together in bowl. Combine buttermilk and vanilla in 2-cup liquid measuring cup. Using stand mixer fitted with paddle, beat butter, cream cheese, and granulated sugar on medium-high speed until light and fluffy, about 2 minutes. Add eggs, one at a time, and beat until combined. Reduce speed to low and add flour mixture in 3 additions, alternating with buttermilk mixture in 2 additions, scraping down bowl as needed. Give dough final stir by hand.

3 Divide dough into 6 equal pieces. Form each piece into 5-inch disk, wrap tightly in plastic wrap, and refrigerate until firm, about 30 minutes.

4 Meanwhile, cut six 9-inch parchment paper rounds. Line 8-inch round cake pan with parchment round and press chilled dough disk into bottom of lined pan with your lightly floured hands. Using parchment, transfer dough round to rimmed baking sheet. Repeat with second dough disk (2 rounds should be about ½ inch apart). Repeat with 2 additional dough disks on second baking sheet. Bake until just golden around edges, 16 to 20 minutes, switching and rotating sheets halfway through baking. Let cake rounds cool on sheets for

10 minutes, then transfer to counter and let cool completely. Repeat with remaining dough disks. (Cake rounds can be frozen for up 1 month; defrost rounds at room temperature.)

5 Place 1 cake round on platter. Spread ½ cup filling evenly over top, leaving ½-inch border around edge of cake. Top with second cake round. Repeat with remaining filling and cake rounds, finishing with cake round. Cover cake with plastic and refrigerate until cake has softened, at least 8 hours or up to 3 days. Dust cake with confectioners' sugar before serving.

Creating the Cake Rounds

1 Using your lightly floured hands, press dough disk evenly into bottom of pan.

2 Lift parchment to transfer rounds to baking sheet. Two rounds should fit on large baking sheet.

Sky-High Cakes

cherry chocolate chip cake

serves 10 to 12

1 (21-ounce) can cherry pie filling

1 cup whole milk, room temperature

6 large egg whites, room temperature

1 teaspoon vanilla extract

2¼ cups (9 ounces) cake flour

1¾ cups (12¼ ounces) sugar

4 teaspoons baking powder

1 teaspoon salt

12 tablespoons unsalted butter,
cut into 12 pieces and softened

2 cups (12 ounces) mini chocolate chips

1 tablespoon vegetable shortening

1 (10-ounce) jar maraschino cherries with
stems, drained and wiped dry

5 drops red food coloring

6 cups Vanilla Buttercream (page 403)

½ cup heavy cream, chilled

why this recipe works Black Forest Cake (page 142) is a decidedly grown-up way to showcase the combination of cherries and chocolate. But we also wanted a more playful pairing of these two affectionate flavors, so we decided to create a beautiful homespun treat for all ages. This cherry-chocolate cake is essentially an ice cream sundae in cake form, and it looks as good as it tastes. Many recipes for cherry-chocolate cake call for adding chopped maraschino cherries to a simple white cake batter, but we found that the cherries in canned pie filling tasted better and had truer cherry flavor. A cheery pink vanilla buttercream and some fluffy whipped cream were a happy topping to our polka-dotted cake. As for the cherry on top? This time we went with maraschinos: Their attractive red stems made them easy to dip in chocolate for the perfect crowning touch to our whimsical cake. Draining the maraschino cherries and drying them with paper towels helps the melted chocolate adhere to them.

1 Adjust oven rack to middle position and heat oven to 350 degrees. Grease three 8-inch round cake pans, line with parchment paper, grease parchment, and flour pans. Drain cherry pie filling and rinse under running water. Press cherries between several layers of paper towels until very dry. Chop cherries fine and reserve ½ cup (discard remaining cherries); set aside.

2 Whisk milk, egg whites, and vanilla together in bowl. Using stand mixer fitted with paddle, mix flour, sugar, baking powder, and salt on low speed until combined. Add butter, 1 piece at a time, until only pea-size pieces remain, about 1 minute. Add all but ½ cup milk mixture, increase speed to medium-high, and beat until light and fluffy, about 1 minute. Reduce speed to medium-low, add remaining ½ cup milk mixture, and beat until incorporated, about 30 seconds (batter may look curdled). Give batter final stir by hand.

3 Gently fold chopped cherries and ½ cup chocolate chips into cake batter. Divide batter evenly among prepared pans and smooth tops with rubber spatula. Bake until toothpick inserted in center comes out clean, 20 to 25 minutes, switching and rotating pans halfway through baking. Let cakes cool in pans on wire rack for 10 minutes. Remove cakes from pans, discarding parchment, and let cool completely on rack, about 2 hours.

4 Line plate with parchment. Microwave shortening and remaining 1½ cups chocolate chips in bowl at 50 percent power, stirring occasionally, until melted, 2 to 3 minutes. Holding stems, partially dip maraschino cherries into chocolate and place on prepared plate. Refrigerate until set, about 15 minutes.

5 Mix food coloring into buttercream in bowl until combined; add more coloring as desired.

6 Using stand mixer fitted with whisk attachment, whip cream on high speed until soft peaks form, about 1 minute; set aside.

7 Line edges of cake platter with 4 strips of parchment to keep platter clean. Place 1 cake layer on platter. Spread ¾ cup buttercream evenly over top, right to edge of cake. Repeat with 1 more cake layer, pressing lightly to adhere, and ¾ cup buttercream. Top with remaining cake layer, pressing lightly to adhere. Spread remaining buttercream evenly over top and sides of cake. Carefully remove parchment strips and decorate with whipped cream and cherries before serving.

blackberry-mascarpone lemon cake

serves 12 to 16

blackberry jam

1 pound (3¼ cups) blackberries, plus extra for garnish

1 cup (7 ounces) granulated sugar

cake

2½ cups (10 ounces) cake flour

2 cups (14 ounces) granulated sugar

1 tablespoon baking powder

½ teaspoon salt

10 large eggs (4 whole, 6 separated), room temperature

12 tablespoons unsalted butter, melted and cooled

¼ cup water

2 teaspoons grated lemon zest plus ¼ cup juice (2 lemons)

4 teaspoons vanilla extract

mascarpone frosting

1 teaspoon unflavored gelatin

2 tablespoons water

8 ounces (1 cup) mascarpone cheese, room temperature

8 ounces cream cheese, softened

¼ cup (1 ounce) confectioners' sugar

1 teaspoon vanilla extract

⅛ teaspoon salt

2 cups heavy cream, chilled

why this recipe works In search of a showstopping cake with a unique combination of flavors, we fell in love with this blackberry-mascarpone lemon cake. It is strikingly beautiful, impressively tall, and features layers of contrasting flavors and textures: tart lemon, sweet blackberries, and a silky rich mascarpone whipped cream. Together, these elements make for a cake that's both light and decadent. Lemon chiffon cake was the perfect base; it has a light fluffy texture but enough structure to stand four layers tall. Making a frosting with mascarpone cheese took some finesse. The high fat content of mascarpone can cause it to separate when overagitated. Replacing half of the mascarpone with tangy cream cheese, which has stabilizers to ensure a creamy texture, made our frosting foolproof. We whipped the two cheeses with sugar until just light and fluffy, making sure not to overwhip. Next we folded in whipped cream, which we enhanced with gelatin to give it more structure; this gave our frosting a lighter texture that was still stable enough to be stacked between the cake layers. The final addition of a vibrant homemade blackberry jam made for a sophisticated frosting that was as beautiful as it was delicious. For a look as modern as the flavor profile, we didn't frost the sides of our cake; instead, we merely scraped them with a thin veil of our frosting so the lovely layers peeked through. Be sure to let the cake pans cool completely before repeating with more batter.

1 *For the blackberry jam* Process blackberries in food processor until smooth, about 1 minute; transfer to large saucepan. Stir sugar into blackberries and bring to boil over medium-high heat. Boil mixture, stirring often and adjusting heat as needed, until thickened and measures 1½ cups, 15 to 20 minutes. Transfer jam to bowl and let cool completely. (Jam can be refrigerated for up to 1 week; stir to loosen and bring to room temperature before using.)

2 *For the cake* Adjust oven rack to lower-middle position and heat oven to 325 degrees. Lightly grease two 8-inch round cake pans, line with parchment paper, grease parchment, and flour pans. Whisk 1¼ cups flour, ¾ cup sugar, 1½ teaspoons baking powder, and ¼ teaspoon salt together in large bowl. Whisk in 2 eggs and 3 yolks, 6 tablespoons butter, 2 tablespoons water, 1 teaspoon lemon zest and 2 tablespoons juice, and 2 teaspoons vanilla until smooth.

3 Using stand mixer fitted with whisk attachment, whip 3 egg whites on medium-low speed until foamy, about 1 minute. Increase speed to medium-high and whip whites to soft, billowy mounds, about 1 minute. Gradually add ¼ cup sugar and whip until glossy, soft peaks form, 1 to 2 minutes. Whisk one-third of whites into batter to lighten. Using rubber spatula, gently fold remaining whites into batter in 2 batches until no white streaks remain.

4 Divide batter evenly between prepared pans and smooth tops with rubber spatula. Bake until toothpick inserted in center comes out clean, 30 to 40 minutes, switching and rotating pans halfway through baking.

5 Let cakes cool in pans on wire rack for 10 minutes. Remove cakes from pans, discarding parchment, and let cool completely on rack, about 2 hours. Repeat steps 2 through 5 with remaining cake ingredients to make two more cake layers.

6 *For the mascarpone frosting* Sprinkle gelatin over water in bowl and let sit until gelatin softens, about 5 minutes. Microwave mixture in 5-second increments until gelatin is dissolved and liquefied.

7 Using clean, dry mixer bowl and whisk attachment, whip mascarpone, cream cheese, sugar, vanilla, and salt on medium speed until light and fluffy, about 30 seconds, scraping down bowl as needed; transfer to large bowl. Using clean, dry mixer bowl and whisk attachment, whip cream on medium-low speed until foamy, about 1 minute. Increase speed to high and whip until soft peaks just begin to form, about 1 minute, scraping down bowl as needed. Slowly pour in gelatin mixture, and continue to beat until stiff peaks form, about 1 minute. Using rubber spatula, stir ⅓ of whipped cream into mascarpone mixture to lighten; gently fold remaining whipped cream into mixture in 2 batches. Stir room temperature blackberry jam to loosen, then gently fold jam into mascarpone mixture until combined. Refrigerate frosting for at least 20 minutes or up to 24 hours before using.

8 Line edges of cake platter with 4 strips of parchment to keep platter clean and place small dab of frosting in center of platter to anchor cake. Place 1 cake layer on platter. Spread 1 cup frosting evenly over top, right to edge of cake. Repeat with 2 more cake layers, pressing lightly to adhere and spreading 1 cup frosting evenly over each layer. Top with remaining cake layer and spread 1½ cups frosting evenly over top. Spread remaining frosting evenly over sides of cake to cover with thin coat of frosting. Run edge of offset spatula around cake sides to create sheer veil of frosting. (Cake sides should still be visible.) Refrigerate cake for 20 minutes. Garnish with blackberries and carefully remove parchment strips before serving. (Cake can be refrigerated for up to 24 hours; bring to room temperature before serving.)

Frosting Blackberry-Mascarpone Lemon Cake

1 After filling cake, spread 1½ cups frosting over top. Spread remaining frosting evenly over sides of cake to cover with thin coat of frosting.

2 Run edge of offset spatula around cake sides to create sheer veil of frosting.

peanut butter pretzel cake

serves 10 to 12

cake

5 ounces thin pretzels, broken into ½-inch pieces (2 cups)

1¼ cups whole milk, room temperature

6 large egg whites, room temperature

3 tablespoons molasses

1 teaspoon vanilla extract

1½ cups (7½ ounces) all-purpose flour

1½ cups (10½ ounces) sugar

5 teaspoons baking powder

2 teaspoons salt

14 tablespoons unsalted butter, cut into 14 pieces and softened

candied peanuts

½ cup dry-roasted peanuts

2 tablespoons sugar

2 tablespoons water

¼ teaspoon salt

6 cups Peanut Butter Frosting (page 401)

1 ounce thin pretzels, broken into ¼-inch pieces (½ cup)

why this recipe works Nutty and rich, sweet and salty, creamy and crunchy—the contrasting flavors and textures of pretzels and peanut butter make them an irresistible combination. We wanted to make a festive cake that would showcase this much-loved pairing in a big way. This meant that rather than use pretzels just for decoration, we actually used a homemade pretzel "flour" in the cake batter. To make the flour, we simply processed thin pretzels in a food processor until they were finely ground. The addition of some regular flour ensured the cake had enough structure and wasn't coarse or dense. A little salt and a dose of molasses reinforced the pretzel flavor of our three-layer cake through and through. Creamy peanut butter frosting added luxurious richness and was the perfect foil to the pretzel element of our cake. A ring of crushed pretzels around the bottom of the frosted cake hinted at the flavor inside, and crunchy candied peanuts were a gorgeous crown for this decadent dessert. We had the best luck using Rold Gold Thin Pretzels.

1 *For the cake* Adjust oven rack to middle position and heat oven to 350 degrees. Grease three 8-inch round cake pans, line with parchment paper, grease parchment, and flour pans. Process pretzels in food processor until finely ground, 1 to 2 minutes; set aside.

2 Whisk milk, egg whites, molasses, and vanilla together in 4-cup liquid measuring cup. Using stand mixer fitted with paddle, mix ground pretzels, flour, sugar, baking powder, and salt on low speed until combined. Add butter, 1 piece at a time, and mix until only pea-size pieces remain, about 1 minute.

3 Add half of milk mixture, increase speed to medium-high, and beat until light and fluffy, about 1 minute. Reduce speed to medium-low, add remaining milk mixture, and beat until incorporated, about 30 seconds (batter may look slightly curdled). Give batter final stir by hand. Divide batter evenly among prepared pans and smooth tops with rubber spatula. Bake until tops are golden and toothpick inserted in center comes out clean, 25 to 30 minutes, switching and rotating pans halfway through baking. Let cakes cool in pans on wire rack for 10 minutes. Remove cakes from pans, discarding parchment, and let cool completely on rack, about 2 hours.

4 *For the candied peanuts* Line rimmed baking sheet with parchment. Bring all ingredients to boil in medium saucepan over medium heat. Cook, stirring constantly, until water evaporates and sugar appears dry and somewhat crystallized and evenly coats peanuts, about 5 minutes. Reduce heat to low and continue to stir peanuts until sugar turns amber color, about 2 minutes. Transfer peanuts to prepared sheet and spread into even layer. Let cool completely, about 10 minutes.

5 Line edges of cake platter with 4 strips of parchment to keep platter clean. Place 1 cake layer on platter. Spread ¾ cup frosting evenly over top, right to edge of cake. Repeat with 1 more cake layer, pressing lightly to adhere, and ¾ cup frosting. Top with remaining cake layer, pressing lightly to adhere. Spread 1 cup frosting evenly over top. Spread remaining frosting over sides of cake. Press pretzel pieces around bottom third of cake. Mound candied peanuts in center of cake. Carefully remove parchment strips before serving.

rhubarb ribbon cake

serves 12 to 16

cake

1½ pounds rhubarb, trimmed

2¼ cups (19¼ ounces) granulated sugar

2½ cups (10 ounces) cake flour

1¼ teaspoons baking powder

¼ teaspoon baking soda

¾ teaspoon salt

1 cup buttermilk, room temperature

10 tablespoons unsalted butter, melted and cooled

3 large eggs, separated, plus 3 large yolks, room temperature

3 tablespoons vegetable oil

2 teaspoons vanilla extract

Pinch cream of tartar

frosting

½ cup granulated sugar

1 pound (4 sticks) unsalted butter, each stick cut into 8 pieces and softened

½ teaspoon salt

4 cups (1 pound) confectioners' sugar

why this recipe works In our opinion, rhubarb might just be the most intriguing produce item there is. Technically a vegetable, its bracing flavor, when tempered, is a bright treat in sweet applications. To get rhubarb into a cake it needs to be cooked; it's woody, stringy, and acerbic when raw. We wanted to incorporate rhubarb in a beautiful and impressive early-summer layer cake. We tossed sliced rhubarb with some sugar and placed it in the cake pans for two of our layers before pouring in buttery yellow cake batter, a rich foil to the tart rhubarb. For the third layer, we took advantage of ruby rhubarb's unique stripey appearance and peeled the rhubarb into ribbons, which we placed in the bottom of the cake pan. We put this special cake on top for a stunning surface. We continued with the ribbon theme by piping the frosting, which we flavored with cooked-down rhubarb puree, in horizontal ribbons across the cake for a stunning dessert that was pretty in pink.

1 *For the cake* Adjust oven rack to middle position and heat oven to 350 degrees. Grease three 8-inch round cake pans, line with parchment paper, and grease parchment. Using vegetable peeler, peel 1 colorful ribbon from each side of each rhubarb stalk. Toss ribbons and ¼ cup granulated sugar together in bowl. Slice remaining peeled rhubarb thin (you should have 4 cups) and toss with ¼ cup granulated sugar in second bowl. Arrange half of rhubarb ribbons in 1 pan in neat single layer to cover entire pan bottom, cutting edges to fit. Arrange remaining ribbons perpendicular over first layer. Arrange 1 cup of sliced rhubarb in even layer in each of remaining 2 pans. (Reserve remaining sliced rhubarb for frosting.)

2 Whisk flour, baking powder, baking soda, salt, and 1½ cups sugar together in bowl. Whisk buttermilk, melted butter, egg yolks, oil, and vanilla together in second bowl.

3 Using stand mixer fitted with whisk attachment, whip egg whites and cream of tartar on medium-low speed until foamy, about 1 minute. Increase speed to medium-high and whip whites to soft billowy mounds, about 1 minute. Gradually add remaining ¼ cup sugar and whip until glossy, stiff peaks form, 2 to 3 minutes; transfer to third bowl.

4 Add flour mixture to now-empty mixer bowl and mix on low speed, gradually adding melted butter mixture and mixing until almost incorporated (a few streaks of dry flour will remain), about 15 seconds. Scrape down bowl, then beat on medium-low speed until smooth and fully incorporated, 10 to 15 seconds. Using rubber spatula, stir one-third of whites into batter to lighten, then gently fold in remaining whites until no white streaks remain.

5 Divide batter evenly among pans and smooth tops with rubber spatula. Bake until tops are light golden and toothpick inserted in center comes out clean, 22 to 25 minutes, switching and rotating pans halfway through baking. Let cakes cool in pans on wire rack for 15 minutes. Run thin knife around edge of pans to loosen cakes, remove cakes from pans, discarding parchment, and let cool completely on wire rack, about 2 hours.

6 *For the frosting* Combine reserved sliced rhubarb and granulated sugar in medium saucepan and bring to boil over medium-high heat. Cook until rhubarb is tender, about 2 minutes. Blend rhubarb mixture with immersion blender until smooth, about 30 seconds; let cool completely. Using stand mixer fitted with whisk attachment, whip butter, salt, and cooled rhubarb mixture on medium-low speed until combined. Slowly add confectioners' sugar and continue to mix until smooth, about 2 minutes. Increase speed to medium-high and whip frosting until light and fluffy, about 5 minutes.

7 Line edges of cake platter with 4 strips of parchment to keep platter clean. Reserve cake with rhubarb ribbons for top layer. Place 1 cake layer (rhubarb side up) on platter. Spread 1 cup frosting evenly over top, right to edge of cake. Repeat with second layer, pressing lightly to adhere, and 1 cup frosting. Top with ribbon cake, pressing lightly to adhere. Spread sides of cake with thin layer of frosting, about ¾ cup. Using basket weave pastry tip, pipe remaining frosting in horizontal bands around sides of cake. Serve.

Placing the Rhubarb Ribbons

1 Arrange half of rhubarb ribbons in 1 pan in neat single layer to cover entire pan bottom.

2 Cut edges of rhubarb ribbons to fit.

3 Arrange remaining ribbons perpendicular over first layer, cutting edges to fit.

Frosting Rhubarb Ribbon Cake

1 Place 1 cake layer (rhubarb side up) on platter. Spread 1 cup frosting evenly over top, right to edge of cake.

2 Repeat with second layer, pressing lightly to adhere, and 1 cup frosting.

3 Top with ribbon cake, pressing lightly to adhere. Spread sides of cake with thin layer of frosting, about ¾ cup.

4 Using basket weave pastry tip, pipe remaining frosting in horizontal bands around sides of cake.

Sky-High Cakes

toasted almond cake

serves 10 to 12

candied almonds

candied almonds

1 tablespoon unsalted butter

2 cups sliced almonds

3 tablespoons granulated sugar

filling

5 large egg yolks

½ cup (3½ ounces) granulated sugar

3 tablespoons cornstarch

2 cups heavy cream

Pinch salt

4 tablespoons unsalted butter,
cut into 4 pieces and chilled

1½ teaspoons vanilla extract

1 teaspoon almond extract

frosting

16 tablespoons unsalted butter, softened

2 tablespoons amaretto

½ cup heavy cream, chilled

2 (9-inch) White Cake Layers
(page 395)

Confectioners' sugar

why this recipe works Sweet almonds, at once delicate and floral and rich and nutty, provide a beautiful flavor base for cakes. While you can grind almonds into a flour to be used for the cake itself (see page 184 for our Italian Almond Cake), their essence is also a nice addition to fillings and frostings. For this cake we incorporated three sources of almond flavor—extract, amaretto, and the nuts themselves—into its many layers. And while this four-layered confection is stacked with contrasts—it's buttery yet light, creamy yet crunchy—the almond flavor throughout unifies the elements. We halved two white cake layers to make four layers and filled them with a foolproof pastry cream that we thickened with cornstarch and flavored with vanilla and almond extract. The addition of a little whipped cream lightened the pastry cream to just the right consistency. We liked this light and creamy filling so much that we used it in between every layer, reserving the frosting—a rich blend of pastry cream and butter flavored with amaretto—for coating the exterior of the cake. For a finishing touch, we caramelized a generous amount of sliced almonds and then coated every inch of the frosting with this crunchy, buttery garnish for the ultimate almond layer cake.

1 *For the candied almonds* Line rimmed baking sheet with parchment paper. Melt butter in 12-inch nonstick skillet over medium heat. Add almonds and cook, stirring frequently, until light golden brown, about 5 minutes. Add sugar and continue to cook, stirring constantly, until sugar has caramelized and almonds are deep golden brown, about 3 minutes longer. Transfer to prepared sheet, spread in even layer, and let cool completely.

2 *For the filling* Whisk egg yolks, 2 tablespoons sugar, and cornstarch in medium bowl until mixture is pale yellow and thick, about 1 minute; set aside. Heat cream, salt, and remaining 6 tablespoons sugar in medium saucepan over medium heat until simmering, stirring occasionally to dissolve sugar.

3 Gradually whisk half of cream mixture into yolk mixture to temper, then slowly whisk tempered egg yolks back into simmering cream mixture. Return to simmer over medium heat and cook, whisking constantly, until pastry cream is thickened and a few bubbles burst on surface, about 1 minute. Off heat, whisk in butter, vanilla, and almond extract until incorporated. Transfer pastry cream to bowl and press plastic wrap directly on surface. Refrigerate pastry cream until cold and set, at least 3 hours or up to 2 days.

4 *For the frosting* Transfer 1 cup pastry cream to small bowl for frosting and let come to room temperature. Using stand mixer fitted with paddle, beat butter on medium speed until smooth and light, about 3 minutes. Add pastry cream in 3 additions, beating for 30 seconds after each addition. Add amaretto and continue to beat until light and fluffy, about 5 minutes longer, scraping down bowl as needed. Set aside frosting.

5 Using clean, dry mixer bowl and whisk attachment, whip cream on medium-low speed until foamy, about 1 minute. Increase speed to high and whip until soft peaks form, 1 to 3 minutes. Using rubber spatula, fold whipped cream into remaining pastry cream; set aside filling.

6 Using long serrated knife, cut 1 horizontal line around sides of each cake layer; then, following scored lines, cut each layer into 2 even layers. Spread each bottom cake layer with 1 cup filling and replace top. Line edges of cake platter with 4 strips of parchment to keep platter clean. Place 1 filled cake on platter. Top with remaining filling and place second filled cake on top. Spread frosting evenly over top and sides of cake. Gently press candied almonds all over cake. Dust top of cake with confectioners' sugar and carefully remove parchment strips before serving.

Making the Candied Almonds

1 Melt butter in 12-inch nonstick skillet over medium heat. Add almonds and cook, stirring frequently, until light golden brown, about 5 minutes.

2 Add sugar and continue to cook, stirring constantly, until sugar has caramelized and almonds are deep golden brown, about 3 minutes longer.

3 Transfer to prepared sheet, spread in even layer, and let cool completely.

blueberry jam cake

serves 10 to 12

3 (8-inch) White Cake Layers (page 395)

jam filling

½ cup (3½ ounces) granulated sugar

2 tablespoons low- or no-sugar-needed fruit pectin

Pinch salt

15 ounces (3 cups) fresh or thawed frozen blueberries

1 tablespoon lemon juice

frosting

8 tablespoons unsalted butter, softened

1½ cups (6 ounces) sifted confectioners' sugar

8 ounces cream cheese, cut into 8 pieces and softened

2 teaspoons vanilla extract

3 (8-inch) White Cake Layers (page 395)

why this recipe works Blueberries sometimes make their way into simple summer cakes like Blueberry Boy Bait (page 301). But we've rarely seen them shine in a more upscale affair—until now. This stunning cake features layers of downy white cake filled with a vibrant blueberry jam. We already had a recipe for tender, fine-crumbed white layer cake, so we turned our attention to the blueberry filling. For the jam, only homemade would do; we made a simple one with blueberries (we found fresh or frozen worked fine), lemon juice, some pectin, and just enough sugar to enhance the natural sweetness of the berries. With the main elements of our simple but elegant cake in place, we could now focus on what really makes this dessert a true showstopper: the beautiful ombre pattern (colors that blend into one another from dark to light) of the frosting. To achieve this effect, we started with a tangy cream cheese frosting and colored it with some of our jam. We found it necessary to pass this portion of the blueberry filling through a fine-mesh strainer, or it left the frosting full of bits of skin that marred the appearance of the cake. And because the filling contains naturally thickening pectin, we found we could simply add more of it to the frosting to get an increasingly darker hue without diluting it. Having a cake stand with a turntable is a must for this cake. If your kitchen is warm, chilling the dark shades of frosting helps.

1 *For the jam filling* Process sugar, pectin, and salt in food processor until combined, about 3 seconds. Add blueberries and pulse until chopped coarse, 6 to 8 pulses. Transfer blueberry mixture to medium saucepan and bring to simmer over medium heat, stirring occasionally, until mixture is bubbling and just starting to thicken, 6 to 8 minutes. Off heat, stir in lemon juice. Transfer 1⅓ cups jam to small bowl, cover, and refrigerate until firm, about 3 hours. Strain remaining jam through fine-mesh strainer set over bowl, cover, and set aside at room temperature. (You should have at least ¼ cup.)

2 *For the frosting* Using stand mixer fitted with paddle, beat butter and sugar on medium-high speed until light and fluffy, about 3 minutes. Add cream cheese, 1 piece at a time, and beat until no lumps remain. Add vanilla and 2 tablespoons strained jam and mix until incorporated. Transfer ⅓ cup frosting to each of 2 small bowls. Add 1 teaspoon strained jam to first bowl and 1 tablespoon strained jam to second bowl, stirring well to combine. (You should have 3 shades of frosting.)

3 Place 1 cake layer on cake turntable. Spread ⅔ cup chilled jam evenly over top. Repeat with 1 more cake layer, pressing lightly to adhere, and remaining chilled jam. Top with remaining cake layer, pressing lightly to adhere. Spread small amount of lightest-colored frosting in even layer over top and sides of cake. Using small offset spatula, spread darkest-colored frosting over bottom third of sides of cake; medium-colored frosting over middle third; and remaining lightest-colored frosting over top third. While spinning cake turntable, run spatula from bottom to top of side of cake to blend frosting colors. While spinning cake turntable, run spatula over top of cake, working from outside in to create spiral. Serve.

Building Blueberry Jam Cake

1 Place 1 cake layer on cake turntable. Spread ⅔ cup chilled jam in even layer over top.

2 Repeat with 1 more cake layer, pressing gently to adhere, and remaining chilled jam. Top with remaining cake layer.

3 Spread small amount of lightest-colored frosting in even layer over top and sides of cake.

4 Spread darkest-colored frosting over bottom third of sides of cake.

5 Spread medium-colored frosting over middle third of cake.

6 Spread remaining lightest-colored frosting over top third of cake.

7 While spinning cake turntable, run spatula from bottom to top of side of cake to blend frosting colors.

8 While spinning cake turntable, run spatula over top of cake, working from outside in to create spiral.

5

ELEGANT CAKES & TORTES

french apple cake

serves 8 to 10

1½ pounds Granny Smith apples, peeled, cored, cut into 8 wedges, and sliced ⅛ inch thick crosswise

1 tablespoon Calvados

1 teaspoon lemon juice

1 cup (5 ounces) plus 2 tablespoons all-purpose flour

1 cup (7 ounces) plus 1 tablespoon granulated sugar

2 teaspoons baking powder

½ teaspoon salt

1 cup vegetable oil

1 cup whole milk

1 large egg plus 2 large yolks

1 teaspoon vanilla extract

Confectioners' sugar

why this recipe works The French have a remarkable apple cake featuring butter-soft apple slices that are tender yet perfectly intact surrounded by a rich—but not the least bit heavy—custard base. Perched above the rich custard sits a layer of airy cake with a golden, crisp top. We opted for Granny Smith apples in our recipe; they're firm and their tartness provided a nice foil to the sweet cake. To ensure that the apple slices softened fully, we gave them a head start in the microwave. Next we needed to find a way to create two cake layers with different textures from one batter. Fortunately, this step was easier than we thought; we simply divided the batter, adding egg yolks to one portion to make the custardy base and then adding flour to the rest to form the cake layer above it. Sprinkling the cake with granulated sugar just before it went into the oven gave the cake an appealingly crisp top. The microwaved apples should be pliable but not completely soft. Take one apple slice and try to bend it. If it snaps in half, it's too firm; microwave it for an additional 30 seconds and test again. If Calvados is unavailable, 1 tablespoon of apple brandy or white rum can be substituted.

1 Adjust oven rack to lower-middle position and heat oven to 325 degrees. Spray 9-inch springform pan with vegetable oil spray. Place prepared pan on aluminum foil–lined rimmed baking sheet. Place apples in pie plate, cover, and microwave until apples are pliable and slightly translucent, about 3 minutes. Toss apples with Calvados and lemon juice and let cool for 15 minutes.

2 Whisk 1 cup flour, 1 cup granulated sugar, baking powder, and salt together in bowl. Whisk oil, milk, whole egg, and vanilla in second large bowl until smooth. Add flour mixture to milk mixture and whisk until just combined. Transfer 1 cup batter to third bowl and set aside.

3 Add egg yolks to remaining batter and whisk to combine. Using spatula, gently fold in cooled apples. Transfer batter to prepared pan; using offset spatula, spread batter evenly to pan edges, gently pressing on apples to create even, compact layer and smooth surface.

4 Whisk remaining 2 tablespoons flour into reserved batter. Pour over batter in pan, spread batter evenly to pan edges, and smooth surface. Sprinkle remaining 1 tablespoon granulated sugar evenly over cake. Bake until center of cake is set, toothpick inserted in center comes out clean, and top is golden brown, about 1¼ hours. Let cake cool in pan on wire rack for 5 minutes. Run thin knife around edge of pan to loosen cake, then let cool completely, 2 to 3 hours. Remove sides of pan and slide thin metal spatula between cake bottom and pan bottom to loosen, then slide cake onto platter. Dust cake lightly with confectioners' sugar before serving.

italian almond cake

serves 8 to 10

1½ cups plus ⅓ cup blanched sliced almonds, toasted

¾ cup (3¾ ounces) all-purpose flour

¾ teaspoon salt

¼ teaspoon baking powder

⅛ teaspoon baking soda

4 large eggs

1¼ cups (8¾ ounces) plus 2 tablespoons sugar

1 tablespoon plus ½ teaspoon grated lemon zest (2 lemons)

¾ teaspoon almond extract

5 tablespoons unsalted butter, melted

⅓ cup vegetable oil

why this recipe works Simple, rich almond cake makes a sophisticated and delicately sweet dessert, but traditional European versions tend to be heavy and dense. For a slightly cakier version with plenty of nutty flavor, we swapped out the usual almond paste for toasted blanched sliced almonds (we disliked the slight bitterness imparted by skin-on almonds) and added a bit of almond extract for extra depth. A generous amount of lemon zest provided subtle brightness. For an even lighter crumb, we increased the flour slightly and added baking powder—an untraditional ingredient—to ensure proper rise. Making the batter in a food processor broke down some of the protein structure in the eggs, ensuring that the cake had a level, not domed, top, which was especially important for this unfrosted dessert. We swapped some butter for oil and lowered the oven temperature to produce an evenly baked, moist cake. For a crunchy finishing touch, we topped the cake with sliced almonds and a sprinkle of lemon-infused sugar. If you can't find blanched sliced almonds, grind slivered almonds for the batter and use unblanched sliced almonds for the topping. Serve with Orange Crème Fraîche (recipe follows), if desired.

1 Adjust oven rack to middle position and heat oven to 300 degrees. Grease 9-inch round cake pan and line with parchment paper. Pulse 1½ cups almonds, flour, salt, baking powder, and baking soda in food processor until almonds are finely ground, 5 to 10 pulses. Transfer almond mixture to bowl.

2 Process eggs, 1¼ cups sugar, 1 tablespoon lemon zest, and almond extract in now-empty processor until very pale yellow, about 2 minutes. With processor running, add melted butter and oil in steady stream until incorporated. Add almond mixture and pulse to combine, 4 to 5 pulses. Transfer batter to prepared pan.

3 Using your fingers, combine remaining 2 tablespoons sugar and remaining ½ teaspoon lemon zest in small bowl until fragrant, 5 to 10 seconds. Sprinkle top of cake evenly with remaining ⅓ cup almonds followed by sugar-zest mixture.

4 Bake until center of cake is set and bounces back when gently pressed and toothpick inserted in center comes out clean, 55 minutes to 1 hour 5 minutes, rotating pan after 40 minutes. Let cake cool in pan on wire rack for 15 minutes. Run thin knife around edge of pan. Invert cake onto greased wire rack, discarding parchment, and reinvert cake onto second wire rack. Let cake cool completely on rack, about 2 hours, before serving. (Cake can be stored at room temperature for up to 3 days.)

orange crème fraîche
makes about 2 cups

2 oranges
1 cup crème fraîche
2 tablespoons sugar
⅛ teaspoon salt

Finely grate 1 teaspoon zest from 1 orange. Cut away
peel and pith from oranges. Slice between membranes
to release segments and cut segments into ¼-inch
pieces. Combine orange pieces and zest, crème fraîche,
sugar, and salt in bowl and mix well. Refrigerate for
1 hour before serving.

cornmeal cake with apricot-bay compote

serves 8 to 10

cake

½ cup (2½ ounces) cornmeal

1 cup (5 ounces) all-purpose flour

1 teaspoon baking powder

⅛ teaspoon baking soda

½ teaspoon salt

¾ cup whole milk

¾ cup (5¼ ounces) sugar

6 tablespoons unsalted butter, melted and cooled

1 large egg plus 1 large yolk

compote

1 cup water

3 tablespoons honey

2 large bay leaves

1 teaspoon vanilla extract

1 cup dried apricots, halved

2 cups Whipped Cream (page 405)

3 tablespoons chopped shelled pistachios

why this recipe works This delicate, fragrant cornmeal cake features a fruit compote with a unique flavor profile, and it's a welcome finish to an elegant summer dinner or a treat on the brunch table. Toasting the cornmeal boosted its flavor, allowing us to use a relatively small amount in proportion to the flour; this helped keep the cake light and tender without compromising its sweet, nutty corn flavor. While the cake layers baked and cooled, we made a sweet, tangy, and aromatic compote from dried apricots, bay leaves, honey, and vanilla. Pureeing the mixture in the food processor ensured a smooth cake filling. We topped the cake with a simple, vanilla-scented whipped cream and a handful of chopped pistachios for textural interest. We do not recommend using medium- or coarse-ground cornmeal in this recipe.

1 *For the cake* Adjust oven rack to middle position and heat oven to 350 degrees. Grease two 9-inch round cake pans, line with parchment paper, grease parchment, and flour pans. Toast cornmeal in 10-inch skillet over medium heat until fragrant, stirring frequently, 2 to 3 minutes. Transfer to large bowl and let cool slightly.

2 Whisk flour, baking powder, baking soda, and salt into cornmeal. Whisk milk, sugar, melted butter, and egg and yolk in second bowl until smooth. Whisk milk mixture into flour mixture until smooth.

3 Divide batter evenly between prepared pans and smooth tops with rubber spatula. Bake until golden brown and toothpick inserted in center comes out clean, 14 to 16 minutes, switching and rotating pans halfway through baking. Let cakes cool in pans on wire rack for 10 minutes. Remove cakes from pans, discarding parchment, and let cool completely on rack, about 1 hour.

4 *For the compote* Bring water, honey, bay leaves, and vanilla to boil in medium saucepan over medium-high heat. Cook, stirring occasionally, until honey has dissolved, about 3 minutes. Stir in apricots and return to boil. Reduce heat to medium-low and simmer, stirring occasionally, until fruit is plump and tender and liquid has reduced by half, about 30 minutes. Discard bay leaves.

5 Transfer apricot mixture to food processor and process until smooth, about 2 minutes, scraping down sides of bowl as needed. Transfer apricot mixture to bowl and set aside to cool.

6 Place 1 cake layer, bottom side up, on cake platter. Spread apricot compote evenly over top, right to edge of cake. Top with second cake layer, bottom side up, and press lightly to adhere. Spread whipped cream evenly over top of cake. Sprinkle with pistachios and serve immediately.

pomegranate walnut cake

serves 10 to 12

cake

2 cups (8 ounces) cake flour

2 teaspoons baking powder

¾ teaspoon salt

1½ cups walnuts, toasted

16 tablespoons unsalted butter, softened

1½ cups (10½ ounces) granulated sugar

4 large eggs, room temperature

½ cup whole milk, room temperature

1 tablespoon pomegranate molasses

2 teaspoons vanilla extract

candied walnuts

⅔ cup walnuts, toasted

2 tablespoons granulated sugar

2 tablespoons water

2 teaspoons pomegranate molasses

¼ teaspoon salt

frosting

20 tablespoons (2½ sticks) unsalted butter, cut into 20 pieces and softened

2¼ cups (9 ounces) confectioners' sugar

⅛ teaspoon salt

2 tablespoons heavy cream

2 tablespoons pomegranate molasses

2 teaspoons vanilla extract

1 cup pomegranate seeds

why this recipe works The combination of earthy walnuts and sweet-tart pomegranates is especially popular in savory dishes of the Middle East. We thought this pairing would also shine in a sweet application and set our sights on creating an elegant layer cake. We fortified a buttery yellow cake with tangy pomegranate molasses and a full cup and a half of finely chopped walnuts; toasting the walnuts deepened their flavor for an unmistakable presence. We tested a few frosting options, but the winner was a simple American buttercream flavored with more pomegranate molasses. We topped the cake with jewel-like fresh pomegranate seeds and stunning quick candied walnuts.

1 *For the cake* Adjust oven rack to middle position and heat oven to 350 degrees. Grease two 9-inch round cake pans, line with parchment paper, grease parchment, and flour pans. Whisk flour, baking powder, and salt together in bowl.

2 Process walnuts in food processor until finely chopped, about 1 minute; transfer to bowl. Process butter, sugar, eggs, milk, pomegranate molasses, and vanilla in now-empty processor until mostly smooth, about 30 seconds (mixture may look slightly curdled). Add flour mixture and pulse until just incorporated, about 5 pulses. Add walnuts; pulse until just combined, about 5 pulses. Divide batter evenly between prepared pans and smooth tops with rubber spatula. Bake until toothpick inserted in center comes out clean, 24 to 28 minutes, switching and rotating pans halfway through baking. Let cakes cool in pans on wire rack for 10 minutes. Remove cakes from pans, discarding parchment, and let cool completely on rack, about 2 hours.

3 *For the candied walnuts* Line rimmed baking sheet with parchment. Bring all ingredients to boil in medium saucepan over medium heat. Cook, stirring constantly, until water evaporates and sugar mixture coats nuts and looks glossy, about 5 minutes. Transfer walnuts to prepared sheet and spread into even layer. Let cool completely, about 10 minutes.

4 *For the frosting* Using stand mixer fitted with paddle, beat butter on medium-high speed until smooth, about 20 seconds. Add sugar and salt and mix on medium-low speed until most of sugar is moistened, about 45 seconds. Scrape down bowl. Add cream, pomegranate molasses, and vanilla and beat on medium-high speed until light and fluffy, about 5 minutes, scraping down bowl as needed.

5 Place 1 cake layer on platter. Spread half of frosting evenly over top, right to edge of cake. Top with second cake layer and press lightly to adhere. Spread remaining frosting evenly over top, right to edge of cake, leaving sides of cake exposed. Arrange candied walnut halves in ring around edge of cake. Spread pomegranate seeds in even layer inside ring of walnuts, covering all of exposed frosting. Serve.

flourless chocolate cake

serves 10 to 12

12 ounces bittersweet chocolate, broken into 1-inch pieces

16 tablespoons unsalted butter

6 large eggs

1 cup (7 ounces) sugar

½ cup water

1 tablespoon cornstarch

1 tablespoon vanilla extract

1 teaspoon instant espresso powder

½ teaspoon salt

why this recipe works Incredibly rich and impossibly smooth, flourless chocolate cake is elegant, refined, and universally beloved. But recipes for this intense, deeply chocolate dessert typically require complicated techniques. Our take on this indulgent cake minimizes fuss without sacrificing flavor or texture. We began by gently melting chocolate and butter in the microwave before incorporating the remaining ingredients. In the absence of flour, we called on eggs for structure, cornstarch for body, and water for a moist, smooth texture. Vanilla and espresso powder underscored the chocolate flavor and deepened its impact. Ensuring a crack-free surface was as easy as straining and resting the batter before tapping out bubbles that rose to the surface. Baking the cake in a low oven produced a perfectly smooth top. This cake needs to chill for at least 6 hours, so we recommend making it the day before serving. An accurate oven thermometer is essential here. We prefer this cake made with 60 percent bittersweet chocolate; our favorite brands are Ghirardelli and Callebaut. Top servings with Whipped Cream (page 405) and shaved chocolate (see page 143), if desired. To slice, dip a sharp knife in very hot water and wipe dry before and after each cut.

1 Adjust oven rack to middle position and heat oven to 275 degrees. Spray 9-inch springform pan with vegetable oil spray. Microwave chocolate and butter in bowl at 50 percent power, stirring occasionally, until melted, about 4 minutes. Let chocolate mixture cool for 5 minutes.

2 Whisk eggs, sugar, water, cornstarch, vanilla, espresso powder, and salt in large bowl until thoroughly combined, about 30 seconds. Whisk in chocolate mixture until smooth and slightly thickened, about 45 seconds. Strain batter through fine-mesh strainer into prepared pan, pressing against strainer with rubber spatula or back of ladle to help batter pass through. Gently tap pan on counter to release air bubbles; let sit on counter for 10 minutes to allow air bubbles to rise to top. Use tines of fork to gently pop any air bubbles that have risen to surface. Bake until edges are set and center jiggles slightly when cake is shaken gently, 45 to 50 minutes.

3 Let cake cool in pan on wire rack for 5 minutes; run thin knife around edge of pan to loosen cake. Let cake cool on rack until barely warm, about 30 minutes. Cover cake tightly with plastic wrap, poke small hole in top, and refrigerate until cold and firmly set, at least 6 hours or up to 2 days. Remove sides of pan and slide thin metal spatula between cake bottom and pan bottom to loosen, then slide cake onto platter. Let cake stand at room temperature for 30 minutes before serving.

chocolate-hazelnut cake

serves 8 to 10

6 ounces bittersweet chocolate, chopped

1⅓ cups hazelnuts, toasted and skinned

1 cup (7 ounces) granulated sugar

2 tablespoons all-purpose flour

¼ teaspoon salt

5 large eggs, separated, plus 1 large yolk

Pinch cream of tartar

8 tablespoons unsalted butter, cut into 8 pieces and softened

Confectioners' sugar

why this recipe works Italian *gianduia* is a confection featuring the much-loved combination of chocolate and hazelnut paste. This irresistible flavor pairing is also commonly found in *torta gianduia*, a cake with a crackly, crisp, meringue-like top and a slightly coarse, very moist interior. Its taste and texture depend on a delicate balance of eggs, butter, sugar, bittersweet chocolate, and ground hazelnuts. In the absence of a chemical leavener, the eggs, whipped to stiff peaks and folded in, provide lift to the cake. While many versions rely on the ground hazelnuts alone for structure, we found that adding a small amount of flour—just 2 tablespoons—lightened the cake enough to give it a melt-in-the-mouth texture. Dusting this super-rich cake with confectioners' sugar gave it rustic charm. Serve with Whipped Cream (page 405), if desired.

1 Adjust oven rack to middle position and heat oven to 350 degrees. Grease 9-inch springform pan, line with parchment paper, and grease pan sides only.

2 Microwave chocolate in bowl at 50 percent power, stirring occasionally, until melted, 2 to 4 minutes; let cool completely. Pulse hazelnuts, ¼ cup granulated sugar, flour, and salt in food processor until hazelnuts are finely ground, about 10 pulses; set aside.

3 Using stand mixer fitted with whisk attachment, whip egg whites and cream of tartar on medium-low speed until foamy, about 1 minute. Increase speed to medium-high and whip until stiff peaks form, 3 to 4 minutes; transfer to large bowl. Return now-empty bowl to mixer. Fit stand mixer with paddle; beat butter and remaining ¾ cup granulated sugar in now-empty mixer bowl on medium-high speed until pale and fluffy, about 3 minutes. Add egg yolks, one at a time, and beat until combined. Reduce speed to low, add cooled chocolate, and mix until just combined. Add hazelnut mixture and mix until just combined, scraping down bowl as needed.

4 Using rubber spatula, stir one-third of whites into batter. Gently fold remaining whites into batter until no white streaks remain. Transfer batter to prepared pan and smooth top with rubber spatula. Gently tap pan on counter to release air bubbles. Bake until toothpick inserted halfway between center and outer rim of cake comes out clean, 45 to 50 minutes. (Center of cake will still be moist.)

5 Let cake cool completely in pan on wire rack, about 3 hours. (Cooled cake can be wrapped in plastic wrap and refrigerated for up to 4 days; let sit at room temperature for 30 minutes before serving.) Run thin knife around edge of pan to loosen cake, then remove sides of pan. Invert cake onto sheet of parchment paper. Peel off and discard parchment baked onto cake. Turn cake right side up onto platter. Dust with confectioners' sugar before serving.

chocolate-raspberry torte

serves 12 to 16

cake

8 ounces bittersweet chocolate, chopped fine

12 tablespoons unsalted butter, cut into ½-inch pieces

2 teaspoons vanilla extract

¼ teaspoon instant espresso powder

1¾ cups sliced almonds, toasted

¼ cup (1¼ ounces) all-purpose flour

½ teaspoon salt

5 large eggs, room temperature

¾ cup (5¼ ounces) sugar

2 (9-inch) cardboard rounds

filling

2½ ounces (½ cup) raspberries, plus 16 raspberries for garnishing

¼ cup seedless raspberry jam

glaze

5 ounces bittersweet chocolate, chopped fine

½ cup plus 1 tablespoon heavy cream

why this recipe works In theory, Sachertorte—a traditional Viennese dessert featuring rich chocolate cake layered with apricot jam and enrobed in a refined chocolate glaze—makes a lavish finish to an elegant meal. In reality, however, this torte always sounds more appealing than it actually tastes: Dry cake, an overly sweet jam with little fruity complexity, and a thin, sugary coating are common pitfalls. We set out to improve this classic dessert, but decided to give it our own unique spin by pairing the rich chocolate cake with tangy raspberries. We wanted a decadent, fudgy base, so we started by baking two thin layers of flourless chocolate cake. But when we tried to stack the layers, the dense cake tore and fell apart. Adding ground almonds (along with a small amount of flour) gave our cake the structure it needed and provided a good flavor boost. The winning approach for our raspberry filling was to combine jam with lightly mashed fresh berries for a sweet-tart mixture that clung to the cake. For the glaze, we kept things simple, melting bittersweet chocolate with heavy cream to create a rich, glossy ganache.

1 *For the cake* Adjust oven rack to middle position and heat oven to 325 degrees. Grease two 9-inch round cake pans, line with parchment paper, grease parchment, and flour pans. Melt chocolate and butter in large heatproof bowl set over saucepan filled with 1 inch barely simmering water, making sure that water does not touch bottom of bowl and stirring occasionally until smooth. Let cool completely, about 30 minutes. Stir in vanilla and espresso powder.

2 Pulse ¾ cup almonds in food processor until coarsely chopped, 6 to 8 pulses; transfer to bowl and set aside. Process remaining 1 cup almonds until very finely ground, about 45 seconds. Add flour and salt and continue to process until combined, about 15 seconds. Transfer almond mixture to second bowl. Process eggs in now-empty processor until lightened in color and almost doubled in volume, about 3 minutes. With processor running, slowly add sugar and process until thoroughly combined, about 15 seconds. Using whisk, gently fold egg mixture into chocolate mixture until some streaks of egg remain. Sprinkle half of ground almond mixture over chocolate mixture and gently whisk until just combined. Sprinkle with remaining ground almond mixture and gently whisk until just combined.

3 Divide batter evenly between prepared pans and smooth tops with rubber spatula. Bake until centers are firm and toothpick inserted in center comes out with few moist crumbs attached, 14 to 16 minutes, switching and rotating pans halfway through baking. Let cakes cool completely in pans on wire rack, about 30 minutes.

4 Run thin knife around edges of pans to loosen cakes, then invert onto cardboard rounds, discarding parchment. Using wire rack, turn 1 cake right side up, then slide from rack back onto cardboard round.

5 *For the filling* Place ½ cup raspberries in bowl and mash coarse with fork. Stir in jam until just combined.

6 Spread raspberry mixture onto cake layer that is right side up. Top with second cake layer, leaving it upside down. Transfer assembled cake, still on cardboard round, to wire rack set in rimmed baking sheet.

7 *For the glaze* Melt chocolate and cream in heatproof bowl set over saucepan filled with 1 inch barely simmering water, making sure that water does not touch bottom of bowl and stirring occasionally until smooth. Off heat, gently whisk until very smooth. Pour glaze onto center of assembled cake. Using offset spatula, spread glaze evenly over top of cake, letting it drip down sides. Spread glaze along sides of cake to coat evenly.

8 Using fine-mesh strainer, sift reserved chopped almonds to remove any fine bits. Gently press sifted almonds onto cake sides. Arrange remaining 16 raspberries around outer edge. Refrigerate cake on rack until glaze is set, at least 1 hour or up to 24 hours. (If refrigerated for more than 1 hour, let cake sit at room temperature for about 30 minutes before serving.) Transfer cake to platter and serve.

gâteau breton

serves 8 to 10

filling

⅔ cup water

½ cup dried California apricots, chopped

⅓ cup (2⅓ ounces) sugar

1 tablespoon lemon juice

cake

16 tablespoons unsalted butter, cut into 16 pieces and softened

¾ cup plus 2 tablespoons (6⅛ ounces) sugar

6 large egg yolks (1 lightly beaten with 1 teaspoon water)

2 tablespoons dark rum

1 teaspoon vanilla extract

2 cups (10 ounces) all-purpose flour

½ teaspoon salt

why this recipe works Hailing from France's Brittany coast, where butter is king, gâteau Breton is a simple yet stately cake, rich in flavor with a dense yet tender crumb that falls somewhere between shortbread cookie and pound cake. Most recipes call for creaming the butter and sugar before incorporating egg yolks and flour, with some specifying upward of 10 minutes of creaming. But extended creaming incorporated too much air into the batter and resulted in a light, fluffy crumb—the opposite of what we wanted. Creaming the butter for a more reasonable 4 to 5 minutes (only 3 minutes of which was with the sugar) produced an ultrathick batter that baked into a firm yet tender cake. Briefly freezing a layer of the batter in the cake pan made easy work of spreading on a bright apricot filling, and a second stint in the freezer firmed up the apricot-topped batter so we could cleanly apply the top layer. We strongly prefer the flavor of California apricots in the filling. Mediterranean or Turkish apricots can be used, but increase the amount of lemon juice to 2 tablespoons.

1 *For the filling* Process water and apricots in blender until uniformly pureed, about 2 minutes. Transfer puree to 10-inch nonstick skillet and stir in sugar. Set skillet over medium heat and cook, stirring frequently, until puree has darkened slightly and rubber spatula leaves distinct trail when dragged across bottom of skillet, 10 to 12 minutes. Transfer filling to bowl and stir in lemon juice. Refrigerate filling until cool to touch, about 15 minutes.

2 *For the cake* Adjust oven rack to lower-middle position and heat oven to 350 degrees. Grease 9-inch round cake pan.

3 Using stand mixer fitted with paddle, beat butter on medium-high speed until smooth and lightened in color, 1 to 2 minutes. Add sugar and continue to beat until pale and fluffy, about 3 minutes longer. Add 5 egg yolks, one at a time, and beat until combined. Scrape down bowl, add rum and vanilla, and mix until incorporated, about 1 minute. Reduce speed to low, add flour and salt, and mix until flour is just incorporated, about 30 seconds. Give batter final stir by hand.

4 Spoon half of batter into bottom of prepared pan. Using small offset spatula, spread batter into even layer. Freeze for 10 minutes. Spread ½ cup filling in even layer over chilled batter, leaving ¾-inch border around edge (reserve remaining filling for another use). Freeze for 10 minutes.

5 Gently spread remaining batter over filling. Using offset spatula, carefully smooth top of batter. Brush with egg yolk wash. Using tines of fork, make light scores in surface of cake, spaced about 1½ inches apart, in diamond pattern, being careful not to score all the way to sides of pan. Bake until top is golden brown and edges of cake start to pull away from sides of pan, 45 to 50 minutes, rotating pan halfway through baking. Let cake cool in pan on wire rack for 30 minutes. Run thin knife around edge of pan, remove cake from pan, and let cool completely on rack, about 1 hour, before serving.

variation
gâteau breton with prune filling
Increase water to 1 cup, substitute 1 cup pitted prunes for apricots, and omit sugar in filling. Bring water and prunes to simmer in small saucepan over medium heat. Reduce heat to medium-low and cook until all liquid is absorbed and prunes are very soft, 10 to 12 minutes. Remove saucepan from heat, add lemon juice, and stir with wooden spoon, pressing prunes against side of saucepan, until coarsely pureed. Transfer filling to bowl and refrigerate until cool to touch, about 15 minutes.

Elegant Cakes and Tortes

chocolate-pecan torte

serves 10 to 12

cake

8 ounces bittersweet chocolate, chopped

6 tablespoons unsalted butter,
cut into 3 pieces

1½ cups pecans, plus about
35 pecans for decorating

1 cup (5 ounces) all-purpose flour

¾ teaspoon ground cinnamon

½ teaspoon salt

4 large eggs, separated

1 cup packed (7 ounces) light brown sugar

2 teaspoons vanilla extract

⅓ cup spiced rum

glaze

8 ounces bittersweet chocolate, chopped

1 cup heavy cream

2 tablespoons corn syrup

Pinch salt

why this recipe works Flourless chocolate-pecan cake may be popular at Passover, but we wanted to incorporate this winning flavor combination into a cake that was suited to any event, any time of year. And don't let the simplicity of the ingredients fool you—this cake is pure decadence. Plenty of ground pecans gave the cake a buttery sweetness, which we complemented with the warm notes of cinnamon and spiced rum. While the pecans added both flavor and structure to the cake, we decided to add some flour too; a moderate amount ensured our cake wouldn't collapse and sink, as flourless chocolate cakes have a tendency to do. We were careful to whip the egg whites just to soft peaks so they were easy to incorporate into the batter. For the glaze, we kept things simple: Hot cream poured over chopped bittersweet chocolate created a rich ganache. Whisking in a little corn syrup to finish gave our ganache a luxurious, glossy sheen.

1 *For the cake* Adjust oven rack to middle position and heat oven to 300 degrees. Grease 9-inch springform pan and line with parchment paper. Microwave chocolate and butter in bowl at 50 percent power, stirring occasionally, until melted, 1 to 2 minutes; let cool slightly. Process 1½ cups pecans, flour, cinnamon, and salt in food processor until finely ground, about 30 seconds.

2 Using stand mixer fitted with whisk attachment, whip egg whites on medium-low speed until foamy, about 1 minute. Increase speed to medium-high and whip whites to soft, billowy mounds, about 1 minute. Gradually add ¼ cup sugar and whip until glossy, soft peaks form, 1 to 2 minutes.

3 Whisk egg yolks, vanilla, and remaining ¾ cup sugar in large bowl until pale and thick, about 30 seconds. Slowly whisk in chocolate mixture until combined. Slowly whisk in rum until combined. Using whisk, fold in one-third of whipped whites. Using rubber spatula, gently fold in half of pecan mixture. Repeat with half of remaining whites and remaining pecan mixture, finishing with remaining whites. Transfer batter to prepared pan and bake until toothpick inserted in center comes out clean, 45 to 50 minutes, rotating pan halfway through baking. Let cake cool completely in pan on wire rack, about 2 hours. Run thin knife around edge of pan to loosen cake, then remove sides of pan. Invert cake onto wire rack set over rimmed baking sheet, discarding parchment.

4 *For the glaze* Place chocolate in bowl. Heat cream in small saucepan over medium-high heat until just simmering. Pour over chocolate and let sit for 5 minutes. Gently whisk mixture, starting in center and working outward, until melted and smooth. Gently stir in corn syrup and salt until combined. Immediately pour glaze evenly over top and sides of cake. Refrigerate until set, about 30 minutes. Transfer cake to platter. Arrange pecan halves along bottom edge. Serve.

triple chocolate mousse cake

serves 12 to 16

bottom layer

6 tablespoons unsalted butter, cut into 6 pieces

7 ounces bittersweet chocolate, chopped fine

¾ teaspoon instant espresso powder

4 large eggs, separated

1½ teaspoons vanilla extract

Pinch cream of tartar

Pinch salt

⅓ cup packed (2⅓ ounces) light brown sugar

middle layer

5 tablespoons hot water

2 tablespoons Dutch-processed cocoa powder

7 ounces bittersweet chocolate, chopped fine

1½ cups heavy cream, chilled

1 tablespoon granulated sugar

⅛ teaspoon salt

top layer

¾ teaspoon unflavored gelatin

1 tablespoon water

1 cup (6 ounces) white chocolate chips

1½ cups heavy cream, chilled

Shaved semisweet chocolate (see page 143) (optional)

why this recipe works Triple chocolate mousse cake, sometimes called tuxedo cake, is a triple-decker stunner that becomes incrementally lighter in texture and richness from bottom to top. For a base layer that had the heft to support the upper two tiers, we chose flourless chocolate cake instead of the typical mousse cake. For the middle layer, we started with a traditional chocolate mousse but found it a little heavy; removing the eggs resulted in a lighter, creamier layer. And for the top tier, we made an easy white chocolate mousse by folding whipped cream into melted white chocolate. To prevent the soft top mousse from oozing during slicing, we added a little gelatin to the mix. This recipe requires a springform pan that is at least 3 inches high. We recommend using our favorite dark chocolate, Ghirardelli 60% Cacao Bittersweet Chocolate Premium Baking Bar, for the bottom and middle layers; the test kitchen's other highly recommended dark chocolate, Callebaut Intense Dark Chocolate, L-60-40NV, may be used, but it will produce drier, slightly less sweet results. For the best results, chill the mixer bowl before whipping the heavy cream in steps 5 and 8. To slice, use a cheese wire or dip a sharp knife in hot water and wipe dry before and after each cut. Top servings with shaved chocolate (see page 143), if desired.

1 *For the bottom layer* Adjust oven rack to middle position and heat oven to 325 degrees. Grease 9-inch springform pan. Combine butter, chocolate, and espresso powder in large heatproof bowl set over saucepan filled with 1 inch barely simmering water, making sure that water does not touch bottom of bowl and stirring occasionally until butter and chocolate are melted. Remove from heat and let cool slightly, about 5 minutes. Whisk in egg yolks and vanilla; set aside.

2 Using stand mixer fitted with whisk attachment, whip egg whites, cream of tartar, and salt on medium-low speed until foamy, about 1 minute. Add half of sugar and whip until combined, about 15 seconds. Add remaining sugar, increase speed to high, and whip until soft peaks form, about 1 minute longer, scraping down bowl halfway through whipping. Using whisk, fold one-third of whipped whites into chocolate mixture to lighten. Using rubber spatula, fold in remaining whites until no white streaks remain. Carefully pour batter into prepared pan and smooth top with rubber spatula.

3 Bake until cake has risen, is firm around edges, and center springs back when pressed gently with your finger, 13 to 18 minutes, rotating pan halfway through baking. Let cake cool completely in pan on wire rack, about 1 hour, before filling. (Cake will collapse as it cools.) Do not remove cake from pan.

4 *For the middle layer* Combine hot water and cocoa in small bowl; set aside. Melt chocolate in large heat-proof bowl set over saucepan filled with 1 inch barely simmering water, making sure that water does not touch bottom of bowl and stirring occasionally until smooth. Remove from heat and let cool slightly, 2 to 5 minutes.

5 Using clean, dry mixer bowl and whisk attachment, whip cream, sugar, and salt on medium-low speed until foamy, about 1 minute. Increase speed to high and whip until soft peaks form, 1 to 3 minutes.

6 Whisk cocoa mixture into melted chocolate until smooth. Using whisk, fold one-third of whipped cream into chocolate mixture to lighten. Using rubber spatula, fold in remaining whipped cream until no white streaks remain. Spoon mousse into pan over cooled cake and smooth top with offset spatula. Gently tap pan on counter to release air bubbles. Wipe inside edge of pan with damp cloth to remove any drips. Refrigerate cake for at least 15 minutes.

7 *For the top layer* Sprinkle gelatin over water in small bowl and let sit until gelatin softens, about 5 minutes. Place chocolate chips in medium heatproof bowl. Bring ½ cup cream to simmer in small saucepan over medium-high heat. Remove from heat, add gelatin mixture, and stir until gelatin is fully dissolved. Pour cream mixture over chocolate chips and let sit, covered, for 5 minutes. Whisk mixture gently until smooth. Let cool completely, stirring occasionally (mixture will thicken slightly).

8 Using clean, dry mixer bowl and whisk attachment, whip remaining 1 cup cream on medium-low speed until foamy, about 1 minute. Increase speed to high and whip until soft peaks form, 1 to 3 minutes. Using hand whisk, fold one-third of whipped cream into white chocolate mixture to lighten. Using rubber spatula, fold in remaining whipped cream until no white streaks remain. Spoon white chocolate mousse into pan over middle layer and smooth top with offset spatula. Refrigerate cake until set, at least 2½ hours. (Cake can be refrigerated for up to 24 hours; let sit at room temperature for up to 45 minutes before releasing from pan and serving.)

9 Garnish top of cake with shaved chocolate, if using. Run thin knife around edge of pan to loosen cake, then remove sides of pan. Run clean knife along outside of cake to smooth. Serve.

Gelatin

Gelatin is a flavorless, nearly colorless substance derived from the collagen in animals' connective tissue and bones. It's a pure protein that works by suspending water in a mesh-like, semisolid matrix. By slowing down the movement of liquids, gelatin has a stabilizing effect, making it harder for water and other liquids to be forced out, essentially fencing them in.

The most commonly available type of gelatin is powdered, which is usually packaged in individual ¼-ounce packets measuring 2½ teaspoons. However, we've found that these packets aren't always accurate and can be off by as much as ¾ teaspoon. If you are making a texture-sensitive dessert, like our Triple Chocolate Mousse Cake, we recommend that you dump a couple of envelopes into a bowl and get out your measuring spoons.

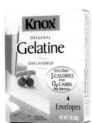

refined strawberry shortcake

serves 8 to 10

strawberries

2 pounds strawberries, hulled and sliced lengthwise ¼ inch thick (6 cups)

¼ cup (1¾ ounces) granulated sugar

2 teaspoons lemon juice

Pinch salt

½ teaspoon cornstarch

cake

4 tablespoons unsalted butter, melted and cooled slightly

1 teaspoon vanilla extract

½ teaspoon grated lemon zest

1¼ cups (5 ounces) cake flour

¼ teaspoon salt

5 large eggs

¾ cup (5¼ ounces) granulated sugar

whipped cream

1 cup heavy cream, chilled

⅓ cup crème fraîche

3 tablespoons confectioners' sugar, plus extra for dusting

why this recipe works While we liked the idea of transforming strawberry shortcake—a summertime favorite—into a whole cake with a presentation more elegant than that of store-bought shells. We decided on a genoise sponge cake, which gets its structure from egg proteins—rather than the weaker gluten proteins a butter cake depends on—making it sturdy enough to support a juicy berry topping without breaking down. Cutting a circle out of one of the cake layers gave us an inset portion to fill with a fresh strawberry filling, and macerating the berries with sugar and a little lemon juice gave them a glossy, vibrant appearance. We thickened some of the juice with cornstarch and then tossed it with the berries for a more cohesive filling. Brushing the remaining juice over the cake before adding the berries ensured it was evenly moistened. Have your equipment ready and ingredients measured before beginning. Cool the melted butter only slightly, to between 95 and 110 degrees.

1 *For the strawberries* Toss strawberries with sugar, lemon juice, and salt in large bowl. Set aside for at least 1½ hours or up to 3 hours.

2 *For the cake* Adjust oven rack to middle position and heat oven to 350 degrees. Spray two 9-inch round cake pans with baking spray with flour, line with parchment paper, and spray parchment with baking spray with flour. Combine melted butter, vanilla, and lemon zest in bowl. Whisk flour and salt together in second bowl.

3 Combine eggs and sugar in bowl of stand mixer; place bowl over saucepan filled with 2 inches simmering water, making sure that water does not touch bottom of bowl. Whisking constantly, heat until sugar is dissolved and mixture registers 115 to 120 degrees, about 3 minutes.

4 Transfer bowl to stand mixer fitted with whisk attachment. Whip on high speed until eggs are pale yellow and have tripled in volume, about 5 minutes. (Egg foam will form ribbon that sits on top of mixture for 5 seconds when dribbled from whisk.) Measure out ¾ cup egg foam, whisk into butter mixture until combined, and set aside.

5 Transfer remaining egg foam to large, wide bowl and sift one-third of flour mixture over egg foam in even layer. Using rubber spatula, gently fold batter 6 to 8 times until small streaks of flour remain. Repeat folding 6 to 8 times with half of remaining flour mixture. Sift remaining flour mixture over batter and gently fold 10 to 12 times until flour is completely incorporated.

6 Pour butter mixture over batter in even layer. Gently fold until just incorporated, taking care not to deflate batter. Divide batter evenly between prepared pans.

7 Bake until center of cakes are set and bounce back when gently pressed and toothpick inserted in center comes out clean, 13 to 16 minutes. Remove cakes from pans, discarding parchment, and let cool completely on wire rack, about 2 hours.

8 Drain berries in fine-mesh strainer set over bowl. Measure out 2 tablespoons juice into small bowl (reserve remaining juice in bowl) and stir in cornstarch until well combined. Microwave, stirring every 10 seconds, until mixture is very thick and translucent, 30 to 45 seconds. Set aside.

9 Place 1 cake layer right side up on platter. Place second layer upside down on cutting board. Using paring knife, cut circle from center of cake on board, leaving 1-inch-wide ring of cake. (Reserve circle for another use.)

Place upside-down cake ring on top of layer on platter. Using pastry brush, brush all of unthickened strawberry juice onto bottom cake layer and inner sides of cake ring. Gently combine berries and reserved thickened juice in now-empty bowl. Spoon berry mixture into cake ring, forming even layer.

10 *For the whipped cream* Using stand mixer fitted with whisk attachment, whip cream and crème fraîche on low speed until foamy, about 1 minute. Add sugar, increase speed to medium-high, and whip until soft peaks form, about 2 minutes. Dollop 2 tablespoons whipped cream onto center of cake. Transfer remaining whipped cream to serving bowl. Dust cake ring with confectioners' sugar. Serve, passing extra whipped cream separately.

Building Refined Strawberry Shortcake

1 Using paring knife, cut circle from center of cake on cutting board, leaving 1-inch-wide ring of cake.

2 Place upside-down cake ring on top of layer on platter.

3 Brush all of unthickened strawberry juice onto bottom cake layer and inner sides of cake ring.

4 Gently combine berries and reserved thickened juice in now-empty bowl. Spoon berry mixture into cake ring, forming even layer.

5 Dollop 2 tablespoons whipped cream onto center of cake.

6 Dust cake ring with confectioners' sugar.

chocolate-espresso dacquoise

serves 10 to 12

meringue

¾ cup blanched sliced almonds, toasted

½ cup hazelnuts, toasted and skinned

1 tablespoon cornstarch

⅛ teaspoon salt

1 cup (7 ounces) sugar

4 large egg whites, room temperature
(reserve yolks for buttercream)

¼ teaspoon cream of tartar

buttercream

¾ cup whole milk

4 large egg yolks

⅓ cup (2⅓ ounces) sugar

1½ teaspoons cornstarch

¼ teaspoon salt

2 tablespoons amaretto or water

1½ tablespoons instant espresso powder

16 tablespoons unsalted butter,
cut into 16 pieces and softened

ganache

6 ounces bittersweet chocolate,
chopped fine

¾ cup heavy cream

2 teaspoons corn syrup

12 hazelnuts, toasted and skinned

1 cup blanched sliced almonds, toasted

why this recipe works It's possible there is no more stunning finale to a meal than a dacquoise, a multilayered showpiece of crisp meringue and rich, silky buttercream coated in a glossy ganache. But preparing one is typically a project to rival all projects. For a more approachable dacquoise, we swapped the traditional individually piped meringue layers for a single sheet that we trimmed into layers; we also shortened the usual 4-plus hours of oven time by increasing the temperature. For the filling, we opted for a German buttercream. Unlike some other buttercreams, it requires no thermometer or hot sugar syrup. And because it calls for equal parts pastry cream and butter, this option enabled us to use the egg yolks leftover from the meringue. Flavoring the buttercream with espresso powder and amaretto contributed another element of sophistication. To slice, dip a sharp knife in hot water and wipe it dry before and after each cut.

1 *For the meringue* Adjust oven rack to middle position and heat oven to 250 degrees. Using ruler, draw 13 by 10½-inch rectangle on piece of parchment paper. Grease baking sheet and place parchment on it, marked side down. Process almonds, hazelnuts, cornstarch, and salt in food processor until nuts are finely ground, 15 to 20 seconds. Add ½ cup sugar and pulse to combine, 1 to 2 pulses.

2 Using stand mixer fitted with whisk attachment, whip egg whites and cream of tartar on medium-low speed until foamy, about 1 minute. Increase speed to medium-high and whip whites to soft, billowy mounds, about 1 minute. Gradually add remaining ½ cup sugar and whip until glossy, stiff peaks form, 2 to 3 minutes. Fold nut mixture into egg whites in 2 batches. Using offset spatula, spread meringue evenly into 13 by 10½-inch rectangle on parchment, using lines on parchment as guide. Using spray bottle, evenly mist surface of meringue with water until glistening. Bake for 1½ hours. Turn off oven and let meringue cool in oven for 1½ hours. (Do not open oven during baking or cooling.) Remove from oven and let cool completely, about 10 minutes. (Meringue can be wrapped tightly in plastic wrap and stored at room temperature for up to 2 days.)

3 *For the buttercream* Bring milk to simmer in small saucepan over medium heat. Meanwhile, whisk egg yolks, sugar, cornstarch, and salt in bowl until smooth. Remove milk from heat and, whisking constantly, add half of milk to yolk mixture to temper. Whisking constantly, return tempered yolk mixture to remaining milk in saucepan. Return saucepan to medium heat and cook, whisking constantly, until mixture is bubbling and thickens to consistency of warm pudding, 3 to 5 minutes. Transfer pastry cream to bowl and press plastic wrap directly on surface. Refrigerate until cold and set, at least 2 hours or up to 24 hours. Warm to room temperature in microwave at 50 percent power, stirring every 10 seconds, before using.

4 Stir together amaretto and espresso powder; set aside. Using stand mixer fitted with paddle, beat butter at medium speed until smooth and light, 3 to 4 minutes. Add pastry cream in 3 batches, beating for 30 seconds after each addition. Add amaretto mixture and continue to beat until light and fluffy, about 5 minutes longer, scraping down bowl thoroughly halfway through mixing.

5 *For the ganache* Place chocolate in heatproof bowl. Bring cream and corn syrup to simmer in small saucepan over medium heat. Pour cream mixture over chocolate; let stand for 1 minute, then stir until smooth. Set aside to cool until chocolate mounds slightly when dripped from spoon, about 5 minutes.

6 Carefully invert meringue and peel off parchment. Reinvert meringue and place on cutting board. Using serrated knife and gentle, repeated scoring motion, trim edges of meringue to form 12 by 10-inch rectangle. Discard trimmings. With long side of rectangle parallel to counter, use ruler to mark both long edges of meringue at 3-inch intervals. Using serrated knife, score surface of meringue by drawing knife toward you from mark on top edge to corresponding mark on bottom edge. Repeat scoring until meringue is fully cut through. Repeat until you have four 10 by 3-inch rectangles. (If any meringues break during cutting, use them as middle layers.)

7 Place 3 rectangles on wire rack set in rimmed baking sheet. Spread ¼ cup ganache evenly over each meringue. Refrigerate until ganache is firm, about 15 minutes. Set aside remaining ganache.

8 Using offset spatula, spread top of remaining rectangle with ½ cup buttercream; place rectangle on wire rack with ganache-coated meringues. Invert 1 ganache-coated meringue, place on top of buttercream, and press gently to level. Repeat, spreading meringue with ½ cup buttercream and topping with inverted ganache-coated meringue. Spread top with buttercream. Invert final ganache-coated meringue on top of cake. Use your hand to steady top of cake and spread half of remaining buttercream to lightly coat sides of cake, then use remaining buttercream to coat top of cake. Smooth until cake resembles box. Refrigerate until buttercream is firm, about 2 hours. (Once buttercream is firm, assembled cake may be wrapped tightly in plastic and refrigerated for up to 2 days.)

9 Warm remaining ganache in heatproof bowl set over saucepan filled with 1 inch barely simmering water, making sure that water does not touch bottom of bowl; stir occasionally until mixture is very fluid but not hot. Keeping assembled cake on wire rack, pour ganache over top of cake. Using offset spatula, spread ganache in thin, even layer over top of cake, letting excess flow down sides. Spread ganache over sides in thin layer (top must be completely covered, but some small gaps on sides are OK).

10 Garnish top of cake with hazelnuts. Holding bottom of cake with your hand, gently press almonds onto cake sides with your other hand. Refrigerate on wire rack, uncovered, for at least 3 hours or up to 12 hours. Transfer cake to platter. Serve.

Assembling Chocolate-Espresso Dacquoise

1 Using offset spatula, spread ¼ cup ganache evenly over 3 meringue rectangles and refrigerate until firm. Spread top of remaining rectangle with ½ cup buttercream.

2 Invert 1 ganache-coated meringue, place on top of buttercream-coated meringue, and press gently to level. Repeat, spreading meringue with ½ cup buttercream and topping with inverted ganache-coated meringue.

3 Spread top with buttercream. Invert final ganache-coated meringue on top of cake. Coat sides and top with remaining buttercream.

chocolate-caramel layer cake

serves 10 to 12

cake

1½ cups (7½ ounces) all-purpose flour

¾ cup (2¼ ounces) unsweetened cocoa powder

1½ cups (10½ ounces) granulated sugar

1¼ teaspoons baking soda

¾ teaspoon baking powder

¾ teaspoon salt

¾ cup buttermilk

½ cup water

¼ cup vegetable oil

2 large eggs

1 teaspoon vanilla extract

caramel filling

1¼ cups (8¾ ounces) granulated sugar

¼ cup light corn syrup

¼ cup water

1 cup heavy cream

8 tablespoons unsalted butter, cut into 8 pieces

1 teaspoon vanilla extract

¾ teaspoon salt

frosting

16 tablespoons unsalted butter, softened

¾ cup (3 ounces) confectioners' sugar

½ cup (1½ ounces) unsweetened cocoa powder

Pinch salt

½ cup light corn syrup

¾ teaspoon vanilla extract

6 ounces bittersweet chocolate, melted and cooled

Flake sea salt (optional)

why this recipe works Chocolate-caramel layer cake is a towering and substantial creation featuring both sweet and salty elements and a sleek, glossy coat of frosting. But in testing existing chocolate-caramel cake recipes, we found that many barely contained enough caramel flavor to merit the name. To ensure rich, salty-sweet caramel flavor in each bite, we sandwiched three layers of thick but spreadable caramel filling between layers of deep, dark, moist chocolate cake. With visions of our layers slipping and sliding, we turned to the techniques we used for our Salted Caramel Cupcakes (page 70); we cooked the caramel until it was dark (but not burnt) and added both cream and butter to finish. Since butter is solid at room temperature, this ensured that the caramel set up once cooled and didn't ooze. After stacking and filling our layers, we draped our cake in a thick, satiny chocolate frosting. And while it's optional, we love the flavor and visual appeal of a sprinkling of coarse flake sea salt to finish. When taking the temperature of the caramel in steps 3 and 4, remove the pot from the heat and tilt the pan to one side. Use your thermometer to stir the caramel back and forth to equalize hot and cool spots and ensure an accurate reading.

1 *For the cake* Adjust oven rack to middle position and heat oven to 325 degrees. Grease two 9-inch round cake pans, line with parchment paper, grease parchment, and flour pans. Sift flour and cocoa into large bowl. Whisk in sugar, baking soda, baking powder, and salt. Whisk buttermilk, water, oil, eggs, and vanilla together in second bowl. Whisk buttermilk mixture into flour mixture until smooth batter forms. Divide batter evenly between prepared pans and smooth tops with rubber spatula.

2 Bake until toothpick inserted in center comes out clean, 22 to 28 minutes, switching and rotating pans halfway through baking. Let cakes cool in pans on wire rack for 15 minutes. Remove cakes from pans, discarding parchment, and let cool completely on rack, at least 2 hours.

3 *For the caramel filling* Lightly grease 8-inch square baking pan. Combine sugar, corn syrup, and water in medium saucepan. Bring to boil over medium-high heat and cook, without stirring, until mixture is amber colored, 8 to 10 minutes. Reduce heat to low and continue to cook, swirling saucepan occasionally, until mixture is dark amber and registers 375 to 380 degrees, 2 to 5 minutes longer.

4 Off heat, carefully stir in cream, butter, vanilla, and salt (mixture will bubble and steam). Return saucepan to medium heat and cook, stirring frequently, until smooth and caramel reaches 240 to 245 degrees, 3 to 5 minutes. Carefully transfer caramel to prepared pan and let cool until just warm to touch (100 to 105 degrees), 20 to 30 minutes.

5 *For the frosting* Process butter, sugar, cocoa, and salt in food processor until smooth, about 30 seconds, scraping down sides of bowl as needed. Add corn syrup and vanilla and process until just combined, 5 to 10 seconds. Scrape down sides of processor, then add chocolate and process until smooth and creamy, 10 to 15 seconds. (Frosting can be made 3 hours in advance. For longer storage, cover and refrigerate frosting. Let stand at room temperature for 1 hour before using.)

6 Using long serrated knife, cut 1 horizontal line around sides of each cake layer; then, following scored lines, cut each layer into 2 even layers.

7 Using rubber spatula or large spoon, transfer one-third of caramel to center of 1 cake layer and use small offset spatula to spread over surface, leaving ½-inch border around edge. Repeat with remaining caramel and 2 of remaining cake layers. (Three of your cake layers should be topped with caramel.)

8 Line edges of cake platter with 4 strips of parchment to keep platter clean. Place 1 caramel-covered cake layer on platter. Top with second and third caramel-covered layers. Top with remaining cake layer and spread frosting evenly over top and sides of cake. To smooth frosting, run edge of offset spatula around cake sides and over top. Carefully remove parchment strips. Let cake stand at room temperature for at least 1 hour. (Cake can be made up to 2 days in advance and refrigerated. Let stand at room temperature for at least 5 hours before serving.) Sprinkle with sea salt, if using, and serve.

Caramel Tips and Tricks

Caramel is simply sugar (sucrose) that's been heated until it melts, browns, and develops complex flavor. You can use it to make a fluid caramel sauce or chewy or hard candy by adding cream, butter, and other flavorings. The longer the mixture cooks, the more water will evaporate and the stiffer the caramel will become. With the right recipe, it's easy to overcome the two main caramel pitfalls: unevenly melted, burnt sugar and crystallized sugar. The latter happens when some of the sucrose molecules aren't hot enough to melt and break down into glucose and fructose. Instead, they bond, creating a grainy texture. Here's what to do.

1 Add Water Water, which makes a "wet caramel," helps the sugar melt evenly, reducing the risk that some sugar burns before the rest caramelizes.

2 Choose Corn Syrup Adding either acid or corn syrup to sugar as it caramelizes can prevent crystallization; both interfere with sucrose's ability to bond with itself. Acid speeds the breakdown of sucrose into fructose and glucose, both of which dilute the remaining sucrose molecules, decreasing the chance they can bond. But corn syrup already contains glucose molecules (and water), so it dilutes sucrose faster.

3 Use a Heavy-Bottomed Saucepan Sugar is prone to burning in lightweight cookware, which doesn't transfer heat evenly.

4 Don't Stir the Pot Stirring the sugar to help it melt isn't necessary. We simply swirl the pan occasionally as the syrup cooks to even out hot spots.

Taking the Temperature of Caramel

Swirl caramel to even out any hot spots. Tilt pot so that caramel pools 1 to 2 inches deep and move thermometer back and forth in caramel for about 5 seconds before taking reading.

raspberry charlotte

serves 12 to 16

filling

1¼ teaspoons unflavored gelatin

2 tablespoons water

3 large egg yolks (whites reserved for cake)

2 teaspoons cornstarch

1 pound (3¼ cups) fresh or thawed frozen raspberries

⅔ cup (4⅔ ounces) sugar

2 tablespoons unsalted butter

Pinch salt

1¾ cups heavy cream, chilled

jam mixture

½ teaspoon unflavored gelatin

1 tablespoon lemon juice

½ cup seedless raspberry jam

cake

⅔ cup (2⅔ ounces) cake flour

6 tablespoons (2⅔ ounces) sugar

¾ teaspoon baking powder

⅛ teaspoon salt

¼ cup vegetable oil

1 large egg plus 3 large whites (reserved from filling)

2 tablespoons water

1 teaspoon vanilla extract

¼ teaspoon cream of tartar

why this recipe works The classic charlotte russe, a grand dessert consisting of Bavarian cream encased in sponge cake, has fallen out of favor—partly because it's fussy to make and partly because it doesn't hold much appeal for modern cooks. But we loved the idea of a light, creamy cake, so we decided to update this dessert by streamlining the technique and adding a fresh, bright raspberry filling. We started from the inside out, creating a raspberry curd that we lightened with whipped cream. After cooking the curd on the stovetop, we poured it into a mixture of gelatin and water and set it aside to cool and thicken. Just a small amount of gelatin ensured the filling would set up without turning as bouncy as Jell-O. For the cake, we settled on the sturdy structure of tender, rich chiffon cake. We baked one round cake and one square cake, using the round as the bottom and slicing the square cake into raspberry jam–filled strips to line the walls of a springform pan. If using frozen berries, thaw completely before using and use any collected juices too. It's important to measure the berries for the filling by weight. If you wish to garnish the top of the charlotte with berries, arrange 1 to 1½ cups fresh raspberries (depending on size) around the edge of the assembled charlotte before refrigerating. To slice, dip a knife in hot water and wipe it dry before and after each cut.

1 *For the filling* Sprinkle gelatin over water in large bowl and set aside. Whisk egg yolks and cornstarch together in bowl until combined. Combine raspberries, sugar, butter, and salt in medium saucepan. Mash lightly with whisk and stir until no dry sugar remains. Cook over medium heat, whisking frequently, until mixture is simmering and raspberries are almost completely broken down, 4 to 6 minutes.

2 Remove raspberry mixture from heat and, whisking constantly, slowly add ½ cup raspberry mixture to yolk mixture to temper. Whisking constantly, return tempered yolk mixture to remaining raspberry mixture in saucepan. Return saucepan to medium heat and cook, whisking constantly, until mixture thickens and bubbles, about 1 minute. Strain through fine-mesh strainer set over gelatin mixture and press on solids with rubber spatula or back of ladle until only seeds remain. Discard seeds and stir raspberry mixture until gelatin is dissolved. Set aside, stirring occasionally, until curd is slightly thickened and reaches room temperature, at least 30 minutes or up to 1¼ hours.

3 *For the jam mixture* Sprinkle gelatin over lemon juice in small bowl and let sit until gelatin softens, about 5 minutes. Heat jam in microwave, whisking occasionally, until hot and fluid, 30 to 60 seconds. Add softened gelatin to jam and whisk until dissolved; set aside.

4 *For the cake* Adjust oven rack to upper-middle position and heat oven to 350 degrees. Lightly grease 8-inch round cake pan and 8-inch square baking pan, line with parchment paper, and lightly grease parchment. Whisk flour, sugar, baking powder, and salt together in bowl. Whisk oil, whole egg, water, and vanilla into flour mixture until smooth batter forms.

5 Using stand mixer fitted with whisk attachment, whip egg whites and cream of tartar on medium-low speed until foamy, about 1 minute. Increase speed to medium-high and whip until soft peaks form, 2 to 3 minutes. Transfer one-third of egg whites to batter; whisk gently until mixture is lightened. Using rubber spatula, gently fold remaining egg whites into batter.

6 Pour 1 cup batter into prepared round pan and spread evenly. Pour remaining batter into prepared square pan and spread evenly. Place pans on rimmed baking sheet and bake until cakes spring back when pressed lightly in center and surface is no longer sticky, 8 to 11 minutes (round cake, which is shallower, will be done before square cake). Cakes should not brown.

7 Let cakes cool in pans on wire rack for 5 minutes. Invert round cake onto wire rack. Carefully remove parchment, then reinvert onto second wire rack. Repeat with square cake. Let cool completely, at least 15 minutes.

8 Place round cake in center of platter. Spread with 2 tablespoons jam mixture. Place ring from 9-inch springform pan around cake, leaving equal space on all sides. Leave clasp of ring slightly loose. Using sharp chef's knife, trim ⅛ inch off all edges of square cake. Spread square cake with 2 tablespoons jam mixture. Cut cake in half. Cut each half lengthwise into 2 pieces to make 4 equal-size long strips. Place cake strips around round cake, jam side in, taking care to nestle ends together neatly. Fasten clasp of springform ring.

9 Using stand mixer fitted with whisk attachment, whip cream on medium-low speed until foamy, about 1 minute. Increase speed to high and whip until soft peaks form, 1 to 2 minutes. Transfer one-third of whipped cream to chilled filling; whisk gently until mixture is lightened. Using rubber spatula, gently fold in remaining cream until mixture is homogeneous.

10 Pour filling into cake ring and spread evenly to edge. (Surface of filling will be above edge of cake.) Drizzle remaining jam mixture over surface of filling. Using knife, swirl jam through surface of filling, making marbled pattern. Refrigerate for at least 5 hours or up to 24 hours.

11 Run thin knife around edge of pan (just ½ inch down), then remove sides of pan. Let stand at room temperature for 20 minutes before serving.

Assembling the Cake Base

1 Spread round cake with 2 tablespoons jam mixture. Place ring from 9-inch springform pan around cake, leaving equal space on all sides. Leave clasp of ring slightly loose.

2 Using sharp chef's knife, trim ⅛ inch off all edges of square cake. Spread square cake with 2 tablespoons jam mixture. Cut cake in half. Cut each half lengthwise into 2 pieces to make 4 equal-size long strips.

3 Place cake strips around round cake, jam side in, taking care to nestle ends together neatly. Fasten clasp of springform ring.

Elegant Cakes and Tortes

6

GREAT AMERICAN CAKES

strawberry dream cake

serves 10 to 12

cake

10 ounces frozen whole strawberries (2 cups)

¾ cup whole milk

6 large egg whites

2 teaspoons vanilla extract

2¼ cups (9 ounces) cake flour

1¾ cups (12¼ ounces) granulated sugar

4 teaspoons baking powder

1 teaspoon salt

12 tablespoons unsalted butter, cut into 12 pieces and softened

frosting

10 tablespoons unsalted butter, softened

2¼ cups (9 ounces) confectioners' sugar

12 ounces cream cheese, cut into 12 pieces and softened

Pinch salt

8 ounces fresh strawberries, hulled and sliced thin (1½ cups)

why this recipe works Strawberries might as well be the official fruit of summer, and a pink-hued strawberry cake is sure to be welcome at any birthday party or cookout. But as we found when developing our recipe for Strawberry Cupcakes (page 68), the vast majority of existing strawberry cake recipes turn to Jell-O for flavor. For our cake, we wanted real strawberry flavor, from real strawberries. As we started testing, however, we were reminded why so many recipes opt for Jell-O: Adding strawberry solids—whether chopped, sliced, or pureed—wreaked havoc on the cake's crumb, making it impossible to achieve the tender, fluffy texture that we wanted. Using just the juice from the strawberries was the answer. Microwaving the berries briefly helped release their liquid, which we strained and then reduced before incorporating it into the batter. We added the strawberry solids to a tangy cream cheese frosting, and also laid thinly sliced strawberries between the two cake layers. Garnished with more fresh berries, this cake packs fresh strawberry flavor into every bite.

1 *For the cake* Adjust oven rack to middle position and heat oven to 350 degrees. Grease two 9-inch round cake pans, line with parchment paper, grease parchment, and flour pans.

2 Microwave strawberries in covered bowl until softened and very juicy, about 5 minutes. Transfer strawberries to fine-mesh strainer set over small saucepan and press firmly with rubber spatula to extract as much liquid as possible; set aside solids for frosting. Boil strained strawberry juice over medium-high heat, stirring occasionally, until syrupy and measures ¼ cup, 6 to 8 minutes. Off heat, whisk in milk. Transfer mixture to clean bowl and whisk in egg whites and vanilla until combined.

3 Using stand mixer fitted with paddle, mix flour, sugar, baking powder, and salt on low speed until combined. Add butter, 1 piece at a time, and mix until only pea-size pieces remain, about 1 minute. Add half of milk mixture, increase speed to medium-high, and beat until light and fluffy, about 1 minute. Reduce speed to medium-low, add remaining milk mixture, and beat until incorporated, about 30 seconds. Give batter final stir by hand.

4 Divide batter evenly between prepared pans and smooth tops with rubber spatula. Gently tap pans on counter to settle batter. Bake until toothpick inserted in center comes out clean, 20 to 25 minutes, switching and rotating pans halfway through baking.

5 Let cakes cool in pans on wire rack for 10 minutes. Remove cakes from pans, discarding parchment, and let cool completely on rack, about 2 hours. (Cakes layers can be stored at room temperature for up to 2 days.)

6 *For the frosting* Using stand mixer fitted with paddle, mix butter and sugar on low speed until combined, about 30 seconds. Increase speed to medium-high and beat until pale and fluffy, about 2 minutes. Add cream cheese, 1 piece at a time, and beat until incorporated, about 1 minute. Add reserved strawberry solids and salt and mix until combined, about 30 seconds. Refrigerate until ready to use. (Frosting can be refrigerated for up to 2 days.)

7 Pat sliced strawberries dry with paper towels. Line edges of cake platter with 4 strips of parchment to keep platter clean. Place 1 cake layer on platter. Spread ¾ cup frosting evenly over top, press 1 cup strawberries into frosting, then spread additional ¾ cup frosting over top, right to edge of cake. Top with remaining cake layer, pressing lightly to adhere, and spread remaining frosting evenly over top and sides of cake. Garnish with remaining strawberries. Carefully remove parchment strips before serving. (Frosted cake can be refrigerated for up to 2 days; bring to room temperature before serving.)

german chocolate cake

serves 10 to 12

filling

4 large egg yolks

1 (12-ounce) can evaporated milk

1 cup (7 ounces) granulated sugar

6 tablespoons unsalted butter, cut into 6 pieces

¼ cup packed (1¾ ounces) light brown sugar

⅛ teaspoon salt

2 teaspoons vanilla extract

2⅓ cups (7 ounces) sweetened shredded coconut

1½ cups pecans, toasted and chopped fine

cake

4 ounces semisweet or bittersweet chocolate, chopped fine

¼ cup (¾ ounce) Dutch-processed cocoa powder

½ cup boiling water

2 cups (10 ounces) all-purpose flour

¾ teaspoon baking soda

12 tablespoons unsalted butter, softened

1 cup (7 ounces) granulated sugar

⅔ cup packed (4⅔ ounces) light brown sugar

¾ teaspoon salt

4 large eggs

1 teaspoon vanilla extract

¾ cup sour cream

why this recipe works German chocolate cake is a distinctly American invention—it gets its name from Baker's German's Sweet Chocolate—and most recipes are similar, if not identical, to the one on the back of the box. The result is a cake that's too sweet, with weak chocolate flavor and a filling so wet and heavy it ruins the texture of the cake. We wanted a German chocolate cake that was just sweet enough, with an unmistakable chocolate presence and a thick—but not dense—coconut-pecan filling that could support the layers of cake. We quickly realized that the chocolate for which this cake is named was simply much too sweet. Using both cocoa powder and semisweet or bittersweet chocolate improved matters, and mixing them with boiling water intensified their chocolate flavor. A combination of brown and white sugars gave this cake the right level of caramel-like sweetness we loved from the original and also contributed to a tender texture. The filling's base of egg yolks, evaporated milk, sugar, and butter is typically simmered, but we found this resulted in a loose consistency. Boiling the filling ensured it thickened properly. We stirred sweetened shredded coconut into the filling before chilling (refrigerating the filling helped it firm up), but we waited until it was time to assemble the cake before adding the toasted pecans to preserve their crunch. For an accurate measurement of boiling water, bring a full kettle of water to a boil and then measure out the desired amount.

1 *For the filling* Whisk egg yolks in medium saucepan, then gradually whisk in evaporated milk. Whisk in granulated sugar, butter, brown sugar, and salt and cook over medium-high heat, whisking constantly, until mixture is boiling, frothy, and slightly thickened, about 6 minutes. Transfer mixture to bowl, whisk in vanilla, then stir in coconut. Let cool until just warm, then refrigerate until cool, at least 2 hours or up to 3 days. (Pecans are added later.)

2 *For the cake* Adjust oven rack to lower-middle position and heat oven to 350 degrees. Grease two 9-inch round cake pans, line with parchment paper, grease parchment, and flour pans. Combine chocolate and cocoa in bowl, add boiling water, cover, and let sit for 5 minutes. Whisk chocolate mixture until smooth, then let cool completely. Whisk flour and baking soda together in second bowl.

3 Using stand mixer fitted with paddle, beat butter, granulated sugar, brown sugar, and salt on medium-high speed until light and fluffy, about 3 minutes. Add eggs, one at a time, and beat until combined. Add vanilla, increase speed to medium-high, and beat until light and fluffy, about 45 seconds. Reduce speed to low, add chocolate mixture, then increase speed to medium and beat until combined, about 30 seconds, scraping down bowl once (batter may look curdled). Reduce speed to low, add flour mixture in 3 additions, alternating with sour cream in 2 additions, scraping down bowl as needed. Give batter final stir by hand (batter will be thick).

4 Divide batter evenly between prepared pans and smooth tops with rubber spatula. Gently tap pans on counter to settle batter. Bake until toothpick inserted in center comes out clean, about 30 minutes, switching and rotating pans halfway through baking.

5 Let cakes cool in pans on wire rack for 10 minutes. Remove cakes from pans, discarding parchment, and let cool completely on rack, about 2 hours. (Cake layers can be stored at room temperature for up to 24 hours or frozen for up to 1 month; defrost cakes at room temperature.)

6 Using long serrated knife, cut 1 horizontal line around sides of each layer; then, following scored lines, cut each layer into 2 even layers. Stir toasted pecans into chilled filling.

7 Place 1 cake layer on platter. Spread 1 cup filling evenly over top, right to edge of cake. Repeat with remaining cake layers, aligning cuts so layers are even and pressing lightly to adhere (leave sides unfrosted). Serve. (Frosted cake can be refrigerated for up to 24 hours; bring to room temperature before serving.)

variations

german chocolate cake with banana, macadamia, and coconut filling

If you cannot find roasted unsalted macadamia nuts, substitute salted ones, but first remove excess salt by spreading them on a dish towel and rubbing them with the towel.

Reduce vanilla in filling to 1 teaspoon and add 2 teaspoons dark rum with vanilla in step 1. Substitute unsalted macadamia nuts for pecans. Just before assembling cake, peel and cut 4 bananas into ⅜-inch-thick slices. Arrange one-quarter of banana slices on first cake layer, then spread filling evenly over; repeat with remaining cake layers, bananas, and filling.

german chocolate cake with coffee, cashew, and coconut filling

Add 2 teaspoons ground coffee to filling mixture with sugars in step 1. Substitute roasted unsalted cashews for pecans.

Sweet Chocolate

There's white chocolate, milk chocolate, semisweet chocolate, and dark chocolate—and then there's sweet chocolate. What's sweet chocolate? Think milk chocolate without the milk. Also called sweet dark chocolate, it is just that—extremely sweet. While it must contain at least 15 percent chocolate liquor, it is often more than 60 percent sugar. Sweet chocolate is sold by Baker's as German's Sweet Chocolate Bar. And it's so cloying that we don't even include it in its namesake cake. You can make German chocolate cake without German's chocolate. We had better results using a combination of cocoa powder and good-quality semisweet or bittersweet chocolate.

jelly roll cake

serves 8 to 10

¾ cup (3¾ ounces) all-purpose flour

1 teaspoon baking powder

¼ teaspoon salt

5 large eggs, room temperature

¾ cup (5¼ ounces) granulated sugar

½ teaspoon vanilla extract

Confectioners' sugar

⅔ cup seedless jam

why this recipe works Filled, rolled sponge cakes are an American classic. They're both beautiful to look at and delicious to eat, but many recipes we tried yielded cakes far too fragile to roll. We discovered that the secret to a flexible cake that wouldn't crack was to use plenty of eggs—our recipe calls for a whopping five. Whipping the eggs until they were thick before adding the dry ingredients enhanced their structure-building abilities. While the cake was still hot, we rolled it into a spiral on a confectioners' sugar–dusted towel and then allowed it to sit for 15 minutes before unrolling it and adding the filling. This early roll gave the cake memory so it stayed snug once rolled again with the jam. To avoid deflating the batter when transferring it to the prepared baking sheet, hold the mixer bowl as close to the bottom of the sheet as possible, using a rubber spatula to gently push the batter into the sheet. Make sure not to overbake the cake, which can cause cracking once rolled. You will need at least a 20 by 15-inch dish towel for this recipe. While raspberry jam is traditional, you can use the flavor of your choice. Serve with Whipped Cream (page 405), if desired.

1 Adjust oven rack to lower-middle position and heat oven to 350 degrees. Grease 18 by 13-inch rimmed baking sheet, line with parchment paper, grease parchment, and flour sheet. Whisk flour, baking powder, and salt together in bowl; set aside.

2 Using stand mixer fitted with whisk attachment, whip eggs at medium-high speed and gradually add granulated sugar and then vanilla, about 1 minute. Continue to whip mixture until very thick and voluminous, 4 to 8 minutes. Sift flour mixture over egg mixture; using rubber spatula, gently fold batter until just incorporated.

3 Pour batter into prepared sheet with rubber spatula and spread into even layer with offset spatula. Bake until cake is firm and springs back when touched, 12 to 17 minutes, rotating baking sheet halfway through baking. Lay dish towel on counter and dust with confectioners' sugar.

4 Immediately run thin knife around edge of baking sheet to loosen cake, then flip hot cake out onto towel, discarding parchment. Starting from short side, roll cake and towel snugly into log. Let cake cool, seam side down, for 15 minutes.

5 Gently unroll cake. Spread jam evenly over cake, leaving ½-inch border along edges. Reroll cake gently but snugly around jam, leaving towel behind as you roll. Trim ends of cake, transfer cake to platter, and let cake cool completely, about 30 minutes. Dust with confectioners' sugar before serving.

Making Jelly Roll Cake

1 Using offset spatula, evenly spread batter in baking sheet, pushing batter against sides and into corners. Smooth top of batter.

2 While cake bakes, sift confectioners' sugar evenly over dish towel measuring at least 20 by 15 inches.

3 When cake is done, immediately run knife around edge of cake, then flip hot cake onto towel. Peel off and discard parchment.

4 Starting from 1 short end of cake, roll cake and sugared towel snugly into log.

5 Let rolled cake cool, seam side down, for 15 minutes. Then gently unroll cake.

6 Using offset spatula, evenly spread thin layer of jam over cake, leaving ½-inch border around edges.

7 Reroll cake gently but snugly around jam, carefully peeling off towel as you roll.

8 Trim both ends of cake.

hummingbird cake

serves 10 to 12

cake

2 (8-ounce) cans crushed pineapple in juice

3 cups (15 ounces) all-purpose flour

2 teaspoons baking powder

1 teaspoon baking soda

1 teaspoon ground cinnamon

1 teaspoon salt

2 cups (14 ounces) granulated sugar

3 large eggs

1 cup vegetable oil

4 very ripe large bananas, peeled and mashed (2 cups)

1½ cups pecans, toasted and chopped

2 teaspoons vanilla extract

frosting

20 tablespoons (2½ sticks) unsalted butter, softened

5 cups (20 ounces) confectioners' sugar

2½ teaspoons vanilla extract

½ teaspoon salt

1¼ pounds cream cheese, cut into 20 pieces and chilled

½ cup pecans, toasted and chopped

why this recipe works This layer cake is a Southern specialty full of bananas, pineapple, and pecans, all covered with a tangy cream cheese frosting. Although this cake's namesake is lighter than air, we found most recipes were anything but; greasy cake, minimal pineapple flavor, and unwieldy chunks of mushy banana are standard. Still, we love the uniqueness of this cake and set out to make a great one. Reducing the oil—traditional recipes contain upward of 1½ cups—was the first logical step in creating a less heavy cake, and tweaking the leavener finished the job, opening up and lightening the cake's crumb. Chunks of banana weighed down the crumb of our newly improved cake; mashing the bananas proved a better approach and distributed banana flavor more evenly throughout the layers. To address the wan pineapple flavor, we more than doubled the amount of fruit, boiling down the juices to concentrate their flavor and eliminate extra moisture. Finished with a rich cream cheese frosting and a sprinkling of chopped toasted pecans, we'd revamped a retro cake for modern tastes. Toast a total of 2 cups of pecans to divide between the cake and the frosting.

1 *For the cake* Adjust oven rack to middle position and heat oven to 350 degrees. Grease two 9-inch round cake pans, line with parchment paper, grease parchment, and flour pans. Drain pineapple in fine-mesh strainer set over bowl, pressing to extract juice; set aside solids. Pour juice into small saucepan and cook over medium heat until reduced to ⅓ cup, about 5 minutes.

2 Whisk flour, baking powder, baking soda, cinnamon, and salt together in bowl. Whisk sugar and eggs together in large bowl; whisk in oil. Stir bananas, pecans, vanilla, reserved pineapple solids, and reduced juice into sugar-egg mixture. Stir in flour mixture until just combined.

3 Divide batter evenly between prepared pans and smooth tops with rubber spatula. Bake until dark golden brown on top and toothpick inserted in center comes out clean, 50 to 55 minutes, switching and rotating pans halfway through baking. Let cakes cool in pans on wire rack for 20 minutes. Remove cakes from pans, discarding parchment, and let cool completely on rack, about 2 hours.

4 *For the frosting* Using stand mixer fitted with paddle, beat butter, sugar, vanilla, and salt on low speed until smooth; continue to mix for 2 minutes, scraping down bowl as needed. Increase speed to medium-low, add cream cheese, 1 piece at a time, and mix until smooth; continue to mix for 2 minutes.

5 Line edges of cake platter with 4 strips of parchment to keep platter clean. Place 1 cake layer on platter. Spread 2 cups frosting evenly over top, right to edge of cake. Top with remaining cake layer, press lightly to adhere, then spread 2 cups frosting evenly over top. Spread remaining frosting evenly over sides of cake. To smooth frosting, run edge of offset spatula around cake sides and over top. Sprinkle top of cake with pecans. Carefully remove parchment strips. Refrigerate cake for at least 1 hour or up to 2 days before serving.

Canned Crushed Pineapple

Our Hummingbird Cake relies on canned crushed pineapple for intense tropical flavor. But are there noticeable differences from can to can? We tested three products packed in pineapple juice (which we prefer to sugary syrup). It turned out that the products varied greatly. Our favorite had small, even chunks that tasted "almost like fresh" and gave the cake textural interest. Our least favorite had a texture like that of "baby food." **Dole Crushed Pineapple in 100% Pineapple Juice**, the least expensive product in our lineup and our winner, was lightly sweet yet tart, with recognizable pineapple chunks.

chocolate blackout cake

serves 10 to 12

pudding

2 cups half-and-half

1 cup whole milk

1¼ cups (8¾ ounces) granulated sugar

¼ cup (1 ounce) cornstarch

½ teaspoon salt

6 ounces unsweetened chocolate, chopped

2 teaspoons vanilla extract

cake

1½ cups (7½ ounces) all-purpose flour

2 teaspoons baking powder

½ teaspoon baking soda

½ teaspoon salt

8 tablespoons unsalted butter

¾ cup (2¼ ounces) Dutch-processed cocoa powder

1 cup brewed coffee

1 cup buttermilk

1 cup packed (7 ounces) light brown sugar

1 cup (7 ounces) granulated sugar

2 large eggs

1 teaspoon vanilla extract

why this recipe works When the Ebinger's chain of bakeries closed its doors more than 40 years ago, Brooklyn residents went into mourning over the loss of their beloved chocolate blackout cake, a tender, decadent chocolate cake layered with a pudding-like filling and covered with cake crumbs. We set out to create our own version. Using an ample amount of cocoa powder, bloomed in butter, in the batter was the first step toward making a cake worthy of the name. The addition of some brewed coffee and brown sugar further underscored the chocolate notes. Because the pudding component needs to cling to the sides of the cake, we added some cornstarch to thicken it to the proper consistency. A combination of milk and half-and-half gave the pudding a velvety, lush quality that complemented the dark, rich cake. Do not substitute natural cocoa powder for the Dutch-processed cocoa powder.

1 *For the pudding* Whisk half-and-half, milk, sugar, cornstarch, and salt together in large saucepan. Set saucepan over medium heat. Add chocolate and whisk constantly until chocolate melts and mixture begins to bubble, 2 to 4 minutes. Off heat, stir in vanilla. Transfer pudding to large bowl and press plastic wrap directly on surface. Refrigerate pudding until cold, at least 4 hours or up to 24 hours.

2 *For the cake* Adjust oven rack to middle position and heat oven to 325 degrees. Grease two 8-inch round cake pans, line with parchment paper, grease parchment, and flour pans. Whisk flour, baking powder, baking soda, and salt together in bowl.

3 Melt butter in large saucepan over medium heat. Stir in cocoa and cook until fragrant, about 1 minute. Off heat, whisk in coffee, buttermilk, brown sugar, and granulated sugar until sugars are dissolved. Whisk in eggs and vanilla, then slowly whisk in flour mixture.

4 Divide batter evenly between prepared pans. Bake until toothpick inserted in center comes out clean, 30 to 35 minutes, switching and rotating pans halfway through baking. Let cakes cool in pans on wire rack for 15 minutes. Remove cakes from pans, discarding parchment, and let cool completely on rack, about 2 hours.

5 Using long serrated knife, cut 1 horizontal line around sides of each layer; then, following scored lines, cut each layer into 2 even layers. Crumble 1 cake layer into medium crumbs and set aside. Line edges of cake platter with 4 strips of parchment to keep platter clean. Place 1 cake layer on platter. Spread 1 cup pudding evenly over top, right to edge of cake. Repeat with 1 more cake layer, pressing lightly to adhere, and 1 cup pudding. Top with remaining cake layer, pressing lightly to adhere. Spread remaining pudding evenly over top and sides of cake. Sprinkle cake crumbs evenly over top and sides of cake, pressing lightly to adhere. Carefully remove parchment strips before serving. (Cake can be refrigerated for up to 2 days.)

boston cream pie

serves 10 to 12

pastry cream

2 cups half-and-half

6 large egg yolks, room temperature

½ cup (3½ ounces) sugar

Pinch salt

¼ cup (1¼ ounces) all-purpose flour

4 tablespoons unsalted butter,
cut into 4 pieces and chilled

1½ teaspoons vanilla extract

cake

1½ cups (7½ ounces) all-purpose flour

1½ teaspoons baking powder

¾ teaspoon salt

¾ cup whole milk

6 tablespoons unsalted butter

1½ teaspoons vanilla extract

3 large eggs, room temperature

1½ cups (10½ ounces) sugar

glaze

½ cup heavy cream

2 tablespoons light corn syrup

4 ounces bittersweet chocolate,
chopped fine

why this recipe works Legend has it that Boston cream pie was invented in the 1850s at Boston's landmark Parker House Hotel. A creative baker produced a wildly popular dessert by pouring chocolate glaze onto a cream-filled cake. So why is this dessert called a pie? Food historians theorize that home cooks transferred the concept to the most common form of bakeware in the mid-19th-century kitchen: a pie plate. These days, Boston cream pie is rarely made at home, owing to its reputation as an intimidating recipe with multiple tricky components. That's too bad because when it hits all the right marks, this dessert is supremely satisfying. A hot-milk sponge cake made a good base for our Boston cream pie; it doesn't call for separating eggs or require any finicky folding techniques, making it a streamlined choice. Adding extra egg yolks to the pastry cream thickened it just enough to prevent it from oozing out of the uncoated sides of our cake. Melted chocolate, heavy cream, and a little corn syrup made an incredibly simple, smooth glaze that clung to the top of our pie and dripped invitingly down its sides for the perfect finishing touch.

1 *For the pastry cream* Heat half-and-half in medium saucepan over medium heat until just simmering. Meanwhile, whisk egg yolks, sugar, and salt in bowl until smooth. Add flour and whisk until incorporated. Whisk about ½ cup half-and-half into yolk mixture to temper, then slowly whisk tempered yolk mixture back into remaining half-and-half in saucepan. Continue to cook, whisking constantly, until mixture thickens slightly, about 1 minute. Reduce heat to medium-low and continue to simmer, whisking constantly, for 8 minutes.

2 Increase heat to medium and cook, whisking vigorously, until bubbles burst on surface, 1 to 2 minutes. Off heat, whisk in butter and vanilla until incorporated. Strain pastry cream through fine-mesh strainer set over medium bowl. Press plastic wrap directly on surface. Refrigerate pastry cream until set, at least 2 hours or up to 24 hours.

3 *For the cake* Adjust oven rack to middle position and heat oven to 325 degrees. Grease two 9-inch round cake pans, line with parchment paper, and grease parchment. Whisk flour, baking powder, and salt together in bowl. Heat milk and butter in small saucepan over low heat until butter is melted. Remove from heat, add vanilla, and cover to keep warm.

4 Using stand mixer fitted with whisk attachment, whip eggs and sugar on high speed until light and airy, about 5 minutes. Add hot milk mixture and whisk by hand until incorporated. Add flour mixture and whisk by hand until incorporated.

5 Divide batter evenly between prepared pans. Bake until tops of cakes are light brown and toothpick inserted in center comes out clean, 20 to 22 minutes, switching and rotating pans halfway through baking. Let cakes cool completely in pans on wire rack, about 2 hours. Run thin knife around edges of pans, remove cakes from pans, discarding parchment, and let cool completely on rack.

6 Place 1 cake layer on platter. Whisk pastry cream briefly, then spoon onto center of cake. Using offset spatula, spread evenly to edge. Place second layer on pastry cream, bottom side up, and press lightly on cake to level. Refrigerate cake while preparing glaze.

7 *For the glaze* Bring cream and corn syrup to simmer in small saucepan over medium heat. Remove from heat, add chocolate, and let sit, covered, for 5 minutes. Whisk mixture gently until smooth.

8 Pour glaze onto center of cake. Using offset spatula, spread glaze to edge of cake, letting excess drip down sides. Refrigerate cake for at least 3 hours before serving. (Cake can be refrigerated for up to 24 hours; bring to room temperature before serving.)

How to Pour the Glaze

1 Pour glaze onto center of cake.

2 Using offset spatula, spread glaze to edge of cake, letting excess drip down sides.

Demystifying Corn Syrup

Is Karo corn syrup the same thing as the high-fructose corn syrup ubiquitous in soft drinks and other processed foods? In a word, no. Corn syrup (the most popular brand being Karo, introduced in 1902) is made by adding enzymes to a mixture of cornstarch and water to break the long starch strands into glucose molecules. It's valuable in candy making because it discourages crystallization; it also helps baked goods retain moisture. And corn syrup makes an excellent addition to glazes; it's less sweet than granulated sugar, and it contributes body and sticking power. High-fructose corn syrup (HFCS) is a newer product that came on the market in the 1960s. It's made by putting regular corn syrup through an additional enzymatic process that converts a portion of the glucose molecules into fructose, boosting its sweetness to a level even higher than that of cane sugar. Because HFCS is considerably less expensive than cane sugar, it's widely used in processed foods, but it's not sold directly to consumers. Corn syrup comes in light and dark varieties, with dark corn syrup having a deeper flavor. Manufacturers turn light corn syrup into dark by adding caramel color and a molasses-like product.

blitz torte

serves 10 to 12

filling

1 teaspoon unflavored gelatin

2 tablespoons water

1 cup heavy cream, chilled

1 teaspoon vanilla extract

½ cup lemon curd

10 ounces (2 cups) raspberries

2 tablespoons orange liqueur

1 tablespoon sugar

cake

½ cup whole milk

4 large egg yolks (reserve whites for meringue)

1½ teaspoons vanilla extract

1¼ cups (5 ounces) cake flour

1 cup (7 ounces) sugar

1½ teaspoons baking powder

½ teaspoon salt

12 tablespoons unsalted butter, cut into 12 pieces and softened

meringue

4 large egg whites (reserved from cake)

¼ teaspoon cream of tartar

¾ cup (5¼ ounces) sugar

½ teaspoon vanilla extract

½ cup sliced almonds

why this recipe works The beauty of blitz torte, a dessert created by German American immigrants, is that you get five impressive layers—cake, meringue, fruit-and-cream filling, more cake, and more meringue—for about the same amount of work as a two-layer cake. That's because the recipe is incredibly clever: Each meringue layer is baked directly atop the yellow cake batter. The recipe is also pleasingly symmetrical; the egg yolks go into the cake, while the whites go into the meringue. In order for the meringue and cake to cook through at the same rate, we baked them for almost an hour in a 325-degree oven—a longer time and lower temperature than we normally would for a yellow cake. For our filling, we folded store-bought lemon curd into whipped cream and stabilized it with gelatin before layering it with raspberries, mimicking the silky richness of a custard without making one. The end result is a masterpiece of flavors and textures: tender cake, soft and crisp meringue, crunchy almonds, and creamy fruit filling. Bliss torte is more like it!

1 *For the filling* Sprinkle gelatin over water in small bowl and let sit until gelatin softens, about 5 minutes. Microwave until mixture is bubbling around edges and gelatin dissolves, 15 to 30 seconds. Using stand mixer fitted with whisk attachment, whip cream and vanilla on medium-low speed until foamy, about 1 minute. Increase speed to medium-high and whip until soft peaks form, about 2 minutes. Add gelatin mixture and whip until stiff peaks form, about 1 minute.

2 Whisk lemon curd in large metal bowl to loosen. Gently fold whipped cream mixture into lemon curd. Refrigerate whipped cream filling for at least 1½ hours or up to 3 hours. (Filling may look slightly curdled before assembling cake.)

3 *For the cake* Meanwhile, adjust oven rack to middle position and heat oven to 325 degrees. Grease two 9-inch round cake pans, line with parchment paper, grease parchment, and flour pans.

4 Beat milk, egg yolks, and vanilla together in 2-cup liquid measuring cup with fork. Using clean, dry mixer bowl and paddle, mix flour, sugar, baking powder, and salt on low speed until combined, about 5 seconds. Add butter, 1 piece at a time, and mix until only pea-size pieces remain, about 1 minute. Add half of milk mixture, increase speed to medium-high, and beat until light and fluffy, about 1 minute. Reduce speed to medium-low, add remaining milk mixture, and beat until incorporated, about 30 seconds (batter may look slightly curdled). Give batter final stir by hand. Divide batter evenly between prepared pans and spread into even layer using small offset spatula.

5 *For the meringue* Using clean, dry mixer bowl and whisk attachment and clean, dry mixer bowl, whip egg whites and cream of tartar on medium-low speed until foamy, about 1 minute. Increase speed to medium-high and whip whites to soft, billowy mounds, 1 to 3 minutes.

Gradually add sugar and whip until glossy, stiff peaks form, 3 to 5 minutes. Add vanilla and whip until incorporated.

6 Divide meringue evenly between cake pans and spread evenly over cake batter to edges of pan. Using back of spoon, create peaks in meringue. Sprinkle meringue with almonds. Bake until meringue is golden and has pulled away from sides of pan, 50 to 55 minutes, switching and rotating pans halfway through baking. Let cakes cool completely in pans on wire rack. (Cakes can be stored, uncovered, in pans at room temperature or up to 24 hours.)

7 Ten minutes before assembling cake, gently toss raspberries, liqueur, and sugar together in bowl and let sit, stirring occasionally.

8 Gently remove cakes from pans, discarding parchment. Place 1 cake layer on platter, meringue side up. Spread half of whipped cream filling evenly over top of meringue. Using slotted spoon, spoon raspberries evenly over filling, leaving juice in bowl. Gently spread remaining whipped cream filling over raspberries, covering raspberries completely. Top with second cake layer, meringue side up. Serve cake within 2 hours of assembly.

Making Blitz Torte

1 Divide batter evenly between prepared pans and spread into even layer using small offset spatula.

2 Divide meringue evenly between cake pans and spread evenly over cake batter to edges of pan.

3 Using back of spoon, create peaks in meringue. Sprinkle meringue with almonds.

4 Bake until meringue is golden and has pulled away from sides of pan, 50 to 55 minutes.

5 Gently remove cakes from pans, discarding parchment. Place 1 cake layer on platter, meringue side up.

6 Spread half of whipped cream filling evenly over top of meringue.

7 Using slotted spoon, spoon raspberries evenly over filling, leaving juice in bowl.

8 Gently spread remaining whipped cream filling over raspberries, covering raspberries completely.

9 Top with second cake layer, meringue side up.

italian cream cake

serves 10 to 12

cake

1½ cups (4½ ounces) sweetened shredded coconut, toasted

1 cup buttermilk, room temperature

2 teaspoons vanilla extract

2½ cups (10 ounces) cake flour

2 teaspoons baking powder

½ teaspoon baking soda

¾ teaspoon salt

12 tablespoons unsalted butter, cut into 12 pieces and softened

4 tablespoons shortening, cut into 4 pieces

1¾ cups (12¼ ounces) granulated sugar

5 large eggs, room temperature

2 cups pecans, toasted and chopped

frosting

12 tablespoons unsalted butter, cut into 12 pieces and softened

2¼ cups (9 ounces) confectioners' sugar

½ cup cream of coconut

½ teaspoon vanilla extract

Pinch salt

1 pound cream cheese, cut into 8 pieces and softened

why this recipe works Although the name is a mystery (there's nothing Italian about this cake), the appeal of this Southern beauty is obvious: Sweet coconut and buttery pecans are folded into layers of tender yellow cake which is draped in tangy cream cheese frosting. While coconut is intended to be the star, most of the recipes we found produced weak coconut flavor. To enhance the flavor of toasted shredded coconut, we processed it to a finely ground meal that ensured flavor in every bite. To moisten and soften this meal, we soaked it in buttermilk before adding it to the batter. And cream of coconut gave the frosting flavor. Toasted, chopped pecans provided welcome texture and complementary rich, nutty flavor both in the cake and as a garnish.

1 *For the cake* Adjust oven rack to middle position and heat oven to 350 degrees. Grease two 9-inch round cake pans, line with parchment paper, grease parchment, and flour pans. Process coconut in food processor until finely ground, about 1 minute. Combine coconut, buttermilk, and vanilla in 2-cup liquid measuring cup and let sit until coconut is slightly softened, about 10 minutes; set aside.

2 Combine flour, baking powder, baking soda, and salt in bowl. Using stand mixer fitted with paddle, beat butter, shortening, and sugar on medium-high speed until pale and fluffy, about 3 minutes. Add eggs, one at a time, and beat until combined. Reduce speed to low and add flour mixture in 3 additions, alternating with coconut-buttermilk mixture in 2 additions, scraping down bowl as needed. Add ¾ cup pecans and give batter final stir by hand.

3 Divide batter evenly between prepared pans. Bake until toothpick inserted in center comes out clean, 28 to 32 minutes, switching and rotating pans halfway through baking. Let cakes cool in pans on wire rack for 10 minutes. Remove cakes from pans, discarding parchment, and let cool completely on rack, about 2 hours. (Cake layers can be stored at room temperature for up to 2 days.)

4 *For the frosting* Using stand mixer fitted with paddle, mix butter and sugar on low speed until combined, about 30 seconds. Increase speed to medium-high and beat until pale and fluffy, about 2 minutes. Add cream of coconut, vanilla, and salt and beat until smooth, about 30 seconds. Add cream cheese, 1 piece at a time, and beat until incorporated, about 1 minute. Refrigerate until ready to use.

5 Line edges of cake platter with 4 strips of parchment to keep platter clean. Place 1 cake layer on platter. Spread 1½ cups frosting evenly over top, right to edge of cake. Top with second cake layer, press lightly to adhere, then spread remaining frosting evenly over top and sides of cake. Gently press remaining 1¼ cups pecans onto sides of cake. Carefully remove parchment strips before serving. (Cake can be refrigerated for up to 2 days; bring to room temperature before serving.)

wellesley fudge cake

serves 10 to 12

cake

2½ cups (12½ ounces) all-purpose flour

2 teaspoons baking soda

1 teaspoon baking powder

½ teaspoon salt

¾ cup hot water

½ cup (1½ ounces) unsweetened cocoa powder

16 tablespoons unsalted butter, cut into 16 pieces and softened

2 cups (14 ounces) granulated sugar

2 large eggs

1 cup buttermilk, room temperature

2 teaspoons vanilla extract

frosting

1½ cups packed (10½ ounces) light brown sugar

1 cup evaporated milk

8 tablespoons unsalted butter, cut into 8 pieces and softened

½ teaspoon salt

8 ounces bittersweet chocolate, chopped

1 teaspoon vanilla extract

3 cups (12 ounces) confectioners' sugar, sifted

why this recipe works Roughly a century ago, when the founder of Wellesley College held that "pies, lies, and doughnuts should never have a place in Wellesley College," students honed their fudge-making skills in secret and produced impressive candy, which led to the creation of a slab of fudge-like frosting for their namesake cake. For our version, we started with a base of evaporated milk, butter, and sugar for a frosting similar to fudge. Brown sugar is less likely to crystallize than granulated sugar, so it was our sugar of choice. Stirring in more butter and evaporated milk off the heat prevented the fat in the chocolate from separating and becoming grainy. The addition of a generous amount of confectioners' sugar thickened it to a spreadable consistency.

1 *For the cake* Adjust oven rack to middle position and heat oven to 350 degrees. Grease two 8-inch square cake pans, line with parchment paper, grease parchment, and flour pans. Whisk flour, baking soda, baking powder, and salt together in bowl. Whisk hot water and cocoa in small bowl until smooth; set aside. Using stand mixer fitted with paddle, beat butter and sugar on medium-high speed until pale and fluffy, about 3 minutes. Add eggs, one at a time, and beat until combined. Reduce speed to low and add flour mixture in 3 additions, alternating with buttermilk in 2 additions, scraping down bowl as needed. Slowly add cocoa mixture and vanilla and mix until incorporated. Give batter final stir by hand.

2 Divide batter evenly between prepared pans and smooth tops with rubber spatula. Bake until toothpick inserted in center comes out with few crumbs attached, 25 to 30 minutes, switching and rotating pans halfway through baking. Let cakes cool in pans on wire rack for 15 minutes. Remove cakes from pans, discarding parchment, and let cool completely on rack, about 2 hours.

3 *For the frosting* Heat brown sugar, ½ cup evaporated milk, 4 tablespoons butter, and salt in large saucepan over medium heat until small bubbles appear around perimeter of pan, 4 to 8 minutes. Reduce heat to low and simmer, stirring occasionally, until large bubbles form and mixture has thickened and turned deep golden brown, about 6 minutes; transfer to large bowl. Stir in remaining ½ cup evaporated milk and remaining 4 tablespoons butter until mixture is slightly cool. Add chocolate and vanilla and stir until smooth. Whisk in confectioners' sugar until incorporated. Let cool completely, stirring occasionally, about 1 hour.

4 Line edges of cake platter with 4 strips of parchment to keep platter clean. Place 1 cake layer on platter. Spread 1 cup frosting evenly over top, right to edge of cake. Top with second cake layer, press lightly to adhere, then spread remaining frosting evenly over top and sides of cake. Refrigerate cake until frosting is set, about 1 hour. Carefully remove parchment strips before serving.

bananas foster cake

serves 10 to 12

caramel and banana filling

½ cup dark rum

½ cup packed (3½ ounces) dark brown sugar

Pinch salt

2 tablespoons unsalted butter, chilled

4 ripe bananas

⅛ teaspoon ground cinnamon

frosting

20 tablespoons (2½ sticks) unsalted butter, cut into 20 pieces and softened

⅛ teaspoon salt

2½ cups (10 ounces) confectioners' sugar

¼ cup dark rum

1 teaspoon vanilla extract

3 (8-inch) Yellow Cake Layers (page 394)

why this recipe works Bananas Foster is an American dessert originating in New Orleans. The ingredients are simple—bananas, butter, sugar, rum—but the preparation is spectacular: The rum is ignited and the bananas flambéed, making for an impressive display. Served warm over ice cream, bananas Foster must be made quickly and eaten right away. For a party-friendly version of this dessert that wouldn't require last-minute prep, we decided to make a bananas Foster–inspired layer cake. We cooked up a rum-laced caramel and added sliced bananas to the warm sauce for a cohesive filling that we could sandwich between layers of buttery yellow cake. The addition of a small amount of ground cinnamon—just ⅛ teaspoon—contributed a warm fragrance to the filling. A simple fluffy frosting flavored with a generous dose of rum mimicked the boozy flavor of plated bananas Foster. To finish the cake in dramatic fashion, we topped it with banana slices and butter-enriched caramel, shingling the bananas and letting the caramel drip enticingly down the sides.

1 *For the caramel and banana filling* Cook rum, sugar, and salt in 10-inch skillet over medium-low heat, stirring frequently, until spatula leaves 2-second trail when dragged through sauce, 7 to 10 minutes. Remove caramel from heat. Whisk 3 tablespoons caramel and butter in small bowl until combined; set aside and let cool completely.

2 Peel 2 bananas and cut into ¼-inch slices. Add sliced bananas and cinnamon to remaining warm caramel in skillet and stir gently to combine. Set aside and let cool completely.

3 *For the frosting* Using stand mixer fitted with paddle, beat butter and salt on medium-low speed until smooth, about 10 seconds. Slowly add sugar and continue to mix until smooth, about 2 minutes longer. Add rum and vanilla; mix until incorporated, about 1 minute, scraping down bowl as needed. Increase speed to medium-high and beat frosting until light and fluffy, about 5 minutes.

4 Line edges of cake platter with 4 strips of parchment to keep platter clean. Place 1 cake round on platter. Spread half of banana filling over top. Repeat with 1 more cake layer and remaining filling. Top with remaining cake layer and spread frosting evenly over top and sides of cake. To smooth frosting, run edge of offset spatula around cake sides and over top. Just before serving, peel remaining 2 bananas, cut into ¼-inch slices, and shingle around top edge of cake. Pour reserved caramel-butter mixture over bananas, allowing excess to drip down sides of cake. Carefully remove parchment strips before serving.

peanut butter and jam cake

serves 10 to 12

cake

1 cup whole milk, room temperature

6 large egg whites, room temperature

1 teaspoon vanilla extract

2¼ cups (9 ounces) cake flour

1¾ cups (12¼ ounces) sugar

4 teaspoons baking powder

1 teaspoon salt

12 tablespoons unsalted butter, cut into 12 pieces and softened

frosting

16 tablespoons unsalted butter, cut into 16 pieces and softened

1 cup creamy peanut butter

3 tablespoons heavy cream

1 teaspoon vanilla extract

2 cups (8 ounces) confectioners' sugar

1¼ cups seedless raspberry jam

1 cup dry-roasted peanuts, chopped

why this recipe works Peanut butter and jelly sandwiches are a lunchbox staple for kids all across America, but there's no denying that adults love them equally. Maybe it's nostalgia, or maybe it's the irresistible combination of salty and sweet that's so appealing. No matter the reason, we wanted to turn this classic favorite into a playful dessert for all by trading the white bread for fluffy cake and the peanut butter for rich, creamy frosting. We baked our White Cake Layers (page 395) in square cake pans rather than round ones for a sandwich-inspired look and then cut each layer in half to make four layers. We filled sets of two layers each with a bright raspberry jam. In between the two jam "sandwiches" we spread a thick layer of supercreamy peanut butter frosting that really put the PB in PB and J. To finish, we coated the whole cake in more peanut butter frosting (after all, peanut butter is the best part, right?) and decorated the top with more jam. Covering the sides with chopped peanuts provided a nice crunch. This cake is so good, you'll want to skip lunch.

1 *For the cake* Adjust oven rack to middle position and heat oven to 350 degrees. Grease two 8-inch square baking pans, line with parchment paper, grease parchment, and flour pans. Whisk milk, egg whites, and vanilla together in bowl.

2 Using stand mixer fitted with paddle, mix flour, sugar, baking powder, and salt on low speed until combined. Add butter, 1 piece at a time, until only pea-size pieces remain, about 1 minute. Add all but ½ cup milk mixture, increase speed to medium-high, and beat until light and fluffy, about 1 minute. Reduce speed to medium-low, add remaining ½ cup milk mixture, and beat until incorporated, about 30 seconds (batter may look curdled). Give batter final stir by hand.

3 Divide batter evenly between prepared pans. Bake until toothpick inserted in center comes out clean, about 25 minutes, switching and rotating pans halfway through baking. Let cakes cool in pans on wire rack for 10 minutes. Run thin knife around edges of pans and remove cakes from pan, discarding parchment. Let cakes cool completely on lightly greased rack, about 2 hours.

4 *For the frosting* Using stand mixer fitted with paddle, beat butter, peanut butter, cream, and vanilla on medium-high speed until smooth, about 30 seconds. Reduce speed to medium-low, slowly add sugar, and beat until incorporated and smooth, 1 to 2 minutes. Increase speed to medium-high and whip until light and fluffy, about 5 minutes.

5 Line edges of cake platter with 4 strips of parchment paper to keep platter clean. Using long serrated knife, cut each layer into 2 even layers. Spread each bottom layer with ½ cup jam and replace top. Place 1 filled cake on platter. Spread 1 cup frosting evenly over top, right to edge of cake, and place second filled cake on top. Spread remaining frosting evenly over top and sides of cake. Press peanuts onto sides of cake.

6 Microwave remaining ¼ cup jam in bowl until melted and smooth, about 20 seconds. Transfer to pastry bag or small zipper-lock bag with 1 corner cut off. Pipe jam in straight lines over cake and lightly drag knife through lines to create marbled appearance. Carefully remove parchment strips before serving.

Great American Cakes

minnehaha cake

serves 10 to 12

2½ cups packed (17½ ounces) dark brown sugar

16 tablespoons unsalted butter, cut into 16 pieces and softened

⅔ cup heavy cream

1¼ cups sliced almonds

⅔ cup raisins

3 (8-inch) White Cake Layers (page 395)

why this recipe works Minnehaha cake is named for the fictional princess in Henry Wadsworth Longfellow's famous 1855 poem *Song of Hiawatha*. By the late 1800s, newspapers and cookbooks across the country were publishing recipes for this popular special-occasion dessert. The cake is traditionally a three-layer affair filled with raisins and almonds and topped with a burnt-sugar frosting. We wanted a confection-like frosting with deep caramel flavor; to ensure a frosting with just the right consistency and flavor, we cooked sugar, butter, and cream until the mixture thickened slightly and used a thermometer to monitor the temperature. Grinding raisins and almonds together made for a fairly sticky filling, but it wasn't sticky enough to hold the cake layers together and it tasted dry. Rather than make a cooked filling in addition to our cooked frosting, we found an easy solution: We mixed a small portion of the frosting with the almonds and raisins in the food processor. This step helped bind the coarsely ground ingredients and brought the filling together. Once frosted, we gave our cake an elegant border of sliced almonds around the bottom perimeter, for a cake fit for a princess.

1 Bring sugar, 10 tablespoons butter, and cream to boil in medium saucepan over medium heat. Cook, stirring occasionally, until mixture is slightly thickened and registers 240 degrees. Carefully transfer sugar mixture to bowl of stand mixer fitted with paddle and beat on medium speed until completely cooled, about 15 minutes. Add remaining 6 tablespoons butter, 1 piece at a time, and beat until well incorporated.

2 Pulse ¾ cup almonds, raisins, and 1 cup frosting in food processor until almonds and raisins are coarsely ground.

3 Line edges of cake platter with 4 strips of parchment paper to keep platter clean. Place 1 cake layer on platter. Spread half of filling evenly over top. Repeat with 1 more cake layer, pressing lightly to adhere, and remaining filling. Top with remaining cake layer, pressing lightly to adhere, and spread frosting evenly over top and sides of cake. Decorate bottom of cake with remaining ½ cup almonds. Carefully remove parchment strips before serving.

blackberry jam cake

serves 10 to 12

cake

2 teaspoons ground cinnamon

¼ teaspoon ground allspice

⅛ teaspoon ground cloves

¾ cup seedless blackberry jam

1 cup buttermilk, room temperature

3 tablespoons water

1 teaspoon vanilla extract

3 cups (15 ounces) all-purpose flour

1 tablespoon baking powder

¾ teaspoon salt

20 tablespoons (2½ sticks) unsalted butter, softened

1⅓ cups (9⅓ ounces) granulated sugar

½ cup packed (3½ ounces) light brown sugar

4 large eggs, room temperature

frosting and jam

1½ cups packed (10½ ounces) dark brown sugar

¼ cup (1¼ ounces) all-purpose flour

3 tablespoons cornstarch

½ teaspoon salt

¼ teaspoon baking soda

1½ cups whole milk

2 teaspoons vanilla extract

24 tablespoons (3 sticks) unsalted butter, cut into 24 pieces and softened

¼ cup seedless blackberry jam

1½ cups walnuts, toasted and chopped (optional)

why this recipe works An Appalachian specialty, blackberry jam cake is close kin to spice cake and applesauce cake but gets its sweetness (and some color) from jam stirred directly into the batter. To bring this cake down from the mountains, we started by toasting cinnamon, allspice, and cloves, which gave the cake an aromatic and gently spicy quality without masking the star ingredient: a generous scoop of vibrant blackberry jam. After baking a couple of cakes, we realized that the baking soda we were using for leavening was interacting with the blackberry jam and turning our cake an odd gray-green color. Switching to baking powder gave us better results; the cake was now a pleasant, plummy brown hue. Thinning the jam in the microwave and adding a little water to the batter created a lighter texture. A frosting with notes of caramel complemented our lightly spiced blackberry cake. We mixed milk with the dry ingredients for the frosting, then strained the mixture to eliminate any lumps before boiling it until thickened. Once cooled, we beat in softened butter to transform the pasty mixture into a silken, custard-like frosting. After coating the first layer in frosting, we spread on a layer of jam to reinforce the bright blackberry flavor. Plan ahead, as the frosting needs time to cool.

1 *For the cake* Adjust oven rack to lower-middle position and heat oven to 350 degrees. Grease two 9-inch round cake pans, line with parchment paper, grease parchment, and flour pans. Heat cinnamon, allspice, and cloves in small skillet over medium heat until fragrant, about 1 minute; set aside. Microwave jam in bowl until thin enough to pour, 35 to 45 seconds, stirring halfway through microwaving.

2 Whisk buttermilk, water, and vanilla into jam. Combine flour, baking powder, salt, and toasted spices in large bowl. Using stand mixer fitted with paddle, beat butter, granulated sugar, and brown sugar on medium-high speed until light and fluffy, about 2 minutes. Reduce speed to medium-low and add eggs, one at a time, until incorporated. Add flour mixture in 3 additions, alternating with jam mixture in 2 additions, stopping occasionally to scrape down bowl.

3 Divide batter evenly between prepared pans and smooth tops with rubber spatula. Gently tap pans on counter to release air bubbles. Bake until deep golden brown and toothpick inserted in center comes out clean, 35 to 40 minutes, switching and rotating pans halfway through baking. Let cakes cool in pans on wire rack for 10 minutes. Remove cakes from pans, discarding parchment, and let cool completely on rack, at least 1 hour.

4 *For the frosting and jam* Whisk sugar, flour, cornstarch, salt, and baking soda together in bowl. Slowly whisk in milk until smooth. Strain mixture through fine-mesh strainer into medium saucepan. Cook over medium heat, whisking constantly, until mixture boils and is very thick, 5 to 7 minutes. Transfer milk mixture to clean bowl and let cool completely, about 2 hours.

5 Using stand mixer fitted with whisk attachment, mix cooled milk mixture and vanilla on low speed until combined, about 30 seconds. Add butter, 1 piece at a time, and whip until incorporated, about 2 minutes. Increase speed to medium-high and whip until frosting is light and fluffy, about 5 minutes. Let sit at room temperature until stiff, about 1 hour.

6 Whisk jam in bowl until smooth. Line edges of cake platter with 4 strips of parchment to keep platter clean. Place 1 cake layer on platter. Spread 1½ cups frosting evenly over top, right to edge of cake. Spread jam over frosting, leaving ½-inch border. Top with remaining cake layer and spread remaining frosting evenly over top and sides of cake. Press walnuts, if using, onto sides of cake. Refrigerate cake until set, about 30 minutes. Carefully remove parchment strips before serving. (Frosted cake can be refrigerated for up to 24 hours; bring to room temperature before serving.)

Great American Cakes

lady baltimore cake

serves 10 to 12

sugared pecans

2 cups pecans

2 tablespoons granulated sugar

½ teaspoon kosher salt

1 tablespoon bourbon, rum, or water

1 tablespoon unsalted butter

2 teaspoons vanilla extract

1 teaspoon packed light brown sugar

cake

1 cup dried mixed fruits (any combination of cherries, dates, figs, pineapple, and raisins)

¼ cup pecans, toasted

2 tablespoons bourbon, rum, or water

6 cups Seven-Minute Frosting (page 402)

3 (8-inch) White Cake Layers (page 395)

why this recipe works Statuesque Lady Baltimore cake is dressed to impress, with three layers of tender white cake, stripes of dried fruit and nut filling, and mounds of sticky meringue-like icing. The cake first gained popularity from author Owen Wister's description of it in the 1906 romance novel, *Lady Baltimore*. The book became a best seller, and bakers started making Lady Baltimore cakes based on Wister's description. One hundred years later, Lady Baltimore Cake is still popular in the South, especially around Christmas. But we couldn't find a reputable recipe for the cake, so we decided to develop our own. We started with our favorite white layer cake recipe, which we baked in three 8-inch rounds. For the cake's filling, we ground plenty of dried fruit— using a mixture of fruits gave the filling the most vibrant flavor—with pecans and a little bourbon. This created a sticky, nutty mixture that we blended with some of our frosting to make it easier to spread. Topped with a sweet, seven-minute frosting and decorated with sugared pecans, we now had our own version of Lady Baltimore cake that's sure to be just as popular today as the original was in 1906.

1 *For the sugared pecans* Adjust oven rack to middle position and heat oven to 350 degrees. Spread pecans in even layer on rimmed baking sheet and toast, tossing occasionally, until fragrant and deepened in color, 6 to 8 minutes. While pecans are toasting, stir granulated sugar and salt together in bowl.

2 Bring bourbon, butter, vanilla, and brown sugar to boil in medium saucepan over medium-high heat, whisking constantly. Stir in pecans and cook, stirring constantly, until pecans are shiny and almost all liquid has evaporated, about 1½ minutes.

3 Toss pecans in bowl with sugar-salt mixture, return to sheet, and let cool completely; set aside.

4 *For the cake* Process dried fruits and pecans in food processor until finely chopped, 20 to 30 seconds. Transfer to bowl and mix in bourbon. Stir in 2 cups frosting.

5 Line edges of cake platter with 4 strips of parchment paper to keep platter clean. Place 1 cake layer on platter. Spread half of dried fruit mixture evenly over top. Repeat with 1 more cake layer, pressing lightly to adhere, and remaining dried fruit mixture. Top with remaining cake layer, pressing lightly to adhere. Spread frosting evenly over top and sides of cake, using back of spoon to create attractive swirls and peaks in icing. Decorate with sugared pecans. Carefully remove parchment strips before serving.

blum's coffee crunch

serves 10 to 12

coffee candy

1½ cups (10½ ounces) sugar

¼ cup brewed coffee

¼ cup light corn syrup

1 tablespoon baking soda

cake

1 cup (7 ounces) sugar

1¼ cups (5 ounces) cake flour

1½ teaspoons baking powder

¼ teaspoon salt

5 large eggs (2 whole, 3 separated), room temperature

6 tablespoons unsalted butter, melted and cooled

2 teaspoons vanilla extract

1 teaspoon grated lemon zest plus 2 tablespoons juice

whipped cream

2 cups heavy cream, chilled

6 tablespoons (2⅔ ounces) sugar

1 tablespoon instant espresso powder

1 teaspoon vanilla extract

why this recipe works In the 1970s, no shopping excursion to San Francisco's I. Magnin department store was complete without a stop at its in-house bakery, Blum's, for a slice of cake. The signature concoction marries an unlikely combination: light-as-a-feather lemon chiffon cake with coffee-kissed whipped cream. The unforgettable part of the dessert is the homemade coffee candy that coats the exterior. It's light and crunchy and makes the cake a textural masterpiece. The bakery has been closed for decades, but the iconic cake lives on. We made the candy by adding baking soda to a simple cooked syrup of sugar, coffee, and corn syrup. Once cooled and smashed, the candy pieces are crunchy, crisp, and airy like honeycomb. For an appropriately light and airy lemon cake, we gently folded whipped egg whites into the batter. And we used plenty of egg yolks and butter to ensure that the final cake was rich and tender. Finally, the light and airy frosting was quick and easy: We added espresso powder to whipped cream. This was a retro cake to remember.

1 *For the coffee candy* Grease 8-inch square baking pan and line with parchment paper, allowing excess to overhang pan edges; grease parchment. Heat sugar, coffee, and corn syrup in large saucepan over medium-high heat, stirring occasionally, until mixture registers 310 degrees. Stir in baking soda until incorporated, about 20 seconds (mixture will puff up significantly). Pour mixture into prepared pan and let cool completely, about 1 hour. Once cooled, remove coffee crunch block from pan, place in large zipper-lock bag, and seal. Using rolling pin, crush into bite-size pieces; set aside.

2 *For the cake* Adjust oven rack to lower-middle position and heat oven to 325 degrees. Grease 9-inch round cake pan, line with parchment paper, grease parchment, and flour pan. Set aside 3 tablespoons sugar. Whisk flour, baking powder, salt, and remaining sugar together in large bowl. Add 2 whole eggs and 3 yolks, melted butter, vanilla, and lemon zest and juice and whisk until smooth.

3 Using stand mixer fitted with whisk attachment, whip remaining 3 egg whites on medium-low speed until foamy, about 1 minute. Increase speed to medium-high and whip whites to soft, billowy mounds, about 1 minute. Gradually add reserved sugar and whip until glossy, soft peaks form, 1 to 2 minutes. Using rubber spatula, stir one-third of whites into batter. Gently fold remaining whites into batter until no white streaks remain.

4 Pour batter into prepared pan. Bake until toothpick inserted in center comes out clean, 30 to 40 minutes, rotating pan halfway through baking. Let cake cool in pan on wire rack for 10 minutes. Remove cake from pan, discarding parchment, and let cool completely on rack, about 2 hours.

5 *For the whipped cream* Using stand mixer fitted with whisk attachment, whip cream, sugar, espresso powder, and vanilla on medium-low speed until foamy, about 1 minute. Increase speed to medium-high and whip until stiff peaks form, 1 to 3 minutes.

6 Using long serrated knife, cut 1 horizontal line around sides of cake; then, following scored line, cut cake into 2 even layers. Line edges of cake platter with 4 strips of parchment paper to keep platter clean. Place 1 cake layer on platter. Spread 2 cups frosting evenly over top, right to edge of cake. Top with second cake layer, press lightly to adhere, then spread remaining 2 cups frosting evenly over top and sides of cake. Gently press crushed coffee crunch all over cake. Carefully remove parchment strips before serving.

swiss hazelnut cake

serves 10 to 12

cake

½ cup skin-on hazelnuts, toasted and cooled

1¼ cups (5 ounces) cake flour

1 cup (7 ounces) granulated sugar

1½ teaspoons baking powder

½ teaspoon salt

3 large eggs, separated, plus 2 large whites

½ cup vegetable oil

¼ cup water

2½ teaspoons vanilla extract

¼ teaspoon cream of tartar

frosting

24 tablespoons (3 sticks) unsalted butter, cut into 24 pieces and softened

¼ teaspoon salt

1¾ cups (7 ounces) confectioners' sugar

12 ounces marshmallow crème

2 tablespoons hazelnut liqueur

6 ounces bittersweet chocolate

why this recipe works The Swiss Haus bakery in Philadelphia has sold this sweet, nutty cake since 1923. It features light, airy hazelnut cake; delicate, pillowy vanilla frosting; and a generous garnish of chocolate shavings. The Swiss Haus pastry chef wouldn't disclose the recipe, so we decided to play detective. For full hazelnut flavor, we ground the toasted nuts (with their skins) in a food processor, then substituted this hazelnut "flour" for a portion of the cake flour in our chiffon base. Since meringue buttercream frosting is quite a project, we found an excellent shortcut using marshmallow crème, as we did for our Hazelnut-Chocolate Crêpe Cake (page 168). We developed this recipe with Fluff brand marshmallow crème. To prevent the chocolate for our cake's festive coating from melting as we handled it, we froze the chocolate before and after shaving it and used parchment paper to gently press the shavings into the frosting. When working with the marshmallow crème, grease the inside of your measuring cup and spatula with vegetable oil spray to prevent sticking. Note that the shredding disk should be placed in the freezer for 15 minutes before shaving the chocolate. You may also use a vegetable peeler or the large holes of a box grater to shave the chocolate.

1 *For the cake* Adjust oven rack to middle position and heat oven to 350 degrees. Line two 9-inch round cake pans with parchment paper; grease parchment but not pan sides.

2 Process hazelnuts in food processor until finely ground, about 30 seconds. Whisk flour, sugar, baking powder, salt, and ground hazelnuts together in large bowl. Whisk egg yolks, oil, water, and vanilla together in second bowl. Whisk egg yolk mixture into flour mixture until smooth batter forms.

3 Using stand mixer fitted with whisk attachment, whip egg whites and cream of tartar on medium-low speed until foamy, about 1 minute. Increase speed to medium-high and whip until soft peaks form, 2 to 3 minutes. Gently whisk one-third of whites into batter. Using rubber spatula, gently fold remaining whites into batter until no white streaks remain.

4 Divide batter evenly between prepared pans. Gently tap pans on counter to release air bubbles. Bake until tops are light golden brown and cakes spring back when pressed lightly in center, 25 to 28 minutes, switching and rotating pans halfway through baking.

5 Let cakes cool in pans on wire rack for 15 minutes. Run thin knife around edges of pans. Remove cakes from pan, discarding parchment, and let cool completely on rack, about 1 hour. (To prepare to make chocolate shavings, place food processor shredding disk in freezer.)

6 *For the frosting* Using clean, dry mixer bowl and whisk attachment, mix butter and salt on medium speed until smooth, about 1 minute.

Reduce speed to low and slowly add sugar. Increase speed to medium and whip until smooth, about 2 minutes, scraping down bowl as needed. Add marshmallow crème, increase speed to medium-high, and whip until light and fluffy, 3 to 5 minutes. Reduce speed to low, add hazelnut liqueur, return speed to medium-high, and whip to incorporate, about 30 seconds.

7 Line rimmed baking sheet with parchment paper. Fit food processor with chilled shredding disk. Turn on processor and feed chocolate bar through hopper. Transfer shaved chocolate to prepared baking sheet and spread into even layer. Place in freezer to harden, about 10 minutes.

8 Line edges of cake platter with 4 strips of parchment to keep platter clean. Place 1 cake layer on platter. Spread 2 cups frosting evenly over top, right to edge of cake. Top with remaining cake layer, press lightly to adhere, then spread remaining 2 cups frosting evenly over top and sides of cake.

9 Fold 16 by 12-inch sheet of parchment into 6 by 4-inch rectangle. Using parchment rectangle, scoop up half of chocolate shavings and sprinkle over top of cake. Once top of cake is coated, scoop up remaining chocolate shavings and press gently against sides of cake to adhere, scooping and reapplying as needed. Carefully remove parchment strips before serving.

7

HOLIDAY CAKES

honey cake

serves 12

cake

2½ cups (12½ ounces) all-purpose flour

1¼ teaspoons salt

1 teaspoon baking powder

½ teaspoon baking soda

½ cup water

4 large eggs

6 tablespoons unsweetened applesauce

¼ cup vegetable oil

¼ cup orange juice

1 teaspoon vanilla extract

1¾ cups honey

glaze

1 cup (4 ounces) confectioners' sugar

4½ teaspoons water

1 teaspoon vanilla extract

Pinch salt

why this recipe works Honey cake—besides being a sweet treat that's as good for breakfast as it is for dessert—is a staple at dinners celebrating Rosh Hashanah, the Jewish new year, and serves as a symbol of the sweet year ahead. But all too often the cake tastes predominantly of spices or fruit; shouldn't honey cake taste like honey? After turning out numerous greasy cakes, our first step was to back off on the large amount of oil that most recipes call for. Just ¼ cup of oil and some applesauce did an able job of keeping this cake moist. Adding orange juice (an acid) helped boost the leavening power of the baking soda, ensuring a light cake. For the mild, subtle flavor of the honey to really make its presence known, we needed to use a whopping 1¾ cups; lowering the oven temperature prevented the sweet cake from burning. Make sure to use unsweetened applesauce in this cake. If you plan to make this cake ahead of time, hold off on glazing it until 30 minutes before serving. You'll need 20 ounces of honey for this recipe. You can bake this cake in a decorative 10-cup Bundt pan (for more information, see page 332); place a baking sheet under the Bundt pan.

1 *For the cake* Adjust oven rack to middle position and heat oven to 325 degrees. Spray 12-cup nonstick Bundt pan heavily with baking spray with flour. Whisk flour, salt, baking powder, and baking soda together in large bowl. Whisk water, eggs, applesauce, oil, orange juice, and vanilla in second bowl until combined. Whisk honey into egg mixture until fully incorporated.

2 Whisk honey mixture into flour mixture until combined. Transfer batter to prepared pan. Bake until skewer inserted in center comes out clean, 45 to 55 minutes, rotating pan halfway through baking.

3 Let cake cool in pan on wire rack for 30 minutes. Using small spatula, loosen cake from sides of pan, invert onto rack set in rimmed baking sheet, and remove pan. Let cake cool completely, about 2 hours. (Cake can be wrapped in plastic wrap and stored at room temperature for up to 3 days.)

4 *For the glaze* Whisk sugar, water, vanilla, and salt together in bowl. Drizzle glaze over cooled cake and let set until dry, about 30 minutes, before serving.

maple-pumpkin stack cake

serves 10 to 12

cake

1½ cups (7½ ounces) all-purpose flour

2 teaspoons pumpkin pie spice

1 teaspoon baking powder

1 teaspoon baking soda

1 teaspoon salt

8 tablespoons unsalted butter, melted and cooled

1¼ cups (8¾ ounces) sugar

3 large eggs

1 (15-ounce) can unsweetened pumpkin puree

whipped cream

1½ cups heavy cream, chilled

¼ cup maple syrup

¼ cup pecans, toasted and chopped

why this recipe works While pumpkin pie certainly tastes good, it doesn't exactly make an impressive holiday centerpiece. We wanted a tall-standing cake featuring the flavors of fall that would provide a stunning end to a Thanksgiving feast. We started with four layers of tender, moist cake (which we baked in two batches) and added pumpkin flavor the same way we would for pumpkin pie: with canned pumpkin puree and a couple of teaspoons of pumpkin pie spice. We like our pie served with whipped cream and so we followed suit with this cake, sandwiching the cake layers with a fluffy cream sweetened with maple syrup. Finally, we topped the whole thing off with more maple whipped cream and a sprinkling of crunchy pecans—another favorite ingredient of the season—that we toasted for warm, rich depth. Leaving the sides uncovered made a stunning presentation for this multitiered cake.

1 *For the cake* Adjust oven rack to middle position and heat oven to 350 degrees. Grease two 8-inch round cake pans, line with parchment paper, grease parchment, and flour pans.

2 Whisk flour, pie spice, baking powder, baking soda, and salt together in bowl. Using stand mixer fitted with paddle, beat melted butter, sugar, and eggs on medium-high speed until pale and fluffy, about 3 minutes. Reduce speed to low, add pumpkin, and mix until incorporated. Slowly add flour mixture and mix until only few small flour streaks remain, about 30 seconds.

3 Spread about 1 cup of batter in even layer in each prepared pan. Bake until toothpick inserted in center comes out clean, 12 to 14 minutes, switching and rotating pans halfway through baking. Let cakes cool in pans on wire rack for 10 minutes. Remove cakes from pans, discarding parchment, and let cool completely on lightly greased rack. Reline pans with parchment, grease parchment, and flour pans. Repeat process with remaining batter.

4 *For the whipped cream* Using clean, dry mixer bowl and whisk attachment, whip cream and maple syrup on medium speed until stiff peaks form, about 3 minutes.

5 Place 1 cake round on platter, then spread one-quarter of whipped cream (scant 1 cup) evenly over top. Repeat with remaining cake layers and whipped cream. Sprinkle pecans over top. Serve.

pumpkin roll

serves 8 to 10

cake

1 cup (4 ounces) cake flour, sifted

2 teaspoons pumpkin pie spice

½ teaspoon baking soda

½ teaspoon salt

5 large eggs

1 cup (7 ounces) granulated sugar

1 cup canned unsweetened pumpkin puree

filling

8 tablespoons unsalted butter, softened but still cool

2 cups (8 ounces) confectioners' sugar

8 ounces cream cheese, cut into 4 pieces and softened

1½ teaspoons vanilla extract

8 Spiced Pecans (recipe follows)

Confectioners' sugar

why this recipe works Perhaps the most famous holiday cake is the Yule Log (page 264), which, for good reason, gets trotted out every holiday season. There's much to be said for this classic, but we wanted to develop a unique variation for the holidays with a pumpkin jelly roll cake encasing a simple filling. We initially thought incorporating pumpkin puree into a flexible sponge cake recipe would weigh down the batter, but happily we were wrong. Each additional ¼ cup of puree we introduced did not make the cake heavier; instead, the puree improved the cake's flavor, gave it a moist texture, and made it more flexible. Cream cheese frosting seemed like a natural filling, but it made our cake too dense to roll. We tweaked the ingredient proportions to lighten the texture and then considered whether or not the order in which the ingredients were being mixed together mattered. The answer was yes: The batches in which the butter was blended with the sugar before we added the cream cheese were far lighter because the creamed butter aerated the mix, making it the perfect filling for this festive cake.

1 *For the cake* Adjust oven rack to middle position and heat oven to 350 degrees. Grease 18 by 13-inch rimmed baking sheet, line with parchment paper, and grease parchment. Whisk flour, pie spice, baking soda, and salt together in bowl; set aside. Using stand mixer fitted with paddle, beat eggs and sugar on medium-high speed until pale yellow and thick, 6 to 10 minutes. Add pumpkin, reduce speed to low, and beat until incorporated, about 30 seconds. Fold in flour mixture until combined. Transfer batter to prepared sheet and spread into even layer. Bake until cake is firm and springs back when touched, about 15 minutes. Lay clean sheet of parchment on counter and dust with confectioners' sugar.

2 Immediately run thin knife around edge of baking sheet to loosen cake, then flip hot cake out onto prepared parchment sheet, discarding parchment attached to cake. Starting from short side, roll cake and bottom parchment snugly into log. Let cake cool, seam side down, for 1 hour.

3 *For the filling* Using clean, dry bowl and paddle attachment, beat butter and sugar on medium-high speed until light and fluffy, about 2 minutes. Add cream cheese, 1 piece at a time, beating thoroughly after each addition, about 1 minute. Add vanilla and mix until no lumps remain, about 30 seconds.

4 Gently unroll cake. Spread filling evenly over cake, leaving 1-inch border along edges. Reroll cake gently but snugly around filling, leaving parchment behind as you roll. Wrap cake firmly in plastic wrap and refrigerate for at least 1 hour or up to 2 days. Trim ends of cake, transfer cake to platter, dust with confectioners' sugar, and garnish with Spiced Pecans. Serve. (Cake can be wrapped loosely in plastic and kept at room temperature for up to 8 hours before serving.)

spiced pecans

makes about 5 cups

This recipe makes more nuts than you need to garnish our Pumpkin Roll Cake, but they won't go to waste. (Trust us; they're a delicious snack.) The recipe can easily be doubled. Be sure not to use salted nuts.

1 large egg white
1 tablespoon water
1 teaspoon salt
4 cups (1 pound) pecans
¾ cup sugar
2 teaspoons ground cinnamon
1 teaspoon ground ginger
1 teaspoon ground coriander

1 Adjust oven racks to upper-middle and lower-middle positions and heat oven to 300 degrees. Line 2 rimmed baking sheets with parchment paper. Whisk egg white, water, and salt together in large bowl. Add pecans and toss to coat. Let drain in colander for 5 minutes.

2 Mix sugar, cinnamon, ginger, and coriander in large bowl. Add drained pecans and toss to coat. Spread pecans evenly on prepared baking sheet and bake until dry and crisp, 40 to 45 minutes, switching and rotating sheets halfway through baking. Let pecans cool completely. Break pecans apart and serve. (Pecans can be stored at room temperature for up to 3 weeks.)

yule log

serves 8 to 10

bark

12 ounces semisweet chocolate
(9 ounces chopped fine, 3 ounces grated)

ganache

6 ounces semisweet chocolate, chopped

¾ cup heavy cream

2 tablespoons unsalted butter

1 tablespoon cognac

filling

6 tablespoons (1½ ounces)
confectioners' sugar

2 tablespoons heavy cream

1 teaspoon instant espresso powder

1 pound (2 cups) mascarpone cheese,
room temperature

cake

6 ounces semisweet chocolate,
chopped fine

2 tablespoons unsalted butter,
cut into 2 pieces

2 tablespoons water

¼ cup (1¼ ounces) all-purpose flour

¼ cup (¾ ounce) Dutch-processed
cocoa powder

¼ teaspoon baking powder

⅛ teaspoon salt

6 large eggs, separated, room temperature

⅛ teaspoon cream of tartar

⅓ cup (2⅓ ounces) granulated sugar

1 teaspoon vanilla extract

why this recipe works A *bûche de Noël*, or yule log, is a classic French dessert that's popular in many countries. The roulade (rolled) shape mimics that of the yule logs burned in fireplaces on Christmas Day. We achieved a not-too-sweet chocolate roulade with a velvety texture using semisweet chocolate, plenty of eggs, and a combination of cocoa and flour for structural support. To complement the rich chocolate cake, we created a filling of whipped mascarpone cheese flavored with espresso and a chocolate ganache coating. Finally, for a modern twist on decorating, we made a thin chocolate bark and broke it into shards to cover our log. For a more intense chocolate flavor, you can use bittersweet chocolate in place of the semisweet for the cake, ganache, and bark. We had the best luck using BelGioioso Mascarpone; some mascarpones are runnier, and you may have to whisk them vigorously before using them. To serve, cut into diagonal slices with a serrated knife.

1 *For the bark* Adjust oven rack to upper-middle position and heat oven to 400 degrees. Line rimmed baking sheet with parchment paper. Microwave finely chopped chocolate in bowl at 50 percent power, stirring every 15 seconds, until melted but not much hotter than body temperature (check by holding bowl in the palm of your hand), 2 to 3 minutes. Add grated chocolate and stir until smooth and chocolate is completely melted (returning to microwave for no more than 5 seconds at a time to finish melting if necessary). Pour chocolate directly onto prepared sheet and spread to edges using small, offset spatula. Drag tines of fork through warm chocolate to make abstract bark pattern. Refrigerate until chocolate is set, at least 30 minutes.

2 *For the ganache* Microwave chocolate, cream, butter, and cognac in bowl at 50 percent power, stirring occasionally, until melted and smooth, about 2 minutes. Measure out 3 tablespoons into small bowl and set aside to cool slightly. Set aside remaining ganache and let cool completely, about 30 minutes.

3 *For the filling* Whisk sugar, cream, espresso powder, and reserved 3 tablespoons ganache together in bowl. Stir mascarpone with rubber spatula in second bowl until softened and smooth, then stir in confectioners' sugar mixture; refrigerate until needed.

4 *For the cake* Grease 18 by 13-inch rimmed baking sheet, line with parchment paper, and grease parchment. Microwave chocolate, butter, and water in large, shallow bowl at 50 percent power, stirring occasionally until chocolate and butter have melted and mixture is smooth and glossy, about 1 minute; set aside to cool slightly.

5 Whisk flour, cocoa, baking powder, and salt together in small bowl; set aside. Using stand mixer fitted with whisk attachment, whip egg whites and cream of tartar on medium-low speed until foamy, about 1 minute. Increase speed to medium-high and whip whites to soft, billowy mounds, about 1 minute. Gradually add sugar and vanilla and whip until glossy, stiff peaks form, 2 to 3 minutes. Do not overwhip.

6 While whites are whipping, stir egg yolks into cooled chocolate-water mixture. Whisk one-quarter of whites into chocolate mixture. Using rubber spatula, gently fold remaining whites into chocolate mixture until almost no white streaks remain. Sprinkle cocoa mixture over top of batter and fold in quickly but gently until just incorporated and no dry flour remains. Pour batter into prepared baking sheet and, working quickly, level surface and smooth batter into sheet corners with offset spatula. Bake until center of cake springs back when touched, 8 to 10 minutes, rotating sheet halfway through baking. Invert second baking sheet, grease bottom lightly, and line with parchment.

7 Immediately run thin knife around edge of baking sheet to loosen cake. Working quickly while cake is warm, place second baking sheet on top, parchment side down, and gently flip pans over, discarding parchment attached to cake. Starting from long side, roll cake and bottom parchment into log. Let cake cool, seam side down, for 15 minutes.

8 Gently unroll cake. Stir filling to loosen, then spread evenly over cake, leaving 1-inch border along bottom edge. Reroll cake around filling, leaving parchment behind as you roll. Using long slicing knife, trim both uneven ends of cake on diagonal; set aside. Line edges of platter with 4 strips of parchment paper to keep platter clean. Transfer cake to platter. Dollop 1 tablespoon ganache off-center on top of log and place 1 cut end piece flat edge down on top of log. Using small offset spatula, gently spread remaining ganache over all of cake, covering ends of log, but leaving top stump edge exposed.

9 Gently break chilled chocolate bark into 1- to 3-inch shards. Press shards gently into ganache, overlapping slightly, covering entire cake; refrigerate, uncovered, until ganache has set, about 20 minutes, before serving. (Cake can be refrigerated for up to 24 hours; let cake stand at room temperature for 30 minutes before serving.)

Assembling Yule Log

1 Using long slicing knife, trim both uneven ends of cake on diagonal; set aside.

2 Dollop 1 tablespoon ganache off-center on top of log. Place 1 cut end piece flat edge down on top of log.

3 Using small offset spatula, gently spread remaining ganache over all of cake, covering ends of log, but leaving top stump edge exposed.

4 Gently break chilled chocolate bark into 1- to 3-inch shards. Press shards gently into ganache, overlapping slightly, covering entire cake.

apricot and cherry modern fruitcake

serves 10 to 12

cake

1½ cups (9 ounces) dried apricots (1 cup chopped fine, ½ cup halved crosswise)

¼ cup dark rum

1 cup dried cherries

1 cup (5 ounces) all-purpose flour

1¼ teaspoons baking powder

¾ teaspoon salt

½ cup packed (3½ ounces) light brown sugar

⅓ cup (2⅓ ounces) granulated sugar

2 large eggs, room temperature

8 tablespoons unsalted butter, melted and cooled

1½ teaspoons vanilla extract

1 teaspoon grated lemon zest

1 teaspoon grated orange zest

¾ cup walnuts, toasted and chopped

soak and glaze

⅓ cup dark rum

2 tablespoons orange juice

2 tablespoons apricot jam

why this recipe works Fruitcake gets a bad rap because so many versions are dense, dry, and laden with artificially colored and sickly sweet candied fruit. We wanted an updated, more refined take on this stodgy cake, with complementary fruits, balanced booziness, and a moist but not overly dense texture. To do away with the neon-colored glacé fruits of cakes past, we landed on a combination of tart dried cherries and sweet apricots; as the fruit cooked in the cake they turned translucent, giving them a naturally glacéed effect. We made a rich, sturdy batter that was able to support a full 2 cups of fruit as well as ¾ cup of crunchy walnuts. Orange and lemon zest and vanilla rounded out the flavors. We found that a small amount of rum in the batter along with a rum and orange juice soak gave us the boozy flavor we were looking for without being harsh or making the cake soggy. As a decorative touch we laid halved pieces of dried apricots around the bottom of the pan before pouring in the batter so that the finished cake would have a festive fruit crown, and we finished it with a simple apricot glaze.

1 *For the cake* Adjust oven rack to middle position and heat oven to 350 degrees. Grease 8-inch round cake pan, line with parchment paper, grease parchment, and flour pan. Arrange halved apricots cut side down, perpendicular to pan edge, in tightly packed ring around bottom of pan. Microwave rum in bowl until steaming, about 30 seconds, stir in chopped apricots and cherries and let sit for 20 minutes, stirring once halfway through cooling.

2 Whisk flour, baking powder, and salt together in bowl. Whisk brown sugar, granulated sugar, and eggs in large bowl until thoroughly combined and thick, about 45 seconds. Slowly whisk in melted butter until combined. Whisk in vanilla, lemon zest, and orange zest. Gently whisk in flour mixture until just combined. Using rubber spatula, fold in rum-soaked fruits and walnuts.

3 Pour batter into prepared pan and smooth top with rubber spatula. Bake until deep golden brown and skewer inserted in center comes out clean, 55 minutes to 1 hour 5 minutes, rotating pan halfway through baking. Let cake cool in pan on wire rack for 5 minutes. Run thin knife around edge of pan to loosen cake, invert cake onto wire rack set in rimmed baking sheet, and remove pan.

4 *For the soak and glaze* Combine rum and orange juice in bowl and microwave until steaming and fragrant, about 30 seconds. Measure out 2 tablespoons rum mixture and whisk with apricot jam. Strain mixture through fine-mesh strainer into small bowl, discarding solids, and set apricot glaze aside. Using skewer, poke 15 to 20 holes over cake. Brush warm cake with remaining rum mixture and let cool completely, at least 3 hours. Brush apricot glaze over cake and let sit for 10 minutes. Serve. (Cooled cake and glaze can be wrapped tightly in plastic wrap, separately, and stored at room temperature for up to 1 week. Brush with apricot glaze just before serving.)

Assembling Fruitcake

1 Arrange halved apricots cut side down, perpendicular to pan edge, in tightly packed ring around bottom of pan.

2 Pour batter into prepared pan and smooth top with rubber spatula.

Dried Apricots

You can purchase either Californian or Mediterranean apricots that are sulfured or unsulfured at the supermarket. What's the difference? We tend to like Mediterranean apricots in cooking and baking (unless a recipe specifies the California variety). They're less expensive and more widely available, and most recipes calling for dried apricots are designed to work with their plump, juicy sweetness. California apricots are more tart and chewy—good attributes for eating out of hand (and we prefer them for this), but not quite as great for cooked applications. Their chewiness comes from the fact that they're halved before drying.

Most of the apricots you find are sulfured, that is, treated with sulfur dioxide to preserve their sunny color and extend their shelf life by fighting the development of mold. The sulfur dioxide does so by drastically slowing the activity of an enzyme in the apricots called polyphenol oxidase, which oxidizes other compounds in the plant tissue and creates brown/gray pigments. We've found unsulfured apricots to be chewier and blander than sulfured, although they work well in baking with their molasses notes. However, here the apricots adorn our Apricot and Cherry Modern Fruitcake like jewels on a crown—they look nice when brilliantly orange. For that aesthetic reason, we prefer sulfured apricots.

Sulfured   *Unsulfured*

eggnog bundt cake

serves 12

3 cups (15 ounces) all-purpose flour

1 teaspoon salt

1 teaspoon baking powder

½ teaspoon baking soda

¾ cup buttermilk, room temperature

1 tablespoon vanilla extract

1 tablespoon lemon juice

18 tablespoons unsalted butter,
cut into 18 pieces and softened

2 cups (14 ounces) granulated sugar

3 large eggs plus 1 large yolk,
room temperature

¼ cup dark rum or brandy

1 teaspoon ground nutmeg

¼ teaspoon ground cinnamon

1½ cups (6 ounces) confectioners' sugar

why this recipe works Bundt cake's rich stores of butterfat, sugar, and eggs mean it retains its moisture and therefore keeps well, making it just the thing to have at the ready during a busy December. We wanted to create a seasonal version that featured the flavors of one of the holidays' most ubiquitous traditions: eggnog. But simply pouring eggnog into the batter didn't make the cake taste like eggnog. We were better off separating the ingredients that make eggnog unique and focusing on how to lengthen their influence. Freshly ground nutmeg and a tablespoon of rum hit the right notes and were a good starting point; rather than simply add them to our buttermilk-based batter, we swirled them into a portion of the batter for a ribbon of flavor that spiced and sweetened the cake. A simple glaze of confectioners' sugar and rum pointed up the flavors. For the best results, use dark rum (or brandy). We recommend that you grind your own nutmeg for this cake. You can bake this cake in a decorative 10-cup Bundt pan (for more information, see page 332); place a baking sheet under the Bundt pan.

1 Adjust oven rack to lower-middle position and heat oven to 350 degrees. Spray 12-cup nonstick Bundt pan with baking spray with flour.

2 Whisk flour, salt, baking powder, and baking soda together in bowl. Whisk buttermilk, vanilla, and lemon juice together in small bowl.

3 Using stand mixer fitted with paddle, beat butter and granulated sugar on medium-high speed until pale and fluffy, about 3 minutes. Add eggs and yolk, one at a time, and beat until combined. Reduce speed to low and add flour mixture in 3 additions, alternating with buttermilk mixture in 2 additions, scraping down bowl as needed. Give batter final stir by hand.

4 Combine 1 cup cake batter, 1 tablespoon rum, nutmeg, and cinnamon in large bowl and stir until just combined. Using rubber spatula, spread remaining batter in prepared pan and smooth top. Spoon spiced batter over top and spread gently in thin, even layer. Bake until skewer inserted in center comes out with few moist crumbs attached, 50 minutes to 1 hour, rotating pan halfway through baking. Let cake cool in pan on wire rack for 25 minutes. Invert cake onto wire rack set in rimmed baking sheet, remove pan, and let cool completely on rack, about 3 hours.

5 Whisk confectioners' sugar and remaining 3 tablespoons rum in bowl until smooth. Drizzle glaze over cooled cake and let set for 25 minutes before serving.

chocolate-peppermint cake

serves 10 to 12

8 ounces white chocolate

5 cups Vanilla Frosting (page 398)

1¾ cups finely ground peppermint candies, plus 6 whole candies for garnish

3 (8-inch) Chocolate Cake Layers (page 395)

why this recipe works Chocolate and peppermint are a classic holiday flavor pairing, so we wanted to dress up a chocolate layer cake for the season with peppermint candies. We knew the icing would need to be substantial enough to support a coating of crushed candies, but we also wanted it to taste good. A white chocolate icing provided a sweet complement to the peppermint, but it wasn't thick enough to hold the coating. To get a frosting with the right amount of body, we simply stirred some melted white chocolate into our trusty Vanilla Frosting. But we only added white chocolate to half of the frosting, which we used to spread on the top and sides of the cake; to the rest we added a generous amount of ground peppermint candies and used this frosting to fill the cake. To finish, we piped beautiful rosettes of white chocolate icing around the top of the cake and topped each one with a single round peppermint candy. For an accurate measurement of boiling water, bring a full kettle of water to a boil and then measure out the desired amount. For this recipe, we used about 76 round peppermint candies: six for the garnish and 70 for the cake's two other peppermint uses (the filling and the coating).

1 Microwave white chocolate in bowl at 50 percent power, stirring occasionally, until melted and smooth, 1 to 3 minutes; let cool. Divide frosting evenly between 2 bowls. Stir white chocolate into 1 portion of frosting. Stir ¾ cup ground peppermints into remaining frosting.

2 Line edges of cake platter with 4 strips of parchment paper to keep platter clean. Place 1 cake layer on platter. Spread half of peppermint frosting evenly over top, right to edge of cake. Repeat with 1 more cake layer, press lightly to adhere, and then spread with remaining peppermint frosting. Top with remaining cake layer, pressing lightly to adhere.

3 Set aside ¾ cup white chocolate frosting; spread remaining white chocolate frosting evenly over top and sides of cake. Gently press remaining 1 cup ground peppermints onto cake sides and sprinkle evenly over top. Carefully remove parchment strips. Using remaining white chocolate icing, pipe ring of dots around base of cake and pipe 6 rosettes on top of cake (for more information on decorating cakes, see page 29). Place 1 whole peppermint candy on each rosette. Serve.

gingerbread layer cake

serves 12 to 16

1¾ cups (8¾ ounces) all-purpose flour

¼ cup (¾ ounce) unsweetened cocoa powder

2 tablespoons ground ginger

1½ teaspoons baking powder

1 teaspoon ground cinnamon

¾ teaspoon salt

½ teaspoon ground white pepper

⅛ teaspoon cayenne pepper

1 cup brewed coffee

¾ cup molasses

½ teaspoon baking soda

1½ cups (10½ ounces) sugar

¾ cup vegetable oil

3 large eggs, lightly beaten

2 tablespoons finely grated fresh ginger

5 cups Miracle Frosting (page 404)

¼ cup chopped crystallized ginger (optional)

why this recipe works Good gingerbread is dark and moist, with an intriguing hint of bitterness and a peppery finish. Usually it's a rustic square cake or maybe even an attractive Bundt (see page 348), but it's never quite sophisticated enough to serve as the centerpiece holiday dessert. We wanted to transform homey gingerbread into a stately layer cake. The problem? Traditional recipes are too moist to be stacked four layers high. We knew we could fix the excess moisture problem by cutting back on the molasses or coffee in our recipe or adding a bit more flour. But both strategies would lighten the color and dull the flavor. Instead, we added a conventional cake ingredient that's unconventional in gingerbread: cocoa powder. Cocoa contains a high proportion of absorbent starch; just ¼ cup of it soaked up the cake's excess moisture, so the crumb was no longer objectionably sticky. The cocoa also deepened the color and flavor of our gingerbread without making the cake taste chocolaty. As a bonus, it diluted some of the gluten, making the cake's crumb more tender. For the frosting, the usual cream cheese variety seemed too ordinary, so we took the opportunity to use our Miracle Frosting; it formed an extremely lush, silky coating and its simple flavor let the spicy cake shine. Sprinkling chopped crystallized ginger over the top of the cake completed the holiday gingerbread revamp. Use a 2-cup liquid measuring cup to portion the cake batter. Do not use blackstrap molasses here as it is too bitter.

1 Adjust oven rack to middle position and heat oven to 350 degrees. Grease and flour two 8-inch round cake pans and line pans with parchment paper. Whisk flour, cocoa, ground ginger, baking powder, cinnamon, salt, pepper, and cayenne together in large bowl. Whisk coffee, molasses, and baking soda in second large bowl until combined. Add sugar, oil, eggs, and fresh ginger to coffee mixture and whisk until smooth.

2 Whisk coffee mixture into flour mixture until smooth. Pour 1⅓ cups batter into each prepared pan. Bake until toothpick inserted in center comes out clean, 12 to 14 minutes. Let cakes cool in pans on wire rack for 10 minutes. Remove cakes from pan, discarding parchment, and let cool completely on rack, about 2 hours. Wipe pans clean with paper towels. Let pans cool completely, regrease and reflour pans, and line with fresh parchment. Repeat process with remaining batter.

3 Line edges of cake platter with 4 strips of parchment to keep platter clean. Place 1 cake layer on platter. Spread ¾ cup frosting evenly over top, right to edge of cake. Repeat with 2 more cake layers, pressing lightly to adhere and spreading ¾ cup frosting evenly over each layer. Top with remaining cake layer and spread remaining frosting evenly over top and sides of cake. Garnish top of cake with crystallized ginger, if using. Refrigerate until frosting is set, about 30 minutes, before serving. (Cake can be refrigerated for up to 2 days; bring to room temperature before serving.)

hot cocoa cake

serves 10 to 12

filling

1 teaspoon unflavored gelatin

¼ cup water

6 tablespoons unsalted butter, cut into 6 pieces and softened

1 teaspoon vanilla extract

Pinch salt

2 cups marshmallow crème

frosting

½ cup (3 ounces) white chocolate chips

1½ cups heavy cream

3 tablespoons Dutch-processed cocoa powder, plus extra for dusting

3 (8-inch) Chocolate Cake Layers (page 395)

24 large marshmallows

why this recipe works Reminiscent of a steaming-hot mug of cocoa on a cold winter morning, this rich layer cake gets its name from the combination of chocolate cake and marshmallow filling. We knew making a marshmallow filling could be a challenge—meringues and other marshmallow-like confections involve cooking and closely monitoring a sugar mixture on the stove—so we wanted to find a way to make it easier. For a foolproof filling, we settled on marshmallow crème, which we stabilized with gelatin. But on its own this mixture was too sticky and cloying. Stirring in some butter and vanilla added creaminess and welcome flavor. We love a dollop of whipped cream on our mug of cocoa so we figured a whipped cream frosting would be the perfect complement to this rich cake. We enhanced the whipped cream with cocoa powder and white chocolate for a stable, flavorful, and ultracreamy frosting. To finish, we topped the cake off just like the drink, with a garnish of marshmallows and a dusting of cocoa.

1 *For the filling* Sprinkle gelatin over water in large bowl and let sit until gelatin softens, about 5 minutes. Microwave until mixture is bubbling around edges and gelatin dissolves, about 15 seconds. Stir in butter, vanilla, and salt until combined. Let mixture cool until just warm to touch, about 5 minutes. Whisk in marshmallow crème until smooth; refrigerate filling until firm enough to spread, about 30 minutes.

2 *For the frosting* Place chocolate chips in small bowl. Bring ½ cup cream and cocoa to simmer in small saucepan over medium-high heat, whisking until smooth. Pour cream mixture over chocolate chips and whisk until melted and smooth. Let chocolate mixture cool completely, about 30 minutes. Using stand mixer fitted with whisk attachment, whip remaining 1 cup cream with cooled chocolate mixture on medium-high speed until soft peaks form, 1 to 1½ minutes.

3 Line edges of cake platter with 4 strips of parchment paper to keep platter clean. Place 1 cake layer on platter. Spread half of filling evenly over top. Repeat with 1 more cake layer, press lightly to adhere, then spread with remaining filling. Top with remaining cake layer, pressing lightly to adhere. Spread frosting evenly over top and sides of cake. To smooth frosting, run edge of offset spatula around cake sides and over top. Arrange marshmallows on top of cake in large mound. Dust with extra cocoa. Serve.

chocolate-raspberry heart cake

Serves 10 to 12

cake

1¼ cups (6¼ ounces) all-purpose flour

¾ cup (2¼ ounces) unsweetened cocoa powder

½ teaspoon baking soda

¼ teaspoon salt

8 ounces semisweet chocolate, chopped

12 tablespoons unsalted butter

1½ cups (10½ ounces) sugar

1 cup buttermilk

4 large eggs

1 teaspoon vanilla extract

frosting

7½ ounces (1½ cups) fresh or thawed frozen raspberries, plus about 20 fresh raspberries

8 ounces white chocolate, chopped

1½ cups (10½ ounces) sugar

6 large egg whites

⅛ teaspoon salt

24 tablespoons (3 sticks) unsalted butter, cut into 24 pieces and softened

,

why this recipe work We wanted to create a special, heart-shaped cake made with the classic Valentine's Day pairing of chocolate and raspberry. And while we knew we could probably find a flimsy heart-shaped cake pan at a craft store, we generally avoid purchasing single-use kitchen items. We wanted to put our love into a Valentine's Day dessert with pans we already had at home. We made enough chocolate cake batter to fit into one 8-inch square and one 8-inch round pan. We leveled the cakes after baking to make sure they were the same height and simply cut the round cake in half vertically to create two ears to attach to two adjacent sides of the square. We thought a pink frosting would be a festive touch, and we knew we didn't need to use food coloring to get there. Instead, we made a classic buttercream and stirred in fresh raspberry puree as well as white chocolate for a silky, fruity accompaniment to the rich chocolate cake. Piping pink roses over the cake and dotting it with whole fresh raspberries were beautiful finishing touches. All that was left to do was enjoy this cake with our loved ones.

1 *For the cake* Adjust oven rack to middle position and heat oven to 325 degrees. Grease 8-inch square baking pan and 8-inch round cake pan, line each with parchment paper, grease parchment, and flour pans.

2 Sift flour, cocoa, baking soda, and salt together in bowl. Microwave chocolate and butter in second bowl at 50 percent power, stirring occasionally, until melted, 2 to 4 minutes. Whisk sugar, buttermilk, eggs, and vanilla together in third large bowl.

3 Whisk chocolate mixture into sugar mixture until combined. Whisk in flour mixture until smooth. Divide batter evenly between prepared pans and bake until toothpick inserted in center of each cake comes out clean, 35 to 45 minutes, switching and rotating pans halfway through baking. Let cakes cool in pans on wire rack for 10 minutes. Run thin knife around edge of pans, remove cakes from pans, discarding parchment, and let cool completely on rack, about 1 hour.

4 *For the frosting* Process 1½ cups raspberries in food processor until smooth, about 30 seconds. Strain puree through fine-mesh strainer into bowl; discard solids and set aside puree. Microwave chocolate in bowl at 50 percent power, stirring occasionally, until melted and smooth, 1 to 2 minutes; let cool slightly. Combine sugar, egg whites, and salt in bowl of stand mixer. Set bowl over saucepan filled with 1 inch barely simmering water, making sure that water does not

touch bottom of bowl. Cook, whisking constantly, until mixture reaches 160 degrees, 5 to 8 minutes. Remove bowl from heat and transfer to stand mixer fitted with whisk attachment. Whip warm egg mixture on medium-high speed until stiff peaks form, about 5 minutes. Reduce speed to medium-low and add butter, 1 piece at a time, and whip until smooth and creamy, about 2 minutes. Add chocolate and mix until just combined. Slowly add raspberry puree and mix until incorporated.

5 Place 1 corner of square cake against lower edge of large (about 16-inch diameter) cake plate or pedestal. Using serrated knife, shave domed top from round cake to make it level with square cake; discard top. Cut round cake in half. Place halves, with cut sides facing in, against top 2 edges of square cake to form heart shape. Spread 2½ cups frosting over top and sides of cake in thin, even layer. Fill pastry bag fitted with star tip with remaining frosting and pipe roses (spiraling from inside out) over top and sides of cake. Place fresh raspberries between roses. Serve.

king cake

serves 12

1 cup plus scant 3 tablespoons whole milk

3 large eggs

8 tablespoons unsalted butter, melted

4½ cups (22½ ounces) all-purpose flour

½ cup (3½ ounces) granulated sugar

2¼ teaspoons instant or rapid-rise yeast

1 teaspoon salt

1¼ cups pecans, toasted and ground fine

¾ cup packed (5¼ ounces) light brown sugar

2 teaspoons ground cinnamon

1 miniature porcelain toy baby (optional)

2 cups (8 ounces) confectioners' sugar

1 tablespoon each yellow, green, and purple sanding sugars

why this recipe works This festive cake, which makes an appearance during Carnival season in New Orleans, is made from rich brioche-like dough and filled with a buttery cinnamon sugar accented with ground pecans. Traditional versions place a small plastic baby in the cake; good luck goes to the one who finds the toy. Baking this cake free-form is common but we found it was difficult to get the yeasted dough to hold in the traditional ring shape, so we decided to make ours in a Bundt pan. Once the dough was formed and had risen once, we rolled it into a rectangle, covered the rectangle with our filling, and rolled it into a log; we then connected the ends to form a ring, and set it in the pan to rise once more. The Bundt pan ensured the dough maintained a nice, even shape. We adorned the baked cake with a simple glaze and decorative bands of purple, green, and gold sanding sugar. For a traditional touch, roll the optional toy baby with the filling.

1 Whisk 1 cup milk, eggs, and melted butter together in bowl of stand mixer. Stir in flour, granulated sugar, yeast, and salt until just combined. Fit stand mixer with dough hook and mix on medium-low speed for 10 minutes. Transfer dough to greased large bowl, cover tightly with plastic wrap, and let rise at room temperature until doubled in size, 1½ to 2 hours.

2 Spray 12-cup nonstick Bundt pan with baking spray with flour. Combine pecans, brown sugar, and cinnamon in bowl. Roll dough into 18 by 14-inch rectangle on lightly floured counter, with long side parallel to counter edge. Spray lightly with water and sprinkle evenly with pecan mixture. Place baby, if using, along bottom edge of dough. Roll dough away from you into log and pinch along seam to seal. Form into ring and seal ends together. Place ring, seam side up, in prepared pan; cover loosely with plastic and let rise at room temperature until doubled in size, about 1 hour. Adjust oven rack to middle position and heat oven to 350 degrees.

3 Bake until deep golden brown and cake registers 190 degrees, 30 to 35 minutes, rotating pan halfway through baking. Let cake cool in pan on wire rack for 10 minutes. Invert cake onto wire rack, remove pan, and let cool completely on rack, about 2 hours.

4 Whisk confectioners' sugar and remaining scant 3 tablespoons milk in bowl until smooth. Drizzle glaze over cooled cake, letting it run down sides of cake. Sprinkle cake top with half of yellow sugar in band, then repeat on opposite side. Repeat sprinkling with green and purple sugars to form alternating bands of color. Serve.

flag cake

serves 12 to 15

Yellow Sheet Cake (page 105)

5 cups Vanilla Frosting (page 398)

5 ounces (1 cup) blueberries

15 ounces (3 cups) raspberries

why this recipe works A big flag sheet cake is the perfect Fourth of July dessert; and at a time when patriotic-colored berries are at their best, vibrant blueberries and red raspberries are a fitting topping. We knew that our work-horse Yellow Sheet Cake was the ideal base for the cake, so our challenge when developing this recipe was simply determining the best frosting. Whipped cream, the most common topping for this summer cake, had little staying power and the juicy berries bled into the cream. A simple American buttercream in the form of our Vanilla Frosting worked much better and ably glued the stars and stripes to the cake. Once our cake was topped with berries, we were able to bring the flag to the table. You may have extra frosting after coating the tops and sides of the cake. Wait until a few hours before serving to arrange the berries to ensure that they taste fresh at serving time.

1 Line edges of cake platter with 4 strips of parchment to keep platter clean. Place cake on platter. Spread frosting evenly over top and sides of cake. Using blueberries, outline 6 by 4½-inch rectangle in top left corner of cake. Make diagonal rows of blueberries within outline, leaving single blueberry's width between rows. Lay additional blue-berries evenly between rows to make blueberry checkerboard. Gently press blueberries to adhere.

2 For red stripes, lay raspberries on their side and gently nestle them next to one another. There should be 4 short rows of raspberry stripes across top of cake and 3 long rows of raspberry stripes across bottom of cake. Gently press raspberries to adhere. Serve.

Decorating Flag Cake

1 Outline 6 by 4½-inch rectangle of blueberries in top left corner of cake.

2 Make diagonal rows of blueberries within outline, leaving single blueberry's width between rows.

3 Lay additional blueberries evenly between rows to make blueberry checkerboard.

4 Lay raspberries on their side and gently nestle them next to one another.

patriotic poke cake

serves 10 to 12

1 cup (5 ounces) blueberries

1¼ cups water

¼ cup (1¾ ounces) sugar

2 tablespoons berry-flavored gelatin

7½ ounces (1½ cups) strawberries, hulled

1 tablespoon strawberry-flavored gelatin

2 (9-inch) White Cake Layers (page 395), cooled completely and still in pans

4 cups Whipped Cream (page 405)

why this recipe works Although poke cake is usually in the form of a sheet cake (as with our Strawberry Poke Cake on page 128), we thought it could make a beautiful and festive layer cake for the Fourth of July. For a cake that was red, white, and blue all the way through, we started by cooking blueberries and strawberries and then combining each with gelatin to create two colorful, brightly flavored syrups. We used a simple white cake as our base; it was tender and flavorful but also had enough structure to handle a syrup soaking. We used a skewer to poke holes into the cake layers while they were still in their pans and then drizzled the blueberry syrup over one layer and the strawberry syrup over the other. A simple filling and frosting of whipped cream kept this cake light and refreshing for the summer holidays.

1 Cook blueberries, ¾ cup water, and 2 tablespoons sugar in medium saucepan over medium-low heat, covered, until blueberries are softened, about 8 minutes. Strain mixture through fine-mesh strainer into bowl; discard solids. Whisk berry-flavored gelatin into juices and let cool slightly, about 15 minutes. Repeat cooking and straining using strawberries, remaining ½ cup water, and remaining 2 tablespoons sugar. Whisk strawberry-flavored gelatin into juices and let cool slightly, about 15 minutes.

2 Using skewer, poke 25 holes in top of each cake, twisting gently to form slightly larger holes. Pour cooled blueberry syrup over 1 cake layer. Repeat with cooled strawberry syrup and remaining cake layer. Cover cake pans with plastic wrap and refrigerate until gelatin is set, at least 3 hours or up to 24 hours.

3 Run thin knife around edge of pans. Invert blueberry cake, discarding parchment, onto wire rack, then reinvert onto platter. Spread 1 cup whipped cream evenly over top. Invert strawberry cake onto rack, discarding parchment, and place, right side up, on whipped cream, pressing lightly to adhere. Spread remaining whipped cream over top and sides of cake. Serve.

confetti cake

Serves 10 to 12

1 cup whole milk, room temperature

6 large egg whites, room temperature

1 teaspoon vanilla extract

2¼ cups (9 ounces) cake flour

1¾ cups (12¼ ounces) sugar

4 teaspoons baking powder

1 teaspoon salt

12 tablespoons unsalted butter, cut into 12 pieces and softened

¾ cup rainbow sprinkles

4–6 drops yellow food coloring

6 cups Vanilla Frosting (page 398)

why this recipe works Kids love confetti cake—and we love its playful speckled interior and friendly vanilla flavor that's perfect for a fun celebration. What we don't like, however, are box versions' artificial aftertaste and greasy crumb. We planned to aim higher—literally—than disappointing store-bought mixes by creating an impressive three-layer version of this birthday party favorite. We knew we already had the right base with our fluffy White Cake Layers (page 395). Mixing whole rainbow sprinkles into the batter made for pockets of color that were too large and marred the cake's downy crumb, so we pulsed the sprinkles in the food processor to just the right size before stirring them into the batter. Three layers ensured an impressively tall, celebration-worthy cake. Our simple Vanilla Frosting gave us the clean, satisfying buttery-vanilla flavor we wanted, but its stark white color didn't do this cake justice. Once we dyed it pale yellow with the help of a little food coloring it made the perfect creamy backdrop for more sprinkles, for a cake that was party-ready.

1 Adjust oven rack to middle position and heat oven to 350 degrees. Grease three 8-inch round cake pans, line with parchment paper, grease parchment, and flour pans. Pulse ½ cup sprinkles in food processor until coarsely ground, 8 to 10 pulses; set aside. Whisk milk, egg whites, and vanilla together in bowl.

2 Using stand mixer fitted with paddle, mix flour, sugar, baking powder, and salt on low speed until combined. Add butter, 1 piece at a time, until only pea-size pieces remain, about 1 minute. Add all but ½ cup milk mixture, increase speed to medium-high, and beat until light and fluffy, about 1 minute. Reduce speed to medium-low, add remaining ½ cup milk mixture, and beat until incorporated, about 30 seconds (batter may look curdled). Give batter final stir by hand. Stir ground sprinkles into cake batter.

3 Divide batter evenly between prepared pans and smooth tops with rubber spatula. Bake until toothpick inserted in center comes out clean, 21 to 25 minutes, switching and rotating pans halfway through baking. Let cakes cool in pans on wire rack for 10 minutes. Remove cakes from pans, discarding parchment, and let cool completely on rack, about 2 hours.

4 Mix food coloring into frosting. Line edges of cake platter with 4 strips of parchment to keep platter clean. Place 1 cake layer on platter. Spread ¾ cup frosting evenly over top, right to edge of cake. Repeat with 1 more cake layer, pressing lightly to adhere, and ¾ cup frosting. Top with remaining cake layer, pressing lightly to adhere. Spread remaining frosting evenly over top and sides of cake. Press remaining ¼ cup sprinkles around bottom edge of cake. Carefully remove parchment strips before serving.

60-minute birthday cake

serves 8 to 10

cake

1¼ cups (6¼ ounces) all-purpose flour

¾ cup (5¼ ounces) granulated sugar

½ teaspoon baking soda

½ teaspoon salt

¾ cup whole milk

4 ounces bittersweet chocolate, chopped fine

⅓ cup (1 ounce) Dutch-processed cocoa powder, plus extra for dusting

1 tablespoon instant espresso powder

6 tablespoons vegetable oil

3 large eggs

1 teaspoon vanilla extract

frosting

4 ounces cream cheese

½ cup (2 ounces) plus 2 tablespoons confectioners' sugar

1½ cups heavy cream

1 teaspoon vanilla extract

⅛ teaspoon salt

⅓ cup seedless raspberry jam

Dutch-processed cocoa powder, for dusting

½ cup plus ⅓ cup fresh raspberries

why this recipe works This book is proof that we love making special occasion cakes for our loved ones. But we know we're not alone in sometimes needing to leave this consideration to the last minute. We wanted a birthday cake recipe built for speed, so we turned to the microwave. Yes, the microwave. In an oven, heat transfers slowly to the cake pan and to the top of the cake, gradually moving inward. But the heat of a microwave penetrates an inch into the cake, cooking it directly in a fast, efficient process. For a cake baked in record time, we simply poured our chocolate batter into a soufflé dish and microwaved it at 50 percent power; depending on the microwave, we discovered our cake was done in as little as 10 minutes. We then simply sliced it in half before filling it with a layer of raspberry preserves and topping it with a rich whipped cream cheese frosting. If you do not have a soufflé dish, you can substitute any other circular, microwave-safe, straight-sided dish that is roughly 7 inches in diameter and 3 inches tall with a volume of at least 7 cups. Be sure to microwave your cake at 50 percent power to ensure even cooking. Microwave ovens vary widely in power so we give a large cooking time range for this cake. We developed and tested this recipe with both 1200-watt and 1000-watt microwaves. If your microwave is lower wattage, you may need to extend the cooking time.

1 *For the cake* Lightly grease 7-inch soufflé dish. Cut 6½-inch round of parchment paper and place on bottom of dish. Whisk flour, sugar, baking soda, and salt together in bowl.

2 Combine milk, chocolate, cocoa, and espresso powder in large saucepan. Place saucepan over low heat and cook, whisking frequently, until chocolate is melted and mixture is smooth. Remove from heat and whisk in oil until combined. Whisk in eggs and vanilla until combined (mixture may look curdled). Whisk in flour mixture until combined, making sure to scrape corners of saucepan.

3 Transfer batter to prepared dish. Microwave at 50 percent power until toothpick inserted in center comes out with few crumbs attached, 10 to 18 minutes. Let cake cool in dish for 15 minutes. Run thin knife or small offset spatula between cake and dish to separate. Place cake round or second parchment round on top of cake. Place inverted 12-inch plate on top of soufflé dish and then invert cake and plate together so soufflé dish is now on top and cake rests on plate. Carefully remove soufflé dish by lifting straight up. Remove parchment from top and let cool for 5 minutes. Using long serrated knife, cut 1 horizontal line around sides of cake; then, following scored lines, cut cake into 2 even layers and transfer to wire rack and let rounds cool for at least 10 minutes.

4 *For the frosting* Meanwhile, place cream cheese in large bowl and microwave on high power until softened, about 15 seconds. Whisk 2 tablespoons sugar into cream cheese until smooth. In bowl of stand

mixer fitted with whisk attachment, whip cream, remaining ½ cup sugar, vanilla, and salt on high speed until stiff peaks form. Fold 1½ cups of whipped cream into cream cheese mixture until smooth and combined. Fold in remaining whipped cream until combined. If mixture is looser than traditional frosting, whisk by hand until stiff, up to 30 seconds.

5 Line edges of cake platter with 4 strips of parchment to keep platter clean. Place 1 cake layer on platter. Spread jam evenly over top, leaving ½-inch border around edge of cake. Top with remaining cake layer, press lightly to adhere, then spread remaining frosting evenly over top and sides of cake. Dust with cocoa and garnish with raspberries. Serve.

Soufflé Dishes
We tested four 2-quart soufflé dishes priced from about $10 to $47. All were classic round, straight-sided ceramic dishes that looked like large ramekins. The most important difference came down to the thickness of each dish's walls. Thick walls are mostly a good thing, making a soufflé dish that isn't flimsy. But there can be too much of a good thing. One dish's walls were more than double the width of the thinnest dish in the lineup, insulating the contents so well that they slowed baking times by 5 to 7 minutes. Our favorite dish, the **HIC 64 Ounce Soufflé** ($15.12), delivered impressive, evenly cooked cakes and soufflés.

SNACK CAKES & RUSTIC FRUIT CAKES

sour cream coffee cake

serves 12 to 16

streusel

¾ cup (3¾ ounces) all-purpose flour

¾ cup (5¼ ounces) granulated sugar

½ cup packed (3½ ounces) dark brown sugar

2 tablespoons ground cinnamon

1 cup pecans, chopped

2 tablespoons unsalted butter, cut into 2 pieces and chilled

cake

1½ cups sour cream

4 large eggs

1 tablespoon vanilla extract

2¼ cups (11¼ ounces) all-purpose flour

1¼ cups (8¾ ounces) granulated sugar

1 tablespoon baking powder

¾ teaspoon baking soda

¾ teaspoon salt

12 tablespoons unsalted butter, cut into ½-inch cubes and softened

why this recipe works Coffee cake abandoned grandma's kitchen many moons ago for supermarket shelves lined with industrial ready-made pastries. Consisting of little more than flat, dry yellow cake topped with hard, pellet-like crumbs and nary a cinnamon swirl in sight, these modern store-bought versions are a far cry from our ideal sour cream coffee cake. We wanted a decadent, ultramoist cake, made pleasantly rich and dense from the addition of sour cream, and there had to be crisp, crunchy, melt-in-your-mouth streusel not just on the top but also inside. Using all-purpose flour and four eggs in our batter gave the cake good structure. Plenty of butter and sour cream were essential for superlative flavor, and using the reverse creaming method (the butter and a portion of the sour cream are mixed into the dry ingredients) ensured a velvety, tight crumb. For the ultimate streusel, we combined nuts, brown sugar, plenty of cinnamon, and cold butter. To ensure that the towering cake cooked through completely, we baked it for a full hour at 350 degrees. Note that the streusel is divided into two parts: one for the inner swirls and one—to which pecans are added—for the topping.

1 *For the streusel* Process flour, granulated sugar, ¼ cup brown sugar, and cinnamon in food processor until combined, about 15 seconds. Transfer 1¼ cups flour-sugar mixture to bowl and stir in remaining ¼ cup brown sugar; set aside for streusel filling. Add pecans and butter to processor and pulse until mixture resembles coarse meal, about 10 pulses; set aside for streusel topping.

2 *For the cake* Adjust oven rack to lowest position and heat oven to 350 degrees. Grease and flour 16-cup tube pan. Whisk 1 cup sour cream, eggs, and vanilla together in bowl.

3 Using stand mixer fitted with paddle, mix flour, sugar, baking powder, baking soda, and salt on low speed until combined. Add butter and remaining ½ cup sour cream and mix until dry ingredients are moistened and mixture resembles wet sand with few large butter pieces remaining, about 1½ minutes. Increase speed to medium and beat until batter comes together, about 10 seconds, scraping down bowl with rubber spatula. Reduce speed to medium-low and gradually add egg mixture in 3 additions, beating for 20 seconds and scraping down bowl after each addition. Increase speed to medium-high and beat until batter is light and fluffy, about 1 minute.

4 Spread 2 cups batter in prepared pan and smooth top with rubber spatula. Sprinkle evenly with ¾ cup streusel filling. Repeat with another 2 cups batter and remaining ¾ cup streusel filling. Spread remaining batter over filling, then sprinkle with streusel topping.

5 Bake until cake feels firm and skewer inserted in center comes out clean, 50 minutes to 1 hour, rotating pan halfway through baking. Let cake cool in pan on wire rack for 30 minutes. Remove cake from pan and let cool completely on rack, about 2 hours. Serve. (Cake can be wrapped in aluminum foil and stored at room temperature for up to 5 days.)

variations
apricot-almond sour cream coffee cake
Substitute 1 cup slivered almonds for pecans and ½ teaspoon almond extract for vanilla extract. Spoon six 2-teaspoon mounds apricot jam over bottom layer of batter before sprinkling with streusel and another six 2-teaspoon mounds jam over middle layer of batter before sprinkling with streusel.

lemon-blueberry sour cream coffee cake
Toss 1 cup frozen blueberries with 1 teaspoon grated lemon zest in small bowl. Sprinkle ½ cup blueberries over bottom layer of batter before sprinkling with streusel and remaining ½ cup blueberries over middle layer of batter before sprinkling with streusel.

sour cream coffee cake with chocolate chips
Sprinkle ½ cup chocolate chips over bottom layer of batter before sprinkling with streusel and another ½ cup chocolate chips over middle layer of batter before sprinkling with streusel.

Snack Cakes and Rustic Fruit Cakes

new york–style crumb cake

serves 9

crumb topping

8 tablespoons unsalted butter, melted and warm

⅓ cup (2⅓ ounces) granulated sugar

⅓ cup packed (2⅓ ounces) dark brown sugar

¾ teaspoon ground cinnamon

⅛ teaspoon salt

1¾ cups (7 ounces) cake flour

cake

1¼ cups (5 ounces) cake flour

½ cup (3½ ounces) granulated sugar

¼ teaspoon baking soda

¼ teaspoon salt

6 tablespoons unsalted butter, cut into 6 pieces and softened

⅓ cup buttermilk

1 large egg plus 1 large yolk

1 teaspoon vanilla extract

Confectioners' sugar

why this recipe works The original crumb cake was brought to New York by German immigrants; sadly, bakery-fresh versions have all but disappeared, and most people know only the store-bought, packaged variety. We wanted a recipe closer to the original that could be made at home. The best crumb cakes strike just the right balance between tender yellow cake and thick, lightly spiced crumb topping. Starting with the cake, we reduced the amount of butter so the richness wouldn't be overwhelming (the crumb topping is already plenty rich). But less butter made our cake drier; to compensate, we added buttermilk and left out an egg white to avoid a rubbery texture. We wanted our crumb topping to be soft and cookie-like, not a crunchy streusel, so we mixed granulated and brown sugars with melted butter for a dough-like consistency; a little bit of cinnamon added familiar warmth and spice. Broken into substantial pieces, our topping held together during baking and created a thick layer of moist crumbs with golden edges. Do not substitute all-purpose flour for the cake flour. When topping the cake, take care not to push the crumbs into the batter. This recipe can be easily doubled and baked in a 13 by 9-inch baking pan; increase the baking time to about 45 minutes.

1 Adjust oven rack to upper-middle position and heat oven to 325 degrees. Make foil sling for 8-inch square baking pan by folding 2 long sheets of aluminum foil so each is 8 inches wide. Lay sheets of foil in pan perpendicular to each other, with extra foil hanging over edges of pan. Push foil into corners and up sides of pan, smoothing foil flush to pan.

2 *For the crumb topping* Whisk melted butter, granulated sugar, brown sugar, cinnamon, and salt in bowl until combined. Add flour and stir with rubber spatula or wooden spoon until mixture resembles thick, cohesive dough; set aside and let cool completely, 10 to 15 minutes.

3 *For the cake* Using stand mixer fitted with paddle, mix flour, granulated sugar, baking soda, and salt on low speed until combined. Add butter, 1 piece at a time, and mix until mixture resembles moist crumbs, with no visible butter chunks remaining, 1 to 2 minutes. Add buttermilk, egg and yolk, and vanilla, increase speed to medium-high, and beat until light and fluffy, about 1 minute, scraping down bowl as needed.

4 Transfer batter to prepared pan. Using rubber spatula, spread batter into even layer. Using your hands, roll pieces of crumb-topping dough between your thumb and forefinger into large pea-size pieces. Spread pieces, breaking up any large chunks, in even layer over batter, beginning with edges and working toward center. Bake until crumbs are golden and toothpick inserted in center of cake comes out clean, 35 to 40 minutes, rotating pan halfway through baking. Let cake cool in pan on wire rack for at least 30 minutes. Using foil overhang, lift cake from pan. Dust with confectioners' sugar before serving. (Leftover cake can be refrigerated for up to 2 days.)

Making Large Crumbs

Using your hands, break apart dough, rolling broken dough between your thumb and forefinger to form crumbs about size of large peas. Continue until all dough has been broken down into crumbs.

Snack Cakes and Rustic Fruit Cakes

cream cheese coffee cake

serves 12 to 16

topping

¼ cup (1¾ ounces) sugar

1½ teaspoons grated lemon zest

½ cup sliced almonds

cake

2¼ cups (11¼ ounces) all-purpose flour

1⅛ teaspoons baking powder

1⅛ teaspoons baking soda

1 teaspoon salt

10 tablespoons unsalted butter, cut into 10 pieces and softened

1⅛ cups (7¾ ounces) plus 5 tablespoons (2¼ ounces) sugar

1 tablespoon grated lemon zest plus 4 teaspoons juice

4 large eggs

5 teaspoons vanilla extract

1¼ cups sour cream

8 ounces cream cheese, softened

why this recipe works This brunch staple is fraught with pitfalls, from dry, bland cake to lackluster fillings that sink to the bottom. Rich sour cream contributed moisture to our cake as well as a subtle tang—a perfect backdrop for the cream cheese swirl. For the filling, we settled on a base mixture of softened cream cheese and sugar and then added lemon juice to cut the richness and a hint of vanilla extract for depth. Incorporating a small amount of the cake batter into the cheese ensured our filling wasn't grainy. The filling not only stayed creamy, but it fused to the cake during baking; this eliminated any gaps and guaranteed perfect swirls of filling. Sliced almonds, sugar, and lemon zest formed a glistening, crackly crust on top of our rich, moist cake.

1 Adjust oven rack to middle position and heat oven to 350 degrees. Spray 16-cup tube pan with vegetable oil spray.

2 *For the topping* Stir sugar and lemon zest in small bowl until combined and sugar is moistened. Stir in almonds; set aside.

3 *For the cake* Whisk flour, baking powder, baking soda, and salt together in bowl; set aside. Using stand mixer fitted with paddle, beat butter, 1⅛ cups sugar, and lemon zest on medium-high speed until pale and fluffy, about 3 minutes. Add eggs, one at a time, and beat until combined. Add 4 teaspoons vanilla and mix to combine. Reduce speed to low and add flour mixture in 3 additions, alternating with sour cream in 2 additions, scraping down bowl as needed. Give batter final stir by hand.

4 Set aside 1¼ cups batter. Using rubber spatula, spread remaining batter in prepared pan and smooth top. Return now-empty bowl to mixer and beat cream cheese, lemon juice, remaining 5 tablespoons sugar, and remaining 1 teaspoon vanilla on medium speed until smooth and slightly lightened, about 1 minute. Add ¼ cup reserved batter and mix until incorporated. Spoon cream cheese mixture evenly over batter, keeping filling about 1 inch from edges of pan; smooth top. Spread remaining 1 cup reserved batter over filling and smooth top. Using butter knife or offset spatula, gently swirl filling into batter using figure-8 motion, being careful not to drag filling to bottom or edges of pan. Gently tap pan on counter to release air bubbles. Sprinkle topping evenly over batter, pressing gently to adhere.

5 Bake until top is golden and just firm and skewer inserted in center of cake comes out clean (skewer will be wet if inserted in cream cheese filling), 45 to 50 minutes, rotating pan halfway through baking. Remove pan from oven and firmly tap on counter 2 or 3 times (top of cake may sink slightly). Let cake cool in pan on wire rack for 1 hour. Remove cake from pan and let cool completely on rack, about 1½ hours. Serve. (Leftover cake can be refrigerated for up to 2 days; bring to room temperature before serving.)

applesauce snack cake

serves 9

1 cup apple cider

¾ cup dried apples, cut into ½-inch pieces

1 cup unsweetened applesauce, room temperature

⅔ cup (4⅔ ounces) sugar

½ teaspoon ground cinnamon

¼ teaspoon ground nutmeg

⅛ teaspoon ground cloves

1½ cups (7½ ounces) all-purpose flour

1 teaspoon baking soda

1 large egg, room temperature

½ teaspoon salt

8 tablespoons unsalted butter, melted and cooled

1 teaspoon vanilla extract

why this recipe works Applesauce cakes don't have a singular definition; they run the gamut from dense, chunky fruitcakes to gummy "health" cakes without much flavor. We wanted a moist and tender cake that actually tasted like apples. To achieve the loose, rustic crumb that's best suited to a snack cake, we used the simple quick-bread mixing method, mixing the wet ingredients separately and then gently adding the dry ingredients by hand. (For more information on mixing methods, see page 20.) The challenge lay in adding more apple flavor. Simply increasing the applesauce made for a gummy cake, and fresh apples added too much moisture. But two other sources worked well: apple cider and dried apples. When reduced to a syrup, the apple cider contributed a pleasing sweetness and a slight tang without excess moisture. And dried apples—plumped in the cider while it was reducing—gave our cake even more apple flavor. We liked the textural contrast provided by a simple sprinkling of spiced granulated sugar over the cake before baking. This cake is very moist, so it's best to err on the side of overbaked when testing its doneness. We prefer the rich flavor of cider, but you can substitute apple juice.

1 Adjust oven rack to middle position and heat oven to 325 degrees. Make foil sling for 8-inch square baking pan by folding 2 long sheets of aluminum foil so each is 8 inches wide. Lay sheets of foil in pan perpendicular to each other, with extra foil hanging over edges of pan. Push foil into corners and up sides of pan, smoothing foil flush to pan.

2 Combine cider and dried apples in small saucepan and simmer over medium heat until liquid evaporates and mixture appears dry, about 15 minutes. Let mixture cool completely, then process with applesauce in food processor until smooth, 20 to 30 seconds.

3 Whisk sugar, cinnamon, nutmeg, and cloves together in bowl; set aside 2 tablespoons mixture for topping. Whisk flour and baking soda together in second bowl.

4 Whisk egg and salt together in large bowl. Whisk in sugar mixture until well combined and light-colored, about 20 seconds. Whisk in melted butter in 3 additions, whisking after each addition until incorporated. Whisk in applesauce mixture and vanilla. Using rubber spatula, fold in flour mixture until just combined.

5 Transfer batter to prepared pan and smooth top with rubber spatula. Gently tap pan on counter to settle batter. Sprinkle reserved sugar mixture evenly over top. Bake until toothpick inserted in center comes out clean, 35 to 40 minutes, rotating pan halfway through baking. Let cake cool completely in pan on wire rack, 1 to 2 hours. Using foil overhang, lift cake from pan. Serve. (Cake can be stored at room temperature for up to 2 days.)

variations

applesauce snack cake with oat-nut streusel

Add 2 tablespoons brown sugar, ⅓ cup chopped pecans or walnuts, and ⅓ cup old-fashioned rolled oats or quick oats to sugar mixture set aside for topping, then add 2 tablespoons softened unsalted butter and pinch with fingers to incorporate and form mixture into hazelnut-size clumps.

ginger-cardamom applesauce snack cake

Substitute ½ teaspoon ground ginger and ¼ teaspoon ground cardamom for cinnamon, nutmeg, and cloves. Add 1 tablespoon finely chopped crystallized ginger to sugar mixture set aside for topping.

blueberry boy bait

serves 12

cake

2 cups (10 ounces) plus 1 teaspoon all-purpose flour

1 tablespoon baking powder

1 teaspoon salt

16 tablespoons unsalted butter, cut into 16 pieces and softened

¾ cup packed (5¼ ounces) light brown sugar

½ cup (3½ ounces) granulated sugar

3 large eggs

1 cup whole milk

2½ ounces (½ cup) fresh or frozen blueberries

topping

2½ ounces (½ cup) fresh or frozen blueberries

¼ cup (1¾ ounces) granulated sugar

½ teaspoon ground cinnamon

why this recipe works This moist cake featuring blueberries and a light streusel topping is so called because the girl who created it for the Pillsbury Bake-Off said that teenage boys found it irresistible. We tracked down a version of the contest-winning recipe and decided to see if we could improve it. The original recipe called for shortening and granulated sugar. We swapped butter for the shortening and brown sugar for some of the granulated sugar; both exchanges resulted in a cake with richer, deeper flavor. Next we doubled the amount of blueberries; half went into the cake and the other half on top. An extra egg in the batter provided enough structure to support the extra fruit so the cake wouldn't be mushy. The topping couldn't be simpler: In addition to the blueberries, just a sprinkling of sugar and cinnamon (instead of a streusel) baked into a light, crisp, sweet coating. Now, it's not only teenage boys who can't refuse a second piece. If using frozen blueberries, do not let them thaw, as they will turn the batter a blue-green color.

1 *For the cake* Adjust oven rack to middle position and heat oven to 350 degrees. Grease 13 by 9-inch baking pan, line with parchment paper, grease parchment, and flour pan.

2 Whisk 2 cups flour, baking powder, and salt together in bowl. Using stand mixer fitted with paddle, beat butter, brown sugar, and granulated sugar on medium-high speed until fluffy, about 2 minutes. Add eggs, one at a time, and beat until just incorporated. Reduce speed to medium and add flour mixture in 3 additions, alternating with milk in 2 additions, scraping down bowl as needed. Toss blueberries with remaining 1 teaspoon flour. Using rubber spatula, gently fold blueberries into batter. Transfer batter to prepared pan and smooth top with rubber spatula.

3 *For the topping* Scatter blueberries over top of batter. Stir sugar and cinnamon together in small bowl and sprinkle over batter. Bake until toothpick inserted in center comes out clean, 45 to 50 minutes, rotating pan halfway through baking. Let cake cool in pan on wire rack for 20 minutes. Remove cake from pan, discarding parchment, and place on serving platter. Cut into squares and serve warm or at room temperature. (Cake can be stored at room temperature for up to 3 days.)

easy chocolate snack cake

serves 9

1½ cups (7½ ounces) all-purpose flour

1 cup (7 ounces) sugar

½ teaspoon baking soda

¼ teaspoon salt

⅔ cup mayonnaise

1 large egg

2 teaspoons vanilla extract

½ cup (1½ ounces) Dutch-processed cocoa powder

2 ounces bittersweet chocolate, chopped fine

1 cup hot brewed coffee

Confectioners' sugar (optional)

why this recipe works We wanted a simple-to-make recipe for chocolate cake, one that would be perfect as a postlunch treat or after-school snack. The problem with many old-fashioned chocolate snack cakes is weak chocolate flavor; we were aiming for a cake that would please all ages and palates with an undeniable but not overly rich chocolate presence. Blooming unsweetened cocoa powder in coffee intensified its flavor, and we supplemented the cocoa with a small amount of bittersweet chocolate. Many recipes for chocolate snack cake call for mayonnaise only—no additional eggs—for richness and moisture. We loved a cake made with mayo, but we found that also adding an egg to the batter gave it moisture, as well as a pleasantly springy texture that we loved. If you want to take the cake out of the pan, grease the pan, line with parchment paper, grease the parchment, and then flour the pan. We like to dust this simple all-purpose cake with confectioners' sugar, but it can also be served plain or dressed up for dessert with Whipped Cream (page 405).

1 Adjust oven rack to middle position and heat oven to 350 degrees. Grease and flour 8-inch square baking pan. Whisk flour, sugar, baking soda, and salt together in large bowl. Whisk mayonnaise, egg, and vanilla together in second bowl.

2 Combine cocoa and chocolate in third bowl, pour hot coffee over top, and whisk until smooth; let cool slightly. Whisk in mayonnaise mixture until combined. Stir chocolate mixture into flour mixture until combined.

3 Transfer batter to prepared pan and smooth top with rubber spatula. Gently tap pan on counter to settle batter. Bake until toothpick inserted in center comes out with few crumbs attached, 30 to 35 minutes, rotating pan halfway through baking. Let cake cool completely in pan on wire rack, 1 to 2 hours. Dust with confectioners' sugar, if using, before serving.

oatmeal cake with broiled icing

serves 9

cake

1 cup (3 ounces) quick oats

¾ cup water, room temperature

¾ cup (3¾ ounces) all-purpose flour

½ teaspoon baking powder

½ teaspoon baking soda

½ teaspoon salt

¼ teaspoon ground cinnamon

⅛ teaspoon ground nutmeg

4 tablespoons unsalted butter, softened

½ cup (3½ ounces) granulated sugar

½ cup packed (3½ ounces) light brown sugar

1 large egg, room temperature

½ teaspoon vanilla extract

icing

¼ cup packed (1¾ ounces) light brown sugar

3 tablespoons unsalted butter, melted and cooled

3 tablespoons milk

¾ cup (2¼ ounces) sweetened shredded coconut

½ cup pecans, chopped

why this recipe works With its chewy coconut, crunchy nuts, and butterscotch flavor, the broiled icing on this classic snack cake is a favorite. But we find that the cake itself is often dense, gummy, and bland. We solved the denseness problem by replacing some of the brown sugar with granulated sugar; less moist than brown sugar, granulated sugar lightened the cake's texture. For the nutty flavor that comes from a strong oat presence, we reduced the proportion of flour to oats. Soaking the oats in room-temperature water rather than the typical boiling water softened them adequately and also minimized the amount of released starch, for a cake that lacked gumminess. Unlike the cake, the classic icing required only a few tweaks: cutting back on sugar, using melted butter rather than softened to simplify the recipe, and adding a splash of milk to make it more pliable. This cake is exceptionally tender; to transfer it to a platter without it crumbling, we created a double foil sling, which gave the cake plenty of support. Keeping the iced cake about 9 inches from the heating element produced the crunchy-chewy texture we wanted. If you have a drawer-style broiler, position the rack as far as possible from the broiler element and monitor the icing carefully as it cooks in step 5. Don't use old-fashioned or instant oats. We always use a metal baking pan for cakes of this variety, but it's especially important here: Glass pans are not recommended when broiling. A vertical sawing motion with a serrated knife works best for cutting through the crunchy icing and tender crumb.

1 *For the cake* Adjust oven rack to middle position and heat oven to 350 degrees. Cut two 16-inch lengths aluminum foil and fold both lengthwise to 5-inch widths. Spray 8-inch square baking pan with vegetable oil spray. Press 1 piece of foil into pan. Repeat with second piece, overlapping pieces by about 1 inch. Spray foil lightly with oil spray.

2 Combine oats and room-temperature water in bowl and let sit until water is absorbed, about 5 minutes. Whisk flour, baking powder, baking soda, salt, cinnamon, and nutmeg together in second bowl.

3 Using stand mixer fitted with paddle, beat butter, granulated sugar, and brown sugar on medium speed until combined and mixture has consistency of damp sand, 2 to 4 minutes, scraping down bowl halfway through mixing. Add egg and vanilla and beat until combined, about 30 seconds. Add flour mixture in 2 additions and mix until just incorporated, about 30 seconds. Add soaked oats and mix until combined, about 15 seconds. Give batter final stir by hand.

4 Transfer batter to prepared pan and smooth top with rubber spatula. Gently tap pan on counter 2 or 3 times to settle batter. Bake until toothpick inserted in center comes out with few crumbs attached, 30 to 35 minutes, rotating pan halfway through baking. Let cake cool in pan on wire rack for 10 minutes.

5 *For the icing* While cake cools, adjust oven rack about 9 inches from broiler element and heat broiler. Whisk sugar, melted butter, and milk together in bowl; stir in coconut and pecans. Spread mixture evenly over warm cake. Broil until topping is bubbling and golden, 3 to 5 minutes.

6 Let cake cool in pan on wire rack for 1 hour. Using foil overhang, lift cake from pan. Serve.

Snack Cakes and Rustic Fruit Cakes

tahini-banana snack cake

serves 8

1½ cups (7½ ounces) all-purpose flour

½ teaspoon salt

½ teaspoon baking soda

4 tablespoons unsalted butter, softened

⅓ cup tahini

1¼ cups (8¾ ounces) sugar

2 large eggs

1 cup mashed ripe bananas
(2 to 3 bananas)

¾ teaspoon vanilla extract

¼ cup whole milk

2 teaspoons sesame seeds

why this recipe works Dense, moist banana bread is great. But tender, fluffy banana snack cake is something else again. And while we were working on transformations, we wanted to give our cake an interesting new flavor profile. Banana and peanut butter is a classic combo, but for this cake we decided to get nutty flavor from sesame tahini. To give our cake a light structure, we creamed softened butter and sugar, which incorporated air into the batter. Adding the tahini at this time (and cutting back on the butter to accommodate for the tahini's fat content) proved to be the best approach; this ensured it was fully incorporated and didn't make the cake greasy. Ripe bananas have nearly three times as much sugar as unripe bananas and were the best choice here; just two or three (depending on the size) yielded a cup of mashed banana, which was just the right amount for a moist cake with unmistakable banana flavor. A final sprinkling of sesame seeds was a playful addition that hinted at the tahini inside. This cake is simple enough to make whenever the need to snack strikes—no special occasion required. Be sure to use speckled bananas in this recipe, or your cake will be bland. It is important to let the cake cool completely before serving.

1 Adjust oven rack to middle position and heat oven to 350 degrees. Grease 8-inch square baking pan, line with parchment paper, grease parchment, and flour pan. Whisk flour, salt, and baking soda together in bowl.

2 Using stand mixer fitted with paddle, beat butter, tahini, and sugar on medium-high speed until light and fluffy, about 3 minutes, scraping down bowl as needed. Add eggs, one at a time, and beat until combined. Add bananas and vanilla and beat until incorporated. Reduce speed to low and add flour mixture in 3 additions, alternating with milk in 2 additions, scraping down bowl as needed. Give batter final stir by hand.

3 Transfer batter to prepared pan and smooth top with rubber spatula. Sprinkle top with sesame seeds. Bake until deep golden brown and toothpick inserted in center comes out clean, 40 to 50 minutes, rotating pan halfway through baking.

4 Let cake cool in pan on wire rack for 10 minutes. Remove cake from pan, discarding parchment, and let cool completely on rack, about 2 hours. Serve. (Cake can be stored at room temperature for up to 2 days.)

summer peach cake

serves 8 to 10

peaches

2½ pounds peaches, peeled, halved, pitted, and cut into ½-inch wedges

5 tablespoons peach schnapps

4 teaspoons lemon juice

3 tablespoons granulated sugar

cake

1 cup (5 ounces) all-purpose flour

1¼ teaspoons baking powder

¾ teaspoon salt

½ cup packed (3½ ounces) light brown sugar

⅓ cup (2⅓ ounces) plus 3 tablespoons granulated sugar

2 large eggs, room temperature

8 tablespoons unsalted butter, melted and cooled

¼ cup sour cream

1½ teaspoons vanilla extract

⅜ teaspoon almond extract

⅓ cup panko bread crumbs, crushed fine

why this recipe works Add ripe peaches to cake and problems abound: All the juice makes for a soggy cake and their delicate flavor gets lost. Roasting the peaches—and tossing them with peach schnapps—concentrated their flavor and expelled moisture. However, the peaches became swathed in a flavorful but gooey film when cooked. Coating our roasted peaches in panko bread crumbs ensured the film was absorbed by the crumbs, which then dissolved into the cake. Peach slices and a sprinkling of almond sugar gave the cake a beautiful finish. To crush the panko, place the crumbs in a zipper-lock bag and smash with a rolling pin. Orange liqueur can be substituted for the schnapps. If using farm-fresh peaches, omit the schnapps.

1 *For the peaches* Adjust oven rack to middle position and heat oven to 425 degrees. Line rimmed baking sheet with aluminum foil and spray with vegetable oil spray. Grease and flour 9-inch springform pan. Gently toss 24 peach wedges with 2 tablespoons schnapps, 2 teaspoons lemon juice, and 1 tablespoon sugar in bowl; set aside.

2 Cut remaining peach wedges crosswise into 3 chunks and gently toss with remaining 3 tablespoons schnapps, 2 teaspoons lemon juice, and 2 tablespoons sugar in second bowl. Spread peach chunks onto prepared baking sheet and bake until exuded juices begin to thicken and caramelize at edges of pan, 20 to 25 minutes. Let peaches cool completely on pan, about 30 minutes. Reduce oven temperature to 350 degrees.

3 *For the cake* Whisk flour, baking powder, and salt together in bowl. Whisk brown sugar, ⅓ cup granulated sugar, and eggs in large bowl until thick and thoroughly combined, about 45 seconds. Slowly whisk in melted butter until combined. Whisk in sour cream, vanilla, and ¼ teaspoon almond extract until combined. Add flour mixture and whisk until just combined.

4 Pour half of batter into prepared pan and spread to pan edges with rubber spatula. Sprinkle crushed panko over roasted peaches and toss gently to combine. Arrange peaches evenly in pan and press gently into batter. Gently spread remaining batter over peaches, smooth top, and arrange reserved peaches attractively over top, also placing wedges in center. Combine remaining 3 tablespoons granulated sugar and remaining ⅛ teaspoon almond extract in bowl; sprinkle over top.

5 Bake cake until golden brown and toothpick inserted in center comes out clean, 50 minutes to 1 hour, rotating pan halfway through baking. Let cake cool in pan on wire rack for 5 minutes. Run thin knife around edge of pan to loosen cake, then remove sides of pan. Let cake cool completely on rack, 2 to 3 hours. Slide thin metal spatula between cake bottom and pan bottom to loosen, then slide cake onto platter. Serve.

rustic plum cake

serves 8 to 10

3 tablespoons brandy

2 tablespoons red currant jelly or seedless raspberry jam

1 pound Italian prune plums, halved and pitted

¾ cup (5¼ ounces) granulated sugar

⅓ cup slivered almonds

¾ cup (3¾ ounces) all-purpose flour

½ teaspoon baking powder

¼ teaspoon salt

6 tablespoons unsalted butter, cut into 6 pieces and softened

1 large egg plus 1 large yolk, room temperature

1 teaspoon vanilla extract

¼ teaspoon almond extract (optional)

Confectioners' sugar (optional)

why this recipe works Plum cake can be anything from an Alsatian tart to a German yeasted bread, but our preference is for an almond cake base. Replacing some of the all-purpose flour with homemade almond flour created a rich, moist cake that was sturdy enough to hold the plums aloft. Poaching the plums in a few tablespoons of brandy and red currant jelly and, in addition to their own juices, heightened their floral flavor and ensured they didn't dehydrate during baking. Arranging the plum slices, slightly overlapped, in two rings on top of the batter made for an elegant presentation. This recipe works best with Italian prune plums. If substituting regular red or black plums, use an equal weight of plums, cut them into eighths, and stir them a few times while cooking in step 1. Don't use canned Italian plums. Don't add the leftover plum cooking liquid to the cake before baking; reserve it and serve with the finished cake. The cake can be served warm or at room temperature; if serving warm, remove the sides of the pan after letting the cake cool for 30 minutes and serve as directed. Serve this cake with Whipped Cream (page 405), if desired.

1 Cook brandy and jelly in 10-inch nonstick skillet over medium heat until thick and syrupy, 2 to 3 minutes. Remove skillet from heat and add plums, cut side down. Return skillet to medium heat and cook, shaking pan to prevent plums from sticking, until plums release their juices and liquid reduces to thick syrup, about 5 minutes. Let plums cool in skillet for 20 minutes.

2 Adjust oven rack to middle position and heat oven to 350 degrees. Grease and flour 9-inch springform pan. Process granulated sugar and almonds in food processor until nuts are finely ground, about 1 minute. Add flour, baking powder, and salt and pulse to combine, about 5 pulses. Add butter and pulse until mixture resembles coarse sand, about 10 pulses. Add egg and yolk, vanilla, and almond extract, if using, and process until smooth, about 5 seconds, scraping down sides of bowl as needed (batter will be very thick and heavy).

3 Transfer batter to prepared pan and smooth top with rubber spatula. Stir plums to coat with syrup. Arrange plum halves, skin side down, evenly over surface of batter (reserve leftover syrup). Bake until golden and toothpick inserted in center comes out with few crumbs attached, 40 to 50 minutes, rotating pan halfway through baking. Run thin knife around edge of pan to loosen cake. Let cake cool completely in pan on wire rack, about 2 hours. Remove sides of pan and dust cake with confectioners' sugar, if using. Slide thin metal spatula between cake bottom and pan bottom to loosen, then slide cake onto platter. Serve with reserved plum syrup.

Snack Cakes and Rustic Fruit Cakes

pineapple upside-down cake

serves 8 to 10

topping

1 pineapple, peeled, cored, and cut into ½-inch pieces (4 cups)

1 cup packed (7 ounces) light brown sugar

3 tablespoons unsalted butter

½ teaspoon vanilla extract

cake

1½ cups (7½ ounces) all-purpose flour

1½ teaspoons baking powder

½ teaspoon salt

8 tablespoons unsalted butter, cut into 8 pieces and softened

¾ cup (5¼ ounces) granulated sugar

1 teaspoon vanilla extract

2 large eggs plus 1 large white, room temperature

⅓ cup whole milk, room temperature

why this recipe works The ideal pineapple upside-down cake features a glistening, caramelized, deep amber topping of plump fruit and a rich, tender butter cake. We tried several classic versions, made with canned pineapple, and found they lacked true pineapple flavor. However, while the flavor of fresh pineapple was much better, its juices turned the cake soggy. We discovered that we could eliminate some of the fruit's moisture by caramelizing the pineapple in a skillet with a generous amount of brown sugar. To further concentrate the flavor of the pineapple, we removed it from the pan as soon as it turned golden brown and reduced the juices to a thick syrup; whisking in some butter added richness. For a cake that would stand up to this substantial topping, we reduced the amount of milk to alleviate gumminess and also added an egg white, which lightened the texture without compromising the structure.

1 Adjust oven rack to lower-middle position and heat oven to 350 degrees. Grease 9-inch round cake pan.

2 *For the topping* Cook pineapple and sugar in 10-inch skillet over medium heat until pineapple is translucent and has light brown hue, 15 to 18 minutes, stirring occasionally during first 5 minutes. Transfer fruit and juice to fine-mesh strainer set over bowl (you should have about 2 cups cooked fruit). Return juices to skillet and simmer over medium heat until thickened, beginning to darken, and mixture forms large bubbles, 6 to 8 minutes, adding any more juices released by fruit to skillet after about 4 minutes. Off heat, whisk in butter and vanilla. Pour caramel mixture into prepared cake pan and set aside while preparing cake. (Pineapple will continue to release liquid as it sits; do not add this liquid to already-reduced juice mixture.)

3 *For the cake* Whisk flour, baking powder, and salt together in bowl. Using stand mixer fitted with paddle, beat butter and sugar on medium-high speed until pale and fluffy, about 3 minutes. Reduce speed to medium, add vanilla, and mix to combine. Increase speed to medium-high, add eggs and white, one at a time, and beat until combined. Reduce speed to low and add flour mixture in 3 additions, alternating with milk in 2 additions, scraping down bowl as needed (batter will be thick). Give batter final stir by hand.

4 Working quickly, distribute drained pineapple in cake pan in even layer, gently pressing fruit into caramel. Using rubber spatula, drop mounds of batter over fruit, then spread batter over fruit and to sides of pan in even layer. Gently tap pan on counter to release air bubbles. Bake cake until golden brown and toothpick inserted in center comes out clean, 45 to 50 minutes, rotating pan halfway through baking. Let cool in pan on wire rack for 10 minutes. Run thin knife around edge of pan to loosen cake. Invert onto rack set in rimmed baking sheet. Remove pan. Let cake cool completely, about 2 hours. Serve.

apple upside-down cake

serves 8 to 10

topping

2 pounds Granny Smith or Golden Delicious apples, peeled and cored

4 tablespoons unsalted butter, cut into 4 pieces

⅔ cup packed (4⅔ ounces) light brown sugar

2 teaspoons lemon juice

cake

1 cup (5 ounces) all-purpose flour

1 tablespoon cornmeal (optional)

1 teaspoon baking powder

½ teaspoon salt

¾ cup (5¼ ounces) granulated sugar

¼ cup packed (1¾ ounces) light brown sugar

2 large eggs

6 tablespoons unsalted butter, melted and slightly cooled

½ cup sour cream

1 teaspoon vanilla extract

why this recipe works There's always room for more than one upside-down cake in your repertoire. Pineapple is undoubtedly a classic, but we find a layer of glistening caramelized apples equally appealing. We wanted our topping to have plenty of fresh apple flavor, but we couldn't pile the cake with raw apple slices without it collapsing. Thinly slicing the apples allowed them to cook through in the oven, but while they had fresh flavor they didn't contribute much apple impact. The trick? Precooking thicker slices of apples in a skillet until caramelized and then stirring in thinner slices—along with some sugar—in the last minute so they just barely cooked before transferring the syrupy mixture to the cake pan. This ensured plentiful fruit infused with caramel flavor and a burst of freshness. For a coarse-crumbed cake that wouldn't buckle under the weight of the fruit, we used the quick-bread mixing method, melting the butter; the melted butter introduced less air into the batter, creating a sturdier crumb. The cornmeal gives the cake a pleasant grit, but is not essential.

1 Adjust oven rack to lowest position and heat oven to 350 degrees. Grease 9-inch round cake pan.

2 *For the topping* Cut half of apples into ¼-inch-thick slices. Cut remaining apples into ½-inch-thick slices. Melt butter in 12-inch skillet over medium-high heat. Add ½-inch-thick apple slices and cook, stirring occasionally, until they begin to caramelize, 4 to 6 minutes (do not fully cook apples).

3 Add ¼-inch-thick apple slices, sugar, and lemon juice. Cook, stirring constantly, until sugar dissolves and apples are coated, about 1 minute. Transfer apple mixture to prepared pan and lightly press into even layer.

4 *For the cake* Whisk flour, cornmeal, if using, baking powder, and salt together in bowl. Whisk granulated sugar, brown sugar, and eggs in large bowl until thick and homogeneous, about 45 seconds. Slowly whisk in melted butter until combined. Whisk in sour cream and vanilla until combined. Add flour mixture and whisk until just combined. Transfer batter to prepared pan and spread evenly over apples. Bake until cake is golden brown and toothpick inserted in center comes out clean, 35 to 40 minutes, rotating pan halfway through baking.

5 Let cake cool in pan on wire rack for 20 minutes. Run thin knife around edge of pan to loosen cake. Invert cake onto rack set in rimmed baking sheet. Let sit until cake releases itself from pan, about 1 minute. Remove pan and gently scrape off any fruit stuck in pan and arrange on top of cake. Let cake cool on rack for at least 20 minutes before serving.

variations

apple upside-down cake with almonds

Process ¼ cup almonds, toasted, in food processor until finely ground, about 45 seconds. Whisk ground almonds with flour, baking powder, and salt, and add 1 teaspoon almond extract to batter with sour cream and vanilla in step 4.

apple upside-down cake with lemon and thyme

Add 1 teaspoon grated lemon zest and 1 teaspoon finely chopped fresh thyme to batter with sour cream and vanilla in step 4.

Snack Cakes and Rustic Fruit Cakes

pear-walnut upside-down cake

Serves 8 to 10

Continued reference: (page 314)

topping

4 tablespoons unsalted butter, melted

½ cup packed (3½ ounces) dark brown sugar

2 teaspoons cornstarch

⅛ teaspoon salt

3 ripe but firm Bosc pears (8 ounces each)

cake

1 cup walnuts, toasted

½ cup (2½ ounces) all-purpose flour

½ teaspoon salt

¼ teaspoon baking powder

⅛ teaspoon baking soda

3 large eggs

1 cup (7 ounces) sugar

4 tablespoons unsalted butter, melted

¼ cup vegetable oil

why this recipe works Despite its title as the queen of fruit, the regal pear doesn't get enough attention in desserts. We thought it was time to explore pear upside-down cake, which would be a perfect way to showcase pears' subtle floral flavor and graceful curved shape. We tried every variety of pear at the store and found that Bosc pears, with their dense flesh, held their shape best after baking. Unlike the hardier apples in our Apple Upside-Down Cake (page 314), delicate pears could be sliced into wedges and baked raw; the slices softened up just enough once baked without falling apart. Instead of the sweet yellow cake base typical of upside-down cakes, we made a walnut-based cake, which was light yet sturdy, earthy-tasting and less sweet, and visually attractive. Lining the cake pan with parchment and removing the cake from the pan after 15 minutes allowed the top to set while preventing the bottom of the cake from steaming and turning soggy. Serve with crème fraîche, lightly sweetened whipped cream, or our Yogurt Whipped Topping (recipe follows).

1 *For the topping* Adjust oven rack to middle position and heat oven to 300 degrees. Grease 9-inch round cake pan and line with parchment paper. Pour melted butter over bottom of pan and swirl to evenly coat. Combine sugar, cornstarch, and salt in small bowl and sprinkle evenly over melted butter.

2 Peel, halve, and core pears. Set aside 1 pear half and reserve for other use. Cut remaining 5 pear halves into 4 wedges each. Arrange pears in circular pattern around prepared pan with tapered ends pointing inward. Arrange two smallest pear wedges in center.

3 *For the cake* Pulse walnuts, flour, salt, baking powder, and baking soda in food processor until walnuts are finely ground, 8 to 10 pulses. Transfer walnut mixture to bowl.

4 Process eggs and sugar in now-empty processor until very pale yellow, about 2 minutes. With processor running, add melted butter and oil in steady stream until incorporated. Add walnut mixture and pulse to combine, 4 to 5 pulses. Pour batter evenly over pears (some pears may show through; cake will bake up over fruit).

5 Bake until center of cake is set and bounces back when gently pressed and toothpick inserted in center comes out clean, 1 hour 10 minutes to 1¼ hours, rotating pan after 40 minutes. Let cake cool in pan on wire rack for 15 minutes. Run thin knife around edge of pan to loosen cake. Invert cake onto rack set in rimmed baking sheet and remove pan, discarding parchment. Let cake cool for 2 hours. Serve.

yogurt whipped topping

Makes 1½ cups

You can sweeten this tangy whipped topping with sugar to taste, if desired.

¾ cup heavy cream, chilled
½ cup plain Greek yogurt

Using stand mixer fitted with whisk attachment, whip cream and yogurt on medium speed until combined, about 10 seconds. Increase speed to high and whip to soft peaks, about 1 minute. If stiff peaks are desired, continue to whip 30 to 60 seconds longer.

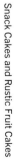

honey-rosemary polenta cake with clementines

serves 8 to 10

cake

1½ cups whole milk

2 sprigs fresh rosemary

1½ cups (8¼ ounces) instant polenta

3 large eggs

5 tablespoons honey

2 teaspoons vanilla extract

1 cup (4 ounces) cake flour

1 teaspoon baking powder

½ teaspoon baking soda

½ teaspoon salt

8 tablespoons unsalted butter, cut into 8 pieces and softened

topping

½ cup heavy cream

1 tablespoon honey

4 clementines, peeled and sliced ⅛ inch thick

why this recipe works We love the Mediterranean flair of polenta cake and thought it would pair nicely with the complementary flavors of honey and rosemary. We didn't want chewy bits of rosemary throughout the cake, however, so we infused the milk in our recipe with a couple of sprigs of rosemary, allowing it to subtly perfume the whole cake. For the topping, we knew a sweet frosting wasn't appropriate; whipped cream was a light and lovely alternative, and a garnish of sliced clementines provided citrusy freshness and an elegant finish. Don't substitute either regular or premade polenta for the instant polenta. Be sure to break up any large clumps of polenta with your fingers before adding it to the batter. Use a serrated knife to cut tidy slices.

1 *For the cake* Adjust oven rack to middle position and heat oven to 350 degrees. Grease 9-inch round cake pan and line with parchment paper.

2 Bring milk and rosemary sprigs to simmer in medium saucepan over medium heat, then let steep off heat for 10 minutes; discard rosemary sprigs. Meanwhile, spread polenta onto rimmed baking sheet and toast in oven until fragrant, about 10 minutes. Stir polenta into milk until combined.

3 Whisk eggs, honey, and vanilla in bowl until combined. Using stand mixer fitted with paddle, mix flour, baking powder, baking soda, and salt on low speed until combined. Add butter, 1 piece at a time, and mix until only pea-size pieces remain, about 1 minute. Add half of egg mixture, increase speed to medium-high, and beat until light and fluffy, about 1 minute. Reduce speed to medium-low, add remaining egg mixture, and beat until incorporated, about 30 seconds. Break up any large clumps of polenta, then beat into batter until combined and smooth, about 2 minutes. Give batter final stir by hand.

4 Transfer batter to prepared pan and smooth top with rubber spatula. Bake until top is golden and toothpick inserted in center comes out clean, 30 to 35 minutes, rotating pan halfway through baking. Let cake cool in pan on wire rack for 10 minutes. Run thin knife around edge of pan. Remove cake from pan, discarding parchment, and let cool completely on rack, about 2 hours. (Unfrosted cake can be stored at room temperature for up to 3 days.)

5 *For the topping* Using stand mixer fitted with whisk attachment, whip cream and honey on medium-low speed until foamy, about 1 minute. Increase speed to high and whip until soft peaks form, 1 to 3 minutes. Spread whipped cream over top of cake, leaving ¼-inch border at edge. Shingle clementines over top. Serve.

POUND CAKES, BUNDT CAKES & TUBE CAKES

pound cake

serves 8

1½ cups (6 ounces) cake flour

1 teaspoon baking powder

½ teaspoon salt

1¼ cups (8¾ ounces) sugar

4 large eggs, room temperature

1½ teaspoons vanilla extract

16 tablespoons unsalted butter, melted and hot

why this recipe works A rich, golden pound cake is a must in any baker's repertoire. But classic pound cake recipes tend to be very particular, requiring ingredients at certain temperatures as well as finicky mixing methods. In our search for a simple, foolproof pound cake recipe, we uncovered two key elements: hot melted (rather than softened) butter and a food processor. The combination of the fast-moving blade of the processor and the hot melted butter emulsified the liquid ingredients quickly before they had a chance to curdle. Sifting the dry ingredients over our emulsified egg mixture in three additions, and whisking them in after each addition, allowed us to incorporate the dry ingredients easily and ensured no pockets of flour marred our finished cake. The test kitchen's preferred loaf pan measures 8½ by 4½ inches; if you use a 9 by 5-inch loaf pan, start checking for doneness 5 minutes early.

1 Adjust oven rack to middle position and heat oven to 350 degrees. Grease and flour 8½ by 4½-inch loaf pan. Whisk flour, baking powder, and salt together in bowl.

2 Process sugar, eggs, and vanilla in food processor until combined, about 10 seconds. With processor running, add hot melted butter in steady stream until incorporated. Transfer to large bowl.

3 Sift flour mixture over egg mixture in 3 additions, whisking to combine after each addition until few streaks of flour remain. Continue to whisk batter gently until almost no lumps remain (do not overmix).

4 Transfer batter to prepared pan and smooth top with rubber spatula. Gently tap pan on counter to settle batter. Bake until toothpick inserted in center comes out with few crumbs attached, 50 minutes to 1 hour, rotating pan halfway through baking.

5 Let cake cool in pan on wire rack for 10 minutes. Run thin knife around edge of pan, remove cake from pan, and let cool completely on rack, about 2 hours. Serve. (Cake can be stored at room temperature for up to 3 days or frozen for up to 1 month; defrost cake at room temperature.)

variations

almond pound cake

Add 1 teaspoon almond extract and ¼ cup slivered almonds to food processor with sugar, eggs, and vanilla. Sprinkle 2 tablespoons slivered almonds over cake before baking.

ginger pound cake

Add 3 tablespoons minced crystallized ginger, 1½ teaspoons ground ginger, and ½ teaspoon ground mace to food processor with sugar, eggs, and vanilla.

lemon pound cake

Add 2 tablespoons grated lemon zest (2 lemons) and 2 teaspoons juice to food processor with sugar, eggs, and vanilla.

orange pound cake

Add 1 tablespoon grated orange zest and 1 tablespoon juice to food processor with sugar, eggs, and vanilla.

Pound Cakes, Bundt Cakes, and Tube Cakes

chocolate pound cake

serves 8

1 cup (5 ounces) all-purpose flour

1 teaspoon salt

¾ cup (2¼ ounces) Dutch-processed cocoa powder

2 ounces milk chocolate, chopped fine

⅓ cup boiling water

16 tablespoons unsalted butter, cut into 16 pieces and softened

1 cup (7 ounces) granulated sugar

¼ cup packed (1¾ ounces) light brown sugar

2 teaspoons vanilla extract

5 large eggs, room temperature

why this recipe works We love pound cake and we love chocolate, but the combination is often a disappointment. That's because most recipes simply add chocolate to a standard pound cake recipe, which mars its finely tuned texture and usually produces lackluster chocolate flavor. We wanted to retool classic pound cake to make it ultrachocolaty without compromising its hallmark velvety-soft crumb. For deep chocolate flavor we used mostly Dutch-processed cocoa powder, which incorporated seamlessly into the batter; a couple ounces of milk chocolate added richness without interfering with the cake's texture. We bloomed both the cocoa and the bar chocolate in hot water to maximize their impact. For an accurate measurement of boiling water, bring a full kettle of water to a boil and then measure out the desired amount. The test kitchen's preferred loaf pan measures 8½ by 4½ inches; if you use a 9 by 5-inch loaf pan, start checking for doneness 5 minutes early.

1 Adjust oven rack to lower-middle position and heat oven to 325 degrees. Grease and flour 8½ by 4½-inch loaf pan. Whisk flour and salt together in bowl.

2 Place cocoa and chocolate in bowl. Pour boiling water over cocoa mixture and stir until chocolate is melted and no dry streaks of cocoa remain. Let mixture cool for 5 minutes.

3 Using stand mixer fitted with paddle, beat butter, granulated sugar, brown sugar, vanilla, and cocoa mixture on medium-high speed until fluffy, 2 to 3 minutes. Add eggs, one at a time, and beat until combined. Reduce speed to low and add flour mixture in 3 additions, scraping down bowl as needed, until just combined (batter may look slightly curdled). Give batter final stir by hand.

4 Transfer batter to prepared pan and gently tap pan on counter to release air bubbles. Bake until toothpick inserted in center comes out clean, 1 hour to 1 hour 10 minutes, rotating pan halfway through baking. Let cake cool in pan on wire rack for 10 minutes. Remove cake from pan and let cool completely on rack, about 2 hours. Serve. (Cake can be stored at room temperature for up to 3 days or frozen for up to 1 month; defrost cake at room temperature.)

cream cheese pound cake

serves 12

3 cups (12 ounces) cake flour

1 teaspoon salt

4 large eggs plus 2 large yolks, room temperature

¼ cup milk

2 teaspoons vanilla extract

24 tablespoons (3 sticks) unsalted butter, softened

6 ounces cream cheese, softened

3 cups (21 ounces) sugar

why this recipe works Adding cream cheese to pound cake is a common variation that adds delightful tang to this rich, dense dessert. While classic pound cake is baked in a loaf pan for a refined yet simple teatime slice, cream cheese versions are typically prepared in a Bundt pan for a big and beautiful presentation. But simply mixing cream cheese—with all its protein, fat, and moisture—into a scaled-up version of our classic pound cake resulted in a cake with a heavy, coarse crumb. For a velvety, tight crumb we left out the leavener, which cut down on the cake's lift. The addition of a couple extra egg yolks (rather than whole eggs, which made the cake gummy) made for a supremely moist and tender cake. Baking our cake in a low oven took a little longer, but it produced a perfect golden-brown crust and a moist, tender interior. We prefer whole milk in this recipe, but any percentage fat will work. You can bake this cake in a decorative 10-cup Bundt pan (for more information, see page 332); place a baking sheet under the Bundt pan. We like to serve this rich cake with sweet-tart Strawberry-Rhubarb Compote (recipe follows).

1 Adjust oven rack to middle position and heat oven to 300 degrees. Spray 12-cup nonstick Bundt pan with baking spray with flour. Whisk flour and salt together in bowl. Whisk eggs and yolks, milk, and vanilla together in 2-cup liquid measuring cup.

2 Using stand mixer fitted with paddle, beat butter, cream cheese, and sugar on medium-high speed until pale and fluffy, about 3 minutes. Reduce speed to low and very slowly add egg mixture, mixing until incorporated (batter may look slightly curdled). Add flour mixture in 3 additions, scraping down bowl as needed. Give batter final stir by hand.

3 Transfer batter to prepared pan. Gently tap pan on counter to release air bubbles. Bake until skewer inserted in center comes out clean, 1 hour 20 minutes to 1½ hours, rotating pan halfway through baking. Let cake cool in pan on wire rack for 15 minutes. Invert cake onto rack, remove pan, and let cool completely, about 2 hours. Serve. (Cake can be stored at room temperature for up to 3 days or frozen for up to 1 month; defrost cake at room temperature.)

strawberry-rhubarb compote

makes about 4 cups

The compote can be refrigerated for up to one week. It makes a great topping for our Cream Cheese Pound Cake, but it's also delicious drizzled on ice cream or stirred into yogurt or oatmeal.

1 pound strawberries, hulled and chopped (3 cups)
1 cup (7 ounces) sugar
1 tablespoon lemon juice
1 pound rhubarb, sliced ¼ inch thick
Pinch salt

1 Toss strawberries with ½ cup sugar and lemon juice in bowl. Transfer strawberry mixture to fine-mesh strainer set over medium saucepan and let stand, stirring occasionally, for 30 minutes. Do not wash bowl.

2 Return strawberries to bowl. Add rhubarb, remaining ½ cup sugar, and salt to strawberry juices in pan and bring to boil over medium-high heat. Reduce heat to medium-low and cook, stirring occasionally, until rhubarb is soft and liquid has thickened, 6 to 8 minutes.

3 Stir strawberries into pan and remove from heat. Transfer compote to bowl and let cool completely, about 45 minutes.

Pound Cakes, Bundt Cakes, and Tube Cakes

7UP pound cake

serves 12

cake

2½ cups (17½ ounces) granulated sugar

5 large eggs, room temperature

½ cup 7UP, room temperature

1 tablespoon grated lemon zest
plus 2 tablespoons juice

1 tablespoon grated lime zest
plus 2 tablespoons juice (2 limes)

½ teaspoon salt

20 tablespoons (2½ sticks) unsalted
butter, melted and slightly cooled

3¼ cups (13 ounces) cake flour

glaze

1 cup (4 ounces) confectioners' sugar

1 tablespoon lemon juice

1 tablespoon lime juice

7UP

Curious if other clear sodas could stand in for 7UP, we compared cakes made with Sprite, Fresca, Mountain Dew, and ginger ale with one made with 7UP. The 7UP cake was indistinguishable from all but one: the Fresca cake, which was pale and tough. Blame it on the artificial sweeteners, and be sure to avoid Diet 7UP for the same reason. We also tried playing soda jerk by creating our own soda from seltzer water, lemon, and lime to equal the pH of 7UP. Our homemade soda worked fine but made for a slightly less sweet cake.

---

why this recipe works In the early 1950s, soda companies began marketing their products as more than mere drinks. Odd recipes like 7UP salad and 7UP parfait pie have mercifully been forgotten, but 7UP pound cake remains a treasured favorite. The effervescent, slightly acidic soda contributes a subtle citrus note; it also provides lift and a uniquely tender texture absent from denser, tight-crumbed classic pound cake. But the buttery richness of pound cake can obscure other flavors so we needed to find a way to accentuate the soda's citrus zing. Cutting back on the amount of sugar called for in the original recipe was our first step. And since finely grated zest could be added without affecting texture, we introduced plenty to awaken the lemon-lime flavor, as well as some fresh lemon and lime juice for a bit of citrusy tartness. Fresh, not flat, 7UP is essential for the best texture and rise.

1 *For the cake* Adjust oven rack to lower-middle position and heat oven to 300 degrees. Grease and flour 16-cup nonstick tube pan. Process sugar, eggs, 7UP, lemon zest and juice, lime zest and juice, and salt in food processor until smooth. With processor running, add melted butter in steady stream until incorporated. Transfer to large bowl. Add flour in 3 additions, whisking to combine after each addition.

2 Transfer batter to prepared pan and gently tap pan on counter to release air bubbles. Bake until skewer inserted in center comes out clean, 1¼ to 1½ hours, rotating pan halfway through baking. Let cake cool in pan on wire rack set in rimmed baking sheet for 10 minutes.

3 *For the glaze* While cake is baking, whisk sugar, lemon juice, and lime juice together in bowl. Remove cake from pan and transfer to rack. Pour half of glaze over warm cake and let cool completely, about 2 hours. Pour remaining glaze over cake and let set for 10 minutes before serving. (Cake can be stored at room temperature for up to 3 days.)

Pound Cakes, Bundt Cakes, and Tube Cakes

cranberry-sour cream pound cake

serves 8

5 large eggs, room temperature

2 teaspoons vanilla extract

1¾ cups (8¾ ounces) all-purpose flour

Salt

½ teaspoon baking powder

⅓ cup sour cream

2 tablespoons milk

14 tablespoons unsalted butter, cut into 14 pieces and softened but still cool

1¼ cups (8¾ ounces) granulated sugar

4 ounces (1 cup) fresh or frozen cranberries, chopped coarse

1 tablespoon confectioners' sugar

why this recipe works Pound cake is simple but elegant; it's also incredibly rich. We thought tart cranberries and tangy sour cream would provide a welcome contrast to the buttery cake, and the bright cranberries would also contribute a burst of color for an extra-special dessert. We wanted this pound cake to have a crumb that wasn't quite as tight as a classic all-butter pound cake, so we used all-purpose flour instead of cake flour and we thoroughly creamed the butter. While cranberries should add tartness, fresh cranberries can border on acerbic. To tame the sourness, we tossed coarsely chopped cranberries with confectioners' sugar before adding them to the batter; this also prevented them from sinking to the bottom of the pan. Baking the loaf slowly (for almost 2 hours) in a low (300 degree) oven ensured that the inside cooked through before the exterior became too brown. If you're using frozen cranberries, there's no need to thaw them first. The ideal temperature for the eggs and butter is 60 degrees. The test kitchen's preferred loaf pan measures 8½ by 4½ inches; if you use a 9 by 5-inch loaf pan, start checking for doneness 5 minutes early.

1 Adjust oven rack to lower-middle position and heat oven to 300 degrees. Spray 8½ by 4½-inch loaf pan with baking spray with flour.

2 Whisk eggs and vanilla together in 2-cup liquid measuring cup. Sift flour, ¾ teaspoon salt, and baking powder into bowl. Whisk sour cream and milk together in second bowl.

3 Using stand mixer fitted with paddle, beat butter on medium-high speed until smooth and creamy, 2 to 3 minutes, scraping down bowl once. Reduce speed to medium and gradually add granulated sugar. Increase speed to medium-high and beat until pale and fluffy, 3 to 5 minutes, scraping down bowl as needed. Reduce speed to medium and gradually add egg mixture in slow, steady stream. Scrape down bowl and continue to mix on medium speed until uniform, about 1 minute (batter may look slightly curdled). Reduce speed to low and add flour mixture in 3 additions, alternating with sour cream mixture in 2 additions, scraping down bowl as needed. Give batter final stir by hand. Toss cranberries with confectioners' sugar and ⅛ teaspoon salt in bowl until evenly coated, then gently but thoroughly fold into batter.

4 Transfer batter to prepared pan and gently tap pan on counter to release air bubbles. Bake until toothpick inserted in center comes out clean, 1¾ hours to 1 hour 55 minutes, rotating pan halfway through baking. Let cake cool in pan on wire rack for 15 minutes. Remove cake from pan and let cool completely on rack, about 2 hours. Serve. (Cake can be stored at room temperature for up to 3 days or frozen for up to 1 month; defrost cake at room temperature.)

ALL ABOUT POUND, BUNDT, AND TUBE CAKES

When we talk about cakes, we often like to categorize them by their flavor, the texture of their crumb, or how they're decorated. And then there are cakes that are defined by the pan in which they're baked. Pound, Bundt, and tube cakes are such cakes. Forming these anytime cakes into their iconic shapes is easy if you have the right information.

BUNDTS OF ALL KINDS

A Bundt pan is a special tube pan with decorative ridges or fluting. It was introduced in 1950 by Nordic Ware at the request of a Minneapolis-area Jewish women's group whose members wanted a lighter, easier-to-use version of the ring-shaped cast-iron pans used to make *kugelhopf*, a Central European yeast cake. But the pan didn't truly become popular until 1966, when the Tunnel of Fudge Cake (see our recipe on page 346) took second place in the Pillsbury Bake-Off. Sales boomed as home bakers across the country sought to make this cake.

Today, Bundt pans are a common sight in kitchens. We love the beautiful, traditional appearance of cakes baked in our favorite pan, the Nordic Ware Anniversary Bundt Pan (for more information on our winning Bundt pan, see page 8). But Nordic Ware also makes a number of other Bundt pan shapes that we had fun experimenting with in the kitchen. We particularly like the Elegant Party, Kugelhopf, and Heritage Bundt pans. The only differences? They don't have the helpful handles found on the anniversary Bundt. And these pans are smaller, holding about 10 cups of batter rather than 12, so they won't accommodate every recipe. We've noted in individual recipes if they work in these pans. Since their designs are intricate, be sure to grease the pan properly so the cakes come out with ease.

Elegant Party Bundt

Kugelhopf Bundt

Heritage Bundt Pan

PREPARING A BUNDT PAN

A Bundt pan makes an attractive cake only if you can get it out in one piece. A generous spray of baking spray with flour did the job for most properly baked cakes (underbaked cakes will stick) except for chocolate. These moist cakes stuck when we simply greased the pan, but if we introduced flour they retained a white coating. Our foolproof solution? Make a paste from 1 tablespoon melted butter and 1 tablespoon cocoa powder and apply it with a pastry brush. This thoroughly coats the surface of the pan, including all the nooks and crannies.

STORING AND FREEZING

The shape of these cakes isn't all they have in common: They also take well to storage. Most cakes, even glazed ones, can be wrapped in plastic wrap or stored in an airtight container at room temperature for as long as 2 to 4 days, depending on the recipe. For long-term storage, the freezer sometimes works better than the refrigerator, which can make some cakes stale. To freeze, wrap the cooled cake in plastic wrap, then in aluminum foil, and freeze for up to 1 month. If you do plan on freezing your cake, avoid glazing until it's defrosted. To defrost a frozen cake, thaw it completely at room temperature (do not unwrap), about 4 hours. (Thawing the cake while still wrapped ensures a nice, firm crust.) We do not recommend freezing angel food or chiffon cakes as their texture is too delicate.

HANGING OUT

To ensure that angel and chiffon cakes have the lightest, fluffiest texture, you'll want to let them cool upside down; if you cool the cake right side up, it will fall flat under its own weight and have a rubbery texture. You can invert it over a large metal kitchen funnel but it's just as easy to grab something you likely already have: a heavy-bottomed bottle (like an empty wine bottle).

Instead of a simple round of parchment, tube pans, naturally, require a parchment "doughnut" to accommodate the tube. This is an important step for cakes like angel food, where you can't grease the pan (it will inhibit the cake's rise).

1 Cut a square of parchment paper slightly bigger than the size of the bottom of the tube pan.

2 Form the paper into a large triangle by folding the top left corner over to meet the bottom right corner.

3 Fold the top right corner over the bottom left corner.

4 Continue to make a smaller triangle by folding the bottom right corner over the bottom left corner.

5 Hold the folded piece of parchment over the tube pan, with the pointed end in the center of the pan. Using scissors, trim both the pointed edge and outside edge so that the parchment just fits inside the pan.

6 Unfold the parchment and lay it over the bottom of the tube pan.

LOAF PAN SIZES

Loaf pans can vary in size by more than an inch, which translates to dramatic differences in the final size and shape of the baked loaf. The pound cakes in this chapter have been designed to work with our favorite pan, the Williams-Sonoma Goldtouch Nonstick Loaf Pan (for more information on loaf pans, see page 8), which measures 8½ by 4½ inches. If you use a larger pan (9 by 5 is common), the cake will look squatter and skimpier when sliced. (There's more room in the pan for the batter to spread out.) The cake, however, will taste the same—just make sure to check for doneness 5 minutes earlier than specified in the recipe to avoid overbaking, as the larger surface area means the cake will bake faster. To accurately measure the size of your loaf pan, measure the top of the pan from inside edge to inside edge, not the bottom.

Baked in 9 by 5-inch Loaf Pan

Baked in 8½ by 4½-inch Loaf Pan

Pound Cakes, Bundt Cakes, and Tube Cakes

lemon bundt cake

serves 12

cake

3 cups (15 ounces) all-purpose flour

1 teaspoon salt

1 teaspoon baking powder

½ teaspoon baking soda

¾ cup buttermilk, room temperature

3 tablespoons grated lemon zest
plus 3 tablespoons juice (3 lemons)

1 tablespoon vanilla extract

18 tablespoons (2¼ sticks) unsalted butter,
cut into 18 pieces and softened

2 cups (14 ounces) granulated sugar

3 large eggs plus 1 large yolk

glaze

2 cups (8 ounces) confectioners' sugar

2–3 tablespoons lemon juice

1 tablespoon buttermilk

why this recipe works Adding lemon flavor to a simple Bundt cake sounds straightforward enough, but in reality it can be really hard to capture lemon's tart, aromatic notes. That's because the flavor of lemon juice is drastically muted when exposed to the heat of an oven, and its acidity can wreak havoc on the delicate nature of baked goods. We wanted to develop a Bundt cake with bold lemon flavor without compromising its texture. We quickly realized we couldn't get the lemon flavor we wanted from lemon juice alone without using so much that the cake fell apart when sliced. We turned to zest and found that three lemons' worth added plenty of well-balanced lemon flavor; a brief soak in lemon juice softened its fibrous texture. Replacing the milk with buttermilk fortified tang. For the glaze, a simple mixture of lemon juice, buttermilk, and confectioners' sugar provided a final layer of citrus flavor. You can bake this cake in a decorative 10-cup Bundt pan (for more information, see page 332); place a baking sheet under the Bundt pan. The cake has a light, fluffy texture when eaten the day it's baked, but if well wrapped and held at room temperature overnight its texture becomes more dense—like that of pound cake—the following day.

1 *For the cake* Adjust oven rack to lower-middle position and heat oven to 350 degrees. Spray 12-cup nonstick Bundt pan with baking spray with flour. Whisk flour, salt, baking powder, and baking soda together in bowl. Whisk buttermilk, lemon zest and juice, and vanilla together in second bowl.

2 Using stand mixer fitted with paddle, beat butter and sugar on medium-high speed until pale and fluffy, about 3 minutes. Add eggs and yolk, one at a time, and beat until combined. Reduce speed to low and add flour mixture in 3 additions, alternating with buttermilk mixture in 2 additions, scraping down bowl as needed. Give batter final stir by hand.

3 Transfer batter to prepared pan and smooth top with rubber spatula. Gently tap pan on counter to settle batter. Bake until wooden skewer inserted in center comes out with few crumbs attached, 50 minutes to 1 hour, rotating pan halfway through baking. Let cake cool in pan on wire rack set in rimmed baking sheet for 10 minutes.

4 *For the glaze* While cake is baking, whisk confectioners' sugar, 2 tablespoons lemon juice, and buttermilk until smooth, adding more lemon juice as needed, teaspoon by teaspoon, until glaze is thick but still pourable.

5 Invert cake onto rack and remove pan. Pour half of glaze over warm cake and let cool for 1 hour. Drizzle remaining glaze evenly over cake and let cool completely, at least 2 hours, before serving.

chocolate sour cream bundt cake

serves 12

¾ cup (2¼ ounces) natural unsweetened cocoa powder, plus 1 tablespoon for pan

12 tablespoons unsalted butter, cut into 12 pieces and softened, plus 1 tablespoon, melted, for pan

6 ounces bittersweet chocolate, chopped

1 teaspoon instant espresso powder (optional)

¾ cup boiling water

1 cup sour cream, room temperature

1¾ cups (8¾ ounces) all-purpose flour

1 teaspoon salt

1 teaspoon baking soda

2 cups packed (14 ounces) light brown sugar

1 tablespoon vanilla extract

5 large eggs, room temperature

Confectioners' sugar (optional)

why this recipe works A chocolate Bundt cake is bound to be pretty; we wanted a recipe that would deliver a cake that tastes every bit as good as it looks, with a fine crumb, moist texture, and rich chocolate flavor. To achieve this, we used both bittersweet chocolate and cocoa powder, dissolving them in boiling water to bloom their flavor. Brown sugar and sour cream provided moisture and a subtle tang. Finally, we enhanced our cake's chocolate flavor with small amounts of espresso powder and vanilla extract. We prefer natural cocoa here; Dutch-processed cocoa will result in a compromised rise. Coating the Bundt pan with baking spray with flour will leave a whitish film on the cake, so we coat the pan with a paste made from cocoa and melted butter, which ensures a clean release. For an accurate measurement of boiling water, bring a full kettle of water to a boil and then measure out the desired amount. You can bake this cake in a decorative 10-cup Bundt pan (for more information, see page 332); place a baking sheet under the Bundt pan. We like to serve this cake with Lightly Sweetened Raspberries and/or Tangy Whipped Cream (recipes follow).

1 Adjust oven rack to lower-middle position and heat oven to 350 degrees. Mix 1 tablespoon cocoa and melted butter into paste. Using pastry brush, thoroughly coat interior of 12-cup nonstick Bundt pan.

2 Combine chocolate, espresso powder, if using, and remaining ¾ cup cocoa in bowl. Pour boiling water over mixture and let sit, covered, for 5 minutes. Whisk mixture gently until smooth. Let cool completely, then whisk in sour cream. Whisk flour, salt, and baking soda together in second bowl.

3 Using stand mixer fitted with paddle, beat softened butter, sugar, and vanilla on medium-high speed until pale and fluffy, about 3 minutes. Add eggs, one at a time, and beat until combined. Reduce speed to low and add flour mixture in 3 additions, alternating with chocolate–sour cream mixture in 2 additions, scraping down bowl as needed. Give batter final stir by hand.

4 Transfer batter to prepared pan and smooth top with rubber spatula. Bake until skewer inserted in center comes out with few crumbs attached, 45 to 50 minutes, rotating pan halfway through baking. Let cake cool in pan on wire rack for 10 minutes. Invert cake onto rack, remove pan, and let cool completely, about 3 hours. Dust with confectioners' sugar, if using, before serving. (Cake can be stored at room temperature for up to 24 hours.)

lightly sweetened raspberries

makes 3 cups

The sweetness of raspberries varies, so start with 1 tablespoon
sugar and then add more to taste.

15 ounces (3 cups) raspberries
1–2 tablespoons sugar

Gently toss raspberries with sugar; let stand until
raspberries have released some juice and sugar has
dissolved, about 15 minutes.

tangy whipped cream

makes about 1½ cups

1 cup heavy cream, chilled
¼ cup sour cream
¼ cup packed (1¾ ounces) light brown sugar
⅛ teaspoon vanilla extract

Using stand mixer fitted with whisk attachment, whip
all ingredients on medium-low speed until foamy, about
1 minute. Increase speed to high and whip until soft
peaks form, 1 to 3 minutes.

honey-oat bundt cake

serves 12

cake

¾ cup (2¼ ounces) old-fashioned rolled oats

2½ cups (12½ ounces) all-purpose flour

1¼ teaspoons salt

1 teaspoon baking powder

½ teaspoon baking soda

½ cup whole milk

8 tablespoons unsalted butter, melted

3 large eggs

6 tablespoons unsweetened applesauce

¼ cup orange juice

1 teaspoon vanilla extract

¾ cup honey

glaze

⅓ cup honey

1 teaspoon vanilla extract

why this recipe works The combination of honey and oats is a classic for good reason: They make a great pairing, with the floral notes of honey underscoring the nuttiness of the oats. These two ingredients make an appearance together in many baked goods and breakfast items such as breads, muffins, and even cereal. We thought hearty oats would make a nice addition to a Bundt cake, but simply mixing in whole oats—whether dry or hydrated in some of the cake's liquid—made the cake's crumb coarse and gummy. The key to success was grinding old-fashioned oats. The ground oats added a pleasant nutty depth to the cake and made the crumb soft and fluffy. To really punch up the honey flavor, we made a simple soaking syrup of honey and vanilla, which we warmed in the microwave until it was thin enough that we could easily brush it over the finished cake. Do not substitute quick oats, instant oats, or steel-cut oats in this recipe. You can bake this cake in a decorative 10-cup Bundt pan (for more information, see page 332); place a baking sheet under the Bundt pan.

1 *For the cake* Adjust oven rack to middle position and heat oven to 325 degrees. Spray 12-cup nonstick Bundt pan generously with baking spray with flour. Process oats in food processor until finely ground, about 1 minute.

2 Whisk ground oats, flour, salt, baking powder, and baking soda together in large bowl. Whisk milk, melted butter, eggs, applesauce, orange juice, and vanilla together in second bowl, then whisk in honey until fully incorporated. Whisk egg mixture into flour mixture until combined.

3 Transfer batter to prepared pan. Bake until skewer inserted in center comes out clean, 45 to 55 minutes, rotating pan halfway through baking. Let cake cool in pan on wire rack set in rimmed baking sheet for 30 minutes. Using thin knife, loosen cake from sides of pan and invert cake onto rack and remove pan.

4 *For the glaze* Microwave honey and vanilla until honey becomes fluid, about 30 seconds. Brush honey mixture over still-warm cake. Let cake cool completely, about 2 hours. Serve.

marbled blueberry bundt cake

serves 12

cake

3 cups (15 ounces) all-purpose flour

1½ teaspoons baking powder

¾ teaspoon baking soda

1 teaspoon salt

½ teaspoon ground cinnamon

¾ cup buttermilk

2 teaspoons grated lemon zest
plus 3 tablespoons juice

2 teaspoons vanilla extract

3 large eggs plus 1 large yolk,
room temperature

18 tablespoons (2¼ sticks) unsalted butter,
cut into 18 pieces and softened

2 cups (14 ounces) sugar

filling

¾ cup (5¼ ounces) sugar

3 tablespoons low- or no-sugar-needed
fruit pectin

Pinch salt

10 ounces (2 cups) fresh or thawed frozen
blueberries

1 teaspoon grated lemon zest
plus 1 tablespoon juice

why this recipe works Blueberry Bundt cake is a summertime favorite, but cultivated blueberries can be oversized and bland, wreaking havoc in a cake. The berries refuse to stay suspended in the batter and burst into bland, soggy pockets when baked. We solved these problems by pureeing the fruit, seasoning it with sugar and lemon, and bumping up its natural pectin content with low-sugar pectin for a thickened, fresh-tasting filling. We swirled our filling throughout the cake for an attractive marbled appearance and bright blueberry flavor in every bite. Spray the pan well in step 1 to prevent sticking. For fruit pectin we recommend both Sure-Jell for Less or No Sugar Needed Recipes and Ball RealFruit Low or No-Sugar Needed Pectin. If using frozen berries, thaw them before blending in step 3. This cake can be served plain or with Whipped Cream (page 405).

1 *For the cake* Adjust oven rack to lower-middle position and heat oven to 325 degrees. Spray 12-cup nonstick Bundt pan generously with baking spray with flour. Whisk flour, baking powder, baking soda, salt, and cinnamon together in large bowl. Whisk buttermilk, lemon zest and juice, and vanilla together in second bowl. Gently whisk eggs and yolk in third bowl to combine.

2 Using stand mixer fitted with paddle, beat butter and sugar on medium-high speed until pale and fluffy, about 3 minutes, scraping down bowl as needed. Reduce speed to medium and beat in half of eggs until incorporated, about 15 seconds. Repeat with remaining eggs, scraping down bowl after incorporating. Reduce speed to low and add one-third of flour mixture, followed by half of buttermilk mixture, mixing until just incorporated after each addition, about 5 seconds. Repeat using half of remaining flour mixture and all of remaining buttermilk mixture. Scrape down bowl, add remaining flour mixture, and mix at medium-low speed until batter is thoroughly combined, about 15 seconds. Remove bowl from mixer and fold batter once or twice with rubber spatula to incorporate any remaining flour. Cover bowl with plastic wrap and set aside while preparing filling (batter will inflate a bit).

3 *For the filling* Whisk sugar, pectin, and salt together in small saucepan. Process blueberries in blender until mostly smooth, about 1 minute. Transfer ¼ cup blueberry puree and lemon zest to saucepan with sugar mixture and stir to thoroughly combine. Heat sugar-blueberry mixture over medium heat until just simmering, about 3 minutes, stirring frequently to dissolve sugar and pectin. Transfer mixture to bowl and let cool for 5 minutes. Add remaining puree and lemon juice to cooled mixture and whisk to combine. Let sit until slightly set, about 8 minutes.

4 Spoon half of batter into prepared pan and smooth top with rubber spatula. Using back of spoon, create ½-inch-deep channel in center of batter. Spoon half of filling into channel. Using butter knife or small offset spatula, thoroughly swirl filling into batter (there should be no large pockets of filling remaining). Repeat swirling step with remaining batter and filling.

5 Bake until top is golden brown and skewer inserted in center comes out clean, 1 hour to 1 hour 10 minutes, rotating pan halfway through baking. Let cake cool in pan on wire rack for 10 minutes. Invert cake onto rack, remove pan, and let cool for at least 3 hours before serving. (Cake can be stored at room temperature for up to 24 hours.)

Marbling the Filling

1 Spoon half of batter into prepared pan and smooth top. Using back of spoon, create ½-inch-deep channel in center of batter.

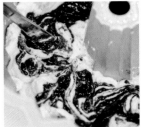

2 Spoon half of filling into channel. Thoroughly swirl filling into batter. Repeat swirling step with remaining batter and filling.

Pound Cakes, Bundt Cakes, and Tube Cakes

saffron-orange bundt cake

serves 12

cake

1 tablespoon boiling water

½ teaspoon saffron threads, crumbled

⅛ teaspoon ground turmeric

¾ cup buttermilk

4 teaspoons grated orange zest, plus 2 tablespoons juice

1 teaspoon vanilla extract

3 cups (15 ounces) all-purpose flour

1 teaspoon salt

1 teaspoon baking powder

½ teaspoon baking soda

18 tablespoons (2¼ sticks) unsalted butter, cut into 18 pieces and softened

2 cups (14 ounces) granulated sugar

3 large eggs plus 1 large yolk

glaze

2 cups (8 ounces) confectioners' sugar

1 teaspoon grated orange zest, plus 2–4 tablespoons juice

why this recipe works Saffron might not be the first ingredient you think about adding to a cake, but the prized spice's floral, earthy notes offer a unique and sophisticated twist to classic Bundt cake. Blooming the saffron in hot water before adding it to the batter released its flavor and aroma, but when we baked the cake we were disappointed to find the interior lacked the bright yellow-orange color that is a defining characteristic of saffron. Adding more saffron was overpowering, so we turned to turmeric; just ⅛ teaspoon dyed the cake a sunny yellow without adding any noticeable flavor. We thought the sweet-sour flavor of orange would pair well with the spice, and we used both zest and juice for an unmistakable orange presence. This grown-up Bundt needed a special finishing touch, so we dressed it up with glaze; a combination of orange juice and confectioner's sugar accentuated the cake's orange notes. You can bake this cake in a decorative 10-cup Bundt pan (for more information, see page 332); place a baking sheet under the Bundt pan. The cake has a light, fluffy texture when eaten the day it is baked, but if well wrapped and held at room temperature overnight its texture becomes denser—like that of pound cake—the following day.

1 *For the cake* Adjust oven rack to lower-middle position and heat oven to 350 degrees. Spray 12-cup nonstick Bundt pan with baking spray with flour. Combine boiling water, saffron, and turmeric in 2-cup liquid measuring cup and let steep for 15 minutes. Whisk in buttermilk, orange zest and juice, and vanilla until combined.

2 Whisk flour, salt, baking powder, and baking soda together in bowl. Using stand mixer fitted with paddle, beat butter and sugar on medium-high speed until pale and fluffy, about 3 minutes. Add eggs and yolk, one at a time, and beat until combined. Reduce speed to low and add flour mixture in 3 additions, alternating with saffron mixture in 2 additions, scraping down bowl as needed. Give batter final stir by hand.

3 Transfer batter to prepared pan and smooth top with rubber spatula. Bake until top is golden and skewer inserted in center comes out clean, 50 to 55 minutes, rotating pan halfway through baking.

4 Let cake cool in pan on wire rack set in rimmed baking sheet for 10 minutes. Invert cake onto rack, remove pan, and let cool completely, at least 2 hours. (Unglazed cake can be stored at room temperature for up to 24 hours.)

5 *For the glaze* Whisk sugar, zest, and 2 tablespoons orange juice in bowl until smooth. Gradually add remaining 2 tablespoons orange juice as needed, teaspoon by teaspoon, until glaze is thick but still pourable. Drizzle glaze over cooled cake and let set for 10 minute before serving.

cider-glazed apple bundt cake

serves 12

4 cups apple cider

3¾ cups (18¾ ounces) all-purpose flour

1½ teaspoons salt

1½ teaspoons baking powder

½ teaspoon baking soda

¾ teaspoon ground cinnamon

¼ teaspoon ground allspice

¾ cup (3 ounces) confectioners' sugar

16 tablespoons unsalted butter, melted

1½ cups packed (10½ ounces) dark brown sugar

3 large eggs

2 teaspoons vanilla extract

1½ pounds Granny Smith apples, peeled and shredded (3 cups)

why this recipe works If you're making an apple cake, there's a very good reason—one that's backed by science—to bake it in a Bundt pan: efficient energy transfer. Apple flavor is relatively mellow, so you really have to pack in a ton of fruit for it have any real presence. To accommodate all that moisture, apple cake batters have to be pretty thick and stiff, which means it takes longer for the oven's heat to penetrate from the outside to the middle. The central hole in a Bundt pan eliminates the problematic middle; plus, it allows heat to flow through the center, producing a more evenly baked apple cake. To bolster the flavor of a hefty 1½ pounds of apples, we made an apple cider reduction and used it three ways: added to the batter, brushed onto the exterior of the baked cake, and stirred into a glaze. For the sake of efficiency, begin boiling the cider before assembling the rest of the ingredients. Reducing the cider to exactly 1 cup is important; if you over-reduce it, make up the difference with water. We like the tartness of Granny Smith apples in this recipe, but any variety of apple will work. You can shred the apples with the shredding disk of a food processor or on the large holes of a paddle or box grater. You can bake this cake in a decorative 10-cup Bundt pan (for more information, see page 332); place a baking sheet under the Bundt pan.

1 Bring cider to boil in 12-inch skillet over high heat; cook until reduced to 1 cup, 20 to 25 minutes. While cider is reducing, adjust oven rack to middle position and heat oven to 350 degrees. Spray 12-cup nonstick Bundt pan with baking spray with flour. Whisk flour, salt, baking powder, baking soda, cinnamon, and allspice in large bowl until combined. Place confectioners' sugar in small bowl.

2 Add 2 tablespoons cider reduction to confectioners' sugar and whisk to form smooth icing. Cover with plastic wrap and set aside. Set aside 6 tablespoons cider reduction.

3 Pour remaining ½ cup cider reduction into large bowl; add melted butter, brown sugar, eggs, and vanilla and whisk until smooth. Pour cider mixture over flour mixture and stir with rubber spatula until almost fully combined (some streaks of flour will remain). Stir in apples and any accumulated juice until evenly distributed. Transfer mixture to prepared pan and smooth top. Bake until skewer inserted in center comes out clean, 55 minutes to 1 hour 5 minutes, rotating pan halfway through baking.

4 Transfer pan to wire rack set in rimmed baking sheet. Brush exposed surface of cake lightly with 1 tablespoon reserved cider reduction. Let cake cool for 10 minutes. Invert cake onto rack, remove pan, and brush top and sides of cake with remaining 5 tablespoons reserved cider reduction. Let cake cool for 20 minutes. Stir icing to loosen, then drizzle evenly over cake. Let cake cool completely, at least 2 hours, before serving. (Cake can be stored at room temperature for up to 3 days.)

Pound Cakes, Bundt Cakes, and Tube Cakes

tunnel of fudge cake

serves 12

cake

¾ cup (2¼ ounces) Dutch-processed cocoa powder, plus 1 tablespoon for pan

20 tablespoons (2½ sticks) unsalted butter, cut into 20 pieces and softened, plus 1 tablespoon, melted, for pan

½ cup boiling water

2 ounces bittersweet chocolate, chopped

2 cups (10 ounces) all-purpose flour

2 cups pecans or walnuts, chopped fine

2 cups (8 ounces) confectioners' sugar

1 teaspoon salt

5 large eggs, room temperature

1 tablespoon vanilla extract

1 cup (7 ounces) granulated sugar

¾ cup packed (5¼ ounces) light brown sugar

chocolate glaze

¾ cup heavy cream

¼ cup light corn syrup

8 ounces bittersweet chocolate, chopped

½ teaspoon vanilla extract

why this recipe works Tunnel of fudge cake is a retro cake that's exactly what it sounds like: an ultrachocolaty moist-crumbed cake with a fudgy, brownie-like interior section. We wanted to resurrect this childhood favorite—and chocoholic's dream—but our first order of business was to ditch the prepackaged cake mix that's typically used. Dutch-processed cocoa gave our cake deep chocolate flavor, and adding melted chocolate to the batter made our cake moister and contributed even more chocolate punch. Replacing some of the granulated sugar with brown sugar and cutting back on the flour and butter provided the perfect environment for the fudgy interior to form. Slightly underbaking the cake was an essential step to achieve the ideal consistency for the chocolate tunnel. For an accurate measurement of boiling water, bring a full kettle of water to a boil and then measure out the desired amount. Do not use a cake tester, toothpick, or skewer to test the cake—the fudgy interior won't give an accurate reading. Instead, remove the cake from the oven when the sides just begin to pull away from the pan and the surface of the cake springs back when pressed gently with your finger. You can bake this cake in a decorative 10-cup Bundt pan (for more information, see page 332); place a baking sheet under the Bundt pan.

1 *For the cake* Adjust oven rack to lower-middle position and heat oven to 350 degrees. Mix 1 tablespoon cocoa and melted butter into paste. Using pastry brush, thoroughly coat interior of 12-cup nonstick Bundt pan. Pour boiling water over chocolate in bowl and whisk until smooth. Let cool completely. Whisk flour, pecans, confectioners' sugar, salt, and remaining ¾ cup cocoa together in large bowl. Whisk eggs and vanilla in 4-cup liquid measuring cup.

2 Using stand mixer fitted with paddle, beat softened butter, granulated sugar, and brown sugar on medium-high speed until fluffy, about 2 minutes. Reduce speed to low and add egg mixture until combined, about 30 seconds. Add chocolate mixture and mix until incorporated, about 30 seconds. Add flour mixture and mix until just combined, about 30 seconds.

3 Transfer batter to prepared pan and smooth top with rubber spatula. Bake until edges are beginning to pull away from pan, about 45 minutes, rotating pan halfway through baking. Let cake cool in pan on wire rack set in rimmed baking sheet for 1½ hours. Invert cake onto rack, remove pan, and let cool completely, at least 2 hours.

4 *For the chocolate glaze* Heat cream, corn syrup, and chocolate in small saucepan over medium heat, stirring constantly, until smooth. Stir in vanilla and set aside until slightly thickened, about 30 minutes. Drizzle glaze over cooled cake and let set for at least 10 minutes before serving. (Cake can be stored at room temperature for up to 2 days.)

bold and spicy gingerbread bundt cake

serves 12

cake

2½ cups (12½ ounces) all-purpose flour

2 teaspoons baking powder

¾ teaspoon baking soda

¾ teaspoon salt

16 tablespoons unsalted butter

2 tablespoons ground ginger

2 teaspoons ground cinnamon

1 teaspoon ground allspice

¼ teaspoon pepper

4 large eggs, room temperature

1½ cups (10½ ounces) granulated sugar

4 teaspoons grated fresh ginger

¾ cup robust or full molasses

¾ cup stout beer

glaze

1¾ cups (7 ounces) confectioners' sugar

3 tablespoons ginger ale

1 teaspoon ground ginger

why this recipe works In our opinion, gingerbread is only worth eating if its flavor is unmistakably bold and spicy. For our gingerbread Bundt cake, the standard liquid combination of mild molasses and water seemed lackluster. Robust molasses had more presence in our scaled-up cake, and we replaced the water with stout for a deeper flavor profile. The beer gave the cake a malty tang that tasters loved. Powdered ginger provided a spicy kick, and a little cinnamon and allspice contributed warm notes. Blooming the spices in melted butter—a technique the test kitchen uses for savory spiced dishes—intensified their flavor, but tasters still wanted more ginger. A bit of grated fresh ginger added another layer of heat that the dried spice alone couldn't muster. And another traditionally savory ingredient, black pepper, added a mild bite that further enhanced the ginger flavor. We used the glaze as one final opportunity to turn up the heat by mixing a little ground ginger in with the confectioners' sugar and adding a few tablespoons of ginger ale to thin the glaze to just the right consistency. Guinness is the test kitchen's preferred brand of stout for this cake. Be sure to use finely ground black pepper here. Do not use blackstrap molasses in this recipe. An equal amount of orange or lemon juice can be substituted for the ginger ale in the glaze. This cake pairs well with Whipped Cream (page 405) or vanilla ice cream.

1 *For the cake* Adjust oven rack to middle position and heat oven to 375 degrees. Spray 12-cup nonstick Bundt pan with baking spray with flour. Whisk flour, baking powder, baking soda, and salt together in bowl.

2 Melt butter in medium saucepan over medium heat. Stir in ground ginger, cinnamon, allspice, and pepper and cook until fragrant, about 30 seconds. Remove from heat and let butter mixture cool slightly.

3 Whisk eggs, sugar, and fresh ginger together in large bowl until light and frothy. Stir in melted butter mixture, molasses, and beer until incorporated. Add flour mixture to egg mixture and whisk until no lumps remain.

4 Transfer batter to prepared pan and smooth top with rubber spatula. Gently tap pan on counter to release air bubbles. Bake until skewer inserted in center comes out clean, about 45 minutes, rotating pan halfway through baking. Let cake cool in pan on wire rack set in rimmed baking sheet for 20 minutes. Invert cake onto rack, remove pan, and let cool completely, about 2 hours.

5 *For the glaze* Whisk sugar, ginger ale, and ginger together in bowl until smooth. Drizzle glaze over cooled cake and let set, about 15 minutes, before serving. (Cake can stored at room temperature for up to 2 days.)

olive oil–yogurt bundt cake

serves 12

cake

3 cups (15 ounces) all-purpose flour

1 tablespoon baking powder

1 teaspoon salt

1¼ cups (8¾ ounces) granulated sugar

4 large eggs

1¼ cups extra-virgin olive oil

1 cup plain whole-milk yogurt

glaze

2 cups (8 ounces) confectioners' sugar

2–3 tablespoons lemon juice

1 tablespoon plain whole-milk yogurt

why this recipe works Popular throughout Spain and France, this simple cake exists in many forms, but the basic recipe is the same: Extra-virgin olive oil and yogurt are combined with eggs, sugar, flour, a leavener, and sometimes citrus to create a moist, delicate cake with a slightly coarse crumb and a subtly tangy, mildly fruity aroma. We tested our way through numerous versions and found we preferred our cake without citrus, which enabled the subtle aroma of the olive oil to shine through. As for the type of yogurt, we found that the most traditional—plain whole-milk yogurt—yielded the best results. The crust and interior crumb of cakes made with Greek yogurt were too thick and dense, and cakes made with low-fat yogurt were too dry and crumbly. Baking our cake in a Bundt pan made for a refined presentation, and we found that an easy-to-make lemon glaze (with a touch of tangy yogurt) further transformed this modest everyday cake into an elegant dessert. For the best flavor, be sure to use high-quality extra-virgin olive oil. You can bake this cake in a decorative 10-cup Bundt pan (for more information, see page 332); place a baking sheet under the Bundt pan.

1 *For the cake* Adjust oven rack to lower-middle position and heat oven to 350 degrees. Spray 12-cup nonstick Bundt pan with baking spray with flour. Whisk flour, baking powder, and salt together in bowl. Whisk sugar and eggs in large bowl until sugar is mostly dissolved and mixture is pale and frothy, about 1 minute. Whisk in oil and yogurt until combined. Using rubber spatula, stir in flour mixture until combined and no dry streaks remain.

2 Pour batter into prepared pan and smooth top with rubber spatula. Gently tap pan on counter to settle batter. Bake until golden brown and skewer inserted in center comes out clean, 40 to 45 minutes, rotating pan halfway through baking. Let cake cool in pan on wire rack set in rimmed baking sheet for 10 minutes.

3 *For the glaze* Whisk sugar, 2 tablespoons lemon juice, and yogurt in bowl until smooth, adding more lemon juice as needed, teaspoon by teaspoon, until glaze is thick but still pourable. Invert cake onto rack and remove pan. Pour half of glaze over warm cake and let cool for 1 hour. Pour remaining glaze over cake and let cool completely, about 2 hours. Serve. (Cake can be stored at room temperature for up to 2 days.)

Pound Cakes, Bundt Cakes, and Tube Cakes

angel food cake

serves 12

¾ cup (3 ounces) cake flour

1½ cups (10½ ounces) sugar

12 large egg whites, room temperature

1 teaspoon cream of tartar

¼ teaspoon salt

1½ teaspoons vanilla extract

1½ teaspoons lemon juice

½ teaspoon almond extract

why this recipe works Angel food cake is sweet, delicate, downy soft, and incredibly light—if you strike the right balance of ingredients and use the proper technique. First, we found it key to create a stable egg white base, starting the whites at medium-low speed just to break them up into a froth and then increasing the mixer speed to medium-high to form soft, billowy mounds. It was also important to add the sugar gradually; once all the sugar was incorporated, the whites became shiny and formed soft peaks when the whisk was lifted. A delicate touch was required when incorporating the flour, which we sifted over the batter and gently folded in. We strongly recommend using a tube pan with a removable bottom, but a pan without one can be lined with parchment paper. (If your tube pan has a removable bottom, you do not need to line it with parchment.) Do not grease the pan; greasing prevents the cake from climbing up and clinging to the sides as it bakes, and a greased pan will produce a disappointingly short cake. Serve this cake as is or dust with confectioners' sugar.

1 Adjust oven rack to lower-middle position and heat oven to 325 degrees. Line 16-cup tube pan with parchment paper but do not grease. Whisk flour and ¾ cup sugar together in bowl.

2 Using stand mixer fitted with whisk attachment, whip egg whites, cream of tartar, and salt on medium-low speed until foamy, about 1 minute. Increase speed to medium-high and whip to soft, billowy mounds, about 1 minute. Gradually add remaining ¾ cup sugar and whip until soft, glossy peaks form, 1 to 2 minutes. Add vanilla, lemon juice, and almond extract and beat until just blended.

3 Sift flour mixture over egg whites, about 3 tablespoons at a time, gently folding mixture into whites after each addition with large rubber spatula.

4 Gently transfer batter to prepared pan and smooth top with rubber spatula. Bake until golden brown and top springs back when pressed firmly, 50 minutes to 1 hour, rotating pan halfway through baking.

5 If pan has prongs around rim for elevating cake, invert pan on them. If not, invert pan over neck of bottle or funnel so that air can circulate all around it. Let cake cool completely in pan, 2 to 3 hours.

6 Run thin knife around edge of pan to loosen cake, then gently tap pan upside down on counter to release cake. Peel off parchment and turn cake right side up onto platter. Serve. (Cake can be stored at room temperature for up to 2 days or refrigerated for up to 4 days.)

chiffon cake

serves 12

1½ cups (10½ ounces) sugar

1⅓ cups (5⅓ ounces) cake flour

2 teaspoons baking powder

½ teaspoon salt

7 large eggs (2 whole, 5 separated),
room temperature

¾ cup water

½ cup vegetable oil

1 tablespoon vanilla extract

½ teaspoon almond extract

½ teaspoon cream of tartar

why this recipe works With the airy height of angel food cake (from whipped egg whites) and the richness of pound cake (from egg yolks and oil), chiffon cake is a win-win. Our starting point for this classic was the original version, as first put before the public by General Mills in *Better Homes and Gardens* in 1948. Sadly, we were disappointed to find this cake was a bit dry—cottony and fluffy rather than moist and foamy, the way we thought chiffon cake should be—and it lacked flavor. Decreasing the flour meant a moister, more flavorful cake but also less structure. Increasing the amount of egg yolks was a step in the right direction, but our cake still wasn't perfect. In the end, instead of whipping all of the egg whites we found that mixing some of them (unbeaten) into the dry ingredients, along with the yolks, water, and oil, provided the structure our cake needed. Serve this cake as is or dust with confectioners' sugar.

1 Adjust oven rack to lower-middle position and heat oven to 325 degrees. Line 16-cup tube pan with parchment paper but do not grease. Whisk sugar, flour, baking powder, and salt together in large bowl. Whisk in whole eggs and yolks, water, oil, vanilla, and almond extract until batter is just smooth.

2 Using stand mixer fitted with whisk attachment, whip egg whites and cream of tartar on medium-low speed until foamy, about 1 minute. Increase speed to medium-high and whip until stiff peaks form, 3 to 4 minutes. Using large rubber spatula, fold whites into batter, smearing any stubborn pockets of egg white against side of bowl.

3 Transfer batter to prepared pan and smooth top with rubber spatula. Gently tap pan on counter to settle batter. Bake until skewer inserted in center comes out clean, 55 minutes to 1 hour 5 minutes, rotating pan halfway through baking.

4 If cake has prongs around rim for elevating cake, invert pan on them. If not, invert pan over neck of bottle or funnel so that air can circulate all around it. Let cake cool completely in pan, 2 to 3 hours.

5 Run thin knife around edge of pan to loosen cake, then gently tap pan upside down on counter to release cake. Peel off parchment and turn cake right side up onto platter. Serve. (Cake can be stored at room temperature for up to 2 days or refrigerated for up to 4 days.)

variations

lemon chiffon cake

Substitute ½ teaspoon baking soda for baking powder.
Reduce water to ⅔ cup, reduce vanilla to 1 teaspoon,
and omit almond extract. Add 3 tablespoons grated
lemon zest plus 2 tablespoons juice (3 lemons) to batter
with vanilla.

mocha-nut chiffon cake

Substitute ¾ cup brewed espresso or strong coffee for
water and omit almond extract. Add ½ cup finely
chopped toasted walnuts and 1 ounce unsweetened
grated chocolate to batter before folding in whites.

orange chiffon cake

Substitute 2 tablespoons grated orange zest plus
¾ cup juice (2 oranges) for water. Reduce vanilla to
1 teaspoon and omit almond extract.

10

CHEESECAKES, ICEBOX CAKES & ICE CREAM CAKES

foolproof new york cheesecake

serves 12 to 16

crust

6 whole graham crackers, broken into pieces

⅓ cup packed (2⅓ ounces) dark brown sugar

½ cup (2½ ounces) all-purpose flour

¼ teaspoon salt

7 tablespoons unsalted butter, melted

filling

2½ pounds cream cheese, cut into chunks and softened

1½ cups (10½ ounces) granulated sugar

⅛ teaspoon salt

⅓ cup sour cream

2 teaspoons lemon juice

2 teaspoons vanilla extract

6 large eggs plus 2 large yolks

why this recipe works New York cheesecake has a plush, luxurious texture, golden brown surface, and buttery graham cracker crust. But it's hard to get right: Different ovens yield different cakes. To achieve the perfect cheesecake for all, we worked from the bottom up. We started by creating a pastry–graham cracker hybrid crust that wouldn't become soggy beneath the moist, dense filling. Using the food processor to combine graham crackers, sugar, flour, and salt with melted butter created a rich, shortbread-like base with nutty wheat flavor. Adding sour cream to our rich cream cheese filling contributed more tang, and straining and resting the filling eliminated any lumps or air pockets. Traditionally, New York–style cheesecakes start in a hot oven so that a burnished outer skin develops before the temperature is dropped to finish, but we found that the time it took for the oven temperature to change varied. We flipped the order, baking at a low temperature to set the filling and then removing it before turning up the heat. Once the oven hit 500 degrees, we put the cheesecake on the upper rack to brown the surface. These tweaks may defy convention, but you can count on this cheesecake to have the same texture, flavor, and appearance no matter what oven is used to bake it. Serve with Fresh Strawberry Topping (page 378), if desired.

1 *For the crust* Adjust oven racks to upper-middle and lower-middle positions and heat oven to 325 degrees. Process crackers and sugar in food processor until finely ground, about 30 seconds. Add flour and salt and pulse to combine, about 2 pulses. Add 6 tablespoons melted butter and pulse until crumbs are evenly moistened, about 10 pulses. Brush bottom of 9-inch springform pan with ½ tablespoon melted butter. Using your hands, press crumb mixture evenly into pan bottom. Using bottom of measuring cup, firmly pack crust into pan. Bake on lower rack until fragrant and beginning to brown around edges, about 13 minutes. Transfer to rimmed baking sheet; set aside and let cool completely. Reduce oven temperature to 200 degrees.

2 *For the filling* Using stand mixer fitted with paddle, beat cream cheese, ¾ cup sugar, and salt on medium-low speed until combined, about 1 minute. Beat in remaining ¾ cup sugar until combined, about 1 minute. Scrape paddle and bowl well; add sour cream, lemon juice, and vanilla and beat at low speed until combined, about 1 minute. Add egg yolks and beat on medium-low speed until thoroughly combined, about 1 minute. Scrape bowl and paddle. Add whole eggs, two at a time, beating until thoroughly combined, about 30 seconds after each addition. Strain filling through fine-mesh strainer set in large bowl, pressing against strainer with rubber spatula or back of ladle to help filling pass through strainer.

3 Brush sides of springform pan with remaining ½ tablespoon melted butter. Pour filling into crust and set aside for 10 minutes to allow air bubbles to rise to top. Gently draw tines of fork across surface of cake to pop air bubbles that have risen to surface.

4 When oven thermometer reads 200 degrees, bake cheesecake on lower rack until center registers 165 degrees, 3 to 3½ hours. Remove cake from oven and increase oven temperature to 500 degrees.

5 When oven is at 500 degrees, bake cheesecake on upper rack until top is evenly browned, 4 to 12 minutes. Let cool for 5 minutes, then run thin knife around edge of pan. Let cheesecake cool in pan on wire rack until barely warm, 2½ to 3 hours. Wrap cheesecake tightly in plastic wrap and refrigerate until cold and firmly set, at least 6 hours or up to 24 hours.

6 To unmold cheesecake, remove sides of pan and slide thin metal spatula between crust and pan bottom to loosen, then slide cheesecake onto platter. Let sit at room temperature for about 30 minutes before serving. (Leftovers can be refrigerated for up to 4 days.)

variation
marble cheesecake
At end of step 2, measure out 1 cup of filling, transfer to small bowl, and stir in 2 tablespoons Dutch-processed cocoa powder until well combined. Pour remaining cheesecake batter into prepared pan in step 3. Using tablespoon, gently spoon chocolate batter onto plain batter around edge and in center of cake, leaving about ½ inch between each spoonful. (If there is extra chocolate batter, add to previous drops.) Using fork, drag tines through batter to make a marbled pattern.

spiced pumpkin cheesecake

serves 12 to 16

crust

**9 whole graham crackers,
broken into 1-inch pieces**

3 tablespoons sugar

½ teaspoon ground ginger

½ teaspoon ground cinnamon

¼ teaspoon ground cloves

7 tablespoons unsalted butter, melted

filling

1⅓ cups (9⅓ ounces) sugar

1 teaspoon ground cinnamon

½ teaspoon ground ginger

½ teaspoon salt

¼ teaspoon ground nutmeg

¼ teaspoon ground cloves

¼ teaspoon ground allspice

**1 (15-ounce) can unsweetened
pumpkin puree**

**1½ pounds cream cheese, cut into chunks
and softened**

1 tablespoon vanilla extract

1 tablespoon lemon juice

5 large eggs, room temperature

1 cup heavy cream

why this recipe works Spiced pumpkin may be a well-trod flavor profile, but it really shines in cheesecake—the tangy cream cheese is a beautiful foil to the earthy pumpkin and warm spices. The only problem? Pumpkin puree holds a lot of moisture that interferes with the creaminess of this custard-based cake, usually resulting in a wet cake and soggy crust. Fortunately, the solution was easy: We thoroughly blotted the pumpkin with paper towels until it became paste-like. To match the pumpkin flavor profile, many recipes call for brown sugar, but we liked white here; its cleaner flavor let the pumpkin take center stage. The addition of some heavy cream fortified the richness of our filling and resulted in an ultracreamy cake. For a complementary crust, we wanted to use spicy gingersnaps, but they refused to retain their crispness when baked beneath the filling, so we spiced up reliable graham crackers with ginger, cinnamon, and cloves. Serve with Brown Sugar and Bourbon Whipped Cream (recipe follows), if desired.

1 *For the crust* Adjust oven rack to lower-middle position and heat oven to 325 degrees. Pulse crackers, sugar, ginger, cinnamon, and cloves in food processor until finely ground, about 15 pulses. Transfer crumbs to bowl, drizzle with 6 tablespoons melted butter, and mix with rubber spatula until evenly moistened. Using your hands, press crumb mixture evenly into bottom of 9-inch springform pan. Using bottom of measuring cup, firmly pack crust into pan. Bake until browned around edges, about 15 minutes, rotating pan halfway through baking. Let crust cool completely on wire rack, about 30 minutes, then wrap outside of pan with two 18-inch square pieces of heavy-duty aluminum foil. Brush inside of pan with remaining 1 tablespoon melted butter. Set springform pan in roasting pan. Bring kettle of water to boil.

2 *For the filling* Whisk sugar, cinnamon, ginger, salt, nutmeg, cloves, and allspice together in bowl. Line rimmed baking sheet with triple layer of paper towels. Spread pumpkin on paper towels in roughly even layer and press with second triple layer of paper towels to wick away moisture. Peel back top layer of paper towels and discard. Grasp bottom layer of paper towels and fold pumpkin in half; peel back paper towels. Repeat and flip pumpkin onto sheet.

3 Using stand mixer fitted with paddle, beat cream cheese on medium-low speed until smooth, about 1 minute. Scrape down bowl, then beat in half of sugar mixture until combined, about 1 minute. Repeat with remaining sugar mixture. Add vanilla, lemon juice, and pumpkin and beat until combined, about 1 minute; scrape down bowl and paddle. Add eggs, one at a time, and beat until combined, about 1 minute. Beat in cream until combined, about 1 minute. Give filling final stir by hand.

4 Pour filling into crust and smooth top with spatula. Set roasting pan on oven rack and pour enough boiling water into roasting pan to come about halfway up sides of springform pan. Bake until cheesecake registers 150 degrees, about 1½ hours. Let cake cool in water bath on wire rack for 45 minutes. Transfer springform pan to rack, discarding foil, and let cheesecake cool until barely warm, about 3 hours. Wrap cheesecake tightly in plastic wrap and refrigerate until cold, at least 3 hours or up to 24 hours.

5 To unmold cheesecake, wrap hot, damp dish towel around springform pan and let stand for 1 minute. Remove sides of pan and slide thin metal spatula between crust and pan bottom to loosen, then slide cheesecake onto platter. Let sit at room temperature for 30 minutes before serving.

variation
pumpkin-bourbon cheesecake with graham-pecan crust
Reduce graham crackers to 5 whole crackers, process ½ cup chopped pecans with crackers, and reduce melted butter to 4 tablespoons. Omit lemon juice from filling, reduce vanilla extract to 1 teaspoon, and add ¼ cup bourbon along with heavy cream.

brown sugar and bourbon whipped cream
Makes 2½ cups

Refrigerating the mixture in step 1 gives the brown sugar time to dissolve.

1 cup heavy cream, chilled
½ cup sour cream
½ cup packed (3½ ounces) light brown sugar
2 teaspoons bourbon
⅛ teaspoon salt

1 Using stand mixer fitted with whisk attachment, mix heavy cream, sour cream, sugar, bourbon, and salt until combined. Transfer to separate bowl, cover with plastic wrap, and refrigerate until ready to serve, at least 4 hours or up to 24 hours, stirring once or twice during chilling to ensure that sugar dissolves.

2 Using clean, dry mixer bowl and whisk attachment, whip mixture on medium-low speed until foamy, about 1 minute. Increase speed to high and whip until soft peaks form, 1 to 3 minutes.

Drying the Pumpkin Puree

 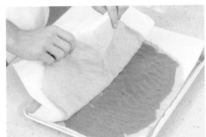 

1 Line rimmed baking sheet with triple layer of paper towels. Spread pumpkin on paper towels in even layer. Press with second triple layer of paper towels to wick away moisture.

2 Peel back top layer of paper towels and discard. Grasp bottom layer of paper towels and fold pumpkin in half; peel back paper towels.

3 Repeat and flip pumpkin onto baking sheet.

Cheesecakes, Icebox Cakes, and Ice Cream Cakes

milk chocolate cheesecake

serves 12 to 16

16 Oreo cookies, broken into rough pieces

1 tablespoon plus ½ cup (3½ ounces) sugar

2 tablespoons unsalted butter, melted

8 ounces milk chocolate, chopped

⅓ cup heavy cream

2 tablespoons unsweetened cocoa powder

¼ teaspoon salt

1½ pounds cream cheese, cut into chunks and softened

4 large eggs, room temperature

2 teaspoons vanilla extract

Melting Milk Chocolate

Because milk chocolate contains milk solids, its protein content is generally higher than that of dark chocolate. The extra protein means that milk chocolate melts at a slightly lower temperature than dark. What's more, when you add heat to protein and sugar, new molecules may form, introducing unwelcome scorched or burned flavors. Microwaves are generally gentle, but notoriously inconsistent, so choose 50 percent power, keep a close eye on the chocolate, and give it a stir every 15 seconds.

---

why this recipe works While chocolate typically makes everything better, cheesecake is a notable exception. The bitter edge of dark chocolate—our go-to—is a poor match for the tang of cream cheese. After making dozens of versions, we figured out that mild-mannered milk chocolate was the secret to a sweet, creamy cheesecake with just the right balance of chocolate and cheese. A small amount of cocoa powder contributed depth. For an easy, crunchy, chocolaty crust, we used Oreo cookies processed with butter and a bit of sugar. Use the entire Oreo—filling and all—for the crust.

1 Adjust oven rack to middle position and heat oven to 350 degrees. Grease bottom and sides of 9-inch springform pan. Process cookies and 1 tablespoon sugar in food processor until finely ground, about 30 seconds. Add melted butter and pulse until crumbs are evenly moistened, about 6 pulses. Using your hands, press crumb mixture evenly into pan bottom. Using bottom of measuring cup, firmly pack crust into pan. Bake until fragrant and set, about 10 minutes. Let crust cool completely on wire rack, about 30 minutes.

2 Reduce oven temperature to 250 degrees. Combine 6 ounces chocolate and cream in bowl and microwave at 50 percent power, stirring occasionally, until melted and smooth, 60 to 90 seconds. Let cool for 10 minutes. Whisk cocoa, salt, and remaining ½ cup sugar in separate bowl until no lumps remain. Using stand mixer fitted with paddle, beat cream cheese and cocoa mixture on medium speed until creamy and smooth, about 3 minutes, scraping down bowl as needed. Reduce speed to medium-low, add chocolate mixture, and beat until combined. Gradually add eggs, one at a time, until incorporated, scraping down bowl as needed. Add vanilla and give batter final stir by hand until no streaks of chocolate remain.

3 Pour filling into crust and smooth top with spatula. Gently tap pan on counter to release air bubbles. Cover pan tightly with aluminum foil (taking care not to touch surface of cheesecake with foil) and place on rimmed baking sheet. Bake for 1 hour, then remove foil. Continue to bake until edges are set and center registers 150 degrees and jiggles slightly when shaken, 30 to 45 minutes. Let cheesecake cool completely in pan on wire rack. Wrap cheesecake tightly in plastic wrap and refrigerate until cold, at least 8 hours or up to 4 days.

4 To unmold cheesecake, remove sides of pan and slide thin metal spatula between crust and pan bottom to loosen, then slide cheesecake onto platter. Microwave remaining 2 ounces chocolate in small bowl at 50 percent power, stirring occasionally, until melted, 60 to 90 seconds. Let cool for 5 minutes. Transfer to small zipper-lock bag, cut small hole in corner, and pipe chocolate in thin zigzag pattern across top of cheesecake. Let cheesecake sit at room temperature for 30 minutes before serving.

red velvet cheesecake

serves 12 to 16

2 (9-inch) Red Velvet Cake Layers (page 396)

frosting

8 tablespoons unsalted butter, cut into 8 pieces and softened

2 cups (8 ounces) confectioners' sugar

8 ounces cream cheese, cut into 4 pieces and softened

¾ teaspoon vanilla extract

Pinch salt

filling

1½ teaspoons unflavored gelatin

1½ cups heavy cream

6 ounces white chocolate, chopped

1 pound cream cheese, cut into chunks and softened

½ cup (3½ ounces) granulated sugar

why this recipe works This inventive and ultradecadent cake combines two classic desserts: red velvet cake and cheesecake. Velvety cake layers encase an easy no-bake cheesecake filling for a striking layered look. We assembled the cake components in a springform pan for stability before refrigerating the cake so the cheesecake portion could set up. A mix of melted white chocolate and gelatin provided structure to the eggless cheesecake layer, and we crumbled a part of each cake round to use as decoration on the side of the finished cake. A simple cream cheese frosting united all three layers of this unique cake.

1 Using long serrated knife, cut 1 horizontal line around sides of each cake layer 1 inch from bottom, then, following scored lines, cut each layer into 2 even layers. Using your fingers, crumble tops into small crumbs; transfer crumbs to airtight container and set aside. Place 1 remaining cake round in 9-inch springform pan; reserve second cake round.

2 *For the frosting* Using stand mixer fitted with paddle, beat butter and sugar on medium-high speed until fluffy, about 2 minutes. Add cream cheese, 1 piece at a time, and continue to beat until incorporated, about 30 seconds. Beat in vanilla and salt. Refrigerate frosting until ready to use.

3 *For the filling* Sprinkle gelatin over ½ cup cream in small saucepan and let sit until gelatin softens, about 5 minutes. Cook mixture over low heat until edges are just bubbling. Add white chocolate and continue to cook, stirring constantly, until just melted and smooth. Set aside and let cool slightly, about 15 minutes. Using clean, dry mixer bowl and whisk attachment, whip remaining 1 cup cream on medium-high speed until soft peaks form, 1 to 2 minutes; transfer to bowl and set aside. Using now-empty stand mixer fitted with paddle, beat cream cheese and sugar on medium-high speed until pale and fluffy, 2 to 3 minutes. Reduce speed to medium-low, add white chocolate mixture, and mix until just combined, scraping down sides of bowl as needed. Using rubber spatula, gently fold in whipped cream until combined.

4 Spread filling over cake in pan and spread into even layer. Place remaining cake round, cut side down, on top. Wrap cheesecake tightly with plastic wrap and refrigerate until set, at least 6 hours or up to 24 hours.

5 Line edges of cake platter with 4 strips of parchment paper to keep platter clean. Run thin knife around edge of pan. Remove sides of pan. Transfer cake to prepared platter. Spread frosting evenly over top and sides of cake. Gently press reserved cake crumbs onto sides of cake. Serve.

Cheesecakes, Icebox Cakes, and Ice Cream Cakes

icebox cheesecake

serves 10 to 12

crust

**8 whole graham crackers,
broken into 1-inch pieces**

1 tablespoon sugar

5 tablespoons unsalted butter, melted

filling

2½ teaspoons unflavored gelatin

1½ cups heavy cream

⅔ cup (4⅔ ounces) sugar

**1 pound cream cheese, cut into 1-inch
pieces and softened**

**1 teaspoon grated lemon zest
plus 2 tablespoons juice**

1 teaspoon vanilla extract

Pinch salt

why this recipe works We love a tall New York–style cheesecake but there's no denying it's a bit of a project. It's also incredibly rich and decadent. Sometimes we want the essence of a cheesecake with less fuss, and we want the tang of a cream cheese–based cake without the weight—something lighter and creamier to finish a meal. Enter no-bake cheesecake: The filling is lightened with whipped cream and the absence of eggs makes for a less rich cake. We achieved the best flavor and texture when we stuck to the tried-and-true combination of heavy cream and cream cheese thickened with gelatin. Allowing the gelatin to hydrate in a portion of the cream and then bringing it to a boil in the microwave fully activated its thickening power. Lemon juice, lemon zest, and a little vanilla added just enough spark to perk up the tangy cream cheese. And with a few simple tweaks, we created a peanut butter lover's variation, using Nutter Butter cookies in the crust and a generous dose of peanut butter in the cake. Serve with Fresh Strawberry Topping (page 378), if desired.

1 *For the crust* Adjust oven rack to middle position and heat oven to 325 degrees. Pulse crackers and sugar in food processor until finely ground, about 15 pulses. Transfer crumbs to bowl, drizzle with melted butter, and mix with rubber spatula until mixture resembles wet sand. Using your hands, press crumb mixture evenly into bottom of 9-inch springform pan. Using bottom of measuring cup, firmly pack crust into pan. Bake until fragrant and beginning to brown, about 13 minutes. Let crust cool completely in pan on wire rack, about 30 minutes.

2 *For the filling* Sprinkle gelatin over ¼ cup cream in 2-cup liquid measuring cup and let sit until gelatin softens, about 5 minutes. Microwave until mixture is bubbling around edges and gelatin dissolves, about 20 seconds; whisk to combine and set aside.

3 Using stand mixer fitted with whisk attachment, whip remaining 1¼ cups cream and sugar on medium-low speed until foamy, about 1 minute. Increase speed to high and whip until soft peaks form, 1 to 3 minutes. Fit stand mixer with paddle, reduce speed to medium-low, add cream cheese, and beat until combined, about 1 minute, scraping down bowl once (mixture may not be completely smooth). Add lemon juice, vanilla, and salt and continue to beat until combined, about 1 minute, scraping down bowl as needed. Increase speed to medium-high and beat until smooth, about 3 minutes. Add dissolved gelatin mixture and lemon zest and continue to beat until smooth and airy, about 2 minutes.

4 Pour filling into crust and spread into even layer with spatula. Wrap cheesecake tightly in plastic wrap and refrigerate until set, at least 6 hours or up to 24 hours.

5 To unmold cheesecake, wrap hot, damp dish towel around pan and let stand for 1 minute. Remove sides of pan and slide thin metal spatula between crust and pan bottom to loosen, then slide cheesecake onto platter. Serve.

variation

icebox peanut butter cheesecake

Omit sugar from crust and lemon zest and juice from filling. Substitute 16 Nutter Butter cookies, broken into rough pieces, for graham crackers. Process cookie pieces in food processor until evenly ground, about 45 seconds (you should have about 1¼ cups crumbs) before combining with butter in step 1. Reduce butter to 2 tablespoons. Reduce sugar in filling to ½ cup (3½ ounces). In step 3, after adding dissolved gelatin mixture, add 1 cup creamy unsalted peanut butter and beat until smooth, about 1 minute. Press ½ cup finely chopped salted peanuts onto sides of cake after unmolding and before serving.

icebox margarita cheesecake

serves 10 to 12

1 cup (3 ounces) sweetened
shredded coconut

1 teaspoon grated lime zest plus 1 lime,
sliced thin

4½ ounces pretzels (3 cups)

6 tablespoons unsalted butter, melted

4 teaspoons unflavored gelatin

¾ cup water

1 (10-ounce) can frozen margarita mix,
thawed

¼ cup tequila

¼ cup triple sec

1½ cups heavy cream, chilled

1 (14-ounce) can sweetened
condensed milk

4 ounces cream cheese, softened

why this recipe works In this dessert, cool, creamy icebox cheesecake meets the salty, pucker-inspiring flavors of a margarita. We started by dissolving gelatin in a mixture of margarita mix, tequila, and triple sec to create a kind of margarita Jell-O (perhaps the best kind of Jell-O). We mixed some of this into the cheesecake filling for flavor and structure, and we strained the remainder to create a glassy "shot" on top of the cake. For a crust that was more in line with our theme, we replaced the traditional graham cracker crust with a pretzel one to hint at the salted rim of a margarita glass. To finish, we garnished the sides of the cake with a mixture of coconut and lime zest and topped it off with slices of lime. This tart and creamy cheesecake is so good and refreshing we'd rather skip cocktail hour and enjoy a slice of cake instead.

1 Adjust oven rack to middle position and heat oven to 350 degrees. Grease 9-inch springform pan and line perimeter with 3-inch-wide strip of parchment paper. Process coconut and lime zest in food processor until coarsely ground, 25 to 30 seconds; reserve ½ cup and set aside. Add pretzels to remaining coconut mixture and process until finely ground, about 1 minute. Add melted butter and pulse to combine, about 5 pulses. Using your hands, press crumb mixture evenly into pan bottom. Using bottom of measuring cup, firmly pack crust into pan. Bake until edges are golden, 10 to 12 minutes. Let crust cool completely on wire rack, about 30 minutes.

2 Sprinkle gelatin over ¼ cup water in small saucepan and let sit until gelatin softens, about 5 minutes. Add margarita mix, tequila, and triple sec and cook over low heat, stirring frequently, until gelatin dissolves, about 5 minutes. Let cool for 15 minutes; set aside.

3 Using stand mixer fitted with whisk attachment, whip cream on medium-low speed until foamy, about 1 minute. Increase speed to high and whip until soft peaks form, 1 to 3 minutes. Transfer whipped cream to bowl; set aside. Using clean, dry mixer bowl and whisk attachment, mix condensed milk and cream cheese until combined, about 1½ minutes. Add 1 cup margarita mixture and whip until incorporated, about 25 seconds. Use whisk to gently fold in one-third of whipped cream, then gently fold in remaining whipped cream. Pour filling into crust. Refrigerate until just set, about 1 hour.

4 Stir remaining ½ cup water into remaining margarita mixture. Strain mixture through fine-mesh strainer into 2-cup liquid measuring cup. Pour over filling and refrigerate until set, at least 4 hours or up to 24 hours. Remove sides of pan and parchment. Press reserved coconut mixture onto sides of cake and top with lime slices. Slide thin metal spatula between crust and pan bottom to loosen, then slide cheesecake onto platter. Serve.

chocolate éclair cake

serves 15

1¼ cups (8¾ ounces) sugar

6 tablespoons cornstarch

1 teaspoon salt

5 cups whole milk

4 tablespoons unsalted butter, cut into 4 pieces

5 teaspoons vanilla extract

1¼ teaspoons unflavored gelatin

2 tablespoons water

2¾ cups heavy cream, chilled

14 ounces graham crackers

1 cup (6 ounces) semisweet chocolate chips

5 tablespoons light corn syrup

why this recipe works Chocolate éclair cake is an instant dessert classic; this no-bake cake features layers of store-bought vanilla pudding and Cool Whip sandwiched between graham crackers and topped off with chocolate frosting. As the graham crackers soften, the whole thing melds into a creamy, sliceable cake. We loved the ease of these convenience items, but our enthusiasm waned when confronted by their flavor. With a couple of easy techniques and very little active time, we produced a from-scratch version that easily trumped its inspiration. Since the cake layers required no more work than lining a pan with graham crackers, we made the effort to prepare a quick stovetop vanilla pudding, folding in whipped cream to lighten it. For the éclair topping, we created a simple microwave-and-stir glaze. Six ounces of finely chopped semisweet chocolate can be used in place of the chips.

1 Combine sugar, cornstarch, and salt in large saucepan. Whisk milk into sugar mixture until smooth and bring to boil over medium-high heat, scraping bottom of pan with heatproof rubber spatula. Immediately reduce heat to medium-low and cook, continuing to scrape bottom, until thickened and large bubbles appear on surface, 4 to 6 minutes. Off heat, whisk in butter and vanilla. Transfer pudding to large bowl and place plastic wrap directly on surface of pudding. Refrigerate until cool, about 2 hours.

2 Sprinkle gelatin over water in bowl and let sit until gelatin softens, about 5 minutes. Microwave until mixture is bubbling around edges and gelatin dissolves, 15 to 30 seconds. Using stand mixer fitted with whisk attachment, whip 2 cups cream on medium-low speed until foamy, about 1 minute. Increase speed to high and whip until soft peaks form, 1 to 3 minutes. Add gelatin mixture and whip until stiff peaks form, about 1 minute.

3 Whisk one-third of whipped cream into chilled pudding, then gently fold in remaining whipped cream, 1 scoop at a time, until combined. Cover bottom of 13 by 9-inch baking dish with layer of graham crackers, breaking crackers as necessary to line bottom of pan. Top with half of pudding–whipped cream mixture (about 5½ cups) and another layer of graham crackers. Repeat with remaining pudding–whipped cream mixture and remaining graham crackers.

4 Combine chocolate chips, corn syrup, and remaining ¾ cup cream in bowl and microwave on 50 percent power, stirring occasionally, until smooth, 1 to 2 minutes. Let glaze cool completely, about 10 minutes. Spread glaze evenly over graham crackers and refrigerate cake for at least 6 hours or up to 2 days before serving.

ALL ABOUT REFRIGERATOR AND FREEZER CAKES

Some of our favorite cakes require time in the fridge or freezer to set up properly. Cheesecakes—both traditional baked egg-based ones and those simply stabilized by gelatin and chilled—are a rich, decadent treat perfect for any special occasion. And there's no arguing that ice cream cakes are the ultimate crowd-pleaser. Use the fridge (or the freezer) to your advantage to make preparing (and storing) these cakes a breeze.

CREATING A CRISP CRUST

While the cakes in this chapter call for a variety of crumb crusts—we like a spiced graham cracker one for our Spiced Pumpkin Cheesecake (page 366) and an Oreo base for our Mexican Chocolate Ice Cream Torte (page 391)—the process of forming them is mostly the same: Mix the crumbs with melted butter and press firmly and evenly into the bottom of a springform pan. We like to use the bottom of a dry measuring cup for this step; its flat bottom and generous surface is perfect for packing the crumbs into an even layer, ensuring a crisp, cohesive crust.

DETERMINING DONENESS

Because cheesecakes have a creamy texture and don't brown the way most cakes do, normal cues like checking with a toothpick or lightly touching the top aren't useful. Gently shaking the cheesecake helps—the center should jiggle slightly—but the best method is checking the internal temperature: Usually the cheesecake should register 150 degrees. The egg proteins begin to coagulate at this point, but the temperature of the dense cake rises and the eggs continue to set once the cake comes out of the oven.

SLICING CREAMY CAKES

Cheesecakes and icebox cakes have super-creamy fillings that will stick to the knife, making it difficult to cut neat pieces. We like to dip our knife in a container of hot water or run it under a hot tap and quickly dry it before cutting so it glides through the cake. Wipe the knife clean before making another cut. Repeat heating the knife as needed.

On the Side

Many cheesecakes and ice cream cakes pair well with a strawberry topping—but not the shellacked or artificial-tasting toppings seen in bakery cases. We prefer a simple accompaniment, made with fresh berries and jam.

fresh strawberry topping
makes about 3 cups

This topping is best the day it's made. Do not use frozen strawberries in this recipe.

1¼ pounds strawberries, hulled and sliced thin (4 cups)
¼ cup (1¾ ounces) sugar
Pinch salt
½ cup strawberry jam
1 tablespoon lemon juice

1 Toss strawberries, sugar, and salt together in bowl and let sit, stirring occasionally, until berries have released their juice and sugar has dissolved, about 30 minutes.

2 Process jam in food processor until smooth, about 8 seconds. Simmer jam in small saucepan over medium heat until no longer foamy, about 3 minutes. Stir warm jam and lemon juice into strawberries. Let cool completely, about 1 hour. Serve at room temperature or chilled.

PREPARING A WATER BATH

Some cakes and cheesecakes, as well as custards, are baked in a water bath (sometimes referred to as a bain-marie). This means that the pan is partially immersed in water to ensure slow, gentle, even baking. A water bath is especially helpful for recipes that use a lot of eggs, which can curdle if they become overheated. The water also increases the humidity inside the oven, preventing the cake or custard from drying out. Here are our easy steps to working with a water bath.

1 To prevent batter from leaking out of the springform pan or water from seeping in, cover the bottom and sides of the pan with two sheets of heavy-duty aluminum foil. Place the pan in the prepared roasting pan.

2 Lifting a roasting pan filled with boiling water is awkward and dangerous. Instead, place the roasting pan with the springform pan on the oven rack. Next, carefully pour the boiling water into the pan. The water should come halfway up the sides of the cake pan.

CHILLING CHEESECAKE

There's a waiting game involved with cheesecakes—and it's essential but worthwhile. After 2 to 3 hours of cooling at room temperature, most cheesecakes require 3 to 5 hours—and even as many as 8 hours—of refrigeration (chilling time depends on the ingredients as well as the thickness and density of the filling). Don't skimp on this time: If cheesecake isn't thoroughly chilled, the filling won't hold its shape. Allowing the cheesecake plenty of time to set up makes for neat, easy slicing and an attractive presentation.

Properly Chilled Cheesecake

Underchilled Cheesecake

---

key cheesecake tips

Cheesecake is certainly a project dessert, but the steps to making it are easy if you keep these tips in mind.

1 Use softened cream cheese Cold cream cheese will lead to a dense, lumpy cheesecake. Softening the cream cheese allows it to mix with the other ingredients and aerate properly for a super-creamy cheesecake.

2 Prebake the crust If the crust is not baked until crisp, the cheesecake's base will become soggy under the moist filling while the cake bakes, and it won't hold together.

3 Scrape down the bowl If you scrape down the mixer bowl often, you'll prevent clumps of cream cheese from being pulled into the batter and appearing as chalky bits in the final cake.

4 Loosen the edges Running a thin knife around the edge of the springform pan before the cake is cool prevents the cheesecake from sticking to the sides of the pan and the top from cracking as the cheesecake contracts.

Cheesecakes, Icebox Cakes, and Ice Cream Cakes

basic ice cream cake

serves 8 to 10

25 Oreo cookies, broken into rough pieces

3 tablespoons unsalted butter, melted

1 pint strawberry ice cream

1 pint vanilla ice cream

1 pint chocolate ice cream

½ cup rainbow sprinkles

why this recipe works The appeal of ice cream cake is obvious: These two beloved desserts belong together, and a cold, creamy slice of ice cream cake is far more satisfying than a scoop of ice cream haphazardly dolloped onto a slice of cake. We wanted to develop a basic ice cream cake that would be a hit at any party. We started with three crowd-pleasing flavors—chocolate, vanilla, and strawberry—to create a striped Neapolitan cake. Oreo crumbs served as a sturdy bottom crust and also provided a welcome bit of chocolaty crunch between each layer of ice cream. When it came to assembling the cake, we found that the key was patience. We didn't start until the crust was completely cool, and allowing the ice cream to soften to a spreadable consistency ensured it wouldn't mar the crust. For clean lines and to avoid a melty mess, it was essential to freeze each layer before adding the next. We dressed up our cake by pressing party-ready rainbow sprinkles into the sides, but you could also use chopped nuts or crushed candies or cookies. You can also pipe a greeting on top once the cake is fully frozen. Use the entire Oreo—filling and all—for the crust. Before removing the cake from the springform pan, run your paring knife under hot tap water for 10 seconds or so.

1 Adjust oven rack to middle position and heat oven to 325 degrees. Process Oreos in food processor until finely ground, about 30 seconds. Add melted butter and process until mixture resembles wet sand, about 10 seconds.

2 Using your hands, press ⅔ cup crumb mixture evenly into bottom of 9-inch springform pan. Using bottom of measuring cup, firmly pack crust into pan. Bake until the crust is fragrant and set, 5 to 10 minutes. Let crust cool completely on wire rack, about 30 minutes.

3 Scoop strawberry ice cream into large bowl and, using large rubber spatula or wooden spoon, break up scoops of ice cream. Stir and fold ice cream to achieve smooth consistency. Spread softened ice cream evenly over crust. Sprinkle ⅔ cup Oreo crumbs over ice cream and pack down lightly. Wrap pan tightly with plastic wrap and freeze until ice cream is just firm, about 30 minutes. Repeat with vanilla ice cream and remaining ⅔ cup Oreo crumbs; wrap tightly and freeze for another 30 minutes. Soften chocolate ice cream, spread evenly in pan, and smooth top. Wrap cake tightly in plastic and freeze until firm, at least 8 hours or up to 1 week.

4 To unmold cake, run hot thin knife around edge of pan. Remove sides of pan and slide thin metal spatula between crust and pan bottom to loosen, then slide cake onto platter. Press sprinkles onto sides of cake. Serve immediately.

tiramisù ice cream cake

serves 8 to 10

2½ cups brewed coffee, room temperature

1½ tablespoons instant espresso powder

6 tablespoons dark rum

14 ounces dried ladyfingers (*savoiardi*)

4 pints coffee ice cream

¼ cup (1½ ounces) mini chocolate chips

8 ounces (1 cup) mascarpone cheese

¾ cup heavy cream, chilled

¼ cup (1¾ ounces) sugar

Unsweetened cocoa powder

why this recipe works We love the classic Italian dessert tiramisù and wanted to reinterpret it for summer as an ice cream cake, filling a ring of coffee-soaked ladyfingers with coffee chip ice cream and crowning it with whipped cream enriched by mascarpone cheese and flavored with rum. To assemble the cake, we needed to take care to soften the ice cream until it was easily spreadable so it wouldn't rip the delicate soaked ladyfinger cookies. While some Italian bakeries make fresh ladyfingers, their soft, cakelike texture became even softer when soaked, which prevented them from standing up straight in the pan. Store-bought dried ladyfingers were sturdier and worked much better. Depending on the brand, 14 ounces is 42 to 60 cookies. Topped with a light dusting of cocoa, this easy-to-assemble ice cream cake is as elegant as the dessert that inspired it.

1 Set wire rack in rimmed baking sheet. Stir coffee, espresso powder, and 5 tablespoons rum in large bowl until espresso powder dissolves. Working with 1 cookie at a time, quickly dunk ladyfingers in coffee mixture and transfer to wire rack; let sit for 5 minutes.

2 Spray 16-cup tube pan with vegetable oil spray and line with parchment paper. Lightly spray parchment with oil spray. Line prepared pan with soaked ladyfingers, with thin sides against pan, packing gently to ensure that there are no spaces between cookies; freeze until firm, about 1 hour. When cookies are firm, scoop ice cream into large bowl and, using large rubber spatula or wooden spoon, break up scoops of ice cream. Stir and fold the ice cream to achieve smooth consistency; fold in chocolate chips. Transfer softened ice cream to cookie-lined pan and smooth top. Wrap cake in plastic wrap and freeze until ice cream is firm, at least 4 hours or up to 4 days.

3 Using stand mixer fitted with whisk attachment, whip mascarpone, cream, sugar, and remaining 1 tablespoon rum on medium-high speed until stiff peaks form, about 2 minutes. Gently invert pan to turn cake onto platter, discarding parchment. Using rubber spatula, top cake with 1 cup mascarpone mixture, then dust lightly with cocoa. Serve immediately with remaining mascarpone mixture.

banana split cake

serves 8 to 10

8 ice cream sandwiches

3 pints strawberry ice cream

1 cup heavy cream

1 cup hot fudge sauce, warmed

⅓ cup walnuts, chopped

1 ripe banana, peeled, halved lengthwise, and sliced

1 maraschino cherry for garnish (optional)

why this recipe works Served with a topping of old-school nostalgia, the banana split is the ultimate ice cream sundae. Our festive ice cream cake is like a massive banana split; it duplicates its flavor and offers an ultracharming appearance. To give the sundae the structure of a cake, we lined the edge of a springform pan with cut store-bought ice cream sandwiches. That took care of the chocolate and vanilla; next we filled the center of the cake with bright strawberry ice cream. We froze the cake at this stage and patiently waited to get to the fun part: the topping. Hot fudge was a must, and store-bought fudge sauce was the perfect frosting substitute for this cake. A generous fluff of whipped cream dolloped in the center, a sprinkling of chopped walnuts, and, of course, banana, were iconic adornments. A cherry on top was the finishing touch for our sundae cake.

1 Chill 9-inch springform pan in freezer. Cut each ice cream sandwich in half lengthwise, then cut it in half crosswise to yield 4 pieces. Transfer sandwich pieces to plate and freeze until very firm. Line outer edge of chilled springform pan with sandwich pieces, arranging them lengthwise. Scoop ice cream into large bowl and, using large rubber spatula or wooden spoon, break up scoops of ice cream. Stir and fold the ice cream to achieve smooth consistency. Fill center of pan with softened ice cream and smooth surface. Wrap cake tightly with plastic wrap and freeze until firm, at least 2 hours or up to 1 week.

2 Using stand mixer fitted with whisk attachment, whip cream on medium-high speed until soft peaks form, about 1 minute. Microwave hot fudge sauce in bowl until warmed. To unmold cake, remove sides of pan and slide thin metal spatula between cake bottom and pan bottom to loosen, then slide cake onto platter. Spoon warmed fudge sauce onto center of cake and spread almost to edge. Dollop with whipped cream and top with walnuts and banana. Top with cherry, if using. Serve immediately

s'mores ice cream cake

serves 8 to 10

4 ounces bittersweet chocolate, chopped fine

½ cup heavy cream

¼ cup light corn syrup

8 whole graham crackers, broken into pieces, plus 8 quartered along dotted seams

4 tablespoons unsalted butter, melted

1 tablespoon sugar

1 cup marshmallow crème

3 pints chocolate ice cream

26 large marshmallows, halved crosswise

why this recipe works The combination of chocolate, graham crackers, and marshmallows is irresistible. We wanted to take each element of s'mores and reimagine this beloved campfire snack as a magnificent ice cream cake. Combining warm, gooey s'mores with ice cream may sound like a mess, but we found a way to add the heat without causing a meltdown. The base of our cake was simple: just a graham cracker crust covered with fudge. The fudge layer provided plenty of chocolate flavor, gave the cake a sundae-like quality, and kept the crust from becoming soggy under the remaining layers. Between the fudge-covered crust and a generous filling of chocolate ice cream, we spread a layer of sweet marshmallow crème—but it wouldn't be s'mores without toasted marshmallows too. We halved large marshmallows so they'd lie flat and covered the top of our cake with them. After freezing the cake until it was very firm, it took just a quick run under a hot broiler to toast the marshmallows without melting the cake. A ring of graham crackers around the outside provided the finishing touch to this playful dessert.

1 Combine chocolate, cream, and corn syrup in bowl and microwave at 50 percent power until melted and smooth, about 1 minute, stirring halfway through microwaving. Let cool completely, about 30 minutes.

2 Adjust oven rack to middle position and heat oven to 325 degrees. Spray 9-inch springform pan with vegetable oil spray and line perimeter with 2½-inch-wide strip of parchment paper. Pulse crackers in food processor until finely ground, about 15 pulses. Combine cracker crumbs, melted butter, and sugar in bowl until mixture resembles wet sand. Using your hands, press crumb mixture evenly into pan bottom. Using bottom of measuring cup, firmly pack crust into pan. Bake until fragrant and beginning to brown, about 12 minutes. Let crust cool completely in pan on wire rack, about 30 minutes.

3 Pour chocolate mixture over crust and smooth into even layer; freeze until firm, about 30 minutes. Spread marshmallow crème over chocolate mixture in even layer; freeze until firm, about 15 minutes. Scoop ice cream into large bowl and, using large rubber spatula or wooden spoon, break up the scoops of ice cream. Stir and fold ice cream to achieve smooth consistency. Spread softened ice cream evenly over marshmallow crème layer. Cover with plastic wrap and freeze until ice cream is very firm, at least 4 hours or up to 24 hours.

4 Adjust oven rack 6 inches from broiler element and heat broiler. Place cake on rimmed baking sheet, discarding plastic, and arrange marshmallow halves, cut sides down, in snug layer over top. Broil until marshmallows are lightly browned, 30 to 60 seconds, rotating sheet halfway through broiling. (Refreeze cake if necessary.) Working quickly, remove sides of pan, discarding parchment, and slide thinmetal spatula between cake bottom and pan bottom to loosen, then slide cake onto platter. Arrange cracker pieces vertically along sides of cake. Serve immediately.

Making the Marshmallow Topping

1 Place cake, still in pan, on baking sheet. Remove plastic wrap and arrange marshmallow halves, cut side down, snugly over top of cake.

2 Broil until marshmallows are lightly browned, 30 to 60 seconds, rotating sheet halfway through broiling for even browning.

watermelon ice cream cake

serves 8 to 10

2 (9-inch) White Cake Layers (page 395)

2½ cups raspberry sorbet

2 ounces semisweet chocolate, chopped fine

12 tablespoons unsalted butter, cut into 12 pieces and softened

3 tablespoons lime juice (2 limes)

½ teaspoon vanilla extract

⅛ teaspoon salt

2 cups (8 ounces) confectioners' sugar

12 drops green food coloring

why this recipe works Cool, a little tart, and incredibly refreshing, sorbet is a favorite summertime treat. We wanted to use sorbet as the jumping-off point for a festive, playful cake in the shape of another summertime favorite: watermelon. To form the rind of the watermelon, we started with a round of tender white cake that we cut into wedges and pressed into a plastic wrap–lined bowl. Next, we softened vibrant raspberry sorbet and mixed in chopped chocolate before pressing the fruity mixture into the bowl with the cake for a filling that resembled the interior of a watermelon, seeds and all. After using the plastic lining to easily unmold the cake from the bowl, we frosted it with a lime-flavored light green frosting and decorated it with strips of dark green frosting for a cake that was cheerfully reminiscent of the real thing. You will need only one white cake layer for this recipe. Freeze the second cake layer for later use.

1 Line 6-cup mixing bowl with plastic wrap. Using serrated knife, cut off domed top of cake so that remaining cake measures ¾ inch thick (reserve top for another use). Cut remaining cake into 8 wedges and line bowl with wedges, arranging as closely as possible to achieve snug fit. Scoop raspberry sorbet into second bowl and, using large rubber spatula or wooden spoon, break up scoops of sorbet. Stir and fold sorbet to achieve smooth consistency; fold in chopped chocolate. Fill cake-lined bowl with sorbet mixture and smooth top. Cover surface with plastic wrap and freeze until very firm, about 6 hours.

2 Using stand mixer fitted with whisk attachment, mix butter, lime juice, vanilla, and salt on medium-low speed until combined. Slowly add sugar and continue to whip until smooth, about 2 minutes. Increase speed to medium-high and whip until light and fluffy, about 5 minutes. Add 6 drops food coloring and mix until combined. Transfer ½ cup frosting to small bowl, add 6 more drops food coloring, and whisk until combined.

3 Remove plastic from cake and turn onto chilled platter; remove remaining plastic wrap. Cover cake with even layer of light green frosting. Spread 8 vertical stripes of dark green frosting evenly around cake. Freeze until frosting is firm, at least 30 minutes or up to 24 hours. Serve immediately.

mexican chocolate ice cream torte

serves 8 to 10

25 Oreo cookies, broken into rough pieces

3 tablespoons unsalted butter, melted

1 pint chocolate ice cream

1 pint coffee ice cream

1 pint vanilla ice cream

1 teaspoon ground cinnamon

1½ cups sliced almonds, toasted

why this recipe works As illustrated in this chapter, we've taken to making our own ice cream cakes since store-bought versions are typically boring assemblages of bland, icy ingredients and too-sweet frosting. This ice cream cake—an ice cream torte, really—is inspired, truly elegant, and sure to win raves. We love the savory spice that cinnamon adds to earthy disks of Mexican chocolate, so for our torte we paired chocolate ice cream with cinnamon-infused vanilla ice cream and bittersweet coffee ice cream for a grown-up frozen treat. Crushed Oreos ably separate the layers. To up the elegance and add a welcome crunch, we sprinkled the top and sides of the cake with sliced almonds, which we toasted to enhance their nutty flavor. Use the entire Oreo—filling and all—for the crust. Before removing the cake from the spring-form pan, run your paring knife under hot tap water for 10 seconds or so.

1 Adjust oven rack to the middle position and heat oven to 325 degrees. Process Oreos in food processor until finely ground, about 30 seconds. Add melted butter and process until mixture resembles wet sand, about 10 seconds.

2 Using your hands, press ⅔ cup crumb mixture evenly into bottom of 9-inch springform pan. Using bottom of measuring cup, firmly pack crust into pan. Bake until the crust is fragrant and set, 5 to 10 minutes. Let crust cool completely on wire rack, about 30 minutes.

3 Scoop chocolate ice cream into large bowl and, using large rubber spatula or wooden spoon, break up scoops of ice cream. Stir and fold the ice cream to achieve a smooth consistency. Spread softened ice cream evenly over crust. Sprinkle ⅔ cup Oreo crumbs over ice cream and pack them down lightly. Wrap pan tightly in plastic wrap and freeze until ice cream is just firm, about 30 minutes. Repeat with coffee ice cream and remaining ⅔ cup Oreo crumbs; wrap tightly and freeze for another 30 minutes. Soften vanilla ice cream, fold in cinnamon, spread evenly in pan, and smooth top. Wrap the cake tightly in plastic and freeze until ice cream is firm, at least 8 hours or up to 1 week.

4 To unmold, run hot thin knife around edge of pan. Remove sides of pan and slide thin metal spatula between crust and pan bottom to loosen, then slide cake onto platter. Press handfuls of almonds gently onto sides of cake, then sprinkle single layer of almonds evenly over top. Serve immediately.

Cheesecakes, Icebox Cakes, and Ice Cream Cakes

APPENDIX
ESSENTIAL CAKE COMPONENTS

cake layers

We find ourselves turning again and again to a few cake flavors—white, yellow, chocolate, red velvet, and devil's food. They're basic enough to pair with lots of different frostings so we can create numerous flavor combinations, and they're crowd-pleasers, so they're great for celebrations. Each of the following cake recipes can make two layers in 9-inch pans or three layers in 8-inch pans. We reference them throughout the book as they're the foundation for project recipes, making those recipes fun and approachable. And in the following pages, we provide different yields of frostings so you can make your own cake combinations and creations, mixing and matching cake layers with frostings and fillings.

yellow cake layers
Makes two 9-inch or three 8-inch cake layers
If making a three-layer cake, start checking doneness a few minutes early.

2½ cups (10 ounces) cake flour
1¼ teaspoons baking powder
¼ teaspoon baking soda
¾ teaspoon salt
1¾ cups (12¼ ounces) sugar
1 cup buttermilk, room temperature
10 tablespoons unsalted butter, melted and cooled
3 large eggs, separated, plus 3 large yolks, room temperature
3 tablespoons vegetable oil
2 teaspoons vanilla extract
Pinch cream of tartar

1 Adjust oven rack to middle position and heat oven to 350 degrees. Grease two 9-inch or three 8-inch round cake pans, line with parchment paper, grease parchment, and flour pans. Whisk flour, baking powder, baking soda, salt, and 1½ cups sugar together in bowl. Whisk buttermilk, melted butter, egg yolks, oil, and vanilla together in second bowl.

2 Using stand mixer fitted with whisk attachment, whip egg whites and cream of tartar on medium-low speed until foamy, about 1 minute. Increase speed to medium-high and whip whites to soft billowy mounds, about 1 minute. Gradually add remaining ¼ cup sugar and whip until glossy, stiff peaks form, 2 to 3 minutes; transfer to third bowl.

3 Add flour mixture to now-empty mixer bowl and mix on low speed, gradually adding buttermilk mixture and mixing until almost incorporated (a few streaks of dry flour will remain), about 15 seconds. Scrape down bowl, then mix on medium-low speed until smooth and fully incorporated, 10 to 15 seconds.

4 Using rubber spatula, stir one-third of whites into batter. Gently fold in remaining whites until no white streaks remain. Divide batter evenly between prepared pans and smooth tops with rubber spatula. Gently tap pans on counter to settle batter. Bake until toothpick inserted in center comes out clean, 20 to 22 minutes, switching and rotating pans halfway through baking. Let cakes cool in pans on wire rack for 10 minutes. Remove cakes from pans, discarding parchment, and let cool completely on rack, about 2 hours. (Cake layers can be stored at room temperature for up to 24 hours or frozen for up to 1 month; defrost cakes at room temperature.)

White Cake Layers

Makes two 9-inch or three 8-inch cake layers
If making a three-layer cake, start checking doneness a few minutes early.

1 cup whole milk, room temperature
6 large egg whites, room temperature
1 teaspoon vanilla extract
2¼ cups (9 ounces) cake flour
1¾ cups (12¼ ounces) sugar
4 teaspoons baking powder
1 teaspoon salt
12 tablespoons unsalted butter, cut into 12 pieces and softened

1 Adjust oven rack to middle position and heat oven to 350 degrees. Grease two 9-inch or three 8-inch round cake pans, line with parchment paper, grease parchment, and flour pans. Whisk milk, egg whites, and vanilla together in bowl.

2 Using stand mixer fitted with paddle, mix flour, sugar, baking powder, and salt on low speed until combined. Add butter, 1 piece at a time, until only pea-size pieces remain, about 1 minute. Add all but ½ cup milk mixture, increase speed to medium-high, and beat until light and fluffy, about 1 minute. Reduce speed to medium-low, add remaining ½ cup milk mixture, and mix until incorporated, about 30 seconds (batter may look curdled). Give batter final stir by hand.

3 Divide batter evenly between prepared pans and smooth tops with rubber spatula. Gently tap pans on counter to settle batter. Bake until toothpick inserted in center comes out with few crumbs attached, 23 to 25 minutes, switching and rotating pans halfway through baking.

4 Let cakes cool in pans on wire rack for 10 minutes. Remove cakes from pans, discarding parchment, and let cool completely on rack, about 2 hours. (Cake layers can be stored at room temperature for up to 24 hours or frozen for up to 1 month; defrost cakes at room temperature.)

Chocolate Cake Layers

Makes two 9-inch or three 8-inch cake layers
Do not substitute natural cocoa powder for the Dutch-processed cocoa powder. If making a three-layer cake, start checking doneness a few minutes early.

4 ounces unsweetened chocolate, chopped coarse
½ cup hot water
¼ cup (¾ ounce) Dutch-processed cocoa powder
1¾ cups (12¼ ounces) sugar
1¾ cups (8¾ ounces) all-purpose flour
1½ teaspoons baking soda
1 teaspoon salt
1 cup buttermilk
2 teaspoons vanilla extract
4 large eggs plus 2 large yolks, room temperature
12 tablespoons unsalted butter, cut into 12 pieces and softened

1 Adjust oven rack to middle position and heat oven to 350 degrees. Grease two 9-inch or three 8-inch round cake pans, line with parchment paper, grease parchment, and flour pans.

2 Combine chocolate, hot water, and cocoa in medium heatproof bowl set over saucepan filled with 1 inch barely simmering water, making sure that water does not touch bottom of bowl and stirring with heat-resistant rubber spatula until chocolate is melted, about 2 minutes. Add ½ cup sugar to chocolate mixture and stir until thick and glossy, 1 to 2 minutes. Remove bowl from heat; set aside to cool.

3 Whisk flour, baking soda, and salt together in bowl. Combine buttermilk and vanilla in second bowl. Using stand mixer fitted with whisk attachment, whip eggs and yolks on medium-low speed until combined, about 10 seconds. Add remaining 1¼ cups sugar, increase speed to high, and whip until light and fluffy, 2 to 3 minutes. Fit stand mixer with paddle. Add cooled chocolate mixture to egg mixture and mix on medium speed until thoroughly combined, 30 to 45 seconds, scraping

continued on next page

down bowl as needed. Add butter, 1 piece at a time, mixing for about 10 seconds after each addition. Add flour mixture in 3 additions, alternating with buttermilk mixture in 2 additions, mixing until incorporated after each addition (about 15 seconds) and scraping down bowl as needed. Reduce speed to medium-low and mix until batter is thoroughly combined, about 15 seconds. Give batter final stir by hand.

4 Divide batter evenly between prepared pans and smooth tops with rubber spatula. Bake until toothpick inserted in center comes out with few moist crumbs attached, 25 to 30 minutes, switching and rotating pans halfway through baking. Let cakes cool in pans on wire rack for 10 minutes. Remove cakes from pans, discarding parchment, and let cool completely on rack, about 2 hours. (Cooled cakes can be stored at room temperature for up to 24 hours or frozen for up to 1 month; defrost cakes at room temperature.)

Red Velvet Cake Layers
Makes two 9-inch or three 8-inch cake layers
Do not substitute Dutch-processed cocoa powder for the natural cocoa powder.

2¼ cups (11¼ ounces) all-purpose flour
1½ teaspoons baking soda
Pinch salt
1 cup buttermilk
2 large eggs
1 tablespoon distilled white vinegar
1 teaspoon vanilla extract
2 tablespoons unsweetened cocoa powder
2 tablespoons (1 ounce) red food coloring
12 tablespoons unsalted butter,
cut into 12 pieces and softened
1½ cups (10½ ounces) sugar

1 Adjust oven rack to middle position and heat oven to 350 degrees. Grease two 9-inch or three 8-inch round cake pans, line with parchment paper, grease parchment, and flour pans. Whisk flour, baking soda, and salt together in bowl. Whisk buttermilk, eggs, vinegar, and vanilla together in second bowl. Mix cocoa and red food coloring in third bowl to smooth paste.

2 Using stand mixer fitted with paddle, beat butter and sugar on medium-high speed until pale and fluffy, about 3 minutes. Reduce speed to low and add flour mixture in 3 additions, alternating with buttermilk mixture in 2 additions, scraping down bowl as needed. Beat in cocoa mixture until batter is uniform. Give batter final stir by hand.

3 Divide batter evenly between prepared pans and smooth tops with rubber spatula. Gently tap pans on counter to settle batter. Bake until toothpick inserted in center comes out clean, about 25 minutes, switching and rotating pans halfway through baking.

4 Let cakes cool in pans on wire rack for 10 minutes. Remove cakes from pans, discarding parchment, and let cool completely on rack, about 2 hours. (Cake layers can be stored at room temperature for up to 24 hours or frozen for up to 1 month; defrost cakes at room temperature.)

Devil's Food Cake Layers

Makes two 9-inch or three 8-inch cake layers

For an accurate measurement of boiling water, bring a full kettle of water to a boil and then measure out the desired amount. Do not substitute natural cocoa powder for the Dutch-processed cocoa powder.

½ cup (1½ ounces) Dutch-processed cocoa powder, plus extra for pan
1½ cups (7½ ounces) all-purpose flour
1 teaspoon baking soda
½ teaspoon baking powder
¼ teaspoon salt
1¼ cups boiling water
4 ounces unsweetened chocolate, chopped
1 teaspoon instant espresso powder or instant coffee powder
10 tablespoons unsalted butter, softened
1½ cups packed (10½ ounces) light brown sugar
3 large eggs, room temperature
½ cup sour cream, room temperature
1 teaspoon vanilla extract

1 Adjust oven rack to middle position and heat oven to 350 degrees. Grease two 9-inch or three 8-inch round cake pans, then dust with cocoa powder and line bottoms with parchment paper.

2 Whisk flour, baking soda, baking powder, and salt together in bowl. Whisk boiling water, chocolate, cocoa, and espresso powder in second bowl until smooth.

3 Using stand mixer fitted with paddle, beat butter and sugar on medium-high speed until pale and fluffy, about 3 minutes. Add eggs, one at a time, and beat until combined, about 30 seconds. Beat in sour cream and vanilla until incorporated. Reduce speed to low and add flour mixture in 3 additions, alternating with chocolate mixture in 2 additions, scraping down bowl as needed. Give batter final stir by hand.

4 Divide batter evenly between prepared pans and smooth tops with rubber spatula. Gently tap pans on counter to settle batter. Bake until toothpick inserted in center comes out with few crumbs attached, 18 to 22 minutes, switching and rotating pans halfway through baking.

5 Let cakes cool in pans on wire rack for 10 minutes. Remove cakes from pans, discarding parchment, and let cool completely on rack, about 2 hours. (Cake layers can be stored at room temperature for up to 24 hours or frozen for up to 1 month; defrost cakes at room temperature.)

frostings and buttercreams

Below is our collection of frostings you can use to fill and coat layer cakes, sheet cakes, and cupcakes. We provide different yields of frosting to accommodate each type of cake. For a guide on how much frosting to put between each layer, see page 24; and for tips on frosting a cake, check out page 23.

vanilla frosting

makes 5 cups, enough for two-layer cake

We cut the butter into pieces and let them soften—but not too much, or the frosting will be greasy. Many recipes for vanilla frosting call for milk; we prefer heavy cream, which gives the frosting a silky quality. For colored frosting, stir in drops of food coloring at the end, but be sure to use a light hand—a little goes a long way.

1 pound (4 sticks) unsalted butter, each stick cut into quarters and softened
¼ cup heavy cream
1 tablespoon vanilla extract
¼ teaspoon salt
4 cups (16 ounces) confectioners' sugar

1 Using stand mixer fitted with paddle, beat butter, cream, vanilla, and salt on medium-high speed until smooth, about 1 minute. Reduce speed to medium-low, slowly add sugar, and beat until incorporated and smooth, about 4 minutes.

2 Increase speed to medium-high and beat until frosting is light and fluffy, about 5 minutes. (Frosting can be refrigerated for up to 3 days; let soften at room temperature, about 2 hours, then rewhip on medium speed until smooth, 2 to 5 minutes.)

makes 3 cups, enough for cupcakes or sheet cake

Reduce butter to 20 tablespoons (2½ sticks), reduce cream to 2 tablespoons, reduce vanilla to 2 teaspoons, reduce salt to ⅛ teaspoon, and reduce confectioners' sugar to 2½ cups (10 ounces).

makes 6 cups, enough for three-layer cake

Increase butter to 1¼ pounds (5 sticks), increase vanilla to 4 teaspoons, and increase confectioners' sugar to 5 cups (1¼ pounds).

flavor variations

almond

For 5 cups frosting substitute 1½ teaspoons almond extract for vanilla.

For 3 cups frosting substitute 1 teaspoon almond extract for vanilla.

For 6 cups frosting substitute 2 teaspoons almond extract for vanilla.

coconut

For 5 cups frosting substitute 1½ teaspoons coconut extract for vanilla.

For 3 cups frosting substitute 1 teaspoon coconut extract for vanilla.

For 6 cups frosting substitute 2 teaspoons coconut extract for vanilla.

coffee

For 5 cups frosting add 3 tablespoons instant espresso powder or instant coffee powder to mixer with butter.

For 3 cups frosting add 1½ tablespoons instant espresso powder or instant coffee powder to mixer with butter.

For 6 cups frosting add ¼ cup instant espresso powder or instant coffee powder to mixer with butter.

orange

For 5 cups frosting add 1 tablespoon grated orange zest and 2 tablespoons juice to mixer with butter.

For 3 cups frosting add 1½ teaspoons grated orange zest and 1 tablespoon juice to mixer with butter.

For 6 cups frosting add 1½ tablespoons grated orange zest and 2½ tablespoons juice to mixer with butter.

peppermint

For 5 cups frosting add 2½ teaspoons peppermint extract to mixer with butter.

For 3 cups frosting add 1½ teaspoons peppermint extract to mixer with butter.

For 6 cups frosting add 1 tablespoon peppermint extract to mixer with butter.

chocolate frosting

makes 5 cups, enough for two-layer cake

We combined a hefty amount of cocoa powder with melted chocolate to give this frosting deep chocolate flavor. A combination of confectioners' sugar and corn syrup made it smooth and glossy. To keep the frosting from separating and turning greasy, we turned to the food processor: The fast-mixing machine virtually eliminated any risk of overbeating, as it blended the ingredients quickly without melting the butter or incorporating too much air. The result was a thick, fluffy foolproof chocolate frosting that spread like a dream. Bittersweet, semisweet, or milk chocolate can be used in this recipe.

30 tablespoons (3¾ sticks) unsalted butter, softened
1½ cups (6 ounces) confectioners' sugar
1 cup (3 ounces) Dutch-processed cocoa powder
⅛ teaspoon salt
1 cup light corn syrup
1½ teaspoons vanilla extract
12 ounces chocolate, melted and cooled

Process butter, sugar, cocoa, and salt in food processor until smooth, about 30 seconds, scraping down sides of bowl as needed. Add corn syrup and vanilla and process until just combined, 5 to 10 seconds. Scrape down sides of bowl, then add chocolate and process until smooth and creamy, 10 to 15 seconds. (Frosting can be kept at room temperature for up to 3 hours or refrigerated for up to 3 days; if refrigerated, let stand at room temperature for 1 hour and stir before using.)

makes 3 cups, enough for cupcakes or sheet cake

Reduce butter to 20 tablespoons (2½ sticks), reduce confectioners' sugar to 1 cup (4 ounces), reduce cocoa powder to ¾ cup (2¼ ounces), reduce corn syrup to ¾ cup, reduce vanilla to 1 teaspoon, and reduce chocolate to 8 ounces.

makes 6 cups, enough for three-layer cake

Increase butter to 1¼ pounds (5 sticks), increase confectioners' sugar to 2 cups (8 ounces), increase cocoa powder to 1½ cups (4½ ounces), and increase chocolate to 1 pound.

chocolate buttercream

makes 5 cups, enough for two-layer cake

When we want a more refined chocolate frosting, we opt for a cooked buttercream of the Swiss meringue variety in which egg whites and granulated sugar are heated over a double boiler and then whipped with knobs of softened butter. This gave us a creamy chocolate frosting that is the perfect crowning touch for any of our chocolate cakes. The melted chocolate should be cooled to between 85 and 100 degrees before being added to the frosting.

1 cup (7 ounces) sugar
5 large egg whites
⅛ teaspoon salt
28 tablespoons (3½ sticks) unsalted butter,
  cut into 28 pieces and softened
14 ounces bittersweet chocolate, melted and cooled
1¼ teaspoons vanilla extract

1 Combine sugar, egg whites, and salt in bowl of stand mixer. Set bowl over saucepan filled with 1 inch of barely simmering water, making sure that water does not touch bottom of bowl. Cook, whisking constantly, until mixture registers 150 degrees, about 3 minutes.

2 Remove bowl from heat and transfer to stand mixer fitted with whisk attachment. Whip warm egg mixture on medium speed until it has consistency of shaving cream and has cooled slightly, about 5 minutes. Add butter, 1 piece at a time, and whip until smooth and creamy, about 2 minutes. (Frosting may look curdled after half of butter has been added; it will smooth out with additional butter.)

3 Add chocolate and vanilla and mix until combined. Increase speed to medium-high and whip until light and fluffy, about 30 seconds, scraping down bowl as needed. If frosting seems too soft after adding chocolate, chill it briefly in refrigerator, then rewhip until

continued on next page

creamy. (Frosting can be refrigerated for up to 24 hours; warm frosting briefly in microwave until just slightly softened, 5 to 10 seconds, then stir until creamy.)

makes 3 cups, enough for cupcakes or sheet cake
Reduce sugar to ½ cup (3½ ounces), reduce egg whites to 3, reduce butter to 16 tablespoons, and reduce chocolate to 8 ounces.

makes 6 cups, enough for three-layer cake
Increase egg whites to 6, increase salt to ¼ teaspoon, increase butter to 1 pound (4 sticks), increase chocolate to 1 pound, and increase vanilla to 1½ teaspoons.

flavor variations

malted milk chocolate buttercream

For 5 cups frosting substitute milk chocolate for bittersweet chocolate. Add ⅓ cup malted milk powder to frosting with chocolate in step 3.

For 3 cups frosting substitute milk chocolate for bittersweet chocolate. Add ¼ cup malted milk powder to frosting with chocolate in step 3.

For 6 cups frosting substitute milk chocolate for bittersweet chocolate. Add ½ cup malted milk powder to frosting with chocolate in step 3.

peanut butter buttercream

For 5 cups frosting substitute 1 cup creamy peanut butter for chocolate. Garnish with ½ cup chopped peanuts.

For 3 cups frosting substitute ⅔ cup creamy peanut butter for chocolate. Garnish with ½ cup chopped peanuts.

For 6 cups frosting substitute 1⅓ cups creamy peanut butter for chocolate. Garnish with ½ cup chopped peanuts.

chocolate ganache frosting

makes 5 cups, enough for two-layer cake
The richest chocolate frosting is also the easiest to make. When we want an intense chocolaty topping for our cake or cupcakes, we go with ganache, made simply from heavy cream and melted semisweet chocolate.

1 pound semisweet chocolate, chopped
2 cups heavy cream

1 Place chocolate in large heatproof bowl. Bring cream to boil in small saucepan. Pour boiling cream over chocolate, and let sit, covered, for 5 minutes. Whisk mixture until smooth, then cover with plastic wrap and refrigerate until cool and slightly firm, about 1 hour.

2 Using stand mixer fitted with whisk attachment, whip cooled chocolate mixture on medium speed until fluffy and mousse-like and soft peaks form, about 2 minutes.

makes 3 cups, enough for cupcakes or sheet cake
Reduce chocolate to 10 ounces and reduce heavy cream to 1¼ cups.

makes 6 cups, enough for three-layer cake
Increase chocolate to 1¼ pounds and increase heavy cream to 2½ cups. Increase chilling time in step 1 to about 2 hours.

peanut butter frosting

makes 5 cups, enough for two-layer cake

This peanut butter frosting is just sweet enough, with undeniable peanut flavor. The butter and heavy cream contributed to a smooth and creamy texture that wasn't greasy. We mixed the cream with the butter and peanut butter before adding the sugar; this helped lighten the butter and made incorporating the sugar easier. Do not use crunchy, old-fashioned, or natural peanut butter in this recipe.

22 tablespoons (2¾ sticks) unsalted butter,
cut into 22 pieces and softened
1⅓ cups creamy peanut butter
3 tablespoons heavy cream
2 teaspoons vanilla extract
⅛ teaspoon salt
2 cups (8 ounces) confectioners' sugar

1 Using stand mixer fitted with paddle, beat butter, peanut butter, cream, vanilla, and salt on medium-high speed until smooth, about 1 minute. Reduce speed to medium-low, slowly add sugar, and beat until incorporated and smooth, about 4 minutes.

2 Increase speed to medium-high and beat until frosting is light and fluffy, about 5 minutes. (Frosting can be refrigerated for up to 3 days; let soften at room temperature, about 2 hours, then rewhip on medium speed until smooth, 2 to 5 minutes.)

makes 3 cups, enough for cupcakes or sheet cake
Reduce butter to 12 tablespoons, reduce peanut butter to ¾ cup, reduce cream to 1½ tablespoons, reduce vanilla to 1½ teaspoons, and reduce confectioners' sugar to 1¼ cups (5 ounces).

makes 6 cups, enough for three-layer cake
Increase butter to 24 tablespoons (3 sticks), increase peanut butter to 1½ cups, and increase confectioners' sugar to 2½ cups (10 ounces).

cream cheese frosting

makes about 5 cups, enough for two-layer cake
We enriched our cream cheese frosting with a little sour cream for extra tang as well as some vanilla for depth of flavor. We found that slowly adding the confectioners' sugar to the other ingredients at a low speed until they were well combined and then turning up the speed gave us more control over the texture, ultimately producing a light, fluffy frosting. Do not use low-fat or fat-free cream cheese or the frosting will have a soupy consistency. This frosting has a softer, looser texture than other frostings; it won't work with a three-layer cake. If the frosting becomes too soft to work with, let it chill in the refrigerator until firm.

1¼ pounds cream cheese, softened
12 tablespoons unsalted butter, cut into 12 pieces
and softened
2 tablespoons sour cream
2 teaspoons vanilla extract
¼ teaspoon salt
2½ cups (10 ounces) confectioners' sugar

1 Using stand mixer fitted with paddle, beat cream cheese, butter, sour cream, vanilla, and salt on medium-high speed until smooth, about 2 minutes. Reduce speed to medium-low, slowly add sugar, and beat until incorporated and smooth, about 4 minutes.

2 Increase speed to medium-high and beat until frosting is light and fluffy, about 4 minutes. (Frosting can be refrigerated for up to 3 days; let soften at room temperature, about 1 hour, then rewhip on medium speed until smooth, about 2 minutes.)

makes 3 cups, enough for cupcakes or sheet cake
Reduce cream cheese to 12 ounces, reduce butter to 6 tablespoons, reduce sour cream to 1½ tablespoons, reduce vanilla to 1 teaspoon, and reduce confectioners' sugar to 1½ cups (6 ounces).

flavor variation
vanilla bean cream cheese frosting
Using paring knife, halve and scrape seeds from 2 vanilla beans and add seeds with cream cheese in step 1.

honey cream cheese frosting

makes 5 cups, enough for two-layer cake

Honey pairs nicely with the tang of cream cheese, giving this frosting a distinct yet nuanced, well-rounded flavor profile. Do not use low-fat or fat-free cream cheese or the frosting will have a soupy consistency. If the frosting becomes too soft to work with, let it chill in the refrigerator until firm.

1¼ pounds cream cheese, softened
12 tablespoons unsalted butter, cut into 12 pieces and softened
1 tablespoon vanilla extract
¼ teaspoon salt
⅔ cup honey

1 Using stand mixer fitted with whisk attachment, whip cream cheese, butter, vanilla, and salt on medium-high speed until smooth, about 2 minutes.

2 Reduce speed to medium-low, add honey, and whip until smooth, about 2 minutes. Increase speed to medium-high and whip until frosting is light and fluffy, 3 to 5 minutes. (Frosting can be refrigerated for up to 3 days; let soften at room temperature, about 1 hour, then rewhip on medium speed until smooth, about 2 minutes.)

makes 3 cups, enough for cupcakes or sheet cake

Reduce cream cheese to 12 ounces, reduce butter to 8 tablespoons, reduce vanilla to 2 teaspoons, reduce salt to ⅛ teaspoon, and reduce honey to 6 tablespoons.

makes 6 cups, enough for three-layer cake

Increase cream cheese to 1½ pounds, increase butter to 16 tablespoons, increase vanilla to 4 teaspoons, and increase honey to ¾ cup.

flavor variation

maple cream cheese frosting
Substitute maple syrup for honey.

seven-minute frosting

makes 5 cups, enough for two-layer cake

Some quick frostings are too sweet or too gritty—but not this one. Taking its name from the time it takes to beat the frosting over simmering water, our easy recipe is the perfect finishing touch to any cake or cupcake. The trick to producing a thick, glossy frosting was to cook a combination of egg whites, sugar, and corn syrup gently over a pan of simmering water before whipping the mixture until cooled and stiff peaks formed. This frosting should be spread on thick and then swept into big, billowy swirls using the back of a spoon.

1½ cups (10½ ounces) sugar
2 large egg whites
6 tablespoons cold water
1½ tablespoons light corn syrup
¼ teaspoon cream of tartar
Pinch salt
1 teaspoon vanilla extract

1 Combine sugar, egg whites, cold water, corn syrup, cream of tartar, and salt in bowl of stand mixer. Set bowl over saucepan filled with 1 inch barely simmering water, making sure that water does not touch bottom of bowl. Cook, whisking constantly, until mixture registers 160 degrees, 5 to 10 minutes.

2 Remove bowl from heat and transfer to stand mixer fitted with whisk attachment. Whip warm egg white mixture on medium speed until soft peaks form, about 5 minutes. Add vanilla, increase speed to medium-high, and continue to whip until mixture has cooled completely and stiff peaks form, 5 to 7 minutes. Use immediately.

makes 3 cups, enough for cupcakes or sheet cake

Reduce sugar to 1 cup (7 ounces), reduce water to ¼ cup, reduce corn syrup to 1 tablespoon, reduce cream of tartar to ⅛ teaspoon, reduce vanilla to ½ teaspoon.

makes 6 cups, enough for three-layer cake

Increase sugar to 1¾ cups (12¼ ounces), increase egg whites to 3, increase water to 7 tablespoons, increase corn syrup to 5 teaspoons, and increase vanilla to 1¼ teaspoons.

vanilla buttercream

makes 5 cups, enough for two-layer cake

Classic French recipes for buttercream rely on sugar alone for the sweetener, but we discovered that substituting corn syrup for some of the sugar gave our buttercream a more fluid—yet stable—consistency. The addition of corn syrup also made it easier to melt the sugar. Some recipes call for whole eggs, but we preferred the richer texture that resulted from using only yolks. It was essential to heat the sugar syrup while the yolks were whipping; the syrup must be hot when added to the egg yolks to ensure they reach a safe temperature. We whipped the yolk-syrup mixture not just to aerate it, but also to cool it off before we added the softened butter; this prevented the butter from melting into pools of grease. Be sure to pour the syrup into the eggs slowly to avoid scrambling the eggs. Because you need to add the hot sugar syrup to the eggs while the mixer is on, using a stand mixer is essential; do not use a handheld mixer. For colored frosting, stir in drops of food coloring at the end, but be sure to use a light hand—a little goes a long way. This buttercream has a natural pale yellow color, but if stored in the refrigerator the buttercream will darken slightly over time.

7 large egg yolks
¾ cup (5¼ ounces) sugar
⅔ cup light corn syrup
2½ teaspoons vanilla extract
⅛ teaspoon salt
1⅛ pounds (4½ sticks) unsalted butter,
each stick cut into quarters and softened

1 Using stand mixer fitted with whisk attachment, whip egg yolks on medium speed until slightly thickened and pale yellow, 4 to 6 minutes.

2 Meanwhile, bring sugar and corn syrup to boil in small saucepan over medium heat, stirring occasionally to dissolve sugar, about 3 minutes.

3 Without letting hot sugar mixture cool off, reduce speed to low and slowly pour hot sugar syrup into whipped egg yolks without hitting sides of bowl or whisk. Increase speed to medium-high and whip until mixture is light and fluffy and bowl is no longer warm, 5 to 10 minutes.

4 Reduce speed to medium-low and add vanilla and salt. Add butter, 1 piece at a time, and whip until completely incorporated, about 2 minutes. Increase speed to medium-high and whip until buttercream is smooth and silky, about 2 minutes. If mixture looks curdled, wrap hot, wet dish towel around bowl and continue to whip until smooth, 1 to 2 minutes. (Buttercream can be refrigerated for up to 3 days; let soften at room temperature, about 2 hours, then rewhip on medium speed until smooth, about 2 minutes.)

makes 3 cups, enough for cupcakes or sheet cake

Reduce egg yolks to 3, reduce sugar to ½ cup (3½ ounces), reduce corn syrup to ⅓ cup, reduce vanilla to 1½ teaspoons, reduce salt to pinch, and reduce butter to 20 tablespoons (2½ sticks).

makes 6 cups, enough for three-layer cake

Increase egg yolks to 8, increase sugar to 1 cup (7 ounces), increase corn syrup to ¾ cup, increase vanilla to 1 tablespoon, increase salt to ¼ teaspoon, and increase butter to 1¼ pounds (5 sticks).

flavor variations
almond buttercream
For 5 cups frosting add 1½ teaspoons almond extract with vanilla.
For 3 cups frosting add 1 teaspoon almond extract with vanilla.
For 6 cups frosting add 2 teaspoons almond extract with vanilla.
coconut buttercream
For 5 cups frosting add 1½ teaspoons coconut extract with vanilla.
For 3 cups frosting add 1 teaspoon coconut extract with vanilla.
For 6 cups frosting add 2 teaspoons coconut extract with vanilla.

miracle frosting

makes 5 cups, enough for two-layer cake

True to its name, this old-fashioned cooked frosting magically transforms from a paste into a fluffy, creamy frosting as you beat it. Most recipes call for cooking the flour and milk together until a thick paste forms, and then creaming the butter and sugar before beating the two mixtures together. But this technique left little lumps of flour suspended in the icing. Adding the sugar to the flour and cooking it with the milk solved the problem. To firm the icing and make it more spreadable, we adjusted the ratio of milk to flour and substituted cornstarch for a small amount of the flour.

1½ cups (10½ ounces) sugar
¼ cup (1¼ ounces) all-purpose flour
3 tablespoons cornstarch
½ teaspoon salt
1½ cups milk
24 tablespoons (3 sticks) unsalted butter, softened
2 teaspoons vanilla extract

1 Whisk sugar, flour, cornstarch, and salt together in medium saucepan. Slowly whisk in milk until smooth. Cook over medium heat, whisking constantly and scraping corners of saucepan, until mixture boils and is very thick, 4 to 8 minutes. Transfer mixture to wide bowl and let cool completely, about 2 hours.

2 Using stand mixer fitted with paddle, beat butter on medium-high speed until light and fluffy, about 5 minutes. Reduce speed to medium, add cooled milk mixture and vanilla, and mix until combined, scraping down sides of bowl as needed. Increase speed to medium-high and beat until frosting is light and fluffy, 3 to 5 minutes.

makes 3 cups, enough for cupcakes or sheet cake

Reduce sugar to ¾ cup (5¼ ounces), reduce flour to 2½ tablespoons, reduce cornstarch to 5 teaspoons, reduce salt to ¼ teaspoon, reduce milk to ¾ cup, reduce butter to 14 tablespoons, and reduce vanilla to 1¼ teaspoons.

makes 6 cups, enough for three-layer cake

Increase sugar to 1¾ cups (12¼ ounces), increase flour to 5 tablespoons (1½ ounces), increase cornstarch to 3 tablespoons plus 2 teaspoons, increase milk to 1¾ cups, increase butter to 30 tablespoons (3¾ sticks), and increase vanilla to 1 tablespoon.

flavor variations

miracle coffee frosting

For 5 cups frosting add 2 tablespoons instant espresso powder to flour mixture in step 1.

For 3 cups frosting add 5 teaspoons instant espresso powder to flour mixture in step 1.

For 6 cups frosting add 2½ tablespoons instant espresso powder to flour mixture in step 1.

miracle milk chocolate frosting

For 5 cups frosting add 5 tablespoons Dutch-processed cocoa powder to flour mixture in step 1 and add 3¾ ounces melted and cooled semisweet chocolate to light and fluffy frosting in step 2 and beat until incorporated, about 30 seconds.

For 3 cups frosting add 3 tablespoons Dutch-processed cocoa powder to flour mixture in step 1 and add 2¼ ounces melted and cooled semisweet chocolate to light and fluffy frosting in step 2 and beat until incorporated, about 30 seconds.

For 6 cups frosting add 6 tablespoons Dutch-processed cocoa powder to flour mixture in step 1 and add 4½ ounces melted and cooled semisweet chocolate to light and fluffy frosting in step 2 and beat until incorporated, about 30 seconds.

creamy vegan chocolate frosting
makes 4 cups, enough for two-layer cake

For a rich, billowy chocolate frosting to top our vegan cakes and cupcakes, we began by melting semisweet chocolate with coconut milk. For an even richer frosting, we discarded the milky liquid from the cans of coconut milk and used just the layer of cream. Chilling the cans of milk overnight helped separate the cream from the milk. Once cooled, we whipped this thick mixture into a light, mousse-like frosting. This frosting tasted downright decadent, but it separated a bit. Using chocolate chips instead of bar chocolate was our fix. Chocolate chips contain emulsifying agents, which stabilized the mixture so it didn't break. Not all semisweet chocolate chips are vegan, so check ingredient lists carefully. Halve this recipe to frost 12 cupcakes (use two cans of coconut milk to obtain the ¾ cup cream); mixing times won't change. Note that this frosting is made over 2 days.

3 (14-ounce) cans coconut milk
3⅓ cups (1¼ pounds) semisweet chocolate chips
¼ teaspoon salt

1 Refrigerate unopened cans of coconut milk for at least 24 hours to ensure that 2 distinct layers form. Skim cream layer from each can and measure out 1½ cups cream (save any extra cream for another use and discard milky liquid).

2 Microwave coconut cream, chocolate chips, and salt in bowl at 50 percent power, whisking occasionally, until melted and smooth, 2 to 4 minutes; transfer to bowl of stand mixer. Press plastic wrap directly on surface of chocolate mixture and refrigerate until cooled completely and texture resembles firm cream cheese, about 3 hours, stirring halfway through chilling. (If mixture has chilled for longer and is very stiff, let stand at room temperature until softened but still cool.) Using stand mixer fitted with whisk attachment, whip at high speed until fluffy, mousse-like soft peaks form, 2 to 4 minutes, scraping down bowl halfway through whipping.

makes 2 cups, enough for cupcakes

Use 2 cans of coconut milk to obtain ¾ cup cream. Reduce chocolate chips to 1⅔ cups (10 ounces) and salt to ⅛ teaspoon.

whipped cream
makes about 2 cups

Whipped cream is the simplest of toppings but is often just right for frosting a cake and letting other components shine. For lightly sweetened whipped cream, reduce the sugar to 1½ teaspoons.

1 cup heavy cream, chilled
1 tablespoon sugar
1 teaspoon vanilla extract

Using stand mixer fitted with whisk attachment, whip cream, sugar, and vanilla on medium-low speed until foamy, about 1 minute. Increase speed to high and whip until soft peaks form, 1 to 3 minutes. (Whipped cream can be refrigerated in fine-mesh strainer set over small bowl and covered with plastic wrap for up to 8 hours.)

makes about 4 cups

Increase cream to 2 cups, sugar to 2 tablespoons, and vanilla to 2 teaspoons.

Whipped Cream Frosting

Need a simple frosting that takes barely a minute to make? Whip some cream, sugar, and vanilla in a food processor. Whereas whipping cream in a stand mixer produces light, billowy peaks, the sharp, fast-moving blades of a food processor can't add as much air. Instead, they produce a dense, creamy consistency that works well as a quick, spreadable topping for snack cakes, angel food and chiffon cakes, and cupcakes. It's also very effective when piped through a pastry bag to make decorative edging. Even better, because the smaller air bubbles created by the food processor are more stable than the bigger bubbles created by a stand mixer, we found that the processed cream kept its thick, dense texture for two full weeks.

---

fillings

Each of the following filling recipes makes enough to fill a three-layer cake. For a two-layer cake, you'll need only half; reserve the remaining filling for another use. Alternatively, try using the jam or preserves of your choice between the cake layers. You will need ⅔ cup of jam between each layer.

chocolate filling
makes 2 cups

For the best flavor, use bittersweet chocolate. Whipping the chilled filling will stiffen it up so it's easier to spread over the cake, but be careful not to overwhip it or it will turn grainy.

1⅓ cups heavy cream
7 ounces bittersweet chocolate, chopped fine
1 teaspoon vanilla extract
⅛ teaspoon salt

Combine cream and chocolate in bowl and microwave at 50 percent power, stirring often, until melted, 2 to 4 minutes. Stir in vanilla and salt. Cover and refrigerate until cold and thickened, at least 4 hours or up to 1 week. Before using, fit stand mixer with paddle and beat on medium-high speed until stiff but spreadable, 30 seconds to 1 minute.

variations
mocha filling

Add 1 tablespoon instant espresso powder or instant coffee powder with chocolate and cream.

white chocolate filling

Do not substitute white chocolate chips here.

Substitute 8 ounces finely chopped white chocolate for bittersweet chocolate and reduce amount of cream to 1 cup. Increase beating time to about 1½ minutes.

fruit filling
makes 3½ cups

We like to use brightly colored dried fruit such as apricots, peaches, cherries, and cranberries. It's important to match the flavor of the jam to that of the dried fruit; if you can't find matching jam, use one with a complementary flavor and color. Add a few drops of food coloring, if desired, to brighten the filling's color.

1 cup (5 ounces) dried fruit
¼ cup orange juice
1 teaspoon unflavored gelatin
1 tablespoon water
3 cups jam, room temperature

1 Bring dried fruit and orange juice to simmer in small saucepan over medium-high heat. Remove from heat, cover, and let sit until fruit is softened, about 10 minutes. Meanwhile, sprinkle gelatin over water in bowl and let sit until gelatin softens, about 5 minutes.

2 Stir gelatin mixture into warm fruit mixture to dissolve, about 1 minute. Process warm fruit mixture and jam in food processor until fruit is finely chopped, 5 to 15 seconds. Transfer mixture to bowl, cover, and refrigerate until set, at least 8 hours or up to 1 week.

lemon curd

makes 2 cups

If you overcook the curd it will be too thick and pasty.

¾ cup lemon juice (4 lemons)
1¼ cups (8¾ ounces) sugar
⅛ teaspoon salt
3 large eggs plus 5 large yolks
6 tablespoons unsalted butter, cut into ½-inch
pieces and frozen

1 Cook lemon juice, sugar, and salt in medium saucepan over medium-high heat, stirring occasionally, until sugar dissolves and mixture is hot (do not boil), about 1 minute.

2 Whisk eggs and yolks in large bowl until combined, then slowly whisk in hot lemon mixture to temper. Return mixture to saucepan and cook over medium-low heat, stirring constantly, until mixture is thickened, registers 170 degrees, and spatula scraped along bottom of pan leaves trail, 3 to 5 minutes.

3 Off heat, stir in frozen butter until melted and incorporated. Strain curd through fine-mesh strainer into bowl and press plastic wrap directly against surface. Refrigerate until curd is firm and spreadable, at least 1½ hours or up to 3 days.

pastry cream

makes 2 cups

You can substitute 1½ teaspoons vanilla extract for the vanilla bean; stir the extract into the pastry cream with the butter in step 4.

2 cups half-and-half
½ cup (3½ ounces) sugar
½ vanilla bean, halved lengthwise, seeds
removed and reserved
Pinch salt
5 large egg yolks
3 tablespoons cornstarch
4 tablespoons unsalted butter, cut into 4 pieces

1 Bring half-and-half, 6 tablespoons of sugar, vanilla bean, vanilla seeds, and salt to simmer in medium saucepan over medium-high heat, stirring occasionally.

2 Meanwhile, whisk egg yolks, cornstarch, and remaining 2 tablespoons sugar in bowl until smooth.

3 Whisk about 1 cup half-and-half mixture into yolk mixture to temper. Slowly whisk tempered egg mixture into remaining half-and-half mixture. Reduce heat to medium and continue to cook, whisking constantly, until pastry cream is thickened and few bubbles burst on surface, about 30 seconds.

4 Off heat, remove vanilla bean and whisk in butter. Transfer pastry cream to bowl and press plastic wrap directly on surface. Refrigerate until cold and set, at least 3 hours or up to 2 days.

variations

almond pastry cream

Omit vanilla bean. Add ¾ teaspoon almond extract with butter in step 4.

mocha pastry cream

Omit vanilla bean. Add 1 teaspoon instant espresso powder or instant coffee powder to half-and-half in step 1.

Conversions and Equivalents

Baking is a science and an art, but geography has a hand in it, too. Flours and sugars manufactured in the United Kingdom and elsewhere will feel and taste different from those manufactured in the United States. So we cannot promise that a cookie you bake in Canada or England will taste the same as a cookie baked in the States, but we can offer guidelines for converting weights and measures. We also recommend that you rely on your instincts when making our recipes. Refer to the visual cues provided. If the dough hasn't "come together in a ball" as described, you may need to add more flour—even if the recipe doesn't tell you to. You be the judge.

The recipes in this book were developed using standard U.S. measures following U.S. government guidelines. The charts below offer equivalents for U.S. and metric measures. All conversions are approximate and have been rounded up or down to the nearest whole number.

EXAMPLE

1 teaspoon	=	4.9292 milliliters, rounded up to 5 milliliters
1 ounce	=	28.3495 grams, rounded down to 28 grams

VOLUME CONVERSIONS

U.S.	METRIC
1 teaspoon	5 milliliters
2 teaspoons	10 milliliters
1 tablespoon	15 milliliters
2 tablespoons	30 milliliters
¼ cup	59 milliliters
⅓ cup	79 milliliters
½ cup	118 milliliters
¾ cup	177 milliliters
1 cup	237 milliliters
1¼ cups	296 milliliters
1½ cups	355 milliliters
2 cups (1 pint)	473 milliliters
2½ cups	591 milliliters
3 cups	710 milliliters
4 cups (1 quart)	0.946 liter
1.06 quarts	1 liter
4 quarts (1 gallon)	3.8 liters

WEIGHT CONVERSIONS

OUNCES	GRAMS
½	14
¾	21
1	28
1½	43
2	57
2½	71
3	85
3½	99
4	113
4½	128
5	142
6	170
7	198
8	227
9	255
10	283
12	340
16 (1 pound)	454

CONVERSIONS FOR COMMON BAKING INGREDIENTS

Because measuring by weight is far more accurate than measuring by volume, and thus more likely to produce reliable results, in our recipes we provide ounce measures in addition to cup measures for many ingredients. Refer to the chart below to convert these measures into grams.

INGREDIENT	OUNCES	GRAMS
Flour		
1 cup all-purpose flour*	5	142
1 cup cake flour	4	113
1 cup whole-wheat flour	5½	156
Sugar		
1 cup granulated (white) sugar	7	198
1 cup packed brown sugar (light or dark)	7	198
1 cup confectioners' sugar	4	113
Cocoa Powder		
1 cup cocoa powder	3	85
Butter†		
4 tablespoons (½ stick or ¼ cup)	2	57
8 tablespoons (1 stick or ½ cup)	4	113
16 tablespoons (2 sticks or 1 cup)	8	227

* U.S. all-purpose flour, the most frequently used flour in this book, does not contain leaveners, as some European flours do. These leavened flours are called self-rising or self-raising. If you are using self-rising flour, take this into consideration before adding leaveners to a recipe.

† In the United States, butter is sold both salted and unsalted. We recommend unsalted butter. If you are using salted butter, take this into consideration before adding salt to a recipe.

OVEN TEMPERATURE

FAHRENHEIT	CELSIUS	GAS MARK
225	105	¼
250	120	½
275	135	1
300	150	2
325	165	3
350	180	4
375	190	5
400	200	6
425	220	7
450	230	8
475	245	9

CONVERTING TEMPERATURES FROM AN INSTANT-READ THERMOMETER

We include doneness temperatures in many of the recipes in this book. We recommend an instant-read thermometer for the job. Refer to the table above to convert Fahrenheit degrees to Celsius. Or, for temperatures not represented in the chart, use this simple formula:

Subtract 32 degrees from the Fahrenheit reading, then divide the result by 1.8 to find the Celsius reading.

example

"Cook caramel until it registers 160 degrees."

To convert:
160°F − 32 = 128°
128° ÷ 1.8 = 71.11°C, rounded down to 71°C

Index

Note: Page references in *italics* indicate photographs.

411

f

Fallen Chocolate Cakes, 96, *97*
Fallen Chocolate Cakes, Orange, 96
Figs
  dried, for recipes, 17
  Lady Baltimore Cake, *250,* 251
Fillings
  Almond Pastry Cream, 407
  Chocolate, 406
  Fruit, 406
  Lemon Curd, 407
  Mocha, 406
  Mocha Pastry Cream, 407
  Pastry Cream, 407
  using jam or preserves for, 406
  White Chocolate, 406
Flag Cake, 282, *283*
Flour
  all-purpose, 10
  cake, 10
  cornmeal, 11
  nut flours, 10
  storing, 11
  whole-wheat, 10
Flourless Chocolate Cake, 190, *191*
Fluffy Yellow Layer Cake, 32, *33*
Food processor, 7
Foolproof New York Cheesecake, 360–61, *361*
French Apple Cake, 182, *183*
French buttercream, about, 24
Fresh Strawberry Topping, 378
Frostings
  Almond, 398
  amounts, 24
  applying, with small offset spatulas, 79
  applying to layer cakes, 23
  Chocolate, 399
  Chocolate, Creamy Vegan, 405
  Chocolate Ganache, 400
  Coconut, 398
  Coffee, 398
  compared with buttercream, 24
  Cream Cheese, 401
  creating flat top with coated sides, 78
  decorating cupcakes with, 78
  ganache, about, 25
  Honey Cream Cheese, 402
  Miracle, 404
  Miracle Coffee, 404
  Miracle Milk Chocolate, 404
  Orange, 398
  Peanut Butter, 401
  Peppermint, 398
  piping, 78

Frostings *(cont.)*
  piping onto cakes, 29
  Seven- Minute, 402
  seven-minute, about, 25
  smoothing, over cakes, 24
  texturing, with a spoon, 26
  using a pastry bag with, 28
  Vanilla, 398
  when to use a crumb coat, 27
  Whipped Cream, 405
  whipped cream used as, 25
  see also Buttercream
Fruit, fresh. *See* Fruit cakes, rustic; *specific fruits*
Fruit cakes, rustic
  Apple Upside-Down Cake, 314–15, *315*
  Apple Upside-Down Cake with Almonds, 315
  Apple Upside-Down Cake with Lemon and Thyme, 315
  Honey-Rosemary Polenta Cake with Clementines, *318,* 319
  Pear-Walnut Upside-Down Cake, 316, *317*
  Pineapple Upside-Down Cake, *312,* 313
  Rustic Plum Cake, *310,* 311
  Summer Peach Cake, 308, *309*
Fruit(s) (dried)
  Apricot and Cherry Modern Fruitcake, *267,* 268–69
  Filling, 406
  Lady Baltimore Cake, *250,* 251
  for recipes, 17

g

Ganache
  about, 25
  Chocolate, Frosting, 400
Gâteau Breton, 196–97, *197*
Gâteau Breton with Prune Filling, 197
Gelatin, about, 201
Genoise Sponge Cake, 40–41, *41*
German buttercream, about, 24
German Chocolate Cake, 222–23, *224*
  with Banana, Macadamia, and Coconut Filling, 223
  with Coffee, Cashew, and Coconut Filling, 223
German Chocolate Sheet Cake, *118,* 119
Ginger
  about, 17
  Bold and Spicy Gingerbread Bundt Cake, 348, *349*
  -Cardamom Applesauce Snack Cake, 299
  Gingerbread Layer Cake, 274, *275*
  Pound Cake, 323
  Spice Cake, 116–17, *117*
Gingerbread Bundt Cake, Bold and Spicy, 348, *349*
Gingerbread Layer Cake, 274, *275*
Gluten-Free Chocolate Layer Cake, 50, *51*
Gluten-Free Confetti Cupcakes, *76,* 77

p

q